MST224

Mathematical methods

Book 3

Scalar and vector fields

Cover image: This shows a simulation of the patterns formed by smoke particles moving in air, which is itself in turbulent motion. The positions of the particles are described by relatively simple differential equations, yet the patterns that they form are complex and intriguing. Similar patterns are also relevant to understanding how clouds produce rain, and are a subject of ongoing research at The Open University.

This publication forms part of an Open University module. Details of this and other Open University modules can be obtained from the Student Registration and Enquiry Service, The Open University, PO Box 197, Milton Keynes MK7 6BJ, United Kingdom (tel. +44 (0)845 300 6090; email general-enquiries@open.ac.uk).

Alternatively, you may visit the Open University website at www.open.ac.uk where you can learn more about the wide range of modules and packs offered at all levels by The Open University.

To purchase a selection of Open University materials visit www.ouw.co.uk, or contact Open University Worldwide, Walton Hall, Milton Keynes MK7 6AA, United Kingdom for a brochure (tel. +44 (0)1908 858779; fax +44 (0)1908 858787; email ouw-customer-services@open.ac.uk).

The Open University has had Woodland Carbon Code Pending Issuance Units assigned from Doddington North forest creation project (IHS ID103/26819) that will, as the trees grow, compensate for the greenhouse gas emissions from the manufacture of the paper in MST224 *Block 3*. More information can be found at https://www.woodlandcarboncode.org.uk/

The Open University, Walton Hall, Milton Keynes, MK7 6AA.

First published 2013.

Edited, designed and typeset by The Open University, using the Open University TeX System.

Printed in the United Kingdom by Halstan & Co. Ltd, Amersham, Bucks.

ISBN 978 1 7800 7481 8

1.1

Contents

Functions of several variables

Introduction

You are familiar with functions such as $f(x) = x^2$ and $g(t) = \sin^2 t$. You know how to differentiate and integrate such functions, and how to find their stationary points (including local maxima and minima). This is the usual stuff of calculus.

In describing the real world, however, we often meet functions of more than one variable. The volume of a brick depends on the lengths of its three sides. The rate of a chemical reaction depends on the concentrations of each of the reacting chemicals, and also on temperature. We may occasionally treat some of the variables as fixed parameters, but in general more than one variable is of interest, and we need to discuss functions of several variables. In this book you will see how we can extend the methods of calculus to functions of two and more variables.

The world that we inhabit has three spatial dimensions, and there are many physical quantities that vary throughout space. For example, the temperature may vary throughout a room. Since each point in the room can be represented by three coordinates (x, y, z), temperature is a function of the three variables x, y and z. We indicate this by writing the temperature function as $T(x, y, z)$.

In physics, quantities that depend on position throughout a whole region of space are called *fields*. There are many examples. We have just mentioned the temperature field; there are also electric fields, magnetic fields, gravitational fields, density fields, wind-velocity fields, and so on. The precise definitions of these fields need not concern us, but they all contain the essential idea of a physical quantity that varies with position.

Some physical quantities are vectors, having both magnitude and direction. For example, the velocity of a particle is a vector describing how fast the particle is moving *and in what direction*. In describing the wind-velocity field, we must specify a vector (the velocity of the wind) at each point in space. We therefore say that the wind-velocity field is a *vector field*. By contrast, the temperature field is a *scalar field* because temperature is a scalar quantity and has no direction associated with it.

This brief introduction has exposed two related ideas:

- We need to extend the methods of calculus to deal with functions of more than one variable.

- Nature provides many examples of functions of more than one variable in the form of fields that vary throughout regions of space. The fields that we will discuss are of two types: scalar fields and vector fields.

With this background, we can now outline the structure of this book.

Unit 7 introduces functions of more than one variable and shows how to differentiate them. This allows us to explore how sensitive these functions are to small changes in their variables, and to locate points at which the functions have maxima and minima.

Unit 8 describes how to integrate functions of more than one variable. For example, given an object of variable density, we will explain how its total mass can be found by integrating over the volume of the object. This is a so-called *volume integral*. We will also discuss integrals over surfaces, allowing us to find the surface areas of shapes such as spheres or cones.

Unit 9 looks at scalar and vector fields, and considers how to differentiate them. Such fields have special properties, and this leads to results beyond those introduced in Unit 7.

Unit 10 completes the book by discussing the integration of fields. Again, there are special results that apply to fields and take us beyond the integrals of Unit 8; these results turn out to be extremely powerful in physics and applied mathematics.

Because much of this book is largely concerned with fields, we will inevitably use physical examples – more so than elsewhere in this module. If you are unfamiliar with physics, be reassured. You need no prior understanding of physics, just a willingness to accept concepts such as temperature or velocity when they are used to illustrate mathematical ideas.

Study guide

This unit introduces functions of two or more variables. It explains how to differentiate these functions, and how to put the derivatives to use.

Section 1 introduces functions of more than one variable, and shows how they can be represented graphically in simple cases. It goes on to describe how these functions are differentiated with respect to individual variables.

Section 2 discusses the chain rule for functions of more than one variable. In fact, a number of different results go under this heading. These rules tell us how sensitive a function is to small changes in its variables, and how to find the derivative of a composite function – a function whose variables depend on other variables.

Section 3 briefly introduces Taylor polynomials for functions of more than one variable.

Finally, Section 4 investigates maxima, minima and other stationary points of functions of several variables. This is an important topic because many of the problems met in science, applied mathematics and economics reduce to finding the conditions under which functions have maximum or minimum values.

1 Partial differentiation

1.1 Notation for functions of one variable

Before describing functions of two and more variables, it is worth reviewing the notation used for functions of one variable. As an example, suppose that

$$z = f(x) = x^2 + 4. \tag{1}$$

Here x is called the *argument* of the function $f(x)$ or the *independent variable*, and z is called the *dependent variable*. If we insert a value for x in the expression $x^2 + 4$ on the right-hand side of equation (1), we get the corresponding function value. For $x = 3$, the function value is $f(3) = 3^2 + 4 = 13$. For $x = a$, the function value is $f(a) = a^2 + 4$.

As noted in Unit 1, similar notation is being used for different things. Equation (1) exhibits the *rule* that defines the function – in this case, 'take the square and add four' – so we may talk about the function $f(x)$. On the other hand, $f(3)$ and $f(a)$ represent particular *values* of the function. In spite of this clash, we will continue to use the $f(x)$ notation (and extend it to functions of more than one variable) – it is simply too useful to avoid.

Such 'abuse of notation' is practically unavoidable in subjects like physics, where mathematical symbols need to be related to physical concepts.

Moreover, in science, the symbols used to represent functions are often chosen in a special way. If we are interested in how a quantity M depends on position x, we may denote the function that describes this dependence by $M(x)$. Note that the symbol M is used for both the quantity and the function. We might also be interested in how M depends on time t, and denote the corresponding function by $M(t)$. This notation keeps us alert to the fact that both functions describe how the quantity M varies, but with respect to different variables. It avoids cluttering our descriptions with arbitrary new symbols whose physical meaning may be rapidly forgotten.

Suppose that the temperature T varies with position x along a rod. With T measured in degrees Celsius and x in metres, we might have

$$T = T(x) = 100e^{-x} \quad \text{for } 0 \le x \le 1.$$

The symbol T on the extreme left is the dependent variable, and x is the independent variable. The way in which T depends on x is described by the function $T(x) = 100e^{-x}$, which has x as its argument. The domain of this function is the region $0 \le x \le 1$.

1.2 Functions of more than one variable

The notation used for functions of a single variable is readily extended to functions of two or more variables. For example, the volume of the cone shown in Figure 1 is given by the formula $V = \frac{1}{3}\pi r^2 h$, where h is the height of the cone and r is the radius of its base. This can be described by a *function of two variables*:

$$V(h, r) = \tfrac{1}{3}\pi r^2 h.$$

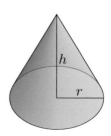

Figure 1 A cone of height h and base radius r

The arguments of this function are h and r. We can also say that h and r are the independent variables, and that the volume of the cone, V, is the dependent variable. For physical reasons, h and r are both positive numbers (measured in metres, say) so the domain of the function $V(h,r)$ is $0 < h < \infty$, $0 < r < \infty$.

The volume of the cone can be expressed in terms of other independent variables. The area of the base of the cone is $A = \pi r^2$, so the volume of the cone is $V = \frac{1}{3}Ah$, and this can be described by the function

$$V(h, A) = \tfrac{1}{3}Ah.$$

Note that the symbol V has been used for the physical quantity 'volume' and for two different functions, $V(h,r)$ and $V(h,A)$. Fortunately, the distinction between quantities and functions is generally clear from context, and the functions $V(h,r)$ and $V(h,A)$ are distinguished by the contents of their round brackets. Where there is a risk of ambiguity, guiding words will be supplied.

A second example is provided by temperature measured over a region. Suppose that we measure temperature on the surface of a horizontal disc of radius $R = 3$ (in metres). We describe points on the surface of the disc by Cartesian coordinates x and y (in metres), with the origin taken to be at the centre of the disc (Figure 2).

The temperature may vary over the disc, but each point on the disc will have a well-defined temperature T, measured in degrees Celsius. We can represent the temperature variation over the entire surface of the disc by a function $T(x, y)$. For example, we might have

$$T(x, y) = 100\, e^{-(x^2+y^2)/10} \quad \text{on the disc.} \tag{2}$$

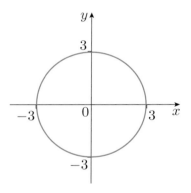

Figure 2 The Cartesian coordinate system used to specify points on a disc

Here we use the symbol T for the temperature function on the disc, and it has arguments x and y. We can also say that x and y are the independent variables, and T is the dependent variable. The values of x and y are restricted because the formula in equation (2) applies only on the disc, and not elsewhere. The domain of the function is therefore the surface of the disc, i.e. the collection of points (x, y) with $x^2 + y^2 \leq 9$.

Given the temperature function, it is a simple matter to calculate the temperature at any point on the disc. For example, at the point $(x, y) = (1, 2)$, the temperature (in degrees Celsius) is

$$T(1, 2) = 100\, e^{-(1^2+2^2)/10} = 100\, e^{-0.5} \simeq 60.7.$$

In this case, the point $(2, 1)$ has the same temperature as the point $(1, 2)$, but this is an accidental feature of the function that we have chosen. In general, the function value $f(a, b)$ is not the same as the function value $f(b, a)$, as you will see in the following exercise.

Exercise 1

Given $f(x, y) = 3x^2 - 2y^2$, evaluate the following.

(a) $f(2, 3)$ (b) $f(3, -2)$ (c) $f(a, b)$ (d) $f(b, a)$

(e) $f(2a, b)$ (f) $f(a - b, 0)$ (g) $f(x, 2)$

1.3 Graphical representations

There are three main ways of visualising functions of two variables:

- Give a perspective view of a surface that represents the function.
- Show one or more slices through the surface.
- Draw a contour map.

All of these methods will be used in this unit, and we briefly introduce them now.

Perspective view of a surface

We can get a good overall understanding of a function $f(x, y)$ by plotting a 'three-dimensional graph'. The two independent variables x and y are plotted in the horizontal xy-plane, and the corresponding function values $z = f(x, y)$ are plotted along the vertical z-axis. Normally, the independent variables cover a continuous range and the function values vary smoothly, so we get a continuous surface, which can be viewed in perspective.

For example, Figure 3(a) is a three-dimensional graph of the function $f(x, y) = x^2 + y^2$. This shape is called a *circular paraboloid*, and is used in radio telescopes to focus a parallel beam to a single point (Figure 4(a)). Figure 3(b) is the graph of $f(x, y) = x^2 - y^2$. This shape is called a *hyperbolic paraboloid*, and has gained popularity with architects because it is eye-catching and relatively easy to construct (Figure 4(b)).

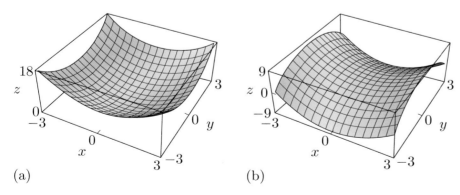

(a)   (b)

Figure 3 Three-dimensional graphs of (a) $f(x, y) = x^2 + y^2$ and (b) $f(x, y) = x^2 - y^2$

(a)   (b)

Figure 4   (a) Radio telescopes have dishes that are circular paraboloids. (b) The roof of a station in Warsaw is shaped as a hyperbolic paraboloid.

An important function of two variables is

$$f(x,y) = Ax + By + C, \tag{3}$$

where A, B and C are constants. This is a *linear function* of x and y, and when we plot it we get a plane. Conversely, the *equation of a plane* in three-dimensional space is given by equation (3). For example, the plane passing through the points $(-2, -2, -3)$, $(0, 0, 3)$ and $(2, 2, 9)$, and extending indefinitely, is given by the surface

$$z = f(x,y) = x + 2y + 3.$$

A portion of this surface is shown in Figure 5.

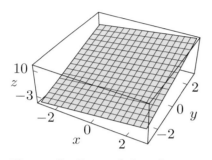

Figure 5   Part of the plane representing the function $f(x,y) = x + 2y + 3$

Graphs of section functions

A second way of visualising a function of more than one variable is to fix the values of all but one of its variables, and then plot a graph showing its dependence on the remaining variable.

For example, given $f(x,y) = x^2 - y^2$, we can set $y = 3$ and then plot a graph of $f(x, 3) = x^2 - 9$ against x, as in Figure 6(a). Or we can set $x = 2$ and plot a graph of $f(2, y) = 4 - y^2$ against y, as in Figure 6(b).

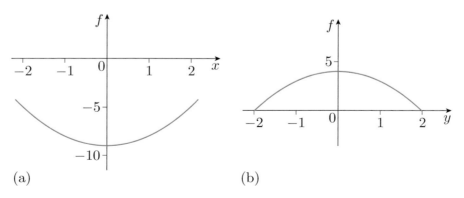

(a)   (b)

Figure 6   Graphs of $f(x,y) = x^2 - y^2$ with one variable held constant: (a) graph of $f(x, 3)$ against x; (b) graph of $f(2, y)$ against y

Figure 6(a) is obtained by taking a vertical section (or slice) through the three-dimensional graph in Figure 3(b). The slice is parallel to the x-axis at the fixed value $y = 3$. Similarly, Figure 6(b) is obtained by taking a vertical slice parallel to the y-axis at the fixed value $x = 2$. Any function of the form $f(x, a)$ or $f(b, y)$, where a and b are constants, is called a **section function**. By itself, a single section function provides limited information: if y is held constant, the section function tells us only about the dependence on x at one fixed value of y, and it tells us nothing about the dependence on y. Nevertheless, a series of section functions taken at various fixed values of y, and various fixed values of x, can provide a great deal of useful information.

Contour maps

Finally, a function of two variables can be visualised using a *contour map*. You may be familiar with this idea from topographical maps (such as those produced by Ordnance Survey in the UK). Here the height of the land is described by a function $h(x, y)$, where x and y are position coordinates in a horizontal plane. The map shows a series of lines joining points of the same height; the example in Figure 7 shows heights between 5000 m below sea level and 3000 m above sea level.

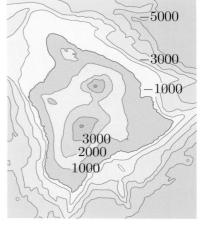

Figure 7   A contour map of Hawaii and the surrounding ocean floor

For any smooth function $f(x, y)$, we can plot a similar contour map. The x and y variables (whether they are position coordinates or not) are plotted in the plane of the page, and a curve is drawn in the xy-plane connecting neighbouring points where the function has a fixed value, say $f = c_1$. This is repeated for a series of values $c_1, c_2, c_3, \ldots$, giving a family of curves. A number is written beside each curve to indicate the value to which it refers. The curves are called **contour lines**, and the entire diagram is called a **contour map**.

Contour maps for the functions $f(x, y) = x^2 + y^2$ and $f(x, y) = x^2 - y^2$ are shown in Figures 8(a) and 8(b). To make sure that you are reading these contour maps correctly, you should compare them with Figures 3(a) and 3(b).

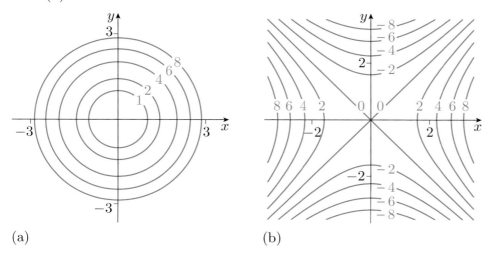

(a)   (b)

Figure 8   Contour maps for: (a) the function $f(x, y) = x^2 + y^2$; (b) the function $f(x, y) = x^2 - y^2$

Beyond two variables

Visualisation of functions of three or more variables is harder. We can always plot section functions, and for a function $f(x, y, z)$ we can plot the equivalent of a contour map, but in three dimensions. Here, neighbouring points with the same function value form a surface, known as a **contour surface**. For example, the function

$$f(x, y, z) = \frac{1}{\sqrt{x^2 + y^2 + z^2}}$$

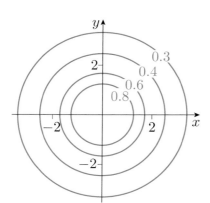

has the fixed value $1/R$ at points where $x^2 + y^2 + z^2 = R^2$. These points lie on the surface of a sphere, so the contour surfaces of this function are concentric spheres centred on the origin. One of these could be shown in a perspective view, or we could show a cross-section through many of them. This is what has been done in Figure 9. Note that the concentric circles in this case are not contour lines, but are cross-sections through spherical contour surfaces, which extend equally above and below the horizontal plane of the page.

Figure 9 A cross-section in the $z = 0$ plane through the spherical contour surfaces of $f(x, y, z) = 1/\sqrt{x^2 + y^2 + z^2}$

Don't worry that you can't see things in more than three dimensions – no one can! This does not matter for our purposes. In order to motivate the key concepts for functions of many variables, the vital step is going from a function $f(x)$ of one variable to a function $f(x, y)$ of two variables. Once this step is made, we can easily extend our methods to functions of many variables without any need for diagrams.

1.4 First-order partial derivatives

Suppose that a variable f depends on x, and this dependence is described by the function $f(x)$. Then we can calculate the derivative df/dx, and this tells us the slope of a graph of $y = f(x)$. Equivalently, it tells us the rate of change of f with respect to x.

We would like to extend these ideas – initially to a function $f(x, y)$ of two variables. Corresponding to the slope of the graph $y = f(x)$, we have the slope of the surface $z = f(x, y)$. Here we run into a new feature: *the slope of a surface depends on our direction of travel.*

Let us imagine that the function $f(x, y)$ represents the height of a hill, expressed in terms of the Cartesian coordinates x and y of points in a horizontal plane. Starting at some point on the hill, you might choose to go in a direction that goes directly up the hill, climbing steeply, or you might choose to go in a more oblique direction across the face of the hill, climbing less steeply. Roads in mountainous country often meander over the terrain, with many hairpin bends designed to keep the magnitude of the slope within safe limits (Figure 10). The slope encountered at any given point depends on the line chosen for the road.

Figure 10 At any given point, the slope of a road depends on the direction that it takes over the terrain

More generally, for any surface $z = f(x, y)$, the slope of the surface depends on the direction in which we move. In the next section, we will find a way of calculating the slope in any given direction, but first, we concentrate on two special directions: the x-direction and the y-direction. For each of these directions, we can define a slope by differentiating $f(x, y)$ in an appropriate way. This leads to the concept of a partial derivative, which we will now explain.

Consider the surface $z = f(x, y)$ obtained from the function

$$f(x, y) = x + y^3 + 2x^2y^2. \tag{4}$$

Suppose that we want to find the slope of this surface in the x-direction at the point $x = 2$, $y = 3$. Because we want the slope in the x-direction, the value of y is fixed at the value $y = 3$, and we can substitute this into equation (4) to obtain the function

$$f(x, 3) = x + 27 + 18x^2.$$

This is the section function at constant y, with $y = 3$. It is a function only of x, and can be differentiated with respect to x to give

$$\frac{d}{dx}f(x, 3) = 1 + 36x. \tag{5}$$

This derivative is the slope of the surface $z = f(x, y)$ in the x-direction for any value of x and for $y = 3$. Finally, substituting $x = 2$ in equation (5), we conclude that the slope in the x-direction at the point $x = 2$, $y = 3$ is equal to $1 + 36 \times 2 = 73$.

A similar calculation gives the slope in the y-direction at $x = 2$, $y = 3$. In this case we substitute $x = 2$ in equation (4) to obtain the section function

$$f(2, y) = 2 + y^3 + 8y^2.$$

This can be differentiated with respect to the remaining variable y to give

$$\frac{d}{dy}f(2, y) = 3y^2 + 16y.$$

Then, substituting in the value $y = 3$, the slope in the y-direction at the point $x = 2$, $y = 3$ is $3 \times 9 + 16 \times 3 = 75$. So the slopes in the x- and y-directions are not the same.

We could carry out similar calculations for any values of x and y in the domain of $f(x, y)$. At any given point, we can find the slope of $z = f(x, y)$ in the x-direction by differentiating with respect to x while treating y as a constant. Similarly, we can find the slope in the y-direction by differentiating with respect to y while treating x as a constant. Derivatives of this type, where certain variables are held constant, are known as *partial derivatives*, and they are written using curly dees as

$$\frac{\partial f}{\partial x} \quad \text{and} \quad \frac{\partial f}{\partial y}$$

or equivalently, as

$$\partial f/\partial x \quad \text{and} \quad \partial f/\partial y.$$

The expression $\partial f/\partial x$ is read as 'partial dee f by dee x'.

Partial derivatives

Given a function $f(x, y)$ of two variables x and y, the **partial derivative** $\partial f / \partial x$ is obtained by differentiating $f(x, y)$ with respect to x while treating y as a constant. Similarly, the partial derivative $\partial f / \partial y$ is obtained by differentiating $f(x, y)$ with respect to y while treating x as a constant.

Both $\partial f / \partial x$ and $\partial f / \partial y$ are also called **first-order partial derivatives** because they involve a *single* differentiation.

The partial derivative $\partial f / \partial x$ is equal to the slope in the x-direction of the surface $z = f(x, y)$. It tells us the rate of change of f with respect to x when we move in the direction of increasing x, keeping y fixed. The partial derivative $\partial f / \partial y$ is equal to the slope in the y-direction of the surface $z = f(x, y)$. It tells us the rate of change of f with respect to y when we move in the direction of increasing y, keeping x fixed.

A more formal definition of first-order partial derivatives is

$$\frac{\partial f}{\partial x} = \lim_{\delta x \to 0} \frac{f(x + \delta x, y) - f(x, y)}{\delta x}, \tag{6}$$

$$\frac{\partial f}{\partial y} = \lim_{\delta y \to 0} \frac{f(x, y + \delta y) - f(x, y)}{\delta y}. \tag{7}$$

It is worth noting that the two terms in the numerator on the right-hand side of equation (6) have the same value of y, which corresponds to treating y as a constant. By contrast, the two terms in the numerator on the right-hand side of equation (7) have the same value of x, and this corresponds to treating x as a constant.

As with ordinary differentiation, we tend to bypass these formal definitions and use the familiar rules of calculus to calculate partial derivatives. The only new feature is that some variables must be treated as constants during the differentiation.

Finding a partial derivative is no harder than finding an ordinary derivative. Just remember that all variables except the one involved in the differentiation must be treated as constants throughout the calculation.

Example 1

Find the partial derivatives $\partial f / \partial x$ and $\partial f / \partial y$ of the function $f(x, y) = x + y^3 + 2x^2 y^2$ in equation (4).

Solution

To find $\partial f / \partial x$, we differentiate with respect to x, treating y as a constant:

$$\frac{\partial f}{\partial x} = 1 + 0 + 4xy^2 = 1 + 4xy^2.$$

The effect of holding y constant differs from term to term. In the term y^3, partial differentiation with respect to x gives zero because the derivative of any constant is zero. In the term $2x^2y^2$, the expression $2y^2$ is a constant coefficient for x^2, and this coefficient is unchanged by the differentiation.

To find $\partial f/\partial y$, we differentiate with respect to y, treating x as a constant:

$$\frac{\partial f}{\partial y} = 0 + 3y^2 + 4x^2y = 3y^2 + 4x^2y.$$

The partial derivatives that we have just calculated are functions of x and y because they refer to a general point (x, y) in the domain of the function f. To find the value of a partial derivative at a particular point, we substitute appropriate values of x and y. For the function in the above example, we see that at the point $x = 2$, $y = 3$, the values of the partial derivatives are

$$\left.\frac{\partial f}{\partial x}\right|_{x=2,\,y=3} = 1 + 4 \times 2 \times 9 = 73,$$

$$\left.\frac{\partial f}{\partial y}\right|_{x=2,\,y=3} = 3 \times 9 + 4 \times 4 \times 3 = 75.$$

These agree with the slopes calculated earlier using section functions. However, the use of partial derivatives is far more efficient because it gives the correct results for *all* values of x and y.

We have seen that the partial derivatives of $f(x, y)$ are functions of x and y. This is sometimes made explicit by using the alternative notations $f_x(x, y)$ and $f_y(x, y)$ instead of $\partial f/\partial x$ and $\partial f/\partial y$. In this case, the subscript x or y indicates the variable with respect to which the derivative is being taken. At a particular point, where $x = a$ and $y = b$, the values of the partial derivatives are denoted by $f_x(a, b)$ and $f_y(a, b)$, which is more compact than curly dee notation.

$f_x(x, y)$ and $f_y(x, y)$ may be abbreviated to f_x and f_y.

Of course, the two independent variables need not be denoted by x and y; any variable names will do, as the next example shows.

Example 2

Given $f(u, v) = u^2 + \sin(uv)$, calculate $f_u\left(\frac{\pi}{2}, 1\right)$ and $f_v\left(\frac{\pi}{2}, 1\right)$.

Solution

Differentiating $f(u, v)$ partially with respect to u gives

$$f_u(u, v) = 2u + v\cos(uv),$$

so

$$f_u\left(\tfrac{\pi}{2}, 1\right) = \pi + \cos\left(\tfrac{\pi}{2}\right) = \pi.$$

Differentiating $f(u, v)$ partially with respect to v gives

$$f_v(u, v) = 0 + u\cos(uv),$$

so

$$f_v\left(\tfrac{\pi}{2}, 1\right) = \tfrac{\pi}{2}\cos\left(\tfrac{\pi}{2}\right) = 0.$$

Exercise 2

Given $g(\theta, \phi) = \sin\theta + \cos\phi\tan\theta$, find $\dfrac{\partial g}{\partial\theta}$ and $\dfrac{\partial g}{\partial\phi}$.

Exercise 3

(a) Given $f(x, y) = (x^2 + y^2)e^{3x}$, find $f_x(x, y)$ and $f_y(x, y)$.

(b) What is the slope of the surface $z = f(x, y)$ in the x-direction at the point $(0, 1)$?

The concept of a partial derivative can easily be extended to functions of more than two variables. For a function $f(x, y, z)$ of three variables, $\partial f/\partial x$ no longer represents the slope of a surface, but it does represent the rate of change of f with respect to x when the other variables y and z have fixed values. The partial derivative $\partial f/\partial x$ is calculated by differentiating $f(x, y, z)$ with respect to x while keeping y *and* z fixed (and similarly for the other partial derivatives). More generally, we keep all but one of the variables fixed and differentiate with respect to the remaining variable.

Example 3

Given $V(x, y, z) = (x^2 + y^2 + z^2)^{-1/2}$, calculate $\partial V/\partial x$, $\partial V/\partial y$ and $\partial V/\partial z$.

Solution

This differentiation uses the 'function of a function' rule.

Partial differentiation with respect to x, with y and z constant, gives

$$\frac{\partial V}{\partial x} = -\tfrac{1}{2}(x^2 + y^2 + z^2)^{-3/2} \times 2x = -\frac{x}{(x^2 + y^2 + z^2)^{3/2}}.$$

Partial differentiation with respect to y, with x and z constant, gives

$$\frac{\partial V}{\partial y} = -\tfrac{1}{2}(x^2 + y^2 + z^2)^{-3/2} \times 2y = -\frac{y}{(x^2 + y^2 + z^2)^{3/2}},$$

and partial differentiation with respect to z, with x and y constant, gives

$$\frac{\partial V}{\partial z} = -\tfrac{1}{2}(x^2 + y^2 + z^2)^{-3/2} \times 2z = -\frac{z}{(x^2 + y^2 + z^2)^{3/2}}.$$

(Because the function $V(x, y, z)$ is symmetric in x, y and z, the answers for $\partial V/\partial y$ and $\partial V/\partial z$ can be obtained from the answer for $\partial V/\partial x$ by interchanging symbols. This is a useful check in this case.)

Exercise 4

(a) Given $f(x, y, z) = (1 + x)^2 + (1 + y)^3 + (1 + z)^4$, calculate the partial derivatives $\partial f / \partial x$, $\partial f / \partial y$ and $\partial f / \partial z$.

(b) Find all the first-order partial derivatives of the function
$$f(x, y, t) = x^2 y^3 t^4 + 4x^2 t^2 - 2xy + y.$$

1.5   Higher-order partial derivatives

You have seen that the first-order partial derivatives of a function $f(x, y)$ are themselves functions of x and y. For example, the first-order partial derivatives of the function $f(x, y) = x + y^3 + 2x^2 y^2$ are

$$\frac{\partial f}{\partial x} = 1 + 4xy^2 \quad \text{and} \quad \frac{\partial f}{\partial y} = 3y^2 + 4x^2 y, \tag{8}$$

as you saw in Example 1. We can go on to differentiate $\partial f / \partial x$ partially with respect to x to obtain

$$\frac{\partial}{\partial x}\left(\frac{\partial f}{\partial x}\right) = \frac{\partial}{\partial x}(1 + 4xy^2) = 4y^2.$$

Each of $\partial f / \partial x$ and $\partial f / \partial y$ can be partially differentiated with respect to either x or y, so equations (8) also give

$$\frac{\partial}{\partial y}\left(\frac{\partial f}{\partial x}\right) = \frac{\partial}{\partial y}(1 + 4xy^2) = 8xy,$$

$$\frac{\partial}{\partial x}\left(\frac{\partial f}{\partial y}\right) = \frac{\partial}{\partial x}(3y^2 + 4x^2 y) = 8xy,$$

$$\frac{\partial}{\partial y}\left(\frac{\partial f}{\partial y}\right) = \frac{\partial}{\partial y}(3y^2 + 4x^2 y) = 6y + 4x^2.$$

These four functions, obtained by partially differentiating $f(x, y) = x + y^3 + 2x^2 y^2$ twice, are called **second-order partial derivatives**.

Second-order partial derivatives are written down using a natural extension of the notation for first-order partial derivatives. In curly-dee notation, we define

$$\frac{\partial^2 f}{\partial x^2} = \frac{\partial}{\partial x}\left(\frac{\partial f}{\partial x}\right), \quad \frac{\partial^2 f}{\partial y \, \partial x} = \frac{\partial}{\partial y}\left(\frac{\partial f}{\partial x}\right),$$

$$\frac{\partial^2 f}{\partial y^2} = \frac{\partial}{\partial y}\left(\frac{\partial f}{\partial y}\right), \quad \frac{\partial^2 f}{\partial x \, \partial y} = \frac{\partial}{\partial x}\left(\frac{\partial f}{\partial y}\right),$$

and in the alternative subscript notation,

$$f_{xx}(x, y) = \frac{\partial^2 f}{\partial x^2}, \quad f_{yx}(x, y) = \frac{\partial^2 f}{\partial y \, \partial x},$$

$$f_{yy}(x, y) = \frac{\partial^2 f}{\partial y^2}, \quad f_{xy}(x, y) = \frac{\partial^2 f}{\partial x \, \partial y}.$$

The value of the partial derivative $f_{xx}(x, y)$ at a particular point $x = a$, $y = b$ is then written as $f_{xx}(a, b)$, with similar notation for the other second-order partial derivatives.

If you can partially differentiate once, then you can partially differentiate again, so you should have no problem in calculating second-order partial derivatives. The following example illustrates the technique.

Example 4

Determine the second-order partial derivatives of the function
$$f(x, y) = e^x \cos y + x^2 - y + 1.$$

Solution

We have
$$\frac{\partial f}{\partial x} = e^x \cos y + 2x, \quad \frac{\partial f}{\partial y} = -e^x \sin y - 1,$$

so
$$\frac{\partial^2 f}{\partial x^2} = \frac{\partial}{\partial x}(e^x \cos y + 2x) = e^x \cos y + 2,$$

$$\frac{\partial^2 f}{\partial y\, \partial x} = \frac{\partial}{\partial y}(e^x \cos y + 2x) = -e^x \sin y,$$

$$\frac{\partial^2 f}{\partial y^2} = \frac{\partial}{\partial y}(-e^x \sin y - 1) = -e^x \cos y,$$

$$\frac{\partial^2 f}{\partial x\, \partial y} = \frac{\partial}{\partial x}(-e^x \sin y - 1) = -e^x \sin y.$$

Exercise 5

Given $f(x, y) = x \sin y$, calculate the second-order partial derivatives f_{xx}, f_{yx}, f_{yy} and f_{xy}, and evaluate them at $(2, \pi)$.

The second-order partial derivatives of a function $f(x, y)$ can be interpreted geometrically. Just as first-order partial derivatives tell us about the slopes of the surface $z = f(x, y)$ in the x- and y-directions, so second-order partial derivatives tell us about the *rates of change* of these slopes when we move in various directions. In a derivative like f_{xx}, we differentiate twice with respect to x, holding y constant. The first differentiation gives us the slope of the surface in the x-direction. In general, this slope varies from point to point, and f_{xx} tells us how rapidly the slope in the x-direction changes as we move in the x-direction. Similarly, f_{yx} tells us how rapidly the slope in the x-direction changes as we move in the y-direction, and so on. Figure 11 illustrates these facts.

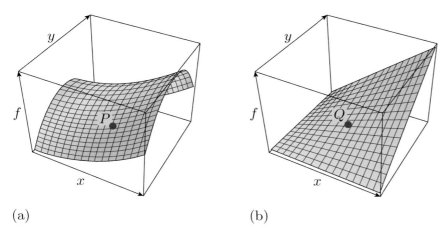

(a)   (b)

Figure 11   (a) At point P, $f_x > 0$ and $f_y > 0$, while $f_{xx} > 0$ and $f_{yy} < 0$. (b) At point Q, $f_x > 0$ and $f_y > 0$, while $f_{xy} > 0$ and $f_{yx} > 0$. Mixed partial derivatives such as f_{xy} and f_{yx} are non-zero for surfaces with a 'twist' in them.

Partial derivatives such as f_{xy} and f_{yx}, which involve differentiations with respect to different variables, are called **mixed partial derivatives**. In Example 4 and Exercise 5 (as well as in the work on the function at the beginning of this subsection) you can see that $f_{xy} = f_{yx}$. In fact, this property is guaranteed by the following theorem, which we do not prove.

Mixed partial derivative theorem

For any function $f(x, y)$ that is sufficiently smooth,

$$\frac{\partial^2 f}{\partial x \, \partial y} = \frac{\partial^2 f}{\partial y \, \partial x}, \quad \text{or equivalently,} \quad f_{xy} = f_{yx}.$$

A similar result applies to a smooth function $f(x_1, x_2, \ldots, x_n)$ of n variables. Again, the order of differentiation does not matter, so

$$\frac{\partial^2 f}{\partial x_i \, \partial x_j} = \frac{\partial^2 f}{\partial x_j \, \partial x_i} \quad \text{for all } x_i \text{ and } x_j.$$

When $x_i = x_j$ this is a trivial identity. The interest lies in the case $x_i \neq x_j$.

You do not need to know precisely what is meant by 'smooth' in this context. In fact, we will assume that the mixed partial derivative theorem applies to all the functions that you will meet in this module.

Exercise 6

Given $f(x, y) = e^{2x+3y}$, calculate $f_{xy}(0, 0)$ and $f_{yx}(0, 0)$.

Exercise 7

Given $f(x, t) = \cos(3x - 2t)$, find expressions for f_{xx} and f_{tt}. Hence write down a relationship between f_{xx} and f_{tt} that applies for all values of x and t for the given function.

---

2 Chain rules and the gradient vector

This section describes a number of rules known as *chain rules*. One of these rules will allow us to find the slope of a surface when we move in an arbitrary direction (not just parallel to the x- or y-axis). In the process, we will use partial derivatives to define a quantity called the *gradient vector*. This will be important later in this unit, and for later units in this book.

2.1   The chain rule for small changes

Suppose that a variable f depends on a single variable x, and this dependence is described by the function $f(x)$. Then we can write

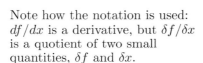

$$\frac{df}{dx} \simeq \frac{\delta f}{\delta x}, \tag{9}$$

Note how the notation is used: df/dx is a derivative, but $\delta f/\delta x$ is a quotient of two small quantities, δf and δx.

provided that δx and the corresponding δf are small enough. Rearranging this equation gives an approximate formula for the change in f that accompanies a very small change in x:

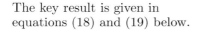

$$\delta f \simeq \frac{df}{dx} \delta x. \tag{10}$$

We therefore see that df/dx determines the *sensitivity* of f to small changes in x. This is important when x is found by measurement and the function value $f(x)$ is deduced from it: if the derivative df/dx has a large magnitude for the value of x of interest, then we need to be very accurate in our measurement of x in order to make a reasonable estimate of f.

The key result is given in equations (18) and (19) below.

We would now like to extend this idea to a function $f(x, y)$ of two variables. In this case, we are interested in the change in f that arises when x and y *both* change by small amounts.

Figure 12 shows a contour map of a function $f(x, y)$.

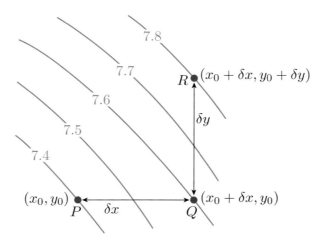

Figure 12   A contour map of a function $f(x, y)$. We consider the change in the value of f as we move from $P = (x_0, y_0)$ to a neighbouring point $R = (x_0 + \delta x, y_0 + \delta y)$.

We consider a point P in the xy-plane with coordinates (x_0, y_0), and a neighbouring point R with coordinates $(x_0 + \delta x, y_0 + \delta y)$. The change in f between these two points is

$$\delta f = f(x_0 + \delta x, y_0 + \delta y) - f(x_0, y_0). \tag{11}$$

The journey from P to R can be taken in two steps. In the first step, the value of y is held constant as we move from P to an intermediate point Q with coordinates $(x_0 + \delta x, y_0)$. In the second step, the value of x is held constant as we move from Q to R.

The change in the value of f in going from P to Q is

$$\delta f_1 = f(x_0 + \delta x, y_0) - f(x_0, y_0), \tag{12}$$

while the change in f in going from Q to R is

$$\delta f_2 = f(x_0 + \delta x, y_0 + \delta y) - f(x_0 + \delta x, y_0). \tag{13}$$

Adding equations (12) and (13), and comparing with equation (11), we see that

$$\delta f = \delta f_1 + \delta f_2. \tag{14}$$

You can check this for the case drawn in Figure 12: in this case, $\delta f = 7.8 - 7.4 = 0.4$, $\delta f_1 = 7.6 - 7.4 = 0.2$ and $\delta f_2 = 7.8 - 7.6 = 0.2$.

More generally, we can say that the change in f is *cumulative*. It is the sum of the change δf_1 obtained when moving in the x-direction and the change δf_2 obtained when moving in the y-direction. Fortunately, we can estimate δf_1 and δf_2 quite easily.

The journey from P to Q starts at the point (x_0, y_0) and makes a displacement δx with y held constant. The resulting change in f is $\delta f = \delta f_1$. By analogy with equation (9), we can therefore write

$$\frac{\partial f}{\partial x} \simeq \frac{\delta f_1}{\delta x}.$$

A partial derivative appears on the left because the journey is made *with y held constant*. This partial derivative is evaluated at point P, and so can be written as $f_x(x_0, y_0)$. Rearranging the equation, we therefore conclude that

$$\delta f_1 \simeq f_x(x_0, y_0)\,\delta x. \tag{15}$$

which is very like equation (10).

A similar argument can be given for the journey from Q to R. In this case, we start from the point Q, with coordinates $(x_0 + \delta x, y)$, and make a displacement δy with x held constant. In this case, we get

$$\delta f_2 \simeq f_y(x_0 + \delta x, y_0)\,\delta y. \tag{16}$$

In fact, this expression is needlessly complicated. If the function f_y varies smoothly, and δx is very small, then we can replace $f_y(x_0 + \delta x, y_0)$ by $f_y(x_0, y_0)$. You might think that this would introduce a small error, but this really does not matter. It turns out that the difference between $f_y(x_0 + \delta x, y_0)$ and $f_y(x_0, y_0)$ is proportional to δx, and because the last term in equation (16) includes a factor δy, the overall error introduced by the replacement is proportional to $\delta x \, \delta y$. Such an error can be neglected in comparison to the terms that we are keeping. It is good enough to say that

$$\delta f_2 \simeq f_y(x_0, y_0) \, \delta y. \tag{17}$$

Finally, using equation (14), we see that the total change in f in going from a point (x_0, y_0) to a neighbouring point $(x_0 + \delta x, y_0 + \delta y)$ is

$$\delta f \simeq f_x(x_0, y_0) \, \delta x + f_y(x_0, y_0) \, \delta y.$$

This equation is valid throughout the domain of the function, so we can replace (x_0, y_0) by (x, y) to obtain our final result, the **chain rule**.

Chain rule for small changes

If $f(x, y)$ is a smooth function, then the change in the dependent variable f that occurs in response to small changes in x and y is

$$\delta f \simeq f_x(x, y) \, \delta x + f_y(x, y) \, \delta y. \tag{18}$$

Using curly dee notation, this rule can also be written in the form

$$\delta f \simeq \frac{\partial f}{\partial x} \, \delta x + \frac{\partial f}{\partial y} \, \delta y. \tag{19}$$

Example 5

The power P output by a star is given by the formula $P = kAT^4$, where A is the star's surface area, T is its surface temperature, and k is a constant. Derive a formula relating the fractional change in power output $\delta P/P$ to the corresponding fractional changes $\delta A/A$ and $\delta T/T$. You may assume that δA and δT are small enough for the chain rule to apply.

Solution

The first-order partial derivatives are

$$\frac{\partial P}{\partial A} = kT^4 \quad \text{and} \quad \frac{\partial P}{\partial T} = 4kAT^3,$$

so the chain rule gives

$$\delta P = \frac{\partial P}{\partial A} \, \delta A + \frac{\partial P}{\partial T} \, \delta T$$

$$= kT^4 \, \delta A + 4kAT^3 \, \delta T.$$

Dividing both sides by $P = kAT^4$, we get

$$\frac{\delta P}{P} \simeq \frac{\delta A}{A} + 4\frac{\delta T}{T}.$$

The coefficient 4 multiplying $\delta T/T$ shows that a 1% increase in temperature produces an approximately 4% increase in power output.

Exercise 8

A quantity f is given by the function

$$f = f(x, y) = \frac{xy}{x + y}.$$

Find $\partial f/\partial x$ and $\partial f/\partial y$, and use the chain rule to estimate the small change in f that occurs when x changes from 1.00 to 1.01, and y changes from 4.00 to 3.99.

Note that $1/f = 1/x + 1/y$. Relationships like this occur when describing electrical circuits and optical lenses.

2.2   Other versions of the chain rule

In ordinary calculus, we often have to differentiate 'a function of a function'. Such a situation arises if the velocity $v = v(x)$ of a particle is given as a function of its position $x = x(t)$, which in turn is a function of time t. We can then write

$$v = v(x) = v(x(t)).$$

You know how to differentiate v with respect to t in such a case. We use the ordinary chain rule of calculus:

$$\frac{dv}{dt} = \frac{dv}{dx} \times \frac{dx}{dt}. \tag{20}$$

So if $v(x) = x^2$ and $x(t) = \sin t$, we have

$$\frac{dv}{dt} = \frac{dv}{dx} \times \frac{dx}{dt} = 2x \times \cos t = 2\sin t \cos t,$$

where we have used $x = \sin t$ in the last step. We could, of course, get the same result by noting that $v = x^2 = \sin^2 t$, and then differentiating $\sin^2 t$ directly; this makes *implicit* use of the chain rule, but we have chosen to be more explicit.

In this subsection, we will look at various generalisations of equation (20) to functions of more than one variable. All these results will be based on equations (18) and (19), and they are all called *chain rules*.

Differentiation with respect to a parameter

Suppose that x and y are both functions of the same variable t. For example, we could have

$$x = R\cos t \quad \text{and} \quad y = R\sin t, \tag{21}$$

where R is a constant and $0 \le t < 2\pi$. The variable t is called a **parameter**. It may represent time, but this is not essential; t could be any quantity that increases as we trace out a given path.

The fact that x and y are both functions of t implies that they are related to one another. In the present case, x and y both lie on a circle of radius R centred on the origin, as indicated in Figure 13, and we say that equations (21) provide a **parametric representation** of this circle. For a given value of t, they specify a definite point on this circle, and as t increases from 0 to 2π, we go once around the circle anticlockwise.

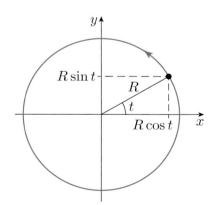

Figure 13   The parametric representation $x = R\cos t$, $y = R\sin t$, $0 \le t < 2\pi$, for points on a circle traced anticlockwise

Suppose that we are given a function $f(x, y)$ with x and y related to the parameter t by equations of the form $x = x(t)$, $y = y(t)$, so that

$$f = f(x(t), y(t)).$$

Then we can ask: what is the rate of change of f with respect to t? The answer is easily found by dividing both sides of equation (19) (the chain rule for small changes) by a small change δt:

$$\frac{\delta f}{\delta t} = \frac{\partial f}{\partial x}\frac{\delta x}{\delta t} + \frac{\partial f}{\partial y}\frac{\delta y}{\delta t}, \tag{22}$$

and then taking the limit as δt tends to zero. This gives the following version of the chain rule.

Chain rule for differentiation with respect to a parameter

If $f = f(x(t), y(t))$, then

$$\frac{df}{dt} = \frac{\partial f}{\partial x}\frac{dx}{dt} + \frac{\partial f}{\partial y}\frac{dy}{dt}. \tag{23}$$

It is worth reflecting on the notation used here. Because $x(t)$ and $y(t)$ are functions of a single variable, we use the ordinary derivatives dx/dt and dy/dt, written with straight dees. By contrast, $f(x, y)$ is a function of two variables, so we use the partial derivatives $\partial f/\partial x$ and $\partial f/\partial y$, written with curly dees. Neither of these should be confused with ratios of small quantities, such as $\delta x/\delta t$ or $\delta y/\delta t$, which appear in equation (22).

Equation (23) is a direct extension of equation (20) to functions of two variables. We could, of course, substitute the functions $x(t)$ and $y(t)$ directly into $f(x, y)$ and carry out an ordinary differentiation with respect to t. Nevertheless, we will use equation (23) in the following example and exercises because this version of the chain rule is a valuable result with many uses and it is important to become familiar with it.

Example 6

With distances measured in metres, the height h of a rock pinnacle depends on horizontal coordinates x and y according to the function

$$h(x, y) = 1000 - 3x^2 - 2xy - 4y^2$$
$$\text{for } -10 < x < 10 \text{ and } -10 < y < 10.$$

A mountaineer follows the blue path shown in Figure 14, with her x- and y-coordinates given by the functions

$$x(t) = 5\cos(2t) \quad \text{and} \quad y(t) = 5\sin(2t) \quad \text{for } 0 \leq t < \pi/2.$$

Use the chain rule to calculate dh/dt as a function of t.

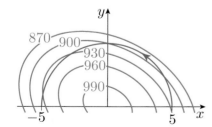

Figure 14 Contour map of a rock pinnacle (orange) with the projection on the xy-plane of the path followed by a mountaineer (blue)

Solution

The chain rule (in the form of equation (23)) tells us that

$$\frac{dh}{dt} = \frac{\partial h}{\partial x}\frac{dx}{dt} + \frac{\partial h}{\partial y}\frac{dy}{dt}.$$

The required partial derivatives are

$$\frac{\partial h}{\partial x} = -6x - 2y, \quad \frac{\partial h}{\partial y} = -2x - 8y,$$

while the derivatives of $x(t)$ and $y(t)$ are

$$\frac{dx}{dt} = -10\sin(2t), \quad \frac{dy}{dt} = 10\cos(2t).$$

We therefore obtain

$$\frac{dh}{dt} = (-6x - 2y)(-10\sin(2t)) + (-2x - 8y)(10\cos(2t))$$
$$= 20\big((3x + y)\sin(2t) - (x + 4y)\cos(2t)\big).$$

Finally, we use the parametric equations for x and y to express everything in terms of t. Direct substitution gives

$$\frac{dh}{dt} = 100\big(3\cos(2t)\sin(2t) + \sin^2(2t) - \cos^2(2t) - 4\sin(2t)\cos(2t)\big)$$
$$= 100\big(\sin^2(2t) - \cos^2(2t) - \sin(2t)\cos(2t)\big).$$

Although it is not essential to do so, we could simplify this answer using trigonometric identities to obtain

$$\frac{dh}{dt} = -50\big(2\cos(4t) + \sin(4t)\big).$$

The final answer is the rate of change of h with respect to the parameter t. The significance of this parameter is left open in this question: it could represent time, in which case dh/dt would be the rate of change of height with respect to time, but this is not essential – in general, t could be any variable that increases along the path.

Exercise 9

Given $z = \sin x - 3\cos y$, use the chain rule to find the rate of change of z with respect to t, where x and y are given by the parametric equations $x = t^2$ and $y = 2t$.

Exercise 10

Given $z = y\sin x$, use the chain rule to find the rate of change of z with respect to t along the curve $(x(t), y(t))$, where $x = e^t$ and $y = t^2$. Evaluate this rate of change at $t = 0$.

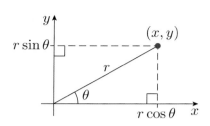

Figure 15 Polar coordinates: a point is defined by the distance r and the angle θ

This is an example of our deliberate 'abuse of notation'. $T(x,y)$ and $T(r,\theta)$ are different mathematical functions representing the same quantity, namely temperature.

The chain rule for a change of variables

At the start of this unit we used the example of temperature measured on the surface of a circular disc. This was described by a function $T(x,y)$ of the Cartesian coordinates x and y of points on the disc. But there is no compelling reason to choose Cartesian coordinates. We could equally well use *polar coordinates* r and θ, which are defined in Figure 15. From Figure 15, you can see that x and y are related to r and θ by the equations

$$x = r\cos\theta \quad \text{and} \quad y = r\sin\theta.$$

These equations imply that x and y are functions of r and θ, and we can express this by writing

$$x = x(r,\theta) \quad \text{and} \quad y = y(r,\theta).$$

The temperature function can then be regarded as a function of r and θ:

$$T(r,\theta) = T(x(r,\theta), y(r,\theta)).$$

We can ask: what is the rate of change of T with respect to r when θ is held constant? This is given by the partial derivative $\partial T/\partial r$, and we will now explain how to calculate this partial derivative from expressions for $T(x,y)$, $x(r,\theta)$ and $y(r,\theta)$ using another form of the chain rule.

Instead of using the r and θ of polar coordinates, let us consider a more general situation. Suppose that we are given a function $f(x,y)$ where the variables x and y are expressed in terms of two other variables, u and v, so that $x = x(u,v)$ and $y = y(u,v)$. Then we can write

$$f = f(x(u,v), y(u,v)),$$

and regard f as a function of u and v.

If x and y change by small amounts, we know that

$$\delta f = \frac{\partial f}{\partial x}\,\delta x + \frac{\partial f}{\partial y}\,\delta y.$$

Now divide both sides of this equation by δu, *under conditions in which v is held constant*. This division gives

$$\frac{\delta f}{\delta u} = \frac{\partial f}{\partial x}\frac{\delta x}{\delta u} + \frac{\partial f}{\partial y}\frac{\delta y}{\delta u},$$

and if we now take the limit as δu tends to zero *while holding v constant*, then the ratios of small quantities become *partial* derivatives. This leads to another form of the chain rule, used when we change variables from (x,y) to (u,v).

Chain rule for a change of variables

If $f = f(x,y)$ with $x = x(u,v)$ and $y = y(u,v)$, then

$$\frac{\partial f}{\partial u} = \frac{\partial f}{\partial x}\frac{\partial x}{\partial u} + \frac{\partial f}{\partial y}\frac{\partial y}{\partial u}. \tag{24}$$

By a similar argument, but dividing by δv while holding u constant,

$$\frac{\partial f}{\partial v} = \frac{\partial f}{\partial x}\frac{\partial x}{\partial v} + \frac{\partial f}{\partial y}\frac{\partial y}{\partial v}. \tag{25}$$

In these equations, $f(x,y)$ is a function of x and y, and $\partial f/\partial x$ implies that y is held constant, while $x(u,v)$ is a function of u and v, and $\partial f/\partial u$ implies that v is held constant, and so on. The best way to see how this works is with an example.

Example 7

Suppose that $f(x,y) = xy^2$, where $x = uv$ and $y = u^2 - v^2$. Use the chain rule to find $\partial f/\partial u$ in terms of u and v.

Solution

We have

$$\frac{\partial f}{\partial x} = y^2 \quad \text{and} \quad \frac{\partial f}{\partial y} = 2xy.$$

Also,

$$\frac{\partial x}{\partial u} = v \quad \text{and} \quad \frac{\partial y}{\partial u} = 2u.$$

So the chain rule (equation (24)) gives

$$\frac{\partial f}{\partial u} = vy^2 + 4uxy = v(u^2 - v^2)^2 + 4u^2 v(u^2 - v^2),$$

which can (optionally) be tidied up to give

$$\frac{\partial f}{\partial u} = v(u^2 - v^2)(5u^2 - v^2).$$

Exercise 11

Suppose that $f(x,y) = x^2 + y^2$, where $x = 2u + 3v$ and $y = 3u - 2v$. Use the chain rule to find the partial derivatives $\partial f/\partial u$ and $\partial f/\partial v$, and evaluate your answers at $(u,v) = (1,2)$.

Exercise 12

Suppose that $f(x,y) = x^2 - y^2$, where $x = r\cos\theta$ and $y = r\sin\theta$. Use the chain rule to find the partial derivatives $\partial f/\partial r$ and $\partial f/\partial \theta$.

2.3   Slope in an arbitrary direction

You saw earlier that the slope of a surface $z = f(x,y)$ depends on the direction of travel. The slope in the x-direction is given by the partial derivative $\partial f/\partial x$, and the slope in the y-direction is given by $\partial f/\partial y$, but what about the slope in an arbitrary direction?

We can answer this question using the chain rule, but first we must say what happens to the x- and y-coordinates when we move away from a given point (x_0, y_0) in a given direction.

In Figure 16, the arrow represents a direction in the xy-plane, and s is the distance travelled away from a starting point (x_0, y_0) in this direction. By simple trigonometry, we see that as we move away from (x_0, y_0), the x- and y-coordinates vary as

$$x = x_0 + s\cos\theta, \quad y = y_0 + s\sin\theta, \tag{26}$$

where θ is the (smaller) angle between the given direction and the positive x-direction. For a given direction, θ has a fixed value, so equations (26) define functions of the form $x = x(s)$ and $y = y(s)$. In other words, they are parametric equations describing a straight-line journey away from (x_0, y_0) in terms of the parameter s.

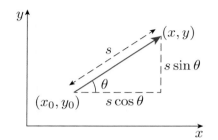

Figure 16 A direction in the xy-plane, starting at (x_0, y_0) and heading at an angle θ to the x-direction

Substituting $x = x(s)$ and $y = y(s)$ in the function $f(x, y)$ gives a function $f(x(s), y(s))$ of s. We can therefore use the chain rule in the form of equation (23) to write down the rate of change of f with respect to s:

$$\frac{df}{ds} = \frac{\partial f}{\partial x}\frac{dx}{ds} + \frac{\partial f}{\partial y}\frac{dy}{ds}.$$

The derivatives dx/ds and dy/ds are immediately found from equations (26), so we conclude that

$$\frac{df}{ds} = \frac{\partial f}{\partial x}\cos\theta + \frac{\partial f}{\partial y}\sin\theta.$$

But what does df/ds mean? It is the rate of change of f, the height of the surface, with respect to the parameter s. In this case, however, the parameter s is the distance travelled in the chosen direction. It follows that at any given point, df/ds is the *slope of the surface in the chosen direction*.

We conclude that at a point (x, y), the slope of the surface $z = f(x, y)$ in a chosen direction is

$$\text{slope} = f_x(x, y)\cos\theta + f_y(x, y)\sin\theta, \tag{27}$$

where θ is related to the chosen direction as shown in Figure 16.

Rather than referring to Figure 16, it is convenient to specify our chosen direction more compactly. The unit vector in the chosen direction is just

$$\widehat{\mathbf{n}} = \cos\theta\,\mathbf{i} + \sin\theta\,\mathbf{j},$$

and this has components $\widehat{n}_x = \cos\theta$ and $\widehat{n}_y = \sin\theta$, so we can restate our conclusion as follows.

Slope of a surface in an arbitrary direction

At any point (x, y), the slope of the surface $z = f(x, y)$ in the direction of the unit vector $\widehat{\mathbf{n}}$ is

$$\text{slope in } \widehat{\mathbf{n}}\text{-direction} = \widehat{n}_x\, f_x(x, y) + \widehat{n}_y\, f_y(x, y). \tag{28}$$

We will rephrase and apply this result in the next subsection, using the important concept of *gradient*.

Exercise 13

Check that equation (28) makes sense in the following special cases.

(a) $\hat{\mathbf{n}}$ points in the x-direction

(b) $\hat{\mathbf{n}}$ points in the y-direction

2.4   The gradient vector and maximum slope

For a given surface $z = f(x, y)$, the slope at a given point depends on the direction chosen for $\hat{\mathbf{n}}$. In one direction, the slope is greatest, and this corresponds to climbing straight up the hill. In another direction, the slope is zero, and this corresponds to skirting the hill, following a contour line.

To investigate the various slopes that can be obtained, it is very useful to define a new quantity. We take the first-order partial derivatives $f_x(x, y)$ and $f_y(x, y)$ and form the vector $f_x(x, y)\,\mathbf{i} + f_y(x, y)\,\mathbf{j}$. This is called the *gradient vector*, and is denoted by $\mathbf{grad}\, f$.

Note that **grad** is printed in bold because the gradient is a vector function. In your written work you should underline it.

The gradient vector

Given a function $f(x, y)$, the **gradient vector** or **gradient** of f is defined by

$$\mathbf{grad}\, f = f_x(x, y)\,\mathbf{i} + f_y(x, y)\,\mathbf{j} = \frac{\partial f}{\partial x}\,\mathbf{i} + \frac{\partial f}{\partial y}\,\mathbf{j}. \qquad (29)$$

This is a vector-valued function of x and y. At a given point (a, b), it is a particular vector:

$$[\mathbf{grad}\, f]_{x=a,\, y=b} = f_x(a, b)\,\mathbf{i} + f_y(a, b)\,\mathbf{j}. \qquad (30)$$

Exercise 14

Calculate the gradient of the function $f(x, y) = xy^2$, and evaluate it at the point $(1, 2)$.

According to definition (29), the components $[\mathbf{grad}\, f]_x$ and $[\mathbf{grad}\, f]_y$ of the gradient vector are just the first-order partial derivatives f_x and f_y, and this allows us to rewrite equation (28) as

In this context, $[\mathbf{grad}\, f]_x$ and $[\mathbf{grad}\, f]_y$ are the x- and y-components of the vector $\mathbf{grad}\, f$.

$$\text{slope in } \hat{\mathbf{n}}\text{-direction} = \hat{n}_x\,[\mathbf{grad}\, f]_x + \hat{n}_y\,[\mathbf{grad}\, f]_y$$
$$= \hat{\mathbf{n}} \cdot \mathbf{grad}\, f. \qquad (31)$$

The right-hand side is the scalar product of two vectors, $\hat{\mathbf{n}}$ and $\mathbf{grad}\, f$.

Recall from Unit 4 that the component of a vector $\mathbf{a}$ in the direction of the unit vector $\hat{\mathbf{n}}$ is given by the scalar product $\hat{\mathbf{n}} \cdot \mathbf{a}$.

Because $\hat{\mathbf{n}}$ is a unit vector, we can say that the slope in the direction of $\hat{\mathbf{n}}$ is equal to the *component* of $\mathbf{grad}\, f$ in the direction of $\hat{\mathbf{n}}$ – a simple and memorable result.

Example 8

Calculate the slope of the function $f(x, y) = xy^3$ at the point $(1, 2)$, in the direction of the unit vector $\hat{\mathbf{n}} = \frac{3}{5}\,\mathbf{i} - \frac{4}{5}\,\mathbf{j}$.

Solution

The gradient of the function is
$$\mathbf{grad}\, f = \frac{\partial f}{\partial x}\,\mathbf{i} + \frac{\partial f}{\partial y}\,\mathbf{j} = y^3\,\mathbf{i} + 3xy^2\,\mathbf{j}.$$

At any point (x, y), the slope in the direction of the unit vector $\hat{\mathbf{n}}$ is
$$\hat{\mathbf{n}} \cdot \mathbf{grad}\, f = \left(\tfrac{3}{5}\,\mathbf{i} - \tfrac{4}{5}\,\mathbf{j}\right) \cdot \left(y^3\,\mathbf{i} + 3xy^2\,\mathbf{j}\right) = \tfrac{3}{5}y^3 - \tfrac{12}{5}xy^2,$$
so at the point $(1, 2)$, the slope is $24/5 - 48/5 = -24/5 = -4.8$.

Exercise 15

Calculate the slope of the function $f(x, y) = 2x^2y^2 + 3xy^3$ at the point $(1, 2)$, in the direction of the (non-unit) vector $\mathbf{i} - \mathbf{j}$.

A note on terminology

When dealing with the graph of a function of one variable, we use the words slope and gradient interchangeably. For a function of two variables, we must be more careful. We refer to the *slope* in a particular direction. The *gradient* is the gradient vector in equation (29). The component of the gradient in a given direction is equal to the slope in that direction, but the gradient vector is not itself a slope.

We can use the properties of scalar products to deduce some properties of the gradient vector. Any scalar product $\mathbf{a} \cdot \mathbf{b}$ can be written as $|\mathbf{a}|\,|\mathbf{b}|\cos\alpha$, where α is the (smaller) angle between the directions of $\mathbf{a}$ and $\mathbf{b}$. Since $\hat{\mathbf{n}}$ is a unit vector, with $|\hat{\mathbf{n}}| = 1$, equation (31) gives
$$\text{slope in } \hat{\mathbf{n}}\text{-direction} = |\hat{\mathbf{n}}|\,|\mathbf{grad}\, f|\cos\alpha = |\mathbf{grad}\, f|\cos\alpha, \qquad (32)$$
where α is the angle between the directions of $\hat{\mathbf{n}}$ and $\mathbf{grad}\, f$. From this equation we can gather a rich harvest.

- The slope varies with α, and the maximum slope arises when $\cos\alpha = 1$ and $\alpha = 0$. This occurs when $\hat{\mathbf{n}}$ points in the same direction as $\mathbf{grad}\, f$. So the maximum slope is found in the direction of the vector $\mathbf{grad}\, f$. Put another way, the direction of $\mathbf{grad}\, f$ has a simple interpretation: it is the direction of maximum slope.

- Setting $\alpha = 0$ in equation (32), the maximum slope is equal to $|\mathbf{grad}\, f|$. So the magnitude of $\mathbf{grad}\, f$ is equal to the maximum slope.

- Along a contour line, the function values are constant and the slope is zero. So if $\hat{\mathbf{n}}$ points along a contour line of f, the slope must be equal to zero. However, equation (32) shows that zero slope corresponds to $\cos \alpha = 0$ and $\alpha = \pi/2$, which tells us that $\hat{\mathbf{n}}$ and $\mathbf{grad}\, f$ are perpendicular. Hence $\mathbf{grad}\, f$ is perpendicular to the contour lines of f.

The properties of the gradient vector may be summarised as follows.

Properties of the gradient vector

For a smooth surface $z = f(x, y)$, at any given point (x, y):

- the gradient vector $\mathbf{grad}\, f$ is a vector in the xy-plane

- $\mathbf{grad}\, f$ points in the direction of maximum slope, and its magnitude is equal to the maximum slope

- $\mathbf{grad}\, f$ is perpendicular to the contour line at the given point.

To illustrate these properties, consider the function $f(x, y) = x^2 + y^2$, plotted in Figure 17(a). In this case, the gradient vector is

$$\mathbf{grad}\, f = 2x\,\mathbf{i} + 2y\,\mathbf{j},$$

and this defines a vector at each point in the xy-plane. Figure 17(b) shows arrows representing the gradient vectors at a selection of points.

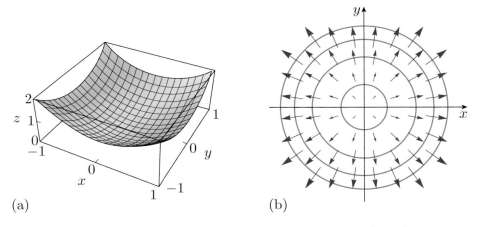

(a)   (b)

Figure 17   (a) A three-dimensional graph of $f(x, y) = x^2 + y^2$. (b) A map in the xy-plane with arrows representing $\mathbf{grad}\, f$ at a selection of points. Contour lines of $f(x, y)$ are shown in orange.

In this case, $\mathbf{grad}\, f$ points radially away from the origin, and its magnitude increases with radial distance from the origin. This makes sense because the slope is steepest in the radially outward direction, and the maximum slope grows as we move outwards. Figure 17(b) also plots the contour lines, which are circles centred on the origin. As expected, the contour line through any given point is perpendicular to the gradient vector at that point.

Exercise 16

Given a function $f(x, y)$, how would you characterise the direction in the xy-plane that gives the steepest *decrease* in $f(x, y)$ at a given point (a, b)?

Exercise 17

A bug in the xy-plane finds itself in a toxic environment. The level of toxicity is given by the function $f(x, y) = 2x^2 y - 3x^3$. The bug is at the point $(1, 2)$. In what direction away from $(1, 2)$ should it initially move in order to lower its exposure to the toxin as rapidly as possible? Specify the direction as a unit vector.

2.5   The chain rule beyond two variables

So far we have focused on functions of two variables. For functions of three or more variables, it is really a case of 'more of the same thing'. For example, if $f = f(x, y, z)$, the chain rule for small changes becomes

$$\delta f = \frac{\partial f}{\partial x}\,\delta x + \frac{\partial f}{\partial y}\,\delta y + \frac{\partial f}{\partial z}\,\delta z.$$

This has the same pattern as for a function of two variables, but with an extra term involving z. The same is true for all the other forms of the chain rule. For example, if $x = x(t)$, $y = y(t)$ and $z = z(t)$, we have

$$\frac{df}{dt} = \frac{\partial f}{\partial x}\frac{dx}{dt} + \frac{\partial f}{\partial y}\frac{dy}{dt} + \frac{\partial f}{\partial z}\frac{dz}{dt}.$$

The calculations get a bit longer, but are essentially the same.

For a function $f(x, y, z)$, the gradient vector is a vector in three-dimensional space, given by

$$\mathbf{grad}\, f = \frac{\partial f}{\partial x}\,\mathbf{i} + \frac{\partial f}{\partial y}\,\mathbf{j} + \frac{\partial f}{\partial z}\,\mathbf{k},$$

where $\mathbf{i}$, $\mathbf{j}$ and $\mathbf{k}$ are Cartesian unit vectors in three-dimensional space. At any given point, this gradient vector is perpendicular to the *contour surfaces* of $f(x, y, z)$ at that point. The direction of $\mathbf{grad}\, f$ is the direction in which the function increases most rapidly, and the magnitude of $\mathbf{grad}\, f$ is the maximum rate of change of f with respect to the distance moved in three-dimensional space.

Exercise 18

(a) Calculate the gradient of the function $f(x, y, z) = x^2 + y^2 + 2z^2$.

(b) The surface of a solid object is given by the equation $f(x, y, z) = 7$, where $f(x, y, z)$ is the function in part (a). Find a unit vector that is perpendicular to this surface at the point $(1, 2, 1)$.

Exercise 19

(a) Use the result of Example 3 to find the gradient of the function
$V(x, y, z) = (x^2 + y^2 + z^2)^{-1/2}$.

(b) Describe in words the direction in which V increases most rapidly.

(c) What is the magnitude of **grad** V at any point $(x, y, z) \neq (0, 0, 0)$?

3 Taylor polynomials

This section is a sort of bridge. Our interest in Taylor polynomials arises mainly because they are needed in the final section of this unit, which deals with the stationary points of functions and their classification. The main point to grasp is the fact that close to a chosen point, functions can be approximated by polynomials. We start by revising the situation for functions of a single variable.

3.1 Review for functions of one variable

You know that a function of one variable can be approximated by a suitable polynomial. For example, Figure 18 shows that the function $f(x) = \sin x$ can be approximated near $x = 0$ by the simple polynomial $p(x) = x$. This approximation is a good one provided that we stay close enough to $x = 0$ (say within 0.1 of it). Similarly, Figure 19 shows that the function $g(x) = \cos x$ can be approximated near $x = \pi$ by the second-order polynomial $p(x) = -1 + \frac{1}{2}(x - \pi)^2$.

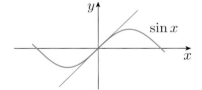

Figure 18   Near $x = 0$, $\sin x$ (orange) is approximated by $p(x) = x$ (blue)

How do we choose a suitable polynomial to use in any particular case? If we want to approximate the function $f(x)$ near the point $x = a$, the secret is to choose a polynomial that matches $f(x)$ in value, and in the values of its first few derivatives, at $x = a$.

For example, let us compare the function $f(x) = \sin x$ with the polynomial $p(x) = x$ at the point $x = 0$. The values match at $x = 0$ because $f(0) = p(0) = 0$. The first derivatives are

$$f'(x) = \cos x \quad \text{and} \quad p'(x) = 1.$$

These also match at $x = 0$ because $f'(0) = p'(0) = 1$. Finally, the second derivatives are

$$f''(x) = -\sin x \quad \text{and} \quad p''(x) = 0,$$

and these also match at $x = 0$ because $f''(0) = p''(0) = 0$.

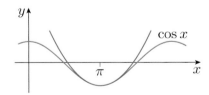

Figure 19   Near $x = \pi$, $\cos x$ (orange) is approximated by $p(x) = -1 + \frac{1}{2}(x - \pi)^2$ (blue)

Show that the function $f(x) = \cos x$ and the polynomial $p(x) = -1 + \frac{1}{2}(x - \pi)^2$ are matched in their values and in the values of their first, second and third derivatives at $x = \pi$.

The problem of finding a suitable polynomial has a general solution. The polynomial that matches $f(x)$ in its values, and in the values of its first n derivatives, at the point $x = a$, is

$$p(x) = f(a) + f'(a)(x - a) + \frac{1}{2!}f''(a)(x - a)^2$$

$$+ \frac{1}{3!}f'''(a)(x - a)^3 + \cdots + \frac{1}{n!}f^{(n)}(a)(x - a)^n, \tag{33}$$

where $f^{(n)}(a)$ is the nth derivative of $f(x)$ evaluated at $x = a$, and $n!$ is factorial n given by $n! = n(n - 1)(n - 2) \ldots 1$.

This polynomial is called the nth-order **Taylor polynomial** for $f(x)$ about $x = a$.

To take a definite case, consider the function $f(x) = \cos x$ of Exercise 20. In this case, successive differentiations give

$$f(x) = \cos x, \quad f'(x) = -\sin x, \quad f''(x) = -\cos x, \quad f'''(x) = \sin x.$$

So at the point $x = \pi$, we have

$$f(\pi) = -1, \quad f'(\pi) = 0, \quad f''(\pi) = 1, \quad f'''(\pi) = 0.$$

Substituting these constants into equation (33) gives the third-order Taylor polynomial for $\cos x$ about the point $x = \pi$:

$$p(x) = -1 + \tfrac{1}{2}(x - \pi)^2,$$

and this is just what we used in Figure 19.

Two points about Taylor polynomials are worth mentioning. First, for many functions, higher-order Taylor polynomials produce successively better approximations. This is illustrated in Figure 20. Second, as we approach the point $x = a$ about which a given low-order Taylor polynomial is calculated, the polynomial becomes increasingly accurate. If we get *extremely* close to the point $x = a$, the function and its low-order Taylor polynomials become practically indistinguishable.

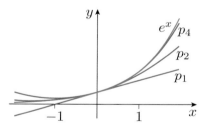

Figure 20   A graph of e^x against x (in orange) compared with Taylor polynomials for e^x of orders 1, 2 and 4 (blue)

(a) Find the first and second derivatives of the function $f(t) = \ln(1 + t^2)$.

(b) Write down the second-order Taylor polynomial for $f(t)$ about the point $t = 0$.

(c) Write down the second-order Taylor polynomial for $f(t)$ about the point $t = 1$.

3.2 Functions of two variables

We now extend the concept of a Taylor polynomial to functions of two or more variables. First we must generalise the idea of a polynomial to cover more than one variable. An expression of the form

$$p(x, y) = A + Bx + Cy, \tag{34}$$

where A, B and C are constants (with B and C not both equal to zero), is called a polynomial of order 1 in x and y. It is also called a *linear polynomial* in x and y.

Polynomials in more than one variable are also called *multinomials*.

An expression of the form

$$p(x, y) = A + Bx + Cy + Dx^2 + Exy + Fy^2, \tag{35}$$

where A, B, C, D, E and F are constants (with D, E and F not all equal to zero), is called a polynomial of order 2. It is also called a *quadratic polynomial* in x and y.

Notice that each term in these polynomials is of the form constant $\times x^n y^m$, where n and m are zero or positive integers. A term in a polynomial is said to be of order N if $n + m = N$. So linear polynomials contain terms up to order 1, and quadratic polynomials contain terms up to order 2.

Given a function $f(x, y)$, we would like to find a suitable polynomial in x and y that approximates the function in the vicinity of a point (a, b). The key is to choose the coefficients in the polynomial in such a way that the function and the polynomial match in their values, and in the values of their first n partial derivatives, at the point (a, b). This is just what an nth-order Taylor polynomial does. In practice, we need Taylor polynomials of only first and second order, so we will concentrate on these.

We will first write down a general expression for the first-order Taylor polynomial for a function $f(x, y)$ about a point (a, b). Then we will check that it has the desired properties. This process will then be repeated for the second-order Taylor polynomial.

First-order Taylor polynomial

The **first-order Taylor polynomial** for $f(x, y)$ about (a, b) is

$$p_1(x, y) = f(a, b) + f_x(a, b)(x - a) + f_y(a, b)(y - b). \tag{36}$$

We can easily check that this polynomial does what is needed. Setting $x = a$ and $y = b$ in equation (36), we see that $p_1(a, b) = f(a, b)$, so the function and the polynomial have the same value at the point (a, b). Moreover, a and b have fixed values, so $f(a, b)$, $f_x(a, b)$ and $f_y(a, b)$ are all constants. Partial differentiation of $p_1(x, y)$ with respect to x and y then gives

$$\frac{\partial p_1}{\partial x} = f_x(a, b) = \left.\frac{\partial f}{\partial x}\right|_{x=a,\, y=b} \quad \text{and} \quad \frac{\partial p_1}{\partial y} = f_y(a, b) = \left.\frac{\partial f}{\partial y}\right|_{x=a,\, y=b}.$$

In particular, the values of $\partial p_1/\partial x$ and $\partial p_1/\partial y$ match those of $\partial f/\partial x$ and $\partial f/\partial y$ at (a,b), so the function and the polynomial $p_1(x,y)$ are matched in their values, and in the values of their *first-order* partial derivatives, at the point (a,b). This is what is required of a first-order Taylor polynomial.

The second-order Taylor polynomial for a function involves its second-order partial derivatives.

Second-order Taylor polynomial

The **second-order Taylor polynomial** for $f(x,y)$ about (a,b) is

$$p_2(x,y) = f(a,b) + f_x(a,b)(x-a) + f_y(a,b)(y-b)$$
$$+ \tfrac{1}{2}\big(f_{xx}(a,b)(x-a)^2 + 2f_{xy}(a,b)(x-a)(y-b)$$
$$+ f_{yy}(a,b)(y-b)^2\big). \tag{37}$$

Be careful to get the second line right: common errors are to not multiply all three terms by $\frac{1}{2}$, or to omit the factor 2 in the middle term.

It is straightforward to check that the value of this polynomial, and the values of all its first- and second-order derivatives, match those of $f(x,y)$ at (a,b). This is done in the following exercise.

Exercise 22

Writing $h(x,y) = p_2(x,y)$, use equation (37) to show that

$$h(a,b) = f(a,b),$$
$$h_x(a,b) = f_x(a,b), \quad h_y(a,b) = f_y(a,b),$$
$$h_{xx}(a,b) = f_{xx}(a,b), \quad h_{yy}(a,b) = f_{yy}(a,b), \quad h_{xy}(a,b) = f_{xy}(a,b).$$

(There is no need to check that $h_{yx}(a,b) = f_{yx}(a,b)$ because this follows from $h_{xy}(a,b) = f_{xy}(a,b)$, thanks to the mixed partial derivative theorem.)

Example 9

Determine the Taylor polynomials of orders 1 and 2 about the point $(2,1)$ for the function $f(x,y) = x^3 + xy - 2y^2$.

Solution

Differentiating the function partially with respect to x and partially with respect to y gives

$$f_x(x,y) = 3x^2 + y, \quad f_y(x,y) = x - 4y.$$

Differentiating partially again gives

$$f_{xx}(x,y) = 6x, \quad f_{xy}(x,y) = 1, \quad f_{yy}(x,y) = -4.$$

It follows that

$$f(2,1) = 8, \quad f_x(2,1) = 13, \quad f_y(2,1) = -2,$$
$$f_{xx}(2,1) = 12, \quad f_{xy}(2,1) = 1, \quad f_{yy}(2,1) = -4,$$

so the first-order Taylor polynomial is

$$p_1(x,y) = 8 + 13(x-2) - 2(y-1),$$

and the second-order Taylor polynomial is

$$\begin{aligned}
p_2(x,y) &= 8 + 13(x-2) - 2(y-1) \\
&\quad + \tfrac{1}{2}\left(12(x-2)^2 + 2(x-2)(y-1) - 4(y-1)^2\right) \\
&= 8 + 13(x-2) - 2(y-1) \\
&\quad + 6(x-2)^2 + (x-2)(y-1) - 2(y-1)^2.
\end{aligned}$$

The answer can be left in this form as, for many purposes, there is no advantage to be gained in collecting terms in powers of x and y.

Exercise 23

Given $f(x,y) = x^2 e^{3y}$, find the first- and second-order Taylor polynomials for $f(x,y)$ about the point $(2,0)$.

The tangent plane

You saw in Subsection 1.3 that a function $f(x,y)$ can be plotted as a surface $z = f(x,y)$ in three-dimensional space. The first-order Taylor polynomial for this function is

$$p_1(x,y) = f(a,b) + f_x(a,b)(x-a) + f_y(a,b)(y-b),$$

and this can also be plotted as a surface

$$z = p_1(x,y).$$

Comparing with equation (3) and the discussion following it, we see that the surface $z = p_1(x,y)$ is a plane. It is called the **tangent plane** of the surface $z = f(x,y)$.

To see why this name is appropriate, first note that $f(a,b) = p_1(a,b)$, so the surface $z = f(x,y)$ coincides with the tangent plane at the point (a,b). We also know that the first partial derivatives of f are the same as those of p_1 at the point (a,b). So we must have

$$[\mathbf{grad}\, p_1]_{x=a,\, y=b} = f_x(a,b)\,\mathbf{i} + f_y(a,b)\,\mathbf{j} = [\mathbf{grad}\, f]_{x=a,\, y=b}. \qquad (38)$$

The slope in any chosen direction in the xy-plane is the component of the gradient vector in that direction, so *the tangent plane and the surface of the function have exactly the same slopes at (a,b) in all directions.* This is why the tangent plane is so-called. It is a natural generalisation of the concept of a tangent line to a curve at a given point (see Figure 21).

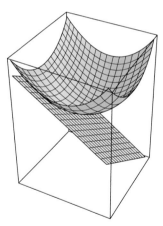

Figure 21   The tangent plane of $f(x,y) = x^2 + y^2$ at the point $x = -1$, $y = -1$

3.3   Matrix representation of Taylor polynomials

Our main interest will be in first- and second-order Taylor polynomials for functions of two or more variables. For future use, it will be helpful to take another look at equations (36) and (37), and recast them in matrix form.

First note that the first-order Taylor polynomial about (a, b) can be written as

$$p_1(x, y) = f(a, b) + f_x(a, b)(x - a) + f_y(a, b)(y - b)$$
$$= f(a, b) + [f_x(a, b) \quad f_y(a, b)] \begin{bmatrix} x - a \\ y - b \end{bmatrix}. \tag{39}$$

By using matrix multiplication on the right-hand side, you can check that this is equivalent to equation (36).

It is convenient to introduce the column vector

$$\mathbf{R} = \begin{bmatrix} x - a \\ y - b \end{bmatrix}, \tag{40}$$

which represents the displacement of the point (x, y) from (a, b) and is called the **displacement vector**. We also define

$$\mathbf{G} = \begin{bmatrix} f_x(a, b) \\ f_y(a, b) \end{bmatrix}, \tag{41}$$

which is a matrix representation of the **gradient vector**.

In terms of these matrices, the first-order Taylor polynomial can be written in the compact form

$$p_1(x, y) = f(a, b) + \mathbf{G}^T \mathbf{R}, \tag{42}$$

where the transpose converts the column matrix $\mathbf{G}$ into the row matrix needed in equation (39).

The second-order Taylor polynomial can also be written in matrix form. We introduce the matrix of second-order partial derivatives

$$\mathbf{H} = \begin{bmatrix} f_{xx}(a, b) & f_{xy}(a, b) \\ f_{yx}(a, b) & f_{yy}(a, b) \end{bmatrix}.$$

Then, using matrix multiplication, you can check that

$$\mathbf{R}^T \mathbf{H} \mathbf{R} = [x - a \quad y - b] \begin{bmatrix} f_{xx}(a, b) & f_{xy}(a, b) \\ f_{yx}(a, b) & f_{yy}(a, b) \end{bmatrix} \begin{bmatrix} x - a \\ y - b \end{bmatrix}$$
$$= [x - a \quad y - b] \begin{bmatrix} f_{xx}(a, b)(x - a) + f_{xy}(a, b)(y - b) \\ f_{yx}(a, b)(x - a) + f_{yy}(a, b)(y - b) \end{bmatrix}$$
$$= f_{xx}(a, b)(x - a)^2 + 2f_{xy}(a, b)(x - a)(y - b) + f_{yy}(a, b)(y - b)^2, \tag{43}$$

where we have used the mixed partial derivative theorem in the last step. Comparing with equation (37), we see that the second-order Taylor polynomial can be written as follows.

Second-order Taylor polynomial in matrix form

$$p_2(x, y) = f(a, b) + \mathbf{G}^T \mathbf{R} + \tfrac{1}{2} \mathbf{R}^T \mathbf{H} \mathbf{R}. \tag{44}$$

A compact formula is all well and good – but you might think that we would need to expand it out to use it. However, in the next section you will see that matrix methods can be applied directly to equation (44) to obtain useful results. In particular, the matrix $\mathbf{H}$ will become a focus of attention. This matrix is called the **Hessian matrix** after the German mathematician Otto Hesse (1811–1874).

Equation (44) is also useful if we need a second-order Taylor polynomial for a function of three (or more) variables. This is because it remains true no matter how many variables the function contains! The only thing that changes is the size of the matrices $\mathbf{R}$, $\mathbf{G}$ and $\mathbf{H}$. For a function $f(x, y, z)$ of three variables, expanded about the point (a, b, c),

$$\mathbf{G} = \begin{bmatrix} f_x(a,b,c) \\ f_y(a,b,c) \\ f_z(a,b,c) \end{bmatrix} \quad \text{and} \quad \mathbf{R} = \begin{bmatrix} x - a \\ y - b \\ z - c \end{bmatrix},$$

while the Hessian matrix of second-order partial derivatives becomes

$$\mathbf{H} = \begin{bmatrix} f_{xx}(a,b,c) & f_{xy}(a,b,c) & f_{xz}(a,b,c) \\ f_{yx}(a,b,c) & f_{yy}(a,b,c) & f_{yz}(a,b,c) \\ f_{zx}(a,b,c) & f_{zy}(a,b,c) & f_{zz}(a,b,c) \end{bmatrix}.$$

You need not bother to multiply out these matrices because when we use equation (44) in the next section, we will need only some very general properties of its constituent matrices.

4 Minima, maxima and saddle points

A very useful aspect of calculus is that it gives us a way of finding the maximum or minimum values of a function, and it lets us find the conditions under which these maxima or minima are attained. In this final section you will see how maxima, minima and other stationary points are found and classified for functions of two or more variables.

Maxima and minima in the natural world

In the natural world, many phenomena are governed by maxima or minima. For example, a mechanical system reaches a condition of stable equilibrium when a quantity known as the *potential energy* reaches its minimum value: a chain suspended between two fixed points will hang in such a way that its potential energy is as small as possible (Figure 22). More complicated systems, that can exchange heat with their surroundings, reach a state of thermal and mechanical equilibrium when a quantity called the *free energy* is minimised. The folding of protein molecules, which determines their biological function, is dictated by the configurations of locally minimum free energy (Figure 23). Even systems in motion, such as planets orbiting the Sun, move in such a way that a quantity called the *action* is minimised. No wonder the great Euler, seeking an ultimate explanation, speculated:

> For since the fabric of the universe is most perfect and the work of a most wise Creator, nothing at all takes place in the universe in which some rule of maximum or minimum does not appear.

Figure 22 A chain hangs in such a way that its potential energy has a minimum value

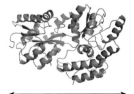

0.000 005 mm

Figure 23 A protein molecule folds in such a way that its free energy has a local minimum value

4.1   Review for functions of one variable

To put our discussion in context, we will briefly remind you of the situation for functions of one variable. The main point is that functions can have local minima and local maxima.

If we are given a function $f(x)$ and a point $x = a$ inside its domain:

- a **local minimum** occurs at $x = a$ if there is a small region around a within which $f(x) > f(a)$ at all points $x \neq a$

- a **local maximum** occurs at $x = a$ if there is a small region around a within which $f(x) < f(a)$ at all points $x \neq a$

- there is an **extremum** at $x = a$ if this point is *either* a local maximum *or* a local minimum.

For example, the function in Figure 24 has local minima at $x = 0.3$ and $x = 1.8$, and a local maximum at $x = 1.3$. All these points are extrema.

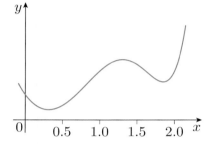

Figure 24   A function $y = f(x)$ with local minima and maxima

There may be several local minima and maxima, so a particular local minimum need not give the smallest possible value of a function (the **global minimum**). Similarly, a particular local maximum need not give the largest possible value of a function (the **global maximum**). The global minimum and global maximum can be found by sifting through all the local minima and maxima. For example, the global minimum of the function in Figure 24 in the region $0 \leq x \leq 2$ is at $x = 0.3$. We will not discuss this point further, but concentrate on the task of finding the local minima and maxima.

We restrict attention to smooth functions $f(x)$, and ignore any minima or maxima that might occur on the boundaries of the domain of $f(x)$. Then calculus can help us to find the local minima and maxima. This is because the tangent line to the graph of $f(x)$ against x is horizontal at a local minimum or maximum. Equivalently, $df/dx = 0$ at such a point. Any point at which the first derivative df/dx is equal to zero is called a **stationary point**. So the extrema (i.e. the local minima and local maxima) are stationary points. However, we can also have stationary points that are not extrema.

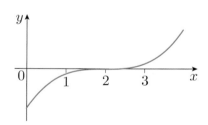

Figure 25   A function $y = f(x)$ with a horizontal point of inflection at $x = 2$

In Figure 25, the stationary point at $x = 2$ is neither a local maximum nor a local minimum. In the immediate vicinity of $x = 2$, points with $x < 2$ have smaller values than $f(2)$, while points with $x > 2$ have larger values than $f(2)$. Such a point is called a **horizontal point of inflection**.

We often need to classify the stationary points – that is, decide whether they are local minima, local maxima or points of inflection. To classify a stationary point at $x = a$, it is helpful to use the second-order Taylor polynomial for $f(x)$ about a:

$$p_2(x) = f(a) + f'(a)(x - a) + \frac{1}{2!}f''(a)(x - a)^2.$$

Since a is a stationary point, we know (by definition) that $f'(a) = 0$, so

$$f(x) \simeq p_2(x) = f(a) + \frac{1}{2!}f''(a)(x - a)^2 \quad \text{(for } x \text{ close to } a\text{).} \tag{45}$$

Now, if we consider a small enough region around $x = a$, then the second-order Taylor polynomial $p_2(x)$ will approximate $f(x)$ extremely well – so well, that we can replace the above $\simeq$ sign by an equals sign with negligible error. Then looking at equation (45), we see that the condition $f''(a) > 0$ guarantees that $f(x) > f(a)$ for all points $x \neq a$. This is precisely the definition of a local minimum. A similar argument, but with $f''(a) < 0$, leads to a local maximum. We therefore have the following test.

> **Second derivative test for stationary points**
>
> Given a function $f(x)$, we can say that:
>
> - when $f'(a) = 0$ and $f''(a) > 0$, we have a local minimum at $x = a$
> - when $f'(a) = 0$ and $f''(a) < 0$, we have a local maximum at $x = a$.

The test works unless $f''(a) = 0$, in which case the test gives us no information; we would need to look at higher-order Taylor polynomials to make a decision. Also note that the second derivative test never identifies a horizontal point of inflection. This is not a great problem because in practical cases the main interest lies in minima and maxima.

4.2 Stationary points for functions of two variables

We will now try to extend the above ideas to a smooth function $f(x, y)$ of two variables. The definitions of local minima and local maxima are essentially the same as before, but take account of the fact that points and regions are now specified by two coordinates.

> **Local minima and maxima**
>
> Given a function $f(x, y)$ and a point (a, b) inside the domain of f:
>
> - a **local minimum** occurs at (a, b) if there is a small region around (a, b) within which $f(x, y) > f(a, b)$ at all points $(x, y) \neq (a, b)$
> - a **local maximum** occurs at (a, b) if there is a small region around (a, b) within which $f(x, y) < f(a, b)$ at all points $(x, y) \neq (a, b)$.

Here, 'inside' implies not on any boundary line.

As before, an **extremum** is a point that is *either* a local minimum *or* a local maximum. For a smooth function $f(x, y)$, the tangent plane to the surface $z = f(x, y)$ is horizontal at any extremum. This means that the slope of the tangent plane is equal to zero for any direction in the xy-plane, so both the partial derivatives f_x and f_y must be zero at an extremum.

Stationary points

A point (a, b) is a **stationary point** of a function $f(x, y)$ if both $f_x(a, b)$ and $f_y(a, b)$ are equal to zero.

All extrema (i.e. all local minima and maxima) are stationary points, but some stationary points are not extrema. Figure 26 shows the three cases that can occur. In all three cases, there is a stationary point at $(0, 0)$ because both the partial derivatives f_x and f_y are equal to zero there.

In Figure 26(a), we have a local minimum because all paths moving smoothly away from $(0, 0)$ initially climb upwards to higher function values. In Figure 26(b), we have a local maximum because all paths moving smoothly away from $(0, 0)$ initially descend downwards to lower function values. But in Figure 26(c), we have something different: some paths moving away from $(0, 0)$ climb upwards, and others descend downwards. This stationary point is neither a local minimum nor a local maximum. It is called a *saddle point* because the shape of the surface is rather like the shape of a saddle placed on a horse's back.

Saddle points

A **saddle point** is a stationary point that is neither a local minimum nor a local maximum. Through such a point, some paths climb to higher function values, while others descend to lower function values.

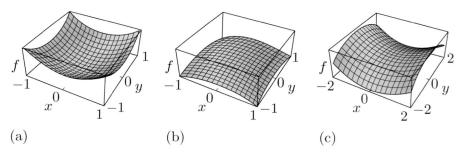

(a)   (b)   (c)

Figure 26 Functions with stationary points at $(0, 0)$: (a) a local minimum; (b) a local maximum; (c) a saddle point

In the next subsection you will see how stationary points can be classified using second-order partial derivatives. For the moment, we concentrate on locating the stationary points using first-order partial derivatives.

Example 10

Locate the stationary point(s) of the function

$$f(x, y) = x^2 + y^2 + (x - 1)(y + 2).$$

Solution

Partially differentiating with respect to x gives

$$f_x(x,y) = 2x + y + 2,$$

and partially differentiating with respect to y gives

$$f_y(x,y) = 2y + x - 1.$$

At a stationary point, $f_x = f_y = 0$, so we need to solve the pair of simultaneous equations

$$2x + \ y = -2,$$
$$x + 2y = 1.$$

These equations have the solution $x = -5/3$, $y = 4/3$, so the only stationary point is at $(x,y) = (-5/3, 4/3)$.

A note of caution! We can always carry out the partial differentiations needed to obtain the simultaneous equations $f_x = 0$, $f_y = 0$. In this unit, such equations can always be solved by hand. More generally, however, the equations may be too complicated for this – they would then be solved numerically on a computer.

Exercise 24

Locate the stationary point(s) of the function

$$f(x,y) = 3x^2 - 4xy + 2y^2 + 4x - 8y.$$

Exercise 25

Locate the stationary point(s) of the function

$$f(x,y) = xy(x + y - 3).$$

4.3   The eigenvalue test

There remains the task of classifying the stationary points – deciding which are local maxima, which are local minima, and which are saddle points. In broad terms, our tactics will be the same as for functions of a single variable: we will use the second-order Taylor polynomial. This method works for functions of any number of variables, but we will initially consider a function $f(x,y)$ of two variables.

Suppose that $f(x,y)$ has a stationary point at (a,b), and that $p_2(x,y)$ is the second-order Taylor polynomial for $f(x,y)$ about (a,b). The full expression for this polynomial is given in equation (37), but there are great advantages in using the matrix version given in equation (44).

This is

$$p_2(x, y) = f(a, b) + \mathbf{G}^T \mathbf{R} + \tfrac{1}{2}\mathbf{R}^T \mathbf{H} \mathbf{R}, \tag{46}$$

where

$$\mathbf{G} = \begin{bmatrix} f_x(a, b) \\ f_y(a, b) \end{bmatrix} \quad \text{and} \quad \mathbf{R} = \begin{bmatrix} x - a \\ y - b \end{bmatrix}$$

are the gradient at (a, b) and the displacement away from (a, b), written as column vectors, and $\mathbf{H}$ is the Hessian matrix of second derivatives at (a, b):

$$\mathbf{H} = \begin{bmatrix} f_{xx}(a, b) & f_{xy}(a, b) \\ f_{yx}(a, b) & f_{yy}(a, b) \end{bmatrix}.$$

Because (a, b) is a stationary point, both $f_x(a, b)$ and $f_y(a, b)$ are equal to zero. The gradient matrix $\mathbf{G}$ therefore has both elements equal to zero, and equation (46) reduces to

$$p_2(x, y) = f(a, b) + \tfrac{1}{2}\mathbf{R}^T \mathbf{H} \mathbf{R}.$$

In the immediate vicinity of (a, b), any small difference between $f(x, y)$ and $p_2(x, y)$ becomes negligible, and we can safely replace $p_2(x, y)$ on the left-hand side by $f(x, y)$. Rearranging slightly, we can write

$$f(x, y) - f(a, b) = \tfrac{1}{2}\mathbf{R}^T \mathbf{H} \mathbf{R}, \tag{47}$$

provided that (x, y) is close enough to the stationary point at (a, b).

Multiplying out the matrix product on the right-hand side of equation (47), it is easy to see that

This matrix multiplication was carried out in equation (43).

$$\begin{aligned} \mathbf{R}^T \mathbf{H} \mathbf{R} = \ & f_{xx}(a, b)(x - a)^2 + f_{yy}(a, b)(y - b)^2 \\ & + 2f_{xy}(a, b)(x - a)(y - b). \end{aligned} \tag{48}$$

Denoting the right-hand side of this equation by $Q(x, y)$, we can write

$$\mathbf{R}^T \mathbf{H} \mathbf{R} = Q(x, y), \tag{49}$$

where $Q(x, y)$ is a quadratic function of x and y with coefficients that depend on the second-order partial derivatives of $f(x, y)$ at the stationary point (a, b).

Now, recall how local minima, local maxima and saddle points are defined.

For a *local minimum*, the function values all around the stationary point are greater than at the stationary point itself. This means that $f(x, y) > f(a, b)$ for all (x, y) that are sufficiently close, but not equal, to (a, b). Using equations (47) and (49), we see that this condition is guaranteed if $Q(x, y) > 0$ for all $(x, y) \neq (a, b)$.

For a *local maximum*, the function values all around the stationary point are smaller than at the stationary point itself. This is guaranteed if $Q(x, y) < 0$ for all $(x, y) \neq (a, b)$.

Saddle points correspond to increases in some directions and decreases in others, so the sign of $Q(x, y)$ must depend on x and y in this case. We therefore have the following criterion.

The nature of a stationary point (a, b) depends on $Q(x, y) = \mathbf{R}^T \mathbf{H} \mathbf{R}$.

- If $Q(x, y) > 0$ for all $(x, y) \neq (a, b)$, then we have a local minimum.
- If $Q(x, y) < 0$ for all $(x, y) \neq (a, b)$, then we have a local maximum.
- If $Q(x, y)$ is positive for some (x, y) and negative for other (x, y), then we have a saddle point.

Given any function $f(x, y)$ with a stationary point at (a, b), we can try to classify this stationary point by examining the sign of $Q(x, y)$ for all x and y around (a, b). Let us take a very simple example. Suppose that

$$f(x, y) = (x - 1)^2 + (y - 1)^2.$$

Then

$$f_x = 2(x - 1) \quad \text{and} \quad f_y = 2(y - 1),$$

so there is a stationary point at $(1, 1)$. The second-order partial derivatives are

$$f_{xx} = 2, \quad f_{yy} = 2, \quad f_{xy} = f_{yx} = 0,$$

which are constants in this case. Hence equation (48) gives

$$Q(x, y) = 2(x - 1)^2 + 2(y - 1)^2.$$

This the sum of two squared terms, neither of which can be negative, so $Q(x, y) > 0$ for all $(x, y) \neq (1, 1)$. We therefore conclude that the stationary point $(1, 1)$ is a local minimum. This is hardly surprising, but illustrates the logic of our method.

Using eigenvalues

In a more general case, the sign of Q may not be so obvious. Fortunately, there is a systematic way to proceed, using the eigenvalues of the Hessian matrix $\mathbf{H}$. The method hinges on the fact that $\mathbf{H}$ is a real symmetric matrix. It is real because f, x and y are all real-valued, so f_{xx}, f_{yy}, f_{xy} and f_{yx} are all real. And it is symmetric because the mixed partial derivative theorem ensures that $f_{xy} = f_{yx}$.

You know from Unit 5 that real symmetric matrices have some special properties. Their eigenvalues are always real, and their eigenvectors can always be chosen to be real, of unit magnitude and mutually orthogonal. For the 2×2 Hessian matrix considered here, there are two real eigenvalues λ_1 and λ_2, corresponding to two real orthogonal eigenvectors $\mathbf{v}_1$ and $\mathbf{v}_2$, so

$$\mathbf{H}\mathbf{v}_1 = \lambda_1 \mathbf{v}_1 \quad \text{and} \quad \mathbf{H}\mathbf{v}_2 = \lambda_2 \mathbf{v}_2. \tag{50}$$

The displacement vector $\mathbf{R}$ can be written as a linear combination of the two real orthogonal eigenvectors:

$$\mathbf{R} = \alpha \mathbf{v}_1 + \beta \mathbf{v}_2,$$

where the components α and β are real (because $\mathbf{R}$, $\mathbf{v}_1$ and $\mathbf{v}_2$ are real).

$\mathbf{R}$, α and β are functions of x and y.

Applying $\mathbf{H}$ to $\mathbf{R}$, and using the eigenvalue equations (50), we get

$$\mathbf{H\,R} = \mathbf{H}(\alpha\mathbf{v}_1 + \beta\mathbf{v}_2) = \alpha(\mathbf{Hv}_1) + \beta(\mathbf{Hv}_2) = \alpha\lambda_1\mathbf{v}_1 + \beta\lambda_2\mathbf{v}_2.$$

We also have

$$\mathbf{R}^T = \alpha\mathbf{v}_1^T + \beta\mathbf{v}_2^T,$$

so

$$Q(x,y) = \mathbf{R}^T\mathbf{H\,R} = (\alpha\mathbf{v}_1^T + \beta\mathbf{v}_2^T)(\alpha\lambda_1\mathbf{v}_1 + \beta\lambda_2\mathbf{v}_2). \tag{51}$$

Finally, we use the fact that $\mathbf{v}_1$ and $\mathbf{v}_2$ are of unit magnitude and mutually orthogonal. In matrix terms, this means that

$$\mathbf{v}_1^T\mathbf{v}_1 = 1, \quad \mathbf{v}_2^T\mathbf{v}_2 = 1, \quad \mathbf{v}_1^T\mathbf{v}_2 = 0, \quad \mathbf{v}_2^T\mathbf{v}_1 = 0.$$

So multiplying out the brackets in equation (51) gives

$$Q(x,y) = \alpha^2\lambda_1 + \beta^2\lambda_2, \tag{52}$$

where α and β vary over a range of real values as x and y vary. Away from the stationary point, the displacement vector $\mathbf{R}$ is non-zero, which means that the components α and β cannot simultaneously be equal to zero. You have already seen that the nature of the stationary point is determined by the sign of $Q(x,y)$. Now we see that this is determined by the signs of the eigenvalues λ_1 and λ_2 of $\mathbf{H}$.

- When both eigenvalues are positive, $Q(x,y) > 0$, and the stationary point is a local minimum.

- When both eigenvalues are negative, $Q(x,y) < 0$, and the stationary point is a local minimum.

- When the eigenvalues have opposite signs, $Q(x,y)$ may be positive or negative, and the stationary point is a saddle point.

This leads to the following procedure.

Procedure 1   The eigenvalue test

Suppose that we are given a smooth function $f(x,y)$ with a stationary point at (a,b). To establish the nature of the stationary point, do the following.

1. Find the second-order partial derivatives, and evaluate them at the stationary point.

2. Construct the Hessian matrix $\mathbf{H}$ at the stationary point, and determine its eigenvalues.

3. Apply the following rules:

   - If all the eigenvalues are positive, we have a local minimum.

   - If all the eigenvalues are negative, we have a local maximum.

   - If the eigenvalues have mixed signs, we have a saddle point.

This procedure does not cover the case where the eigenvalues do not have mixed signs but include a zero; in this case, the test is inconclusive.

Example 11

Locate the stationary point(s) of the function $f(x, y) = e^{-(x^2+y^2)}$, and use the eigenvalue test to classify them.

Solution

Partial differentiation gives

$$f_x = -2xe^{-(x^2+y^2)} \quad \text{and} \quad f_y = -2ye^{-(x^2+y^2)}.$$

Since $f_x = 0$ only when $x = 0$, and $f_y = 0$ only when $y = 0$, there is a single stationary point, at $(0,0)$.

The second-order partial derivatives are

$$f_{xx} = -2e^{-(x^2+y^2)} + 4x^2 e^{-(x^2+y^2)},$$
$$f_{yy} = -2e^{-(x^2+y^2)} + 4y^2 e^{-(x^2+y^2)},$$
$$f_{xy} = 4xy e^{-(x^2+y^2)}.$$

At the stationary point $(0,0)$, we have $f_{xx}(0,0) = -2$, $f_{yy}(0,0) = -2$ and $f_{xy}(0,0) = 0$. So the Hessian matrix at $(0,0)$ is

$$\mathbf{H} = \begin{bmatrix} f_{xx}(0,0) & f_{xy}(0,0) \\ f_{yx}(0,0) & f_{yy}(0,0) \end{bmatrix} = \begin{bmatrix} -2 & 0 \\ 0 & -2 \end{bmatrix}.$$

The eigenvalues satisfy

$$0 = \det(\mathbf{H} - \lambda\mathbf{I}) = \begin{vmatrix} -2-\lambda & 0 \\ 0 & -2-\lambda \end{vmatrix} = (2+\lambda)^2,$$

so they are $\lambda_1 = -2$ and $\lambda_2 = -2$. These are both negative, so the stationary point $(0,0)$ is a local maximum.

For a diagonal matrix, the eigenvalues are equal to the diagonal matrix elements.

Exercise 26

Locate and classify the stationary point of the function

$$f(x, y) = 2x^2 - xy - 3y^2 - 3x + 7y.$$

A minor shortcut is available for functions of two variables. You may recall from Unit 5 that the eigenvalues λ_1 and λ_2 of a 2×2 matrix $\mathbf{A}$ have the following properties:

- Their product is equal to the determinant of $\mathbf{A}$.

- Their sum is equal to the trace of $\mathbf{A}$.

In the case of the Hessian matrix, we have

$$\lambda_1 \lambda_2 = \det \mathbf{H},$$
$$\lambda_1 + \lambda_2 = \operatorname{tr} \mathbf{H}.$$

From the first of these equations we see that the condition $\det \mathbf{H} < 0$ corresponds to eigenvalues of opposite signs, and therefore to a saddle point. The condition $\det \mathbf{H} > 0$ corresponds to eigenvalues of the same sign, and therefore to an extremum – a local minimum if both eigenvalues are positive, and a local maximum if they are both negative.

In order to distinguish between these two types of extremum, we can consider $\operatorname{tr} \mathbf{H}$, which is positive for a local minimum and negative for a local maximum. We can find the sign of $\operatorname{tr} \mathbf{H}$ from its definition

$$\operatorname{tr} \mathbf{H} = f_{xx}(a,b) + f_{yy}(a,b).$$

However, there is an even simpler test. Because

$$\det \mathbf{H} = f_{xx}(a,b)\, f_{yy}(a,b) - f_{xy}^2(a,b),$$

we see that $f_{xx}(a,b)$ and $f_{yy}(a,b)$ must have the same sign if $\det \mathbf{H} > 0$. It follows that a local minimum is characterised by $\det \mathbf{H} > 0$ and $f_{xx}(a,b) > 0$, and a local maximum is characterised by $\det \mathbf{H} > 0$ and $f_{xx}(a,b) < 0$. The following box summarises the situation.

Determinant test for functions of two variables

Suppose that $f(x,y)$ is a smooth function, with a stationary point at (a,b) and a corresponding Hessian matrix $\mathbf{H}$. Then the stationary point is:

We could equally well use $f_{yy}(a,b)$ instead of $f_{xx}(a,b)$ in this test.

- a local minimum if $\det \mathbf{H} > 0$ and $f_{xx}(a,b) > 0$
- a local maximum if $\det \mathbf{H} > 0$ and $f_{xx}(a,b) < 0$
- a saddle point if $\det \mathbf{H} < 0$.

The test is inconclusive if $\det \mathbf{H} = 0$.

Exercise 27

Check that the determinant test reproduces the results derived in Example 11 and Exercise 26.

The determinant test saves a small amount of time because it avoids the need to find the eigenvalues of the Hessian matrix, but it is really an aside to our main discussion. This is because it is restricted to functions of two variables. By contrast, the eigenvalue test can be extended to functions with any number of variables. We will briefly describe how this extension works.

The definitions of stationary point, extremum, local minimum, local maximum and saddle point can all be extended in a natural way. For example, any stationary point is identified by the fact that all of its first-order partial derivatives are equal to zero. So for a function $f(x,y,z)$ of three variables, (a,b,c) is a *stationary point* if and only if

$$f_x(a,b,c) = f_y(a,b,c) = f_z(a,b,c) = 0.$$

This point is a local minimum if $f(x, y, z)$ is *greater* than $f(a, b, c)$ at all points $(x, y, z) \neq (a, b, c)$ in the immediate vicinity of (a, b, c), and so on.

The arguments leading to the eigenvalue test are also similar to those given earlier. The only difference is that the matrices $\mathbf{G}$, $\mathbf{H}$ and $\mathbf{R}$ all grow in dimension as the number of variables in the function increases. For a function of n variables, the Hessian matrix is an $n \times n$ real symmetric matrix. This has n real eigenvectors $\lambda_1, \lambda_2, \ldots, \lambda_n$, corresponding to n real orthogonal eigenvectors. So equation (52) is replaced by

$$Q(x, y) = c_1^2 \lambda_1 + c_2^2 \lambda_2 + \cdots + c_n^2 \lambda_n,$$

where $c_1, c_2, \ldots, c_n$ are all real. Just as before, this leads directly to Procedure 1, which is already phrased in such a way that it applies to any number of eigenvalues. Here is an example for a function of three variables.

Example 12

The function

$$f(x, y, z) = x^2 + y^2 + z^2 + 3xy - 2yz$$

has a stationary point at $(0, 0, 0)$. Use the eigenvalue test to classify it.

Solution

The first-order partial derivatives of $f(x, y, z)$ are

$$f_x = 2x + 3y, \quad f_y = 2y + 3x - 2z, \quad f_z = 2z - 2y,$$

and the second-order partial derivatives are

$$f_{xx} = 2, \quad f_{yy} = 2, \quad f_{zz} = 2,$$
$$f_{xy} = f_{yx} = 3, \quad f_{xz} = f_{zx} = 0, \quad f_{yz} = f_{zy} = -2.$$

These are constants, so the Hessian matrix at $(0, 0, 0)$ is

$$\mathbf{H} = \begin{bmatrix} 2 & 3 & 0 \\ 3 & 2 & -2 \\ 0 & -2 & 2 \end{bmatrix}.$$

The eigenvalues of $\mathbf{H}$ satisfy the characteristic equation

$$\begin{aligned} 0 &= \begin{vmatrix} 2 - \lambda & 3 & 0 \\ 3 & 2 - \lambda & -2 \\ 0 & -2 & 2 - \lambda \end{vmatrix} \\ &= (2 - \lambda)((2 - \lambda)^2 - 4)) - 3(3)(2 - \lambda) \\ &= (2 - \lambda)(\lambda^2 - 4\lambda - 9). \end{aligned}$$

So one of the eigenvalues is 2, and the other two eigenvalues are given by the solutions of $\lambda^2 - 4\lambda - 9 = 0$, i.e.

$$\lambda = \frac{4 \pm \sqrt{16 + 36}}{2} = 2 \pm \sqrt{13}.$$

So the eigenvalues are 2, $2 + \sqrt{13}$ and $2 - \sqrt{13}$. There are both positive and negative eigenvalues, so the stationary point is a saddle point.

Exercise 28

Find the stationary point of the function
$$f(x,y,z) = \tfrac{5}{2}(x^2 + y^2) + 2xy + z^2,$$
and use the eigenvalue test to classify it.

Exercise 29

The following functions all have stationary points at $(0,0,0)$. Where possible, use the eigenvalue test to classify these stationary points.

(a) $f(x,y,z) = x^2 + 2y^2 + 3z^2$

(b) $f(x,y,z) = x^2 + 2y^2 - 3z^2$

(c) $f(x,y,z) = x^2 + 2y^2 + 3z^4$

(d) $f(x,y,z) = x^2 + 2y^2 - 3z^4$

4.4 Constrained extrema

This final subsection is optional. It is included for interest and because it may be useful if you read other texts. It will not be assessed or examined.

So far, we have considered extrema in situations where the independent variables can vary freely. In real life, constraints must often be taken into account. For example, we might ask 'what is the maximum volume of a rectangular box?'. This question is rather pointless as posed, because we can obviously make the volume as large as we choose by building a large enough box! By contrast, the question 'what is the maximum volume of a rectangular box with a total surface area of 4 square metres?' is much more interesting. In this example, the quantity that we are maximising (the volume of the box) is subject to a constraint (the fixed surface area of the box). We are to maximise the volume *while keeping the surface area fixed*. This is a new type of problem, which we now tackle.

Constrained extrema in the real world

The problem of finding extrema subject to constraints is important in economics, business administration and many other aspects of life. Very often, we need to maximise or minimise something – a company would like to maximise its profits, or a hospital would like to minimise its fatalities. But this must be achieved with known, fixed assets.

Economists often represent the desire for a given commodity by a function called the utility function, and they assume that consumers maximise this function, subject to their budget constraints. The question that we face is: given a fixed set of assets, how can we distribute them to achieve a certain goal as fully as possible?

A whole branch of physics (statistical mechanics) is based on similar ideas. In this case, the fixed asset is energy and we work out how to distribute the total energy among the various particles in a system in such a way as to maximise the probability of a particular distribution. It turns out that some distributions are overwhelmingly more likely than others, giving us the power to predict, with practical certainty, how complicated systems containing billions of billions of particles will behave. This works for gases containing 10^{24} molecules and galaxies containing 10^{11} stars, where it would be hopeless to try to predict the detailed motion of every particle.

Suppose that we want to find the maxima or minima of a function $f(x, y)$ subject to a constraint specified by the equation $g(x, y) = c$, where c is a constant. If we could solve the equation $g(x, y) = c$ to obtain y as a function of x, we could substitute this into the function f to obtain $f(x, y(x))$. This depends only on the single variable x, so we could use the rules of ordinary calculus to find its maxima and minima. But what if we cannot solve the equation $g(x, y) = c$ for y?

Problems where the constraint is specified by an inequality are also of interest, but will not be discussed here.

The key to solving this problem is provided by Figure 27, which shows contour lines for the function $f(x, y)$ (in orange) and the curve for the function $g(x, y) = c$ (in blue). In searching for a stationary point of $f(x, y)$, we are obliged to travel along the blue curve in order to satisfy the constraint. At a point like A, the blue curve crosses contour lines of $f(x, y)$, which indicates that f is changing, so A is not a stationary point. At point B, however, the blue curve is tangential to a contour line of $f(x, y)$, and this means that f is not changing as we travel along the blue curve in the vicinity of B. We can therefore say that B is a stationary point of $f(x, y)$ subject to the constraint $g(x, y) = c$.

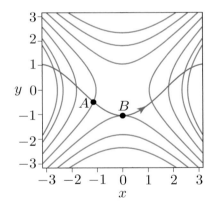

Figure 27 A situation in which we are constrained to move along the blue curve over terrain whose contour lines are shown in orange

The distinguishing feature of point B is that there is a contour line of $f(x, y)$ that is parallel to the curve $g(x, y) = c$ at point B. The corresponding gradient vectors $\mathbf{grad}\, f$ and $\mathbf{grad}\, g$ are perpendicular to these curves, so they are also aligned (parallel or antiparallel). We can therefore write

$$\mathbf{grad}\, f = \lambda\, \mathbf{grad}\, g, \tag{53}$$

where λ is a non-zero constant whose value is at present unknown. Writing down the components of equation (53), together with the original constraint, gives three equations:

We cannot say that $\lambda = 1$, because $\mathbf{grad}\, f$ and $\mathbf{grad}\, g$ may have different magnitudes.

$$\frac{\partial f}{\partial x} - \lambda \frac{\partial g}{\partial x} = 0, \quad \frac{\partial f}{\partial y} - \lambda \frac{\partial g}{\partial y} = 0, \quad g(x, y) = c. \tag{54}$$

These are 3 equations for 3 unknowns (x, y and λ), so the problem is now solved, at least in principle, by eliminating the unknown constant λ and finding values for x and y. If we let

$$L(x,y) = f(x,y) - \lambda g(x,y),$$

we see that equations (54) can also be written as

$$\frac{\partial L}{\partial x} = 0, \quad \frac{\partial L}{\partial y} = 0, \quad g(x,y) = c, \tag{55}$$

which leads to the following procedure.

Procedure 2   Finding stationary points with a constraint

To find the stationary points of the function $f(x,y)$ subject to the constraint $g(x,y) = c$, where c is a constant, do the following.

1. Construct the function $L(x,y) = f(x,y) - \lambda g(x,y)$, where λ is an unknown constant.

2. Partially differentiate $L(x,y)$ with respect to x and y, and form the equations $L_x = 0$ and $L_y = 0$.

3. Find the stationary points of $f(x,y)$ subject to the given constraint.

The following example shows how this procedure is used.

Example 13

Find the stationary points of $f(x,y) = x^2 + y^2$ subject to the constraint $xy = 4$. What are the values of f at these stationary points?

Solution

We form the function $L(x,y) = x^2 + y^2 - \lambda xy$ and calculate its first-order partial derivatives $L_x = 2x - \lambda y$ and $L_y = 2y - \lambda x$. Combining the stationary point conditions $L_x = 0$ and $L_y = 0$ with the constraint equation gives

$$2x - \lambda y = 0, \quad 2y - \lambda x = 0, \quad xy = 4.$$

We require the solutions to be real, so imaginary solutions are rejected.

Eliminating λ, we get $x^2 - y^2 = 0$. Combining this with the constraint equation then gives $x^2 - 16/x^2 = 0$, or $x^4 = 16$, which has real solutions $x = \pm 2$. Putting these values back into the constraint equation $xy = 4$, we see that there are two stationary points: $(2, 2)$ and $(-2, -2)$. In each case, the corresponding value of f is $2^2 + 2^2 = 8$.

Figure 28 shows a contour map of $f(x,y) = x^2 + y^2$, with the constraint curve $xy = 4$ overlaid in blue (there is one branch for $x > 0$ and another branch for $x < 0$). You can see that the constraint curve meets the contour lines of $f(x,y)$ tangentially at the stationary points $(2,2)$ and $(-2,-2)$, and that the function f has the value 8 at these points. This is the smallest value encountered on the curve $xy = 4$, so the stationary points are local minima when the constraint is satisfied. They are not the same as the local minimum $(x,y) = (0,0)$ obtained in the absence of any constraints.

The constant λ is called a **Lagrange multiplier**, after Joseph-Louis Lagrange (1736–1813), who devised the method that we have just described. This method works for functions of three or more variables in a very similar way, but it is not always easy to classify the stationary points. Applying the eigenvalue test to the function $L(x,y)$, for example, does not necessarily tell us the nature of the stationary points of $f(x,y)$ in the presence of a constraint. If necessary, a graph such as that in Figure 28 can be used to distinguish between the various possibilities.

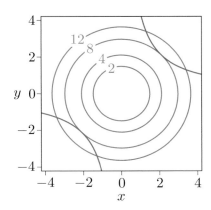

Figure 28 Contour map for $f(x,y) = x^2 + y^2$, with contour lines (orange) and constraint curve $xy = 4$ (blue)

Exercise 30

Find the stationary points of $f(x,y) = 5x - 3y$ subject to the constraint $x^2 - y^2 = 1$.

Learning outcomes

After studying this unit, you should be able to do the following.

- Interpret surfaces, section functions and contour maps used to represent functions of two variables.

- Calculate first- and second-order partial derivatives of a function of several variables.

- Use various versions of the chain rule.

- Calculate the first- and second-order Taylor polynomials for a function of two variables.

- Locate the stationary points of a function of two (or more) variables by solving a system of two (or more) simultaneous equations.

- Classify the stationary points of a function of two (or more) variables using the eigenvalue or determinant test.

Solutions to exercises

Solution to Exercise 1

(a) $f(2,3) = 3 \times 2^2 - 2 \times 3^2 = -6.$

(b) $f(3,-2) = 3 \times 3^2 - 2 \times (-2)^2 = 19.$

(c) $f(a,b) = 3 \times a^2 - 2 \times b^2 = 3a^2 - 2b^2.$

(d) $f(b,a) = 3 \times b^2 - 2 \times a^2 = 3b^2 - 2a^2.$

(e) $f(2a,b) = 3 \times (2a)^2 - 2 \times b^2 = 12a^2 - 2b^2.$

(f) $f(a-b,0) = 3 \times (a-b)^2 - 2 \times 0^2 = 3(a-b)^2.$

(g) $f(x,2) = 3 \times x^2 - 2 \times 2^2 = 3x^2 - 8.$

Solution to Exercise 2

We have

$$\frac{\partial g}{\partial \theta} = \cos\theta + \cos\phi\sec^2\theta \quad \text{and} \quad \frac{\partial g}{\partial \phi} = -\sin\phi\tan\theta.$$

Solution to Exercise 3

(a) Partially differentiating with respect to x, with y held constant, and using the product rule for differentiation, we get

$$f_x(x,y) = 2xe^{3x} + 3(x^2 + y^2)e^{3x} = (3x^2 + 2x + 3y^2)e^{3x}.$$

Partially differentiating with respect to y, with x held constant, gives

$$f_y(x,y) = 2ye^{3x}.$$

(b) At the point $(0,1)$, the slope of the surface in the x-direction is given by

$$f_x(0,1) = (3 \times 0^2 + 2 \times 0 + 3 \times 1^2)e^0 = 3.$$

Solution to Exercise 4

(a) Holding y and z constant,

$$\frac{\partial f}{\partial x} = 2(1+x).$$

Similarly,

$$\frac{\partial f}{\partial y} = 3(1+y)^2 \quad \text{and} \quad \frac{\partial f}{\partial z} = 4(1+z)^3.$$

(b) Holding y and t constant,

$$\frac{\partial f}{\partial x} = 2xy^3t^4 + 8xt^2 - 2y.$$

Holding x and t constant,

$$\frac{\partial f}{\partial y} = 3x^2y^2t^4 - 2x + 1.$$

Finally, holding x and y constant,

$$\frac{\partial f}{\partial t} = 4x^2 y^3 t^3 + 8x^2 t.$$

Solution to Exercise 5

Differentiating $f(x, y) = x \sin y$ with respect to x and treating y as a constant gives

$$f_x(x, y) = \frac{\partial}{\partial x}(x \sin y) = \sin y.$$

Differentiating $f(x, y)$ with respect to y and treating x as a constant gives

$$f_y(x, y) = \frac{\partial}{\partial y}(x \sin y) = x \cos y.$$

Differentiating f_x with respect to x gives

$$f_{xx}(x, y) = \frac{\partial}{\partial x}(\sin y) = 0,$$

while differentiating f_x with respect to y gives

$$f_{yx}(x, y) = \frac{\partial}{\partial y}(\sin y) = \cos y.$$

Differentiating f_y with respect to y gives

$$f_{yy}(x, y) = \frac{\partial}{\partial y}(x \cos y) = -x \sin y,$$

while differentiating f_y with respect to x gives

$$f_{xy}(x, y) = \frac{\partial}{\partial x}(x \cos y) = \cos y.$$

Evaluating these four second-order partial derivatives at $(2, \pi)$, we get

$$f_{xx}(2, \pi) = 0,$$
$$f_{yx}(2, \pi) = \cos \pi = -1,$$
$$f_{yy}(2, \pi) = -2 \sin \pi = 0,$$
$$f_{xy}(2, \pi) = \cos \pi = -1.$$

Solution to Exercise 6

The first-order partial derivatives are

$$\frac{\partial f}{\partial x} = 2e^{2x+3y} \quad \text{and} \quad \frac{\partial f}{\partial y} = 3e^{2x+3y}.$$

Partially differentiating the first of these functions with respect to y and the second with respect to x, we get

$$f_{yx}(x, y) = \frac{\partial}{\partial y}\left(\frac{\partial f}{\partial x}\right) = 6e^{2x+3y},$$

$$f_{xy}(x, y) = \frac{\partial}{\partial x}\left(\frac{\partial f}{\partial y}\right) = 6e^{2x+3y}.$$

At the point $(x, y) = (0, 0)$, we have $f_{xy}(0, 0) = f_{yx}(0, 0) = 6$.

Solution to Exercise 7

The first-order partial derivatives are

$$\frac{\partial f}{\partial x} = -3\sin(3x - 2t) \quad \text{and} \quad \frac{\partial f}{\partial t} = 2\sin(3x - 2t).$$

The required second-order partial derivatives are then

$$\frac{\partial^2 f}{\partial x^2} = \frac{\partial}{\partial x}(-3\sin(3x - 2t)) = -9\cos(3x - 2t),$$

$$\frac{\partial^2 f}{\partial t^2} = \frac{\partial}{\partial t}(2\sin(3x - 2t)) = -4\cos(3x - 2t).$$

Comparing these two expressions, we see that

$$\frac{\partial^2 f}{\partial x^2} = \frac{9}{4}\frac{\partial^2 f}{\partial t^2}, \quad \text{or equivalently,} \quad f_{xx} = \frac{9}{4}f_{tt}.$$

Solution to Exercise 8

Using the quotient rule, the first-order partial derivatives are

$$f_x(x, y) = \frac{(x + y)y - xy}{(x + y)^2} = \frac{y^2}{(x + y)^2},$$

$$f_y(x, y) = \frac{(x + y)x - xy}{(x + y)^2} = \frac{x^2}{(x + y)^2}.$$

At the initial point $(x, y) = (1, 4)$, we have $f_x(1, 4) = 16/25$ and $f_y(1, 4) = 1/25$. We also have $\delta x = 0.01$ and $\delta y = -0.01$. The chain rule then gives

$$\delta f = f_x(1, 4)\,\delta x + f_y(1, 4)\,\delta y = \frac{16}{25} \times 0.01 + \frac{1}{25} \times (-0.01) = 0.006.$$

Solution to Exercise 9

Carrying out the necessary differentiations, we obtain

$$\frac{\partial z}{\partial x} = \cos x, \quad \frac{\partial z}{\partial y} = 3\sin y,$$

$$\frac{dx}{dt} = 2t, \quad \frac{dy}{dt} = 2.$$

The chain rule then gives

$$\frac{dz}{dt} = \frac{\partial z}{\partial x}\frac{dx}{dt} + \frac{\partial z}{\partial y}\frac{dy}{dt} = 2t\cos x + 6\sin y = 2t\cos(t^2) + 6\sin(2t).$$

Solution to Exercise 10

The required derivatives are

$$\frac{\partial z}{\partial x} = y\cos x, \quad \frac{\partial z}{\partial y} = \sin x,$$

$$\frac{dx}{dt} = e^t, \quad \frac{dy}{dt} = 2t.$$

So the chain rule gives

$$\frac{dz}{dt} = \frac{\partial z}{\partial x}\frac{dx}{dt} + \frac{\partial z}{\partial y}\frac{dy}{dt} = e^t y \cos x + 2t \sin x = t^2 e^t \cos(e^t) + 2t \sin(e^t).$$

At $t = 0$, $dz/dt = 0$.

Solution to Exercise 11

We have

$$\frac{\partial f}{\partial x} = 2x \quad \text{and} \quad \frac{\partial f}{\partial y} = 2y.$$

Also,

$$\frac{\partial x}{\partial u} = 2, \quad \frac{\partial y}{\partial u} = 3, \quad \frac{\partial x}{\partial v} = 3, \quad \frac{\partial y}{\partial v} = -2.$$

The chain rule then gives

$$\frac{\partial f}{\partial u} = \frac{\partial f}{\partial x}\frac{\partial x}{\partial u} + \frac{\partial f}{\partial y}\frac{\partial y}{\partial u}$$
$$= 2x \times 2 + 2y \times 3 = 4(2u + 3v) + 6(3u - 2v) = 26u$$

and

$$\frac{\partial f}{\partial v} = \frac{\partial f}{\partial x}\frac{\partial x}{\partial v} + \frac{\partial f}{\partial y}\frac{\partial y}{\partial v}$$
$$= 2x \times 3 + 2y \times (-2) = 6(2u + 3v) - 4(3u - 2v) = 26v.$$

At the point $(u, v) = (1, 2)$, we get $f_u(1, 2) = 26$ and $f_v(1, 2) = 52$.

Solution to Exercise 12

We have

$$\frac{\partial f}{\partial x} = 2x, \quad \frac{\partial f}{\partial y} = -2y.$$

Also,

$$\frac{\partial x}{\partial r} = \cos\theta, \quad \frac{\partial y}{\partial r} = \sin\theta, \quad \frac{\partial x}{\partial \theta} = -r\sin\theta, \quad \frac{\partial y}{\partial \theta} = r\cos\theta.$$

So

$$\frac{\partial f}{\partial r} = \frac{\partial f}{\partial x}\frac{\partial x}{\partial r} + \frac{\partial f}{\partial y}\frac{\partial y}{\partial r}$$
$$= 2x\cos\theta - 2y\sin\theta = 2r\cos^2\theta - 2r\sin^2\theta = 2r\cos(2\theta)$$

and

$$\frac{\partial f}{\partial \theta} = \frac{\partial f}{\partial x}\frac{\partial x}{\partial \theta} + \frac{\partial f}{\partial y}\frac{\partial y}{\partial \theta}$$
$$= 2x \times (-r\sin\theta) - 2y(r\cos\theta) = -4r^2\cos\theta\sin\theta = -2r^2\sin(2\theta).$$

Solution to Exercise 13

(a) When $\widehat{\mathbf{n}}$ points in the x-direction, $\widehat{n}_x = 1$ and $\widehat{n}_y = 0$, so the slope is $f_x(x, y)$. This agrees with our previous interpretation of $\partial f / \partial x$ as the slope in the x-direction.

(b) When $\widehat{\mathbf{n}}$ points in the y-direction, $\widehat{n}_x = 0$ and $\widehat{n}_y = 1$, so the slope is $f_y(x, y)$. This agrees with our previous interpretation of $\partial f / \partial y$ as the slope in the y-direction.

Solution to Exercise 14

With $f = xy^2$, the gradient is

$$\mathbf{grad}\, f = \frac{\partial f}{\partial x}\,\mathbf{i} + \frac{\partial f}{\partial y}\,\mathbf{j} = y^2\,\mathbf{i} + 2xy\,\mathbf{j}.$$

At $(1, 2)$, this gradient has the value $2^2\,\mathbf{i} + (2 \times 1 \times 2)\,\mathbf{j} = 4\,\mathbf{i} + 4\,\mathbf{j}$.

Solution to Exercise 15

The partial derivatives are

$$\frac{\partial f}{\partial x} = 4xy^2 + 3y^3 \quad \text{and} \quad \frac{\partial f}{\partial y} = 4x^2y + 9xy^2,$$

so the gradient is

$$\mathbf{grad}\, f = (4xy^2 + 3y^3)\,\mathbf{i} + (4x^2y + 9xy^2)\,\mathbf{j}.$$

The vector $\mathbf{i} - \mathbf{j}$ is not a unit vector, but the corresponding unit vector is $\widehat{\mathbf{n}} = \frac{1}{\sqrt{2}}\,\mathbf{i} - \frac{1}{\sqrt{2}}\,\mathbf{j}$. At any point (x, y), the slope in the direction of $\widehat{\mathbf{n}}$ is

$$\widehat{\mathbf{n}} \cdot \mathbf{grad}\, f = \frac{1}{\sqrt{2}}(4xy^2 + 3y^3) - \frac{1}{\sqrt{2}}(4x^2y + 9xy^2)$$

$$= \frac{1}{\sqrt{2}}(3y^3 - 4x^2y - 5xy^2).$$

Hence at $(1, 2)$, the slope in the direction of the vector $\mathbf{i} - \mathbf{j}$ is $(24 - 8 - 20)/\sqrt{2} = -2\sqrt{2} = -2.83$ (to three significant figures).

Solution to Exercise 16

Using equation (32), we see that the slope of the surface $z = f(x, y)$ is most negative when $\cos \alpha = -1$, that is, when $\alpha = \pi$. So the direction of steepest decrease at (a, b) is *opposite* to the direction of $\mathbf{grad}\, f$ at (a, b).

Solution to Exercise 17

We first calculate

$$\mathbf{grad}\, f = \frac{\partial f}{\partial x}\,\mathbf{i} + \frac{\partial f}{\partial y}\,\mathbf{j} = (4xy - 9x^2)\,\mathbf{i} + 2x^2\,\mathbf{j}.$$

At the point $(1, 2)$, this has the value

$$[\mathbf{grad}\, f]_{x=1,\, y=2} = -\mathbf{i} + 2\,\mathbf{j}.$$

This vector has magnitude $\sqrt{(-1)^2 + 2^2} = \sqrt{5}$, so the unit vector in the direction of $\mathbf{grad}\, f$ at $(1, 2)$ is $\widehat{\mathbf{n}} = (-\mathbf{i} + 2\,\mathbf{j})/\sqrt{5}$.

This is the direction of steepest *increase* of the function $f(x, y)$. The bug should move in the *opposite* direction, which is the direction of steepest *decrease* of the toxicity function. This is along the unit vector $(\mathbf{i} - 2\mathbf{j})/\sqrt{5}$.

Solution to Exercise 18

(a) The gradient is

$$\mathbf{grad}\, f = \frac{\partial f}{\partial x}\,\mathbf{i} + \frac{\partial f}{\partial y}\,\mathbf{j} + \frac{\partial f}{\partial z}\,\mathbf{k} = 2x\,\mathbf{i} + 2y\,\mathbf{j} + 4z\,\mathbf{k}.$$

(b) The surface of the object is a contour surface for the function $f(x, y, z)$. At each point on this surface, the gradient vector is perpendicular to the surface. At $(1, 2, 1)$ this gradient vector is

$$[\mathbf{grad}\, f]_{(1,2,1)} = 2\,\mathbf{i} + 4\,\mathbf{j} + 4\,\mathbf{k},$$

which has magnitude $\sqrt{4 + 16 + 16} = 6$. So a unit vector perpendicular to the surface at $(1, 2, 1)$ is

$$\widehat{\mathbf{n}} = \tfrac{1}{3}\,\mathbf{i} + \tfrac{2}{3}\,\mathbf{j} + \tfrac{2}{3}\,\mathbf{k}.$$

Solution to Exercise 19

(a) Example 3 found the three partial derivatives $\partial V/\partial x$, $\partial V/\partial y$ and $\partial V/\partial z$ for the function $V(x, y, z)$. Using these results, the gradient vector is

$$\mathbf{grad}\, V = -\frac{x\,\mathbf{i} + y\,\mathbf{j} + z\,\mathbf{k}}{(x^2 + y^2 + z^2)^{3/2}}.$$

(b) Because of the minus sign, $\mathbf{grad}\, V$ points in the opposite direction to the position vector $\mathbf{r} = x\,\mathbf{i} + y\,\mathbf{j} + z\,\mathbf{k}$, so we can say that at each point (x, y, z), the gradient vector $\mathbf{grad}\, V$ points towards the origin. This is the direction in which V increases most rapidly.

(c) The square of the magnitude of $\mathbf{grad}\, V$ is

$$|\mathbf{grad}\, V|^2 = \frac{x^2 + y^2 + z^2}{(x^2 + y^2 + z^2)^3} = \frac{1}{(x^2 + y^2 + z^2)^2},$$

so

$$|\mathbf{grad}\, V| = \frac{1}{x^2 + y^2 + z^2} \quad \text{for } (x, y, z) \neq (0, 0, 0).$$

Solution to Exercise 20

We have

$$f(x) = \cos x, \quad f'(x) = -\sin x, \quad f''(x) = -\cos x, \quad f'''(x) = \sin x,$$

and

$$p(x) = -1 + \tfrac{1}{2}(x - \pi)^2, \quad p'(x) = x - \pi, \quad p''(x) = 1, \quad p'''(x) = 0.$$

Hence $f(\pi) = p(\pi) = -1$, $f'(\pi) = p'(\pi) = 0$, $f''(\pi) = p''(\pi) = 1$ and $f'''(\pi) = p'''(\pi) = 0$, as required.

Solution to Exercise 21

(a) Differentiating once, and then again, gives

$$f'(t) = \frac{1}{1+t^2} \times 2t = \frac{2t}{1+t^2},$$

$$f''(t) = \frac{(1+t^2) \times 2 - 2t \times 2t}{(1+t^2)^2} = \frac{2(1-t^2)}{(1+t^2)^2}.$$

(b) At the point $t = 0$, we have $f(0) = \ln(1) = 0$, $f'(0) = 0$ and $f''(0) = 2$. So the required second-order Taylor polynomial is

$$p(t) = 0 + 0 \times t + \frac{1}{2!} 2 \times (t-0)^2 = t^2.$$

(c) At the point $t = 1$, we have $f(1) = \ln(2)$, $f'(1) = 1$ and $f''(1) = 0$. So the required second-order Taylor polynomial is

$$p(t) = \ln(2) + 1 \times (t-1) + \frac{1}{2!} 0 \times (t-1)^2$$
$$= \ln(2) - 1 + t.$$

Note that this is the *second*-order Taylor polynomial, even though it is a polynomial of order 1. This is because it takes account of the second derivative $f''(1)$, even though this turns out to be equal to zero.

Solution to Exercise 22

Setting $x = a$ and $y = b$ in equation (37), we see that $h(a,b) = p_2(a,b) = f(a,b)$, so the polynomial and the function have the same value at (a,b).

Taking first-order partial derivatives on both sides of equation (37) gives

$$h_x(x,y) = \frac{\partial p_2}{\partial x} = f_x(a,b) + f_{xx}(a,b)(x-a) + f_{xy}(a,b)(y-b),$$

$$h_y(x,y) = \frac{\partial p_2}{\partial y} = f_y(a,b) + f_{xy}(a,b)(x-a) + f_{yy}(a,b)(y-b),$$

so at $x = a$ and $y = b$ we have $h_x(a,b) = f_x(a,b)$ and $h_y(a,b) = f_y(a,b)$, confirming that the first-order partial derivatives match.

Finally, differentiating again to get the second-order partial derivatives gives

$$h_{xx}(x,y) = f_{xx}(a,b), \quad h_{yy}(x,y) = f_{yy}(a,b), \quad h_{xy}(x,y) = f_{xy}(a,b).$$

In particular, we see that $h_{xx}(a,b) = f_{xx}(a,b)$, $h_{yy}(a,b) = f_{yy}(a,b)$ and $h_{xy}(a,b) = f_{xy}(a,b)$, so the second-order partial derivatives match as well.

Solution to Exercise 23

We have

$$f(x,y) = x^2 e^{3y}, \quad f_x(x,y) = 2xe^{3y}, \quad f_y(x,y) = 3x^2 e^{3y}.$$

So at $(2,0)$, we have

$$f(2,0) = 4, \quad f_x(2,0) = 4, \quad f_y(2,0) = 12.$$

Hence the first-order Taylor polynomial about $(2,0)$ is

$$\begin{aligned} p_1(x,y) &= f(2,0) + f_x(2,0)(x-2) + f_y(2,0)(y-0) \\ &= 4 + 4(x-2) + 12y \\ &= -4 + 4x + 12y. \end{aligned}$$

The second-order partial derivatives are

$$f_{xx}(x,y) = 2e^{3y}, \quad f_{xy}(x,y) = 6xe^{3y}, \quad f_{yy}(x,y) = 9x^2 e^{3y}.$$

So at $(2,0)$, we have

$$f_{xx}(2,0) = 2, \quad f_{xy}(2,0) = 12, \quad f_{yy}(2,0) = 36.$$

Hence the second-order Taylor polynomial is

$$\begin{aligned} p_2(x,y) &= p_1(x,y) + \tfrac{1}{2}\left(f_{xx}(2,0)(x-2)^2 + 2f_{xy}(x-2)(y-0)\right.\\ &\qquad\qquad \left. + f_{yy}(2,0)(y-0)^2\right) \\ &= -4 + 4x + 12y + (x-2)^2 + 12(x-2)y + 18y^2. \end{aligned}$$

Solution to Exercise 24

Partially differentiating with respect to x and with respect to y, we obtain

$$f_x(x,y) = 6x - 4y + 4 \quad \text{and} \quad f_y(x,y) = -4x + 4y - 8.$$

Setting these first-order partial derivatives equal to zero gives

$$\begin{aligned} 6x - 4y &= -4, \\ -4x + 4y &= 8. \end{aligned}$$

These equations have the unique solution $x = 2$, $y = 4$. So $(2,4)$ is the only stationary point.

Solution to Exercise 25

We can write $f(x,y) = x^2 y + xy^2 - 3xy$. Partially differentiating with respect to x and with respect to y gives

$$\begin{aligned} f_x(x,y) &= 2xy + y^2 - 3y = y(2x + y - 3), \\ f_y(x,y) &= x^2 + 2xy - 3x = x(x + 2y - 3). \end{aligned}$$

Setting these first-order partial derivatives equal to zero gives

$$\begin{aligned} y(2x + y - 3) &= 0, \\ x(x + 2y - 3) &= 0. \end{aligned}$$

Solving the first equation for y gives either $y = 0$ or $y = 3 - 2x$. For $y = 0$, the second equation becomes $x(x - 3) = 0$, which is satisfied by $x = 0$ and $x = 3$. For $y = 3 - 2x$, the second equation becomes $x(3 - 3x) = 0$, which is satisfied by $x = 0$ (for which $y = 3$) and $x = 1$ (for which $y = 1$). Collecting together the complete set of solutions, the stationary points occur at $(0,0)$, $(3,0)$, $(0,3)$ and $(1,1)$.

Solution to Exercise 26

The first-order partial derivatives are

$$f_x = 4x - y - 3 \quad \text{and} \quad f_y = -x - 6y + 7.$$

Setting these equal to zero, we obtain the simultaneous equations

$$4x - y = 3,$$
$$-x - 6y = -7,$$

which have the solution $x = 1$, $y = 1$. So the only stationary point is at $(1, 1)$.

The second-order partial derivatives are $f_{xx} = 4$, $f_{yy} = -6$ and $f_{xy} = -1$. Evaluating these constant functions at $(1, 1)$ then gives $f_{xx}(1, 1) = 4$, $f_{yy}(1, 1) = -6$ and $f_{xy}(1, 1) = -1$. So the Hessian matrix at $(1, 1)$ is

$$\mathbf{H} = \begin{bmatrix} 4 & -1 \\ -1 & -6 \end{bmatrix}.$$

The eigenvalues satisfy

$$0 = \det(\mathbf{H} - \lambda\mathbf{I}) = \begin{vmatrix} 4 - \lambda & -1 \\ -1 & -6 - \lambda \end{vmatrix} = (\lambda - 4)(\lambda + 6) - 1.$$

So $\lambda^2 + 2\lambda - 25 = 0$, and the eigenvalues are

$$\lambda = \frac{-2 \pm \sqrt{104}}{2} = -1 \pm \sqrt{26}.$$

These have opposite signs, so the stationary point is a saddle point.

Solution to Exercise 27

In Example 11, the Hessian matrix at the stationary point $(0, 0)$ is

$$\mathbf{H} = \begin{bmatrix} -2 & 0 \\ 0 & -2 \end{bmatrix},$$

so $\det \mathbf{H} = 4 > 0$ and $f_{xx}(0, 0) = -2 < 0$. By the determinant test, $(0, 0)$ is a local maximum.

In Exercise 26, the Hessian matrix at the stationary point $(1, 1)$ is

$$\mathbf{H} = \begin{bmatrix} 4 & -1 \\ -1 & -6 \end{bmatrix},$$

so $\det \mathbf{H} = -25 < 0$. By the determinant test, $(1, 1)$ is a saddle point.

Solution to Exercise 28

The first-order partial derivatives of $f(x, y, z)$ are

$$f_x = 5x + 2y, \quad f_y = 5y + 2x, \quad f_z = 2z.$$

The set of simultaneous equations $f_x = 0$, $f_y = 0$ and $f_z = 0$ has the unique solution $x = y = z = 0$, so the only stationary point is at $(0, 0, 0)$.

The non-zero second-order partial derivatives are

$$f_{xx} = 5, \quad f_{yy} = 5, \quad f_{zz} = 2, \quad f_{xy} = f_{yx} = 2.$$

These are constants, so the Hessian matrix at the stationary point is

$$\mathbf{H} = \begin{bmatrix} 5 & 2 & 0 \\ 2 & 5 & 0 \\ 0 & 0 & 2 \end{bmatrix}.$$

The eigenvalues of this matrix are given by the characteristic equation

$$
\begin{aligned}
0 &= \begin{vmatrix} 5 - \lambda & 2 & 0 \\ 2 & 5 - \lambda & 0 \\ 0 & 0 & 2 - \lambda \end{vmatrix} \\
&= (5 - \lambda)(5 - \lambda)(2 - \lambda) - 2(2)(2 - \lambda) \\
&= (2 - \lambda)(\lambda^2 - 10\lambda + 21) \\
&= (2 - \lambda)(\lambda - 3)(\lambda - 7),
\end{aligned}
$$

so the eigenvalues are 2, 3 and 7. Since these are all positive, the eigenvalue test tells us that $(0, 0, 0)$ is a local minimum.

Solution to Exercise 29

(a) The non-zero second-order partial derivatives are $f_{xx} = 2$, $f_{yy} = 4$, $f_{zz} = 6$. These values are constants, so at the stationary point $(0, 0, 0)$ the Hessian matrix is

$$\mathbf{H} = \begin{bmatrix} 2 & 0 & 0 \\ 0 & 4 & 0 \\ 0 & 0 & 6 \end{bmatrix}.$$

This is a diagonal matrix, so its eigenvalues are 2, 4 and 6. These are all positive, so the eigenvalue test tells us that the stationary point is a local minimum.

(b) By an argument similar to that in part (a), the eigenvalues are 2, 4 and -6. These have mixed signs, so the stationary point is a saddle point.

(c) The non-zero second-order partial derivatives are $f_{xx} = 2$, $f_{yy} = 4$, $f_{zz} = 36z^2$. At the stationary point $(0, 0, 0)$, these have values 2, 4 and 0, giving the Hessian matrix

$$\mathbf{H} = \begin{bmatrix} 2 & 0 & 0 \\ 0 & 4 & 0 \\ 0 & 0 & 0 \end{bmatrix}.$$

This is a diagonal matrix, so its eigenvalues are 2, 4 and 0. These include a zero eigenvalue, so the eigenvalue test is inconclusive. In fact, this stationary point is a local minimum, but that is not revealed by the eigenvalue test.

(d) The non-zero second-order partial derivatives are $f_{xx} = 2$, $f_{yy} = 4$, $f_{zz} = -36z^2$. At the stationary point $(0, 0, 0)$, these have values 2, 4 and 0, giving the same Hessian matrix as in part (c). The eigenvalue test is again inconclusive. In fact, this stationary point is a saddle point, but that is not revealed by the eigenvalue test.

Multiple integrals

Introduction

The previous unit introduced functions of two and more variables, and explained how to differentiate them. In this unit we will integrate such functions.

Suppose that a thin rod lies along the x-axis, with one end at $x = 0$ and the other end at $x = L$. If the rod has a uniform composition, its **linear density** λ (its mass per unit length) is constant everywhere along its length, and the total mass of the rod is $M = \lambda L$.

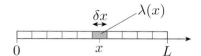

Figure 1 A rod with linear density $\lambda(x)$. The mass contributed by an element centred on x and of length δx is $\lambda(x)\,\delta x$.

A more interesting case arises when the rod is non-uniform (Figure 1). In this case the linear density $\lambda(x)$ is a function of position, and a small element of the rod, centred on x and of length δx, has mass

$$\delta M \simeq \lambda(x)\,\delta x. \tag{1}$$

This equation may be regarded as the definition of the linear density $\lambda(x)$.

Strictly speaking, this is an approximation because we have ignored any variation of $\lambda(x)$ within the element, but the approximation becomes increasingly accurate as the element becomes smaller.

The total mass of the rod can be found be adding together the masses of all its elements. We consider this sum in the limit where the number of elements tends to infinity and the length of each element becomes vanishingly small. In this limit, any approximation involved in equation (1) becomes negligible, and the sum becomes the definite integral

$$M = \int_0^L \lambda(x)\,dx. \tag{2}$$

To find the total mass of the rod, we calculate this integral using the standard rules of calculus. The integral takes a formula for each tiny part and gives an answer for the whole. Not surprisingly, the word *integral* comes from the medieval Latin *integralis* meaning 'forming a whole'.

Crucially for this unit, the tiny elements need not be straight-line segments laid end to end. They could be rectangular elements covering a surface, or tiny brick-shaped elements filling out a volume in three-dimensional space.

Suppose that an oval metal plate of non-uniform composition lies in the xy-plane. In this case each point on the plate can be labelled by its (x, y) coordinates, and the non-uniform composition of the plate can be characterised by a **surface density function** $f(x, y)$, which represents the mass per unit area at any given point (x, y).

The plate can be approximately covered by tiny rectangular area elements aligned with the x- and y-axes, as shown in Figure 2. With rectangular elements the coverage is only approximate, but the approximation is a good one if the elements are small enough.

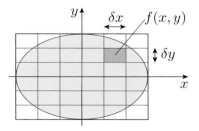

Figure 2 A typical rectangular area element

A typical area element is centred on the point (x, y) and has sides of length δx and δy. This element has area $\delta A = \delta x\,\delta y$, and its mass is

$$\delta M \simeq f(x, y)\,\delta A, \tag{3}$$

where an approximation sign is used because the surface density may vary slightly within the element. However, the approximation becomes increasingly accurate as the element becomes smaller and smaller.

The total mass of the plate is the sum of the masses of all its elements. We consider this sum in the limit where the number of elements tends to infinity and the area of each element becomes vanishingly small. In this limit, the total area occupied by the rectangular elements becomes identical to the area occupied by the plate, and any approximation involved in equation (3) becomes negligible. This is just like the process that led from equation (1) to equation (2), so the sum over all the tiny elements can be regarded as an integral over the area of the plate. The mass of the plate is written as

$$M = \int_S f(x, y)\, dA,$$

where the subscript S on the integral sign indicates that elements exactly cover the surface S of the plate. This expression is called an *area integral*. Of course, we have not told you how to evaluate such an integral, but Section 1 will explain how this is done: by performing *two* definite integrals in succession – one over x and the other over y.

The ideas behind this example can be extended. For instance, instead of integrating over a region in a plane, we can integrate over a curved surface, such as the almost spherical surface of the Earth. If you know the population density (the average number of people per unit area) at each point on Earth, the total human population is found by integrating this population density over the surface of the Earth. Such an integral is called a *surface integral* (rather than an area integral, which is a term that is restricted to planar surfaces).

We can also consider three-dimensional objects rather than surfaces. A three-dimensional object can be approximated by many tiny cuboid volume elements aligned with the x-, y- and z-axes. A typical volume element has coordinates (x, y, z) and sides of length δx, δy and δz. Its volume is $\delta V = \delta x\, \delta y\, \delta z$, and its mass is given by

$$\delta M \simeq f(x, y, z)\, \delta V,$$

where $f(x, y, z)$ is the density of the object (its mass per unit volume) at the point (x, y, z). The total mass of the object is the sum of the masses of all the volume elements. We consider this sum in the limit of infinitely many volume elements, each of vanishingly small volume. In this limit, the sum can be expressed as an integral over the volume of the object. We write

$$M = \int_R f(x, y, z)\, dV,$$

where the subscript R shows that the volume elements exactly cover the region R occupied by the object. Such an expression is called a *volume integral*. We have not told you how to evaluate such an integral, but Section 2 will show how this is done: by performing *three* definite integrals in succession – over x, y and z.

A cuboid is a rectangular box.

The above examples used Cartesian coordinates, but it always possible, and often preferable, to use non-Cartesian coordinates. For example, a given area integral can be evaluated using either Cartesian coordinates or polar coordinates. All coordinate systems give the same answer, but one choice may make life easier than another, and part of the skill of evaluating area, surface and volume integrals is to choose a suitable coordinate system. You will see how to use non-Cartesian coordinates in the second half of this unit.

Uses of surface and volume integrals

Scientists and engineers often need to evaluate area, surface or volume integrals. For example, Figure 3 shows the Hoover Dam in the Colorado River, built in the 1930s to provide irrigation and hydroelectric power. The quantity of concrete used in this structure can be calculated using a volume integral (it is 2.5 million cubic metres). If the curved surface of the dam were to be painted, we could work out the area to be covered by evaluating a surface integral.

Figure 3 The Hoover Dam

In general, volume and surface integrals are useful whenever we have a quantity, such as mass or volume, that is additive. An **additive quantity** is one whose value over a region is equal to the sum of contributions from the region's constituent parts. For example, the mass of any object subdivided into many volume elements is the sum of the masses of these elements. This is what allows us to express the mass of the object first as a sum, and then as an integral.

Some scientists use the term *extensive* instead of additive.

There are many other physical quantities that are additive, including electric charge, energy and particle number. Each of these quantities can be characterised by a density, which may be per unit area or per unit volume. For example, we may talk about the energy density in the Sun at a given time (Figure 4). The total energy is found by integrating this energy density over the volume of the Sun. We may also talk about the number density of bacteria per unit area on the surface of a laboratory dish. If this number density is modelled by a smooth function of position, then the total number of bacteria on the surface of the dish is found by integrating the number density over the surface of the dish.

Figure 4 The surface of the Sun imaged by NASA's Solar Dynamics Observatory

Not all physical quantities are additive. For example, we *cannot* say that the temperature of an object is the sum of the temperatures of its parts, and there is no meaningful physical quantity corresponding to the temperature per unit volume. Nevertheless, if temperature is a function $T(x, y, z)$ of position, we may integrate this function over a region, and divide by the volume of the region to give a measure of the *average* temperature in the region.

Study guide

This unit shows you how to evaluate surface and volume integrals by performing two or three definite integrals in succession. Some of the techniques of integration described in Unit 1 will be used. The unit also uses properties of vector products and determinants that were covered in Unit 4, and the chain rule of partial differentiation, which was introduced in Unit 7.

Section 1 explains how to evaluate area integrals using Cartesian coordinates, and Section 2 deals with volume integrals in Cartesian coordinates.

Section 3 introduces several non-Cartesian coordinate systems and shows how they are used to simplify the evaluation of area and volume integrals. Section 4 gives a review of different types of coordinate system. It unifies all the discussion given earlier in the unit by introducing two important new concepts: *scale factors* and *Jacobian factors*. Finally, Section 5 discusses *surface integrals* over curved surfaces.

1 Area integrals in Cartesian coordinates

In this section, we consider area integrals of functions $f(x, y)$, where x and y are the *Cartesian coordinates* of points in a plane. The regions over which these functions are integrated will also be specified in Cartesian coordinates.

1.1 Area integrals over rectangular regions

We begin with a simple case. Given a function $f(x, y)$ of Cartesian coordinates x and y, we will show how to integrate it over a *rectangular* region in the xy-plane.

Figure 5 shows a rectangular slab in the xy-plane. This could be a small courtyard, for example. One corner of the slab is at the origin, and the slab extends to $x = 3$ and $y = 2$ (measured in metres). The slab is unevenly covered with a layer of snow whose mass per unit area (measured in kilograms per square metre) at the point (x, y) is

$$f(x, y) = xy^2 \quad \text{for } 0 \leq x \leq 3 \text{ and } 0 \leq y \leq 2. \tag{4}$$

The function $f(x, y)$ is defined everywhere on the surface of the slab, and represents the *surface density* of the snow. We can find the total mass of snow on the slab by carrying out a suitable integral.

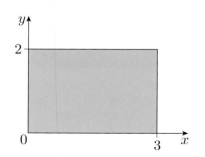

Figure 5   A rectangular slab in the xy-plane

First, consider the narrow shaded strip in Figure 6, which is centred on $y = y_0$ and has width δy. This strip is made up of many tiny rectangular elements placed end to end, parallel to the x-axis, just as in Figure 1. The mass of a single element in the strip, with linear dimensions δx and δy, centred on the point (x, y_0), is found by multiplying the surface density by the area of the element. From equation (4), the surface density at (x, y_0) is $f(x, y_0) = xy_0^2$, so the mass of the element is

$$\delta M_{\text{element}} \simeq xy_0^2 \, \delta x \, \delta y. \tag{5}$$

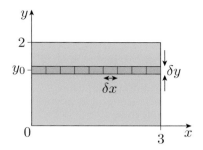

Figure 6 A narrow strip parallel to the x-axis is made up of many tiny elements

An approximation sign is used here because the surface density varies within the element. However, an equals sign will be used from now on, on the understanding that any error will become negligible when we take the limit of vanishingly small elements and integrate.

We can calculate the mass of the strip in Figure 6 by integrating along the x-axis, from one end of the strip to the other. All elements in the strip are centred on $y = y_0$, so this value of y remains constant during the integration. Integrating equation (5) from $x = 0$ to $x = 3$, we get

$$\delta M_{\text{strip}} = \left(\int_{x=0}^{x=3} xy_0^2 \, dx \right) \delta y = \left[\tfrac{1}{2} x^2 y_0^2 \right]_{x=0}^{x=3} \delta y = \tfrac{9}{2} y_0^2 \, \delta y.$$

Notice that the integration has been with respect to x, with y held at a constant value $y = y_0$. This is reminiscent of partial differentiation, where we differentiate with respect to x, while holding y constant. In effect, we have *partially integrated* the function $f(x, y)$ with respect to x (although this terminology is rarely used in practice). Notice too that the limits in the integral have been written explicitly as $x = 0$ and $x = 3$, rather than simply as 0 and 3. This is a useful precaution when dealing with a function that depends on more than one variable.

We denoted the constant value of y by y_0 to emphasise the fact that the value of y was held constant during the integration with respect to x. Nevertheless, our formula for the mass of a strip is valid for any value $y = y_0$ within the region of the slab. We can therefore replace y_0 by y to give the mass of snow in *any* narrow strip of width δy, centred on y:

$$\delta M_{\text{strip}} = \tfrac{9}{2} y^2 \, \delta y. \tag{6}$$

To find the total mass of snow on the slab, we must add up contributions from all the narrow strips between $y = 0$ and $y = 2$ (see Figure 7). We do this in the limit of vanishingly thin strips, which allows us to replace the sum by a definite integral. Equation (6) gives the mass of a strip, and $9y^2/2$ is the corresponding mass per unit length in the y-direction. To find the total mass of snow on the slab, we integrate $9y^2/2$ with respect to y, from $y = 0$ to $y = 2$. This gives a total mass of

$$M = \int_{y=0}^{y=2} \tfrac{9}{2} y^2 \, dy = \tfrac{9}{2} \left[\tfrac{1}{3} y^3 \right]_{y=0}^{y=2} = 12,$$

so we conclude that the total mass of snow on the slab is 12 kilograms.

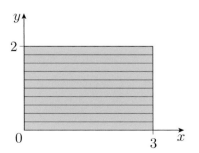

Figure 7 The slab is composed of many narrow strips

Once the principles behind this calculation are understood, it just amounts to doing two integrals in succession, one with respect to x and the other with respect to y. We can write this double integral as

$$M = \int_{y=0}^{y=2} \left(\int_{x=0}^{x=3} xy^2 \, dx \right) dy,$$

In some texts, the brackets enclosing the inner integral are omitted. This is on the strict understanding that the innermost integral is always evaluated first.

where the definite integral in brackets is calculated first, treating y as a constant. After the inner integral has been evaluated, and the upper and lower limits for x have been applied, we have a function of y only. This function is integrated with respect to y, and the final answer is obtained by applying the limits for y. This procedure is readily generalised.

> **Area integral over a rectangular region**
>
> The area integral of a function $f(x,y)$ over a region S is denoted by
>
> $$\int_S f(x,y) \, dA.$$
>
> If S is rectangular and bounded by the lines $x = a$, $x = b$ and $y = c$, $y = d$, the area integral can be obtained as two successive integrals:
>
> $$\int_S f(x,y) \, dA = \int_{y=c}^{y=d} \left(\int_{x=a}^{x=b} f(x,y) \, dx \right) dy. \qquad (7)$$
>
> In the integral over x we treat y as a constant.

We assume here that $a < b$ and $c < d$.

In equation (7), there is an inner integral (enclosed by brackets) and an outer integral. The inner integral is always performed first. But there is nothing to prevent us from doing things the other way round, integrating first with respect to y and then with respect to x.

Returning to the example of the mass of snow on a slab, we could equally well begin by finding the mass of a narrow strip parallel to the y-axis (such as that in Figure 8), and then find the total mass of all such strips.

Integrating the surface density xy^2 first with respect to y and then with respect to x gives

$$M = \int_{x=0}^{x=3} \left(\int_{y=0}^{y=2} xy^2 \, dy \right) dx$$

$$= \int_{x=0}^{x=3} \left[\tfrac{1}{3} xy^3 \right]_{y=0}^{y=2} dx$$

$$= \int_{x=0}^{x=3} \tfrac{8}{3} x \, dx = \tfrac{8}{3} \left[\tfrac{1}{2} x^2 \right]_{x=0}^{x=3} = \tfrac{8}{3} \times \tfrac{9}{2} = 12,$$

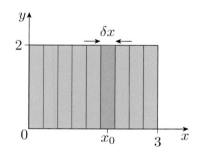

Figure 8 A narrow strip parallel to the y-axis

which is the same as our previous answer. This is just as expected: our decision to subdivide the rectangular slab into thin horizontal strips (as in Figure 7) or into thin vertical strips (as in Figure 8) cannot affect the amount of snow on the slab.

More generally, the area integral in equation (7) can be rewritten as

$$\int_S f(x,y)\, dA = \int_{x=a}^{x=b} \left(\int_{y=c}^{y=d} f(x,y)\, dy \right) dx. \tag{8}$$

Although the ordering of the integrations makes no difference to the final answer, one ordering may involve easier integrations than the other. You are free to choose whichever order makes the calculation easier.

Example 1

Find the value of the area integral of the function $f(x,y) = y\cos(xy)$ over the rectangle S bounded by the lines $x = 0$, $x = 2$ and $y = \pi/2$, $y = \pi$.

Solution

The region of integration is shown in Figure 9. Choosing to integrate over x first, the required area integral is

$$\int_S y\cos(xy)\, dA = \int_{y=\pi/2}^{y=\pi} \left(\int_{x=0}^{x=2} y\cos(xy)\, dx \right) dy.$$

The integral in brackets may look tricky but it is easily evaluated because, when integrating over x, we treat y as a constant. For constant y we have

$$\int_{x=0}^{x=2} y\cos(xy)\, dx = \left[\frac{y\sin(xy)}{y} \right]_{x=0}^{x=2} = \sin(2y).$$

So

$$\begin{aligned}
\int_S y\cos(xy)\, dA &= \int_{y=\pi/2}^{y=\pi} \sin(2y)\, dy \\
&= \left[-\tfrac{1}{2}\cos(2y) \right]_{y=\pi/2}^{y=\pi} \\
&= -\tfrac{1}{2}\cos(2\pi) + \tfrac{1}{2}\cos(\pi) = -1.
\end{aligned}$$

The negative answer is not a problem: it arises because the function $f(x,y) = y\cos(xy)$ is more negative than positive in the given region S.

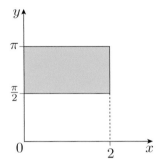

Figure 9 The region of integration for Example 1

Remember: if a is a constant,

$$\int a\cos(ax)\, dx = \frac{a\sin(ax)}{a} + C.$$

In the above example, the decision to integrate first with respect to x was key. In theory, we could have integrated first with respect to y, but the integrals would then have been harder. There is no merit is taking a tough route when an easier one lies open, so be prepared to switch the order of integration if your first choice leads to an impasse.

Product functions integrated over rectangular regions

A special case arises when the function to be integrated over a rectangle takes the form $f(x,y) = h(x)\,g(y)$, which is the *product* of a function $h(x)$ of x only and a function $g(y)$ of y only. In this case, the area integral of $h(x)\,g(y)$ over a rectangular region is simply the product of two ordinary integrals:

$$\int_{y=c}^{y=d} \left(\int_{x=a}^{x=b} h(x)\,g(y)\, dx \right) dy = \left(\int_{x=a}^{x=b} h(x)\, dx \right) \times \left(\int_{y=c}^{y=d} g(y)\, dy \right).$$

For example, integrating $f(x,y) = xy^2$ over the region of Figure 5, we have

$$\int_S f(x,y)\, dA = \left(\int_{x=0}^{x=3} x\, dx \right) \times \left(\int_{y=0}^{y=2} y^2\, dy \right)$$

$$= \left[\tfrac{1}{2}x^2 \right]_{x=0}^{x=3} \times \left[\tfrac{1}{3}y^3 \right]_{y=0}^{y=2} = \tfrac{9}{2} \times \tfrac{8}{3} = 12,$$

in agreement with both our earlier calculations.

However, you must be very careful: splitting an area integral into two factors works only under very special circumstances.

- The integrand $f(x,y)$ must be a product of the form $h(x)\,g(y)$.

- All the limits of integration must be constants: for Cartesian coordinates (x,y), this means that the region of integration must be a rectangle with its edges aligned with the x- and y-axes.

Other area integrals cannot be split in this way. For example, if the integrand is a *sum* of the form $g(x) + h(y)$, the area integral does *not* split into the sum of an integral over x and an integral over y (see Exercise 2).

Exercise 1

Find the value of the area integral of the function $f(x,y) = x^2 y^3$ over the square S bounded by the lines $x = 0$, $x = 2$, $y = 1$ and $y = 3$.

Exercise 2

Evaluate the area integral of the function $f(x,y) = 1 + x + y$ over the rectangle S bounded by the lines $x = 1$, $x = 4$, $y = 0$ and $y = 3$.

Exercise 3

Evaluate the area integral

$$I = \int_S \cos(x+y)\, dA,$$

where S is the square region $0 \le x \le \pi$, $0 \le y \le \pi$.

1.2   Area integrals over non-rectangular regions

The area integrals considered so far have all been over rectangular regions aligned with the coordinate axes. This made it easy to determine the limits of integration. For non-rectangular regions we must be more careful in setting up the integrals because the strips are no longer of the same length and the limits on the inner integral depend on the variable in the outer integral. To illustrate this, consider the following example.

Example 2

In this context, the word 'curve' includes straight lines!

Find the value of the area integral of the function $f(x,y) = xy$ over the region S bounded by the curves $y = x^2$ and $y = x$ for $0 \le x \le 1$.

Solution

We begin by drawing a diagram of the region of integration (Figure 10) and choose to integrate first over y and then over x. To determine the limits of the integration over y, consider a vertical strip drawn at an arbitrary fixed value of x within the given region. The ends of the strip lie on the curves $y = x^2$ and $y = x$. So for a given value of x, the lower limit for the y-integration is $y = x^2$, and the upper limit is $y = x$. These limits are the right way round because $x^2 \leq x$ for $0 \leq x \leq 1$, as shown in the diagram.

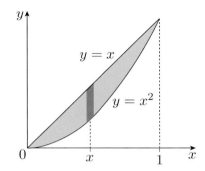

Figure 10   The region of integration for Example 2

The contribution to the area integral from the narrow vertical strip of width δx, centred on x, is found by integrating along the length of the strip:

$$\text{contribution of strip} = \left(\int_{y=x^2}^{y=x} xy \, dy \right) \delta x,$$

where x has a fixed value for a given strip.

A subsequent integration over x sums over all the vertical strips in the region. In this example, the first strip is at $x = 0$ and the last strip is at $x = 1$. Hence the lower and upper limits for the x-integration are $x = 0$ and $x = 1$, and the complete area integral is

$$\int_S xy \, dA = \int_{x=0}^{x=1} \left(\int_{y=x^2}^{y=x} xy \, dy \right) dx. \tag{9}$$

The integral enclosed by brackets is carried out first. This is with respect to y and is evaluated by treating x as a constant, giving

$$\int_{y=x^2}^{y=x} xy \, dy = \left[\tfrac{1}{2} xy^2 \right]_{y=x^2}^{y=x} = \tfrac{1}{2}(x^3 - x^5).$$

The result is a function of x only. This is finally integrated over x to give the area integral:

$$\int_S xy \, dA = \int_{x=0}^{x=1} \tfrac{1}{2}(x^3 - x^5) \, dx = \tfrac{1}{2} \left[\tfrac{1}{4} x^4 - \tfrac{1}{6} x^6 \right]_{x=0}^{x=1} = \tfrac{1}{24}.$$

Let us review this example. We started by drawing a diagram that helped us to find the limits of integration. This is an essential step. We chose to integrate first with respect to y, with x held constant. The limits of the inner y-integral were functions of x, and the limits of the outer x-integral were constants. The area integral was then found by two successive integrations, the first over y (with x held constant) and the second over x.

Although the integrand in this case is a product of a function of x and a function of y, the area integral does *not* reduce to the product of two ordinary integrals. This is because the limits of integration are not all constants. In equation (9), the limits of the y-integral depend on x, so we must do this integral first, and then integrate the result over x.

The general method is readily extended to other area integrals.

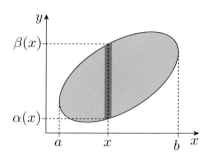

Figure 11 The region of integration for an area integral. The y-limits are given by the equations $y = \alpha(x)$ and $y = \beta(x)$ of the boundary curves.

Procedure 1   Evaluating an area integral

To evaluate an area integral $\int_S f(x,y)\,dA$ over any given region S of the xy-plane, we must decide which integral to do first – that over x or that over y. The following steps assume that we have chosen to integrate first with respect to y, and then with respect to x.

1. Draw a diagram showing the region of integration S.

2. Draw a vertical strip parallel to the y-axis, centred on x, and spanning the region (as in Figure 11). Determine the lower limit $y = \alpha(x)$ and the upper limit $y = \beta(x)$ for this strip. These are the limits for the y-integration (the inner integration). For non-rectangular regions, they are non-constant functions of x.

3. Determine the minimum value $x = a$ and the maximum value $x = b$ for x-values throughout the region. These are the limits for the x-integration (the outer integration), and are always constants.

4. Write down the area integral as

$$\int_S f(x,y)\,dA = \int_{x=a}^{x=b} \left(\int_{y=\alpha(x)}^{y=\beta(x)} f(x,y)\,dy \right) dx. \qquad (10)$$

5. Evaluate the inner integral over y first, holding x constant, and substituting in the limits of integration. This gives a function

$$g(x) = \int_{y=\alpha(x)}^{y=\beta(x)} f(x,y)\,dy,$$

which remains to be integrated over x.

6. Evaluate the remaining definite integral of $g(x)$ over x.

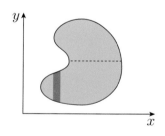

Figure 12 A region for which Procedure 1 fails. The problem is overcome by dividing the region into parts, as shown by the dashed line.

Step 2 of this procedure may sometimes fail. In Figure 12, for example, a strip parallel to the y-axis reaches the boundary of the region before it has spanned the whole region. Such cases are dealt with by breaking the region into smaller parts, but you will not meet this complication in this module.

Exercise 4

Evaluate the area integral of the function $f(x,y) = x - y$ over the triangular region S bounded by the lines $y = x - 1$, $x = 3$ and $y = 0$.

The simplest application of an area integral is to find the area of a given region S in the xy-plane. The area is given by integrating the constant function $f(x,y) = 1$ over the region.

$$\text{Area of region } S = \int_S 1\,dA. \qquad (11)$$

Exercise 5

Find the area of the region between the curve $y = \cos x$ and the straight line $y = 1 - 2x/\pi$, for $0 \le x \le \pi/2$.

Note that $\cos x \ge 1 - 2x/\pi$ for $0 \le x \le \pi/2$.

In Procedure 1 we chose to organise the area into vertical strips and integrate first with respect to y. We can also organise the area into horizontal strips and integrate first with respect to x. In effect, we would then continue to use Procedure 1 but with x and y interchanged. In this alternative ordering the area integral takes the form

$$\int_S f(x, y)\, dA = \int_{y=a}^{y=b} \left(\int_{x=u(y)}^{x=v(y)} f(x, y)\, dx \right) dy. \tag{12}$$

Here, the inner integration is over x with limits of integration that are functions of y, and the outer integration is over y with limits of integration that are constants. The inner integration is carried out first; it yields a function of y, which is then integrated to produce the final answer (which does not depend on x or y). For well-behaved functions, the final answer does not depend on whether we divide the area into vertical or horizontal strips, so equation (12) gives the same answer as equation (10); the choice of method is just one of convenience.

In the special case of an area integral over a rectangular region aligned with the coordinate axes, the limits of integration are all constants. But usually, the limits of the inner integral are not constants. This has an important consequence for calculations.

Rethinking the limits of integration

If we choose to do the x-integral first, as in equation (12), then the limits of integration must be rethought from scratch. This is done by drawing a new sketch of the region, with horizontal strips running parallel to the x-axis, rather than vertical strips parallel to the y-axis.

Let us return to the area integral of $f(x, y) = x - y$ over the triangle S bounded by the lines $y = x - 1$, $x = 3$ and $y = 0$. This was evaluated in Exercise 4 by integrating first over y and then over x. Now we will evaluate the same integral, but with the integrals performed in the opposite order.

A new sketch is needed, and this is given by Figure 13, which shows a typical horizontal strip across the region of integration. This stretches from $x = y + 1$ to $x = 3$. The minimum and maximum values of y are $y = 0$ and $y = 2$, and these are the lower and upper limits of the y-integration. So the area integral is expressed as

$$\int_S f(x, y)\, dA = \int_{y=0}^{y=2} \left(\int_{x=y+1}^{x=3} (x - y)\, dx \right) dy.$$

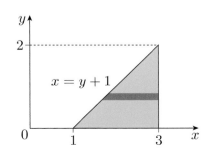

Figure 13

This area integral looks different to that in Exercise 4, but it leads to the same answer. Integrating over x while treating y as a constant gives

$$\int_S f(x,y)\, dA = \int_{y=0}^{y=2} \left[\tfrac{1}{2}x^2 - xy\right]_{x=y+1}^{x=3} dy$$

$$= \int_{y=0}^{y=2} \left(\tfrac{9}{2} - 3y - \tfrac{1}{2}(y+1)^2 + y(y+1)\right) dy$$

$$= \int_{y=0}^{y=2} \left(4 - 3y + \tfrac{1}{2}y^2\right) dy.$$

The final integral over y then gives

$$\int_S f(x,y)\, dA = \left[4y - \tfrac{3}{2}y^2 + \tfrac{1}{6}y^3\right]_{y=0}^{y=2}$$

$$= 8 - 6 + \tfrac{4}{3} = \tfrac{10}{3},$$

as before.

Exercise 6

Sketch the areas of integration for each of the following area integrals, and write down alternative expressions for the same integrals, but with the order of integration reversed.

(a) $\displaystyle\int_{x=0}^{x=2} \left(\int_{y=x/2}^{y=1} f(x,y)\, dy\right) dx$

(b) $\displaystyle\int_{x=0}^{x=2} \left(\int_{y=0}^{y=x/2} f(x,y)\, dy\right) dx$

Exercise 7

The shaded region in the figure below is bounded by the y-axis and the curve $x = 4 - y^2$.

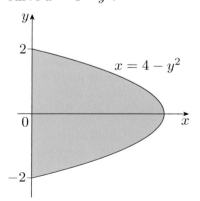

Find the area of this region by integrating first over x and then over y.

Exercise 8

Evaluate the area integral of the function $f(x, y) = x$ over the shaded region S in the figure below, which is a quarter-disc $x^2 + y^2 \leq 1$ with $x \geq 0$ and $y \geq 0$.

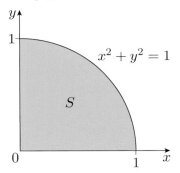

(*Hint*: In this case, it is easier to integrate over x first, and then over y.)

Exercise 9

Evaluate the area integral of $f(x, y) = \exp(x^2)$ over the triangular region in the figure below, which is enclosed by the lines $x = 1$, $y = 0$ and $y = x$.

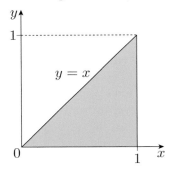

(*Hint*: The integrals over x and y can be written down in either order, but only one of these orderings gives integrals that can be done!)

2 Volume integrals in Cartesian coordinates

We now consider volume integrals. This section uses Cartesian coordinates to evaluate volume integrals over cuboid and some non-cuboid regions. The approach is similar to that used for area integrals, but there are now three coordinates, x, y and z, to consider, and three integrals to perform in succession.

2.1 Volume integrals over cuboid regions

Suppose that we want to find the total mass of an object from its density. Within the object, the density is described by a function $f(x, y, z)$ of Cartesian coordinates (x, y, z). This function allows us to find the mass of a small volume element. An element of volume δV, centred on the point (x, y, z), has mass

$$\delta M = f(x, y, z) \, \delta V.$$

Strictly speaking, this is an approximation because the density function may vary slightly within the volume element, but if the volume element is small enough, any such variation is negligible.

Now imagine subdividing the object into a vast number of tiny non-overlapping volume elements. The total mass of the object is the sum of the masses of its elements. Rather than adding up an immense number of small masses, we take the limit of the sum as the volume of each element tends to zero, and the number of elements tends to infinity. In this limit, the sum becomes an integral and the approximations become exact. The mass of the object can then be written as a volume integral:

$$M = \int_R f(x, y, z) \, dV,$$

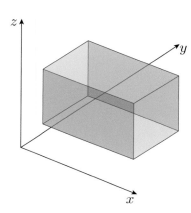

where R is the region occupied by the object, and $f(x, y, z)$ is the density function.

In this subsection, we explain how volume integrals are calculated in the special case where the region of integration is a **cuboid** (i.e. a rectangular block). We choose a Cartesian coordinate system with axes aligned with the faces of the block (Figure 14). These faces lie in the coordinate planes $x = a_1$, $x = a_2$, $y = b_1$, $y = b_2$, $z = c_1$ and $z = c_2$, where $a_1, a_2, \ldots, c_2$ are constants. (Here we use subscripts to distinguish the six constants that define the cuboid. This is neater than using six different letters of the alphabet.)

Figure 14   A cuboid

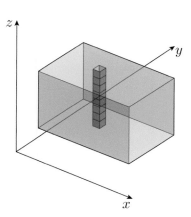

Suppose that we want to integrate the density function $f(x, y, z)$ over this cuboid. We start with a tiny volume element, which is a tiny block with linear dimensions δx, δy and δz, centred on the point (x, y, z). The volume of this element is $\delta V = \delta x \, \delta y \, \delta z$, and its mass is

$$\text{mass of element} = f(x, y, z) \, \delta x \, \delta y \, \delta z.$$

Figure 15 shows how similar tiny elements can be stacked on top of one another to produce a vertical column extending from the bottom to the top face of the cuboid. All the tiny blocks are centred on the same values of x and y, but the value of z varies from $z = c_1$ on the bottom face to $z = c_2$ on the top face. The mass of the column is the sum of the masses of the volume elements that it contains, and in the limit of very small volume elements this can be expressed as an integral:

Figure 15   A narrow column within a cuboid

$$\text{mass of column} = \left(\int_{z=c_1}^{z=c_2} f(x, y, z) \, dz \right) \delta x \, \delta y,$$

where x and y are held constant during the integration over z. The mass of the column remains a function of x and y because the density function may vary from point to point.

Next, we stick many columns together to form a slice running across the cuboid at constant x (Figure 16). The mass of the slice is the sum of the masses of the columns that it contains, and in the limit of very narrow columns this can be expressed as the integral

$$\text{mass of slice} = \left(\int_{y=b_1}^{y=b_2} \left(\int_{z=c_1}^{z=c_2} f(x,y,z) \, dz \right) dy \right) \delta x,$$

where x is held constant during the integration over y. The mass of each slice is a function of x only.

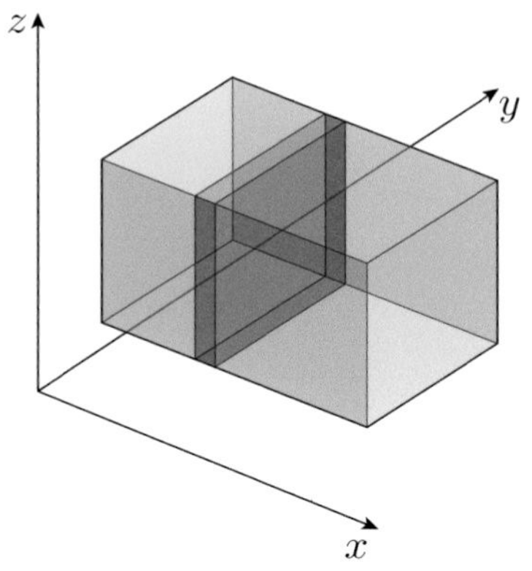

Finally, we join all the slices together to form the complete cuboid. The mass of the cuboid is the sum of the masses of the slices that it contains, and in the limit of very thin slices this can be expressed as

$$\text{mass of cuboid} = \int_{x=a_1}^{x=a_2} \left(\int_{y=b_1}^{y=b_2} \left(\int_{z=c_1}^{z=c_2} f(x,y,z) \, dz \right) dy \right) dx. \qquad (13)$$

Figure 16   A thin slice within a cuboid

This is a typical volume integral over a cuboid. There is no need to go through the steps of dividing the cuboid into blocks, columns and slices every time. You can go straight to the conclusion given by equation (13). More generally, the volume integral of any function $f(x,y,z)$ over a cuboid is given by a similar expression.

Volume integral over a cuboid

Given a function $f(x,y,z)$ of Cartesian coordinates x, y and z, and a cuboid region R, with faces lying in the coordinate planes $x = a_1$, $x = a_2$, $y = b_1$, $y = b_2$, $z = c_1$ and $z = c_2$, the volume integral of f over R is given by

$$\int_R f(x,y,z) \, dV = \int_{x=a_1}^{x=a_2} \left(\int_{y=b_1}^{y=b_2} \left(\int_{z=c_1}^{z=c_2} f(x,y,z) \, dz \right) dy \right) dx.$$

$$(14)$$

We assume here that $a_1 < a_2$, $b_1 < b_2$ and $c_1 < c_2$.

If $f(x,y,z)$ represents density (the mass per unit volume), then the volume integral in equation (14) gives the total mass contained in the region R. If $f(x,y,z) = 1$, then the integral gives the volume of the region R.

In all cases, this volume integral is evaluated from the inside out. First, we integrate over z, holding x and y constant. Then we integrate over y, holding x constant. Finally, we integrate over x. None of this should surprise you. It follows exactly the same pattern as for area integrals over rectangular regions, but we must now integrate over the three coordinates x, y and z, rather than just two.

As for area integrals over rectangular regions, the order of integration makes no difference to the final answer. For example, the above integral can also be written as

$$\int_R f(x, y, z)\, dV = \int_{z=c_1}^{z=c_2} \left(\int_{y=b_1}^{y=b_2} \left(\int_{x=a_1}^{x=a_2} f(x, y, z)\, dx \right) dy \right) dz.$$

Although the final result is the same, the effort needed for the integration may depend on the choice made.

For area integrals, you saw that product functions integrated over rectangular regions can be expressed as the product of two ordinary integrals. A similar result applies to volume integrals. The volume integral of a product function $f(x, y, z) = u(x)\, v(y)\, w(z)$ over a *cuboid* region is simply the product of three ordinary integrals:

$$\int_R f(x, y, z)\, dV = \int_{z=c_1}^{z=c_2} w(z)\, dz \times \int_{y=b_1}^{y=b_2} v(y)\, dy \times \int_{x=a_1}^{x=a_2} u(x)\, dx.$$

But you must be very careful: splitting a volume integral into three factors works only under very special circumstances.

- The integrand $f(x, y, z)$ must be a product of the form $u(x)\, v(y)\, w(z)$.

- All the limits of integration must be constants: for Cartesian coordinates (x, y, z), this means that the region of integration must be a cuboid with its faces aligned with the x-, y- and z-axes.

Other volume integrals cannot be split in this way.

Example 3

A cube has faces at $x = 0$, $x = 1$, $y = 0$, $y = 1$, $z = 0$ and $z = 1$, where lengths are measured in metres. The non-uniform density of the cube (in kilograms per cubic metre) is described by $f(x, y, z) = x^2 + y^2 + z^2$. Determine the mass of the cube.

Solution

The mass of the cube is given by the volume integral

$$M = \int_R (x^2 + y^2 + z^2)\, dV,$$

where R is the volume occupied by the cube. Inserting the appropriate limits, we have

$$M = \int_{x=0}^{x=1} \left(\int_{y=0}^{y=1} \left(\int_{z=0}^{z=1} (x^2 + y^2 + z^2)\, dz \right) dy \right) dx.$$

The inner integral is evaluated first. This is an integral over z with x and y treated as constants. We get

$$M = \int_{x=0}^{x=1} \left(\int_{y=0}^{y=1} \left[x^2 z + y^2 z + \tfrac{1}{3} z^3 \right]_{z=0}^{z=1} dy \right) dx$$

$$= \int_{x=0}^{x=1} \left(\int_{y=0}^{y=1} \left(x^2 + y^2 + \tfrac{1}{3} \right) dy \right) dx.$$

Next, we integrate over y with x treated as a constant. We get

$$M = \int_{x=0}^{x=1} \left[x^2 y + \tfrac{1}{3}y^3 + \tfrac{1}{3}y \right]_{y=0}^{y=1} dx$$

$$= \int_{x=0}^{x=1} \left(x^2 + \tfrac{2}{3} \right) dx.$$

Finally, we integrate over x to obtain

$$M = \left[\tfrac{1}{3}x^3 + \tfrac{2}{3}x \right]_{x=0}^{x=1} = 1.$$

So the mass of the cube is 1 kilogram.

Exercise 10

A cuboid block R has faces at $x = 0$, $x = 2$, $y = 1$, $y = 2$, $z = 2$ and $z = 5$, where lengths are measured in metres. The non-uniform density of the block (in kilograms per cubic metre) is given by $f(x, y, z) = x + y + z$. Find the mass of the block.

Exercise 11

Show that the function $f(x, y, z) = xyz\, e^{-(x^2+y^2+z^2)}$ can be expressed as a product of the form $u(x)\, v(y)\, w(z)$. Hence evaluate the volume integral

$$I = \int_R xyz\, e^{-(x^2+y^2+z^2)}\, dV,$$

where R is a cube with faces at $x = 0$, $x = 1$, $y = 0$, $y = 1$, $z = 0$ and $z = 1$.

2.2   Volume integrals over non-cuboid regions

A cuboid region of integration is, of course, an exceptional case. For shapes other than cuboids, Cartesian coordinates can still be used, but care is needed with the limits of integration.

Remember what happened for area integrals over non-rectangular regions – the limits of the inner integral depended on the variable of integration in the outer integral. Something very similar happens for volume integrals over non-cuboid regions.

Volume integral over a non-cuboid region

The volume integral of a function $f(x, y, z)$ over a non-cuboid region R can be written in the form

$$\int_R f(x, y, z)\, dV = \int_{x=a}^{x=b} \left(\int_{y=\alpha(x)}^{y=\beta(x)} \left(\int_{z=u(x,y)}^{z=v(x,y)} f(x, y, z)\, dz \right) dy \right) dx.$$

$$(15)$$

This involves three integrations performed successively, from the innermost to the outermost. In this case, we integrate first with respect to z (holding x and y constant). This gives us a function of x and y, which is integrated with respect to y (holding x constant). This finally gives a function of x, which is integrated over x.

The limits for the innermost integral depend on the variables of integration x and y in the outer two integrals. The limits for the middle integral depend on the variable of integration x in the outermost integral, and the limits of the outermost integral are constants.

In the special case where $f(x, y, z) = 1$, equation (15) gives the volume of the region.

$$\text{Volume of region} = \int_{x=a}^{x=b} \left(\int_{y=\alpha(x)}^{y=\beta(x)} \left(\int_{z=u(x,y)}^{z=v(x,y)} 1 \, dz \right) dy \right) dx. \quad (16)$$

Sometimes the trickiest part of the calculation is finding the limits of integration that define the region R. This is best done by sketching *two* diagrams, as illustrated in the following example.

Example 4

Find the volume integral of the function $f(x, y, z) = z^2$ over a pyramid R whose faces are given by $x = 0$, $y = 0$, $z = 0$ and $x + y + z = 1$. This pyramid has vertices at points $(0, 0, 0)$, $(1, 0, 0)$, $(0, 1, 0)$ and $(0, 0, 1)$.

Solution

The pyramid is sketched in Figure 17. The plane $x + y + z = 1$ meets the xy-plane in the line $x + y = 1$, so the triangular base of the pyramid is as shown in Figure 18.

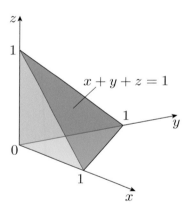

Figure 17 The region of integration for Example 4

The limits of integration can now be determined from our sketches. Above any tiny rectangular area element in the base of the pyramid, we can imagine a narrow column extending up to the blue shaded plane in Figure 17. By summing over all such columns, we cover the whole region of integration inside the pyramid. For a single column, rising from a point (x, y), we integrate over z from $z = 0$ to $z = 1 - x - y$. From Figure 18, we see that a slice at constant x can be produced by integrating over y from $y = 0$ to $y = 1 - x$. And to include all the slices, we must integrate over x from $x = 0$ to $x = 1$.

The order of integration can be checked from the nature of the limits. The z-integral *must* be placed innermost because its limits depend on both x and y. The y-integral comes next because its limits depend on x. Finally, the x-integral is outermost because its limits are constants. The function to be integrated is $f(x, y, z) = z^2$, so the required volume integral is

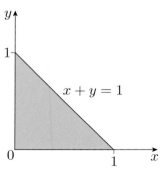

Figure 18 Projection of the region of integration onto the xy-plane

$$\int_R f(x, y, z) \, dV = \int_{x=0}^{x=1} \left(\int_{y=0}^{y=1-x} \left(\int_{z=0}^{z=1-x-y} z^2 \, dz \right) dy \right) dx.$$

The hardest part of the problem is over; now we just need to do the three integrations. We begin by integrating over z, holding both x and y constant:

$$\int_{z=0}^{z=1-x-y} z^2 \, dz = \left[\tfrac{1}{3}z^3\right]_{z=0}^{z=1-x-y} = \tfrac{1}{3}(1-x-y)^3.$$

We then integrate this function over y, holding x constant. You can see by inspection that when k is a constant,

$$\int (k-y)^3 \, dy = -\tfrac{1}{4}(k-y)^4 + \text{constant},$$

This integral can be checked by differentiation. Alternatively, you could use the change of variable $u = k - y$.

so, replacing k by $1-x$, we get

$$\int_{y=0}^{y=1-x} \tfrac{1}{3}(1-x-y)^3 \, dy = \left[-\tfrac{1}{12}(1-x-y)^4\right]_{y=0}^{y=1-x} = \tfrac{1}{12}(1-x)^4.$$

Finally, we integrate over x to obtain

$$\int_R f(x,y,z) \, dV = \int_{x=0}^{x=1} \tfrac{1}{12}(1-x)^4 \, dx = \left[\tfrac{1}{12}\left(-\tfrac{1}{5}(1-x)^5\right)\right]_{x=0}^{x=1} = \tfrac{1}{60}.$$

The same volume integral can be written in a variety of ways, depending on how we order the integrals. For example, we could have projected the region onto the yz-plane, and chosen to integrate first over x, then over y, and finally over z. The volume integral in Example 4 would then be written as

$$\int_R f(x,y,z) \, dV = \int_{z=0}^{z=1} \left(\int_{y=0}^{y=1-z} \left(\int_{x=0}^{x=1-y-z} z^2 \, dx\right) dy\right) dz. \qquad (17)$$

This gives the same answer as the volume integral in Example 4, as you can now check.

Exercise 12

Verify that equation (17) gives the same answer as that in Example 4.

Finding the limits of integration is a key step in all problems of this kind, and requires great care. Let us review how this is done. It is usually helpful to draw *two* diagrams to visualise the geometry – a perspective view of the three-dimensional region of integration and a plan view showing the projection of the region onto a coordinate plane (the xy-plane in Example 4).

Focusing on a tiny element with coordinates (x,y) in the projection onto the xy-plane, and extending upwards in a column within the region, we obtain limits for the inner integration over z. In general, these limits depend on x and y. Then we imagine sticking many columns together, producing a slice across the region at constant x. The y-values at the extremities of a typical slice are evident in the sketch showing the projection of the region onto the xy-plane. These are the limits for the middle integral over y, which in general depend on x. Finally, the minimum and maximum values of x in the projection onto the xy-plane give the constant limits for the outer integral over x.

When you nest the three integrals to form a triple integral, it is worth checking that the following rule is obeyed.

> **Rule for the ordering of integrals in a triple integral**
>
> The limits of integration of a given integral can depend only on the variables of integration of integrals that lie further *outside* it (and are done after it). The limits of the outer integral are always constants.

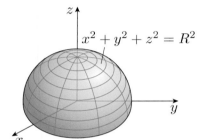

Figure 19   A hemisphere

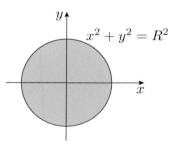

Figure 20   Projection of the hemisphere onto the xy-plane

Example 5

Figure 19 shows a hemisphere of radius R, with its base in the xy-plane, centred on the origin. In Cartesian coordinates, points on the curved surface of the hemisphere have $x^2 + y^2 + z^2 = R^2$. Write down an integral expression that gives the volume of this hemisphere. Do not spend any time evaluating the integrals.

Solution

Consider Figure 19 and the given equation for the curved surface of the hemisphere. For a given element with coordinates (x, y), the limits of the inner integration are $z = 0$ and $z = \sqrt{R^2 - x^2 - y^2}$.

We draw a two-dimensional view of the projection of the hemisphere onto the xy-plane. This is the disc of radius R shown in Figure 20. Choosing to integrate next over y, we see that for a strip centred on x, the limits are $y = -\sqrt{R^2 - x^2}$ and $y = +\sqrt{R^2 - x^2}$. The limits for the final x-integration are $x = -R$ and $x = +R$.

To find the volume of the hemisphere, we integrate the function $f(x, y, z) = 1$ over the hemispherical region. So the volume is given by

$$V = \int_{x=-R}^{x=R} \left(\int_{y=-\sqrt{R^2-x^2}}^{y=\sqrt{R^2-x^2}} \left(\int_{z=0}^{z=\sqrt{R^2-x^2-y^2}} 1 \, dz \right) dy \right) dx.$$

This illustrates the process of finding suitable limits, but the integrals are lengthy and will not be done here. Later in this unit you will see that there are better methods to use in this case, based on *non-Cartesian coordinates*.

Exercise 13

Find the value of the volume integral of the function $f(x, y, z) = x^2 yz$ over the wedge-shaped region shown in the margin, which is bounded by the planes $z = 0$, $y = 0$, $x = 0$, $x = 1$ and $y + z = 1$.

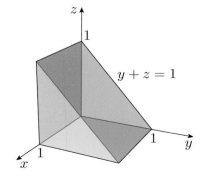

Sometimes the mathematical statement of a problem already specifies the limits of integration, and we can skip the stage of drawing diagrams, as in the following exercise.

Exercise 14

A region in three-dimensional space is defined by

$$0 \leq x \leq y^2 + z^2, \quad 0 \leq y \leq z, \quad 0 \leq z \leq 1,$$

where lengths are measured in metres. What is the volume of this region?

3 Using non-Cartesian coordinates

In principle, it is possible to use the methods of Sections 1 and 2 to evaluate any area or volume integral in Cartesian coordinates x, y and z – possible, but not always wise! For simple shapes such as discs, cylinders and spheres, it is generally much easier to use a different approach based on *non-Cartesian coordinates*. This section gives an introduction to the three most commonly used non-Cartesian systems: *polar coordinates*, *cylindrical coordinates* and *spherical coordinates*.

3.1 Area integrals in polar coordinates

Polar coordinates

Points in a plane are often specified by Cartesian coordinates (x, y), but this is not essential. An alternative choice is to use **polar coordinates** (r, ϕ), as shown in Figure 21.

Sometimes, the polar coordinate is denoted by θ rather than ϕ. Our present choice is deliberate and will have advantages when we compare polar, cylindrical and spherical coordinates.

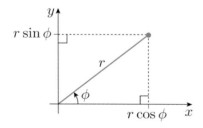

Figure 21   Polar coordinates

- The **radial coordinate** r is the distance of the point from the origin and lies in the range $0 \leq r < \infty$.

- The **angular coordinate** ϕ is the angle measured anticlockwise from the positive x-direction, measured in radians. The value of ϕ is not unique because we can add any integer multiple of 2π radians to it, and still be describing the same point. We often take ϕ to lie in the range $0 \leq \phi < 2\pi$, but other choices (such as $-\pi \leq \phi < \pi$) are equally valid.

Using trigonometry in Figure 21, we see that Cartesian and polar coordinates are related as follows.

$$x = r \cos \phi, \quad y = r \sin \phi. \tag{18}$$

So if we know the polar coordinates (r, ϕ) of a point, we can easily find its Cartesian coordinates (x, y).

Area integrals in polar coordinates

When an area integral is set up in a given coordinate system, a key step is to subdivide the region of integration into a set of tiny area elements.

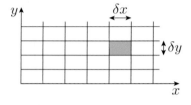

Figure 22   A Cartesian grid

In Cartesian coordinates, this is achieved by drawing lines parallel to the coordinate axes (Figure 22). Along each horizontal line, x varies at constant y. Along each vertical line, y varies at constant x. These lines produce a rectangular grid that divides the xy-plane into tiny rectangular area elements, such as that shaded in Figure 22. This element has area

$$\delta A = \delta x \, \delta y.$$

Something similar is done for polar coordinates. As shown in Figure 23, we create a grid from a set of radial lines (spokes) and a set of circles. Each spoke is a line along which r increases at constant ϕ. Each circle is a curve along which ϕ varies at constant r. Taken together, the spokes and circles divide the xy-plane into tiny area elements, such as that shaded in Figure 23.

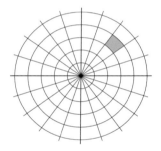

Figure 23   A polar grid

Figure 24 shows a tiny area element, with its size exaggerated for clarity. The element is bounded by radial spokes with $\phi = \phi_0$ and $\phi = \phi_0 + \delta\phi$, and circular arcs with $r = r_0$ and $r = r_0 + \delta r$. The spokes and circular arcs meet at right angles to one another, so if the element is *extremely* small, it can be approximated by a rectangle. The sides running along the spokes have length δr. Because the angle ϕ is measured in radians, the sides running round the circular arcs have length $r_0 \, \delta\phi$. So the element has area

Recall the formula $r \, \delta\phi$ for the length of an arc subtended on a circle of radius r by the angle $\delta\phi$, where $\delta\phi$ is measured in radians.

$$\delta A \simeq \delta r \times r_0 \, \delta\phi = r_0 \, \delta r \, \delta\phi.$$

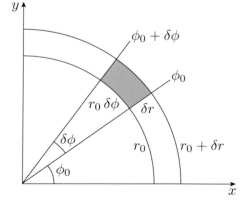

Figure 24   An area element in polar coordinates (enlarged for clarity)

Of course, there is nothing special about the values $r = r_0$ and $\phi = \phi_0$, so we can drop the subscripts and say that an area element centred on (r, ϕ) has area

$$\delta A \simeq r\, \delta r\, \delta \phi, \tag{19}$$

and if we are interested in the area integral of a function $f(r, \phi)$ over some region of the plane, the contribution made by the area element is

$$f(r, \phi)\, \delta A \simeq f(r, \phi)\, r\, \delta r\, \delta \phi.$$

The area integral of $f(r, \phi)$ over a given region in the plane is obtained by adding contributions from all the area elements that make up the region. We do this in the limit of an infinite number of infinitesimally small elements. Then our approximations become exact, and at the same time the sum becomes an integral.

As a definite case, let us take the region of integration to be a disc of radius R, centred on the origin. Then the limits for the r-integral are $r = 0$ and $r = R$, and the limits for the ϕ-integral may be taken to be $\phi = 0$ and $\phi = 2\pi$. The area integral can therefore be written as follows.

Area integral over a disc in polar coordinates

The area integral of $f(r, \phi)$ over a disc S of radius R centred on the origin is

$$\int_S f(r, \phi)\, dA = \int_{\phi=0}^{\phi=2\pi} \left(\int_{r=0}^{r=R} f(r, \phi)\, r\, dr \right) d\phi, \tag{20}$$

where we have chosen to integrate first over r, and then over ϕ.

The reverse order is also valid: with the inner integral over ϕ, and the outer integral over r.

Take careful note of the factor r that appears in equation (20) – and never make the mistake of leaving it out! It occurs in all area integrals based on polar coordinates. There are two ways of seeing why this factor must be included:

- Figure 23 shows that the area elements grow in size as we move away from the origin. If the area element were simply $\delta r\, \delta \phi$, this fact would not be respected.

- The expression $\delta r\, \delta \phi$ has the dimensions of length (because δr is a length and $\delta \phi$ is dimensionless). This is not suitable for an area element; the extra factor r ensures that the area element has the required dimensions of length squared.

The significance of the area integral in equation (20) is similar to that of an area integral in Cartesian coordinates. For example, if $f(r, \phi)$ is the surface density (the mass per unit area) at a point on the disc with polar coordinates (r, ϕ), then equation (20) gives the total mass of the disc.

If $f(r, \phi) = 1$, then equation (20) gives the area of the disc. This evaluates to

$$\int_S 1 \, dA = \int_{\phi=0}^{\phi=2\pi} \left(\int_{r=0}^{r=R} r \, dr \right) d\phi$$

$$= \int_{\phi=0}^{\phi=2\pi} \left[\tfrac{1}{2} r^2 \right]_{r=0}^{r=R} d\phi$$

$$= \int_{\phi=0}^{\phi=2\pi} \tfrac{1}{2} R^2 \, d\phi = \pi R^2,$$

as you would expect. The calculation is much easier in polar coordinates than in Cartesian coordinates. This is because when we integrate over a disc in polar coordinates, the limits of integration are constants that are easily determined.

A similar simplification occurs for the regions of integration in Figure 25, which also have constant limits of integration in polar coordinates. Polar coordinates are usually the preferred choice for such regions. This is true even if the integrand is initially specified in Cartesian coordinates because it can be easily converted to polar coordinates using equations (18).

Figure 25 Some regions of integration suitable for polar coordinates

Example 6

Evaluate the area integral of the function $f(x, y) = xy^2$ over the annular sector S shown in Figure 26. In polar coordinates, S is defined by $1 \leq r \leq 2$ and $0 \leq \phi \leq \pi/2$.

Solution

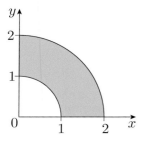

Figure 26 The annular region of integration in Example 6

The shape of the region of integration suggests the use of polar coordinates. Using equations (18) we have

$$xy^2 = (r \cos \phi) \times (r \sin \phi)^2 = r^3 \sin^2 \phi \cos \phi,$$

so the required area integral is

$$\int_S f(x, y) \, dA = \int_{\phi=0}^{\phi=\pi/2} \left(\int_{r=1}^{r=2} r^3 \sin^2 \phi \cos \phi \times r \, dr \right) d\phi$$

$$= \int_{\phi=0}^{\phi=\pi/2} \left(\int_{r=1}^{r=2} r^4 \sin^2 \phi \cos \phi \, dr \right) d\phi.$$

Note that the integrand contains a factor r^4 rather than r^3. The extra factor of r comes from the area element in polar coordinates. Carrying out the integral over r gives

$$\int_S f(x, y) \, dA = \int_{\phi=0}^{\phi=\pi/2} \left[\tfrac{1}{5} r^5 \right]_{r=1}^{r=2} \sin^2 \phi \cos \phi \, d\phi$$

$$= \tfrac{31}{5} \int_{\phi=0}^{\phi=\pi/2} \sin^2 \phi \cos \phi \, d\phi.$$

The integral over ϕ can be done by noting that the integrand is a product of a function of $\sin \phi$ times the derivative of $\sin \phi$ (namely, $\cos \phi$). This suggests that we make the substitution $u = \sin \phi$, giving $du/d\phi = \cos \phi$.

The $\phi = 0$ limit corresponds to $u = \sin 0 = 0$, and the $\phi = \pi/2$ limit corresponds to $u = \sin(\pi/2) = 1$. Putting everything together, we get

$$\int_S f(x,y)\,dA = \tfrac{31}{5} \int_{\phi=0}^{\phi=\pi/2} u^2 \frac{du}{d\phi}\,d\phi$$

$$= \tfrac{31}{5} \int_{u=0}^{u=1} u^2\,du$$

$$= \tfrac{31}{5} \times \tfrac{1}{3} = \tfrac{31}{15}.$$

Note: In this example, the integrand is a *product* of a function of r and a function of ϕ, and the limits of integration are all *constants*. In cases like this, it is legitimate to split the integral into the product of two integrals (just as we did in Cartesian coordinates). We can therefore write

$$\int_S f(x,y)\,dA = \int_{r=1}^{r=2} r^4\,dr \times \int_{\phi=0}^{\phi=\pi/2} \sin^2 \phi \cos \phi\,d\phi.$$

Evaluation of these integrals gives the same answer as before: $\frac{31}{5} \times \frac{1}{3} = \frac{31}{15}$.

Exercise 15

A circular laboratory dish of radius R is covered with bacteria. Relative to an origin at the centre of the dish, the *surface number density* of bacteria is given by the function

$$f(x,y) = \frac{C}{R^4}\left(2R^2 - x^2 - y^2\right),$$

where x and y are Cartesian coordinates, and C is a constant. Find the total number of bacteria on the dish.

The surface number density is the number per unit area at a given point. This is modelled as a smoothly-varying function.

Exercise 16

Use polar coordinates to evaluate the area integrals $\int_S x\,dA$ and $\int_S y\,dA$, where S is the semicircular area shown below.

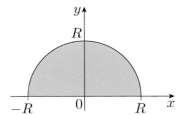

Exercise 17

The function $f(r,\phi) = e^{-r^2}$ is expressed in polar coordinates. Evaluate the area integral of this function over the entire xy-plane.

(*Hint*: An area integral over the entire xy-plane can be carried out in polar coordinates by letting ϕ range from 0 to 2π, and r range from 0 to ∞.)

3.2   Volume integrals in cylindrical coordinates

Cylindrical coordinates are a natural extension of polar coordinates to three dimensions. This subsection introduces cylindrical coordinates and uses them to evaluate volume integrals.

The alternative term **cylindrical polar coordinates** is also used.

Figure 27 shows how the **cylindrical coordinates** (r, ϕ, z) of a point P are defined.

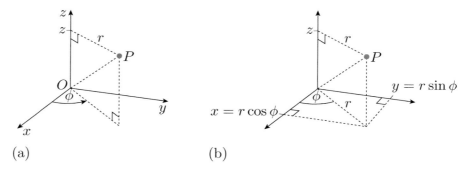

(a)   (b)

Figure 27   A cylindrical coordinate system: (a) coordinates (r, ϕ, z); (b) relationship to Cartesian coordinates

Note carefully: in cylindrical coordinates, r is *not* defined as the distance of P from the origin O.

- The **radial coordinate** r is the perpendicular distance from the z-axis to P. It ranges from 0 on the z-axis to infinity.

- The **angular coordinate** ϕ is the angle (measured in radians) between the positive x-axis and the projection of OP onto the xy-plane. The allowed range of ϕ corresponds to a complete circuit, and may be taken to be between 0 and 2π. The sense of increasing ϕ is as shown in the diagram (anticlockwise when viewed from a point on the positive z-axis).

- The **axial coordinate** z is identical to the z-coordinate of Cartesian coordinates.

In effect, cylindrical coordinates use the Cartesian z-coordinate parallel to the z-axis and polar coordinates perpendicular to the z-axis. Using Figure 27(b), it is easy to see that a point with cylindrical coordinates (r, ϕ, z) has the following Cartesian coordinates.

$$x = r \cos \phi, \quad y = r \sin \phi, \quad z = z. \tag{21}$$

To carry out a volume integral in cylindrical coordinates, we must first construct a volume element and find an expression for its volume. A suitable volume element is shown in Figure 28(a). This is obtained by starting at a point P with cylindrical coordinates (r, ϕ, z), and making small positive increments δr, $\delta \phi$ and δz in each of these coordinates. The edges of the volume element are formed by *coordinate lines* – that is, lines or curves along which *one* cylindrical coordinate increases while the other two coordinates have constant values. In Figure 28, the green, red and blue curves correspond to small increases in r, ϕ and z, respectively. A wider perspective of these coordinate lines is shown in Figure 28(b).

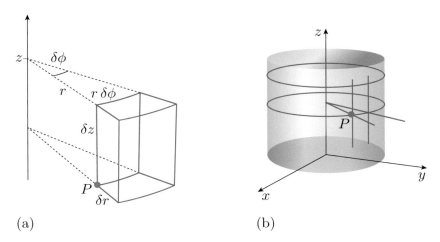

(a)   (b)

Figure 28   A volume element in cylindrical coordinates: (a) a close-up view; (b) a wider perspective

As its dimensions become very small, the volume element approaches a cuboid in shape. You can see from Figure 28(a) that this cuboid has sides of length δr, $r\,\delta\phi$ and δz. The element therefore has volume

$$\delta V = r\,\delta r\,\delta\phi\,\delta z. \tag{22}$$

Recall that a circular arc of radius r subtending an angle $\delta\phi$ (in radians) has length $r\,\delta\phi$.

Now, suppose that $f(r,\phi,z)$ is a function of cylindrical coordinates. Then the volume integral of f over any given region is approximated by adding contributions of the form

$$f(r,\phi,z)\,\delta V \simeq f(r,\phi,z)\,r\,\delta r\,\delta\phi\,\delta z$$

from all the volume elements that make up the region. We do this in the limit of an infinite number of infinitesimally small volume elements; then our approximations become exact, and at the same time the sum becomes a volume integral. If $f(r,\phi,z)$ is the density (the mass per unit volume) inside a given region, this volume integral gives the total mass contained in the region.

To take a definite case, suppose that the region of integration is a cylinder of radius R and height h, aligned on the z-axis and with its base in the xy-plane (see Figure 29). Then the limits for the r-integral are $r = 0$ and $r = R$, the limits for the ϕ-integral are $\phi = 0$ and $\phi = 2\pi$, and the limits for the z-integral are $z = 0$ and $z = h$. The volume integral of $f(r,\phi,z)$ over this cylinder can therefore be written as follows.

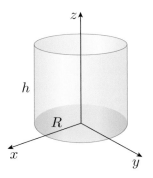

Figure 29   A cylindrical region D

Volume integral over a cylinder in cylindrical coordinates

The volume integral of $f(r,\phi,z)$ over the cylindrical region D in Figure 29 is given by

$$\int_D f(r,\phi,z)\,dV = \int_{z=0}^{z=h} \left(\int_{\phi=0}^{\phi=2\pi} \left(\int_{r=0}^{r=R} f(r,\phi,z)\,r\,dr \right) d\phi \right) dz. \tag{23}$$

The factor r inside the integral must not be forgotten!

The brackets show that we have chosen to integrate first over r, then over ϕ, and finally over z – but any other ordering would be equally valid in this case. For each of the integrations, all variables other than the variable of integration are held constant. For example, ϕ and z are held constant when we integrate over r.

There is nothing unexpected here. The first two integrals, over r and ϕ, correspond to integrating over a planar region in polar coordinates, with z treated as a constant. Only the final integration over z is new.

Example 7

A cylinder of height h and radius R has its central axis along the z-axis, with its base in the xy-plane as in Figure 29. The density of this cylinder is given by

$$f(x, y, z) = \frac{m}{R^5}(x^2 + y^2 + z^2),$$

where x, y and z are Cartesian coordinates, and m is a constant. Find the total mass of the cylinder in terms of m, h and R. Evaluate your answer in the special case where $h = 2R$.

Solution

The total mass of the cylinder is given by the volume integral

$$M = \int_{\text{cylinder}} f(x, y, z)\, dV.$$

Because the region of integration is cylindrical in shape, cylindrical coordinates are the natural choice. We therefore need to express the given density function in cylindrical coordinates. Using equations (21), we get

$$f(r, \phi, z) = \frac{m}{R^5}(r^2 \cos^2 \phi + r^2 \sin^2 \phi + z^2) = \frac{m}{R^5}(r^2 + z^2),$$

where, as usual, we have used the same symbol f for the density function irrespective of the coordinate system.

The total mass is then given by the integral

Any multiplicative *constants*, such as m/R^5, can be taken outside all the integral signs.

$$M = \int_{z=0}^{z=h} \left(\int_{\phi=0}^{\phi=2\pi} \left(\int_{r=0}^{r=R} \frac{m}{R^5}(r^2 + z^2)\, r\, dr \right) d\phi \right) dz$$

$$= \frac{m}{R^5} \int_{z=0}^{z=h} \left(\int_{\phi=0}^{\phi=2\pi} \left(\int_{r=0}^{r=R} (r^3 + z^2 r)\, dr \right) d\phi \right) dz.$$

Integrating over r and applying the limits of integration gives

$$M = \frac{m}{R^5} \int_{z=0}^{z=h} \left(\int_{\phi=0}^{\phi=2\pi} \left(\tfrac{1}{4}R^4 + \tfrac{1}{2}R^2 z^2 \right) d\phi \right) dz.$$

The integration over ϕ is easy. It gives a factor of 2π, which can be taken outside the integral. So

$$M = \frac{2\pi m}{R^5} \int_{z=0}^{z=h} \left(\tfrac{1}{4}R^4 + \tfrac{1}{2}R^2 z^2 \right) dz.$$

Finally, the integral over z gives

$$M = \frac{2\pi m}{R^5} \left(\tfrac{1}{4} R^4 h + \tfrac{1}{6} R^2 h^3 \right).$$

In the special case where $h = 2R$, the mass of the cylinder is

$$M = \frac{2\pi m}{R^5} \left(\tfrac{1}{2} R^5 + \tfrac{4}{3} R^5 \right) = \tfrac{11}{3} \pi m.$$

It is sensible to use cylindrical coordinates for all shapes based on cylinders – such as hollow cylinders or segments of a cylinder. Of course, the limits of integration must be adjusted for each particular case.

Exercise 18

A hollow cylinder, with its central axis of symmetry along the z-axis, has inner radius 2 and outer radius 5. The two flat ends of the cylinder are at $z = -1$ and $z = +1$. Find the volume integral of the function $f(r, \phi, z) = rz^2$ over the volume of this hollow cylinder, where r is the distance from the z-axis.

Volumes with axial symmetry

Consider the shape in Figure 30. This shape is unchanged if we rotate it through any angle around the red axis. Such a shape is said to have **axial symmetry**, and the red axis is called the **axis of symmetry**. If a volume integral is over a region with axial symmetry, it is generally advisable to use cylindrical coordinates rather than Cartesian coordinates, with the z-axis coincident with the axis of symmetry.

We now consider calculating the volumes of objects with axial symmetry. In general, the limits of integration for these volumes are not all constants, but axial symmetry is a very useful simplifying feature: it means that the limits of integration of the r- and z-integrals cannot depend on ϕ. So the volume V of any axially-symmetric region can be expressed in cylindrical coordinates as

$$V = \int_{\phi=0}^{\phi=2\pi} \left(\int_{z=z_1}^{z=z_2} \left(\int_{r=r_{\min}(z)}^{r=r_{\max}(z)} 1 \times r\, dr \right) dz \right) d\phi. \tag{24}$$

Here, the functions $r_{\min}(z)$ and $r_{\max}(z)$ give the minimum and maximum values of the radial coordinate r at a given value of z. If the object is hollow around the z-axis, then $r_{\min}(z)$ is non-zero for at least some values of z, but a solid object has $r_{\min}(z) = 0$ for all z. The values $z = z_1$ and $z = z_2$ are the minimum and maximum values of the z-coordinate in the object.

We can complete the inner integral over r in equation (24) to obtain

$$V = \int_{\phi=0}^{\phi=2\pi} \left(\int_{z=z_1}^{z=z_2} \tfrac{1}{2} \left(r_{\max}^2(z) - r_{\min}^2(z) \right) dz \right) d\phi. \tag{25}$$

Figure 30   A shape with axial symmetry relative to the red axis

Recall that in cylindrical coordinates, the radial coordinate is the distance from the z-axis.

The remaining limits of integration are all constants, so we can reverse the order of the integrals to get

$$V = \int_{z=z_1}^{z=z_2} \left(\int_{\phi=0}^{\phi=2\pi} \tfrac{1}{2} \left(r_{\max}^2(z) - r_{\min}^2(z) \right) d\phi \right) dz.$$

Integrating over ϕ and taking constants outside the remaining integral, we get the following result.

> **Volume of an axially symmetric object**
>
> $$V = \pi \int_{z=z_1}^{z=z_2} \left(r_{\max}^2(z) - r_{\min}^2(z) \right) dz. \tag{26}$$

In the special case of a solid object, $r_{\min}(z) = 0$ for all z, so

$$V = \pi \int_{z=z_1}^{z=z_2} r_{\max}^2(z)\, dz. \tag{27}$$

This formula can be interpreted by imagining that the object is made up of many thin discs, each of thickness δz, stacked one on top of the other. For a given value of z, the appropriate disc has radius $r_{\max}(z)$, area $\pi r_{\max}^2(z)$ and volume $\pi r_{\max}^2(z)\,\delta z$. Adding together the volumes of all the discs and taking the limit as δz tends to zero, we recover equation (27).

The following example shows how this result is used.

Example 8

Use cylindrical coordinates to find the volume of the cone in Figure 31. This cone has height h and base radius a; its axis of symmetry is the z-axis, and its base lies in the xy-plane.

Solution

Figure 32 shows a cross-section through the central axis of the cone. At a given value of z, the surface of the cone has radial coordinate $r = r_{\max}(z)$, as shown in the figure. From similar triangles we see that

$$\frac{h-z}{r_{\max}(z)} = \frac{h}{a}, \quad \text{so} \quad r_{\max}(z) = a\left(1 - \frac{z}{h}\right).$$

Using equation (27), the volume of the cone is

$$V = \pi a^2 \int_{z=0}^{z=h} \left(1 - \frac{z}{h}\right)^2 dz.$$

This integral can be done in a variety of ways. We choose to make the substitution $u = 1 - z/h$, so that $z = h - hu$. Then $dz/du = -h$, and we can make the replacement $dz = -h\,du$. The limits $z = 0$ and $z = h$ correspond to $u = 1$ and $u = 0$, respectively. So the integral becomes

$$V = \pi a^2 \int_{u=1}^{u=0} u^2(-h\,du) = -\pi a^2 h \left[\tfrac{1}{3}u^3\right]_{u=1}^{u=0} = \tfrac{1}{3}\pi a^2 h.$$

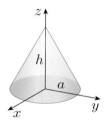

Figure 31   A cone of height h and base radius a

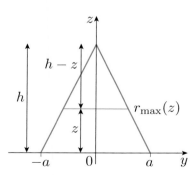

Figure 32   A cross-section through the cone

Exercise 19

A rugby ball has an axis of symmetry along the z-axis, as shown in the margin. In cylindrical coordinates, its surface can be modelled by the equation

$$r_{\max} = a\sqrt{1 - z^2/b^2},$$

where a and b are positive constants. The smallest and largest values of z on the surface of the ball are $z = -b$ and $z = b$. Use equation (27) to find the volume of the ball.

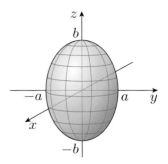

Exercise 20

A sphere of radius R, centred on the origin, is sliced across by a horizontal plane $z = R/2$. The part of the sphere above the plane is a spherical cap. What is the volume of this spherical cap?

3.3   Volume integrals in spherical coordinates

Finally, we discuss **spherical coordinates**, which are used extensively throughout the physical sciences. Figure 33 shows how the spherical coordinates (r, θ, ϕ) of a point P are defined.

The alternative term **spherical polar coordinates** is also used.

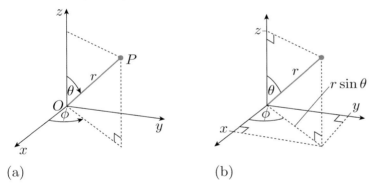

(a)   (b)

Figure 33   A spherical coordinate system: (a) coordinates (r, θ, ϕ); (b) relationship to Cartesian coordinates

- The **radial coordinate** r is the distance of the point from the origin O. It ranges from 0 at the origin to infinity, and is never negative. Note that this radial coordinate is *not* the same as the radial coordinate in cylindrical coordinates. It is therefore always important to state which coordinate system is being used.

- The **polar angle** θ is the smaller of the angles (in radians) between the positive z-axis and the line OP. It ranges from 0 along the positive z-axis to π along the negative z-axis.

- The **azimuthal angle** ϕ is the angle (in radians) between the positive x-axis and the projection of OP in the xy-plane. It increases in the sense shown, and is the same as the angular coordinate ϕ in cylindrical coordinates. The allowed range of ϕ corresponds to a complete circuit, and may be taken to lie between 0 and 2π.

At first sight, it may seem surprising that θ does not range from 0 to 2π. To see why this is so, consider the Earth with $\theta = 0$ at the North pole and $\theta = \pi$ at the South pole. Then it is clear that all latitudes are covered by letting θ range from 0 to π, and all longitudes are covered by letting ϕ range from 0 to 2π. If we gave θ a range larger than $0 \le \theta \le \pi$, we would be in danger of 'double-counting' in volume or surface integrals.

Spherical coordinates (r, θ, ϕ) can be related to Cartesian coordinates (x, y, z) using the trigonometry of right-angled triangles in Figure 33(b).

$$x = r \sin\theta \cos\phi, \quad y = r \sin\theta \sin\phi, \quad z = r \cos\theta. \tag{28}$$

These equations can be used to express any function of x, y and z in terms of r, θ and ϕ. For example,

$$\begin{aligned} z^2 - (x^2 + y^2) &= r^2 \cos^2\theta - (r^2 \sin^2\theta \cos^2\phi + r^2 \sin^2\theta \sin^2\phi) \\ &= r^2 \cos^2\theta - r^2 \sin^2\theta(\cos^2\phi + \sin^2\phi) \\ &= r^2(\cos^2\theta - \sin^2\theta) \\ &= r^2 \cos(2\theta). \end{aligned}$$

Recall that $\sin^2\phi + \cos^2\phi = 1$ and $\cos(2\theta) = \cos^2\theta - \sin^2\theta$.

To carry out a volume integral in spherical coordinates, we need to identify an appropriate volume element and find an expression for its volume. The required volume element is shown in Figure 34(a). This is obtained by starting at a point P with spherical coordinates (r, θ, ϕ), and making small positive increments δr, $\delta \theta$ and $\delta \phi$ in each of these coordinates.

- The edge PQ corresponds to an increase in r (with θ and ϕ constant).
- The edge PR corresponds to an increase in θ (with r and ϕ constant).
- The edge PS corresponds to an increase in ϕ (with r and θ constant).

A wider perspective is shown in Figure 34(b), where the curves along which a single spherical coordinate varies are shown in green, blue and red for r, θ and ϕ, respectively.

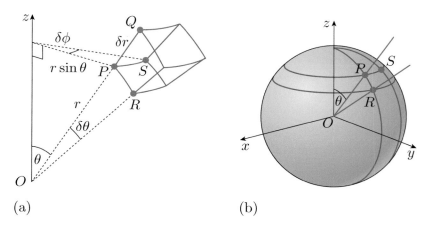

(a)   (b)

Figure 34   A volume element in spherical coordinates: (a) a close-up view; (b) a wider perspective

As its dimensions become very small, the volume element approaches a cuboid in shape, so its volume δV is given by

$$\delta V \simeq PQ \times PR \times PS.$$

The length of PQ is simply δr. In Figure 34(a), PR is an arc of a blue circle of radius r. This arc is generated by an angular change $\delta\theta$ in θ, so its length is $r\,\delta\theta$. Finally, PS is an arc of a red circle. Using the trigonometry in Figure 34(a), you can see that the radius of this circle is $r\sin\theta$. The arc PS is generated by an angular change $\delta\phi$ in ϕ, so its length is $r\sin\theta\,\delta\phi$. We therefore have

$$\delta V \simeq \delta r \times r\,\delta\theta \times r\sin\theta\,\delta\phi = r^2\sin\theta\,\delta r\,\delta\theta\,\delta\phi. \qquad (29)$$

The volume integral over a given region is then found in the usual way: we cover the region with tiny volume elements, then take the limit as the number of elements increases and the volume of each element tends to zero. A sum over volume elements then becomes a volume integral, with limits of integration appropriate for the given region. Here is the result for a sphere.

> **Volume integral over a sphere in spherical coordinates**
>
> The volume integral of $f(r,\theta,\phi)$ over a spherical region of radius R, centred on the origin, is given by
>
> $$I = \int_{\phi=0}^{\phi=2\pi} \left(\int_{\theta=0}^{\theta=\pi} \left(\int_{r=0}^{r=R} f(r,\theta,\phi)\,r^2\sin\theta\,dr \right) d\theta \right) d\phi. \qquad (30)$$

Do not forget the factor $r^2\sin\theta$ inside the integral. It appears in all volume integrals based on spherical coordinates.

This result is easily adapted to other regions by changing the limits of integration. For example, a hollow spherical shell corresponds to taking $R_1 \leq r \leq R_2$, and a hemisphere with $z \geq 0$ is obtained by taking $0 \leq \theta \leq \pi/2$. Spherical coordinates are particularly useful when the limits in all three integrals are constants.

If the function $f(r,\theta,\phi)$ represents density (the mass per unit volume), then the volume integral is the total mass in the given region. If $f(r,\theta,\phi) = 1$, then the volume integral is the volume of the region. For example, the volume of a hollow spherical shell with inner radius R_1 and outer radius R_2 is given by

$$V = \int_{\phi=0}^{\phi=2\pi} \left(\int_{\theta=0}^{\theta=\pi} \left(\int_{r=R_1}^{r=R_2} r^2\sin\theta\,dr \right) d\theta \right) d\phi.$$

As always, we work from the inside outwards. The first integration is over r, with θ and ϕ held constant. This gives

$$V = \int_{\phi=0}^{\phi=2\pi} \left(\int_{\theta=0}^{\theta=\pi} \left[\tfrac{1}{3}r^3\sin\theta \right]_{r=R_1}^{r=R_2} d\theta \right) d\phi$$

$$= \frac{R_2^3 - R_1^3}{3} \int_{\phi=0}^{\phi=2\pi} \left(\int_{\theta=0}^{\theta=\pi} \sin\theta\,d\theta \right) d\phi.$$

The remaining angular integrals are easily done. We get

$$V = \frac{R_2^3 - R_1^3}{3} \int_{\phi=0}^{\phi=2\pi} \left[-\cos\theta \right]_{\theta=0}^{\theta=\pi} d\phi$$

$$= \frac{R_2^3 - R_1^3}{3} \int_{\phi=0}^{\phi=2\pi} 2 \, d\phi = \tfrac{4}{3}\pi(R_2^3 - R_1^3).$$

This is the difference between the volume of a solid sphere of radius R_2 and the volume of a solid sphere of radius R_1, just as you would expect. The calculation is a good advertisement for using spherical coordinates in spherically symmetric situations; going through the lengthy chore of calculating the volume of a sphere in Cartesian coordinates is not the smart option!

The ordering of the integrals in equation (30) implies that we integrate first over r, then over θ, and finally over ϕ. However, if the limits of integration are all constants – as they are in equation (30) – we can write the integrals in a different order and still get the same answer. The choice of order can sometimes affect the ease of the integrations.

Example 9

In spherical coordinates, a function of position takes the form

$$f(r, \theta, \phi) = \frac{1}{(a^2 + r^2 - 2ar\cos\theta)^{1/2}},$$

where a is a positive constant. Integrate this function over the volume of a sphere of radius $R < a$, centred on the origin.

(*Hint*: You may find the following integral useful:

This integral can be confirmed by differentiating the result.

$$\int \frac{\sin\theta}{(a^2 + b^2 - 2ab\cos\theta)^{1/2}} \, d\theta = \frac{1}{ab}(a^2 + b^2 - 2ab\cos\theta)^{1/2} + C,$$

where a and b are constants, and C is an arbitrary constant of integration.)

Solution

In spherical coordinates we write the volume integral in the form

$$I = \int_{r=0}^{r=R} \left(\int_{\phi=0}^{\phi=2\pi} \left(\int_{\theta=0}^{\theta=\pi} \frac{r^2 \sin\theta}{(a^2 + r^2 - 2ar\cos\theta)^{1/2}} \, d\theta \right) d\phi \right) dr,$$

where the factor $r^2 \sin\theta$ comes from the expression for the volume element.

Here, we have chosen to integrate over θ first, then over ϕ, and finally over r. Our motivation for tackling the integrals in this order is that the task of integrating $f(r, \theta, \phi)$ over r looks tough. We integrate over the angles first, in the hope that things will get easier!

Using the symbol J to denote the integral over θ, we have

$$J = \int_{\theta=0}^{\theta=\pi} \frac{r^2 \sin\theta}{(a^2 + r^2 - 2ar\cos\theta)^{1/2}} \, d\theta.$$

Holding r constant and using the integral given in the question with $b = r$, we get

$$J = \left[\frac{r^2}{ar} (a^2 + r^2 - 2ar\cos\theta)^{1/2} \right]_{\theta=0}^{\theta=\pi}$$
$$= \frac{r}{a} \left((a^2 + r^2 + 2ar)^{1/2} - (a^2 + r^2 - 2ar)^{1/2} \right)$$
$$= \frac{r}{a} \left(((a+r)^2)^{1/2} - ((a-r)^2)^{1/2} \right).$$

Within the sphere, we know that $0 \le r \le R$, and the question tells us that $R < a$, so we have $0 \le r < a$. Hence the appropriate square roots are

$$((a+r)^2)^{1/2} = a+r \quad \text{and} \quad ((a-r)^2)^{1/2} = a-r,$$

giving

$$J = \frac{r}{a} \left((a+r) - (a-r) \right) = \frac{2r^2}{a}.$$

Our gamble has paid off: the integration over θ has simplified things considerably. The volume integral then becomes

$$I = \int_{r=0}^{r=R} \left(\int_{\phi=0}^{\phi=2\pi} \frac{2r^2}{a} \, d\phi \right) dr = \int_{r=0}^{r=R} \frac{4\pi r^2}{a} \, dr = \frac{1}{a} \frac{4\pi R^3}{3}.$$

A groundbreaking discovery

Using some additional arguments, physicists can use the result of Example 9 to show that the gravitational effect of a uniform sphere of mass M, measured at any point outside the sphere, is the same as that of a particle of mass M placed at the centre of the sphere.

This discovery was of great historic importance. As early as 1666, Isaac Newton took the gravitational effect of a sphere as being equivalent to a particle placed at its centre, but initially assumed this to be a crude working approximation. Nearly twenty years later, in 1685, he finally succeeded in proving the fact. (Newton's calculation followed a slightly different route to that given here, but the physical conclusions are the same.) We know from his own words that he had no expectation of so beautiful a result until it emerged from his mathematical investigation. The discovery was groundbreaking; it removed the barrier to precise astronomical calculations, and the next year Newton felt able to publish his masterpiece, *Philosophiae Naturalis Principia Mathematica* (Figure 35).

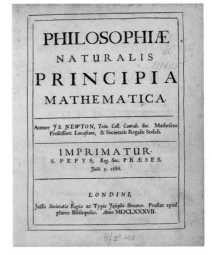

Figure 35   The title page of Newton's masterpiece, usually known as the *Principia*

Frequently, the limits of integration are constants *and* the function to be integrated is a product of single-variable functions of r, θ and ϕ:

$$f(r, \theta, \phi) = u(r)\, v(\theta)\, w(\phi).$$

Under these circumstances, we can write the volume integral in equation (30) as the product of three ordinary integrals:

$$I = \int_{r=0}^{r=R} u(r)\, r^2 \, dr \times \int_{\theta=0}^{\theta=\pi} v(\theta) \sin\theta \, d\theta \times \int_{\phi=0}^{\phi=2\pi} w(\phi) \, d\phi.$$

Example 10

Find the mass of a sphere of radius R, centred on the origin, with a density function given by $f(x, y, z) = mz^2/R^5$, where m is a constant. Convert from Cartesian coordinates to spherical coordinates before carrying out an appropriate volume integral.

Solution

Using equations (28), the density function in spherical coordinates is

$$f(r, \theta, \phi) = \frac{m}{R^5} r^2 \cos^2 \theta,$$

so the mass of the sphere is

$$M = \int_{\phi=0}^{\phi=2\pi} \left(\int_{\theta=0}^{\theta=\pi} \left(\int_{r=0}^{r=R} \frac{mr^2}{R^5} \cos^2 \theta \times r^2 \sin \theta \, dr \right) d\theta \right) d\phi.$$

The integrand is a product function, and the limits of integration are all constants, so the volume integral can be split into a product of three ordinary integrals:

$$M = \frac{m}{R^5} \int_{\phi=0}^{\phi=2\pi} 1 \, d\phi \times \int_{\theta=0}^{\theta=\pi} \cos^2 \theta \sin \theta \, d\theta \times \int_{r=0}^{r=R} r^4 \, dr.$$

The integral over θ can be done by making the substitution $u = \cos \theta$. Then $du/d\theta = -\sin \theta$, and the new lower and upper limits are $u = 1$ and $u = -1$, respectively. Hence

$$\int_{\theta=0}^{\theta=\pi} \cos^2 \theta \sin \theta \, d\theta = \int_{\theta=0}^{\theta=\pi} u^2 \left(-\frac{du}{d\theta} \right) d\theta = -\int_{u=1}^{u=-1} u^2 \, du = \tfrac{2}{3}.$$

The remaining integrals over ϕ and r are easily done. Collecting everything together, we get

$$M = \frac{m}{R^5} \times 2\pi \times \tfrac{2}{3} \times \tfrac{1}{5} R^5 = \tfrac{4}{15} \pi m.$$

Exercise 21

The function

$$f(r, \theta, \phi) = \frac{\sin \theta}{r} \quad (r \neq 0)$$

is expressed in spherical coordinates. Find the volume integral of this function over the region between two concentric spheres, centred on the origin, and of radii $r = 1$ and $r = 2$.

Exercise 22

(a) Given a function $f(r)$, where r is the distance from the origin, show that the volume integral of $f(r)$ over a sphere of radius R, centred on the origin, can be expressed as

$$\int_{\text{sphere}} f \, dV = 4\pi \int_0^R f(r) \, r^2 \, dr.$$

(b) Use your answer to part (a) to find the volume integral of

$$g(x, y, z) = \sqrt{x^2 + y^2 + z^2}$$

over a sphere of radius R, centred on the origin.

4 A review of coordinate systems

You have now met several coordinate systems:

- Cartesian coordinates in two and three dimensions
- polar coordinates in two dimensions
- cylindrical coordinates in three dimensions
- spherical coordinates in three dimensions.

In each case, we defined area or volume elements, and used these elements to calculate area and volume integrals. All of these area and volume elements can be treated from a unified point of view, using the concept of *scale factors*. The basic concept of a scale factor is explained in Subsection 4.1, while Subsection 4.2 gives further details.

4.1 Orthogonal coordinate systems and scale factors

In any given coordinate system, we can define lines or curves along which just one coordinate varies, while the other coordinates remain fixed. Such lines or curves are called **coordinate lines**.

For example, in polar coordinates (r, ϕ), there are r-coordinate lines and ϕ-coordinate lines (Figure 36). The r-coordinate lines are shown in blue: these are radial lines along which r varies and ϕ has a constant value. The ϕ-coordinate lines are shown in orange: these are circles around which ϕ varies and r has a constant value.

Each coordinate has a corresponding coordinate line. In Cartesian coordinates, the x-, y- and z-coordinate lines are all straight lines, parallel to the axes. In polar, cylindrical and spherical coordinate systems, at least one type of coordinate line is not straight; for this reason they are often described as being **curvilinear coordinate systems**.

All the coordinate systems discussed so far share an important property. In each system, *the coordinate lines corresponding to different coordinates meet at right angles*. For example, in Cartesian coordinates, the x-, y- and z-coordinate lines are perpendicular to one another. In polar coordinates, the radial r-coordinate lines are perpendicular to the circular ϕ-coordinate lines, and so on. Coordinate systems with this property are said to be *orthogonal*.

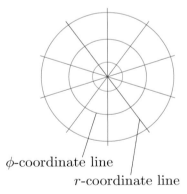

ϕ-coordinate line

r-coordinate line

Figure 36 Coordinate lines in polar coordinates

103

Orthogonal coordinate systems

A coordinate system is said to be **orthogonal** if its coordinate lines, corresponding to different coordinates, meet at right angles.

Cartesian, polar, cylindrical and spherical coordinate systems are all orthogonal.

Now consider the process of forming an area or volume element in an orthogonal coordinate system. First, we review the argument for polar coordinates.

Figure 37 shows a tiny area element in this coordinate system at a point P with polar coordinates (r, ϕ). This element has adjacent sides PQ and PR, and its size has been exaggerated for clarity. Note that PQ is part of an r-coordinate line, and PR is part of a ϕ-coordinate line. Because the polar coordinate system is orthogonal, PQ and PR meet at right angles. This is a great simplifying feature because it means that the tiny area element can be approximated by a rectangle. Such an element has area

$$\delta A = PQ \times PR.$$

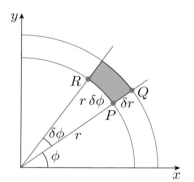

Figure 37   An area element in polar coordinates (r, ϕ)

The lengths PQ and PR are easily found from Figure 37. We have $PQ = \delta r$ and $PR = r\,\delta\phi$, so we conclude that

$$\delta A = r\,\delta r\,\delta\phi.$$

Note that this area element is not just the product of the coordinate increments δr and $\delta\phi$. The angular increment $\delta\phi$ is dimensionless, and it must be multiplied by the factor r to produce the length $PR = r\,\delta\phi$. That is why the formula for δA contains a factor of r.

Now consider a more general case. Suppose that we have a two-dimensional coordinate system with coordinates (u, v). To keep the argument general, we do not specify the nature of these coordinates – they could be polar coordinates (r, ϕ), or some other choice, but we do insist that the coordinate system is *orthogonal*. This means that the u- and v-coordinate lines (the curves along which just one coordinate varies) meet at right angles.

Starting from a given point with coordinates (u, v), we can make a small increment in u, with v held constant. This small increment generates a small step along the u-coordinate line. However, the length of this step need not be equal to δu. You saw this in the case of polar coordinates, where an increment $\delta\phi$ generates a step of length $r\,\delta\phi$. To deal with this point in a general way, we introduce the concept of a scale factor.

Scale factors

For any coordinate u, the length of the segment of the u-coordinate line between u and $u + \delta u$, where $\delta u > 0$, is expressed as

$$\text{length of segment} = h_u\,\delta u, \qquad (31)$$

where h_u is called the **scale factor** for the u-coordinate; this may be a function of the coordinates.

For example, the scale factors for polar coordinates (r, ϕ) are $h_r = 1$ and $h_\phi = r$, corresponding to the segment lengths δr and $r\,\delta\phi$.

Using scale factors, we can write down a general expression for the area of an area element in any orthogonal coordinate system. An area element at a point (u, v) is produced as follows. Starting from the point (u, v) in Figure 38, we step out along the u-coordinate line until u has increased to $u + \delta u$. We also step out along the v-coordinate line until v has increased to $v + \delta v$. This gives two adjacent sides of the area element. From the definition of scale factors, we know that these sides have lengths $h_u\,\delta u$ and $h_v\,\delta v$, respectively. However, the coordinate system is assumed to be *orthogonal*. This means that the coordinate lines meet at right angles, and the area element can be approximated by a rectangle whose area is given by multiplying the lengths of two adjacent sides. We therefore reach the following conclusion.

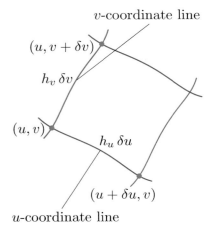

Figure 38   An area element in a general orthogonal coordinate system (u, v)

Area element in orthogonal coordinates

In any orthogonal coordinate system (u, v), an area element has area

$$\delta A = h_u h_v\,\delta u\,\delta v, \qquad (32)$$

where h_u and h_v are appropriate scale factors.

Similar ideas apply to orthogonal coordinate systems in three dimensions. There are now three coordinates, (u, v, w). Since the coordinate system is assumed to be orthogonal, the u-, v- and w-coordinate lines meet at right angles, and a tiny volume element can be approximated by a cuboid. The volume of this element is given by multiplying the lengths of three adjacent sides. By the definition of scale factors, these lengths are $h_u\,\delta u$, $h_v\,\delta v$ and $h_w\,\delta w$. So we have the following result.

Volume element in orthogonal coordinates

In any orthogonal coordinate system (u, v, w), a volume element has volume

$$\delta V = h_u h_v h_w\,\delta u\,\delta v\,\delta w, \qquad (33)$$

where h_u, h_v and h_v are appropriate scale factors.

The products $h_u h_v$ in two dimensions, and $h_u h_v h_w$ in three dimensions, are called **Jacobian factors**. They occur wherever an area or volume integral uses orthogonal coordinates. Do not make the mistake of leaving them out!

Equations (32) and (33) apply in all orthogonal coordinate systems, but to use these equations in a given coordinate system, you need to know the scale factors. There is a trivial case: in Cartesian coordinates, all the scale factors are equal to 1, and the corresponding area and volume elements are $\delta A = \delta x\,\delta y$ and $\delta V = \delta x\,\delta y\,\delta z$. For other coordinate systems, we can use the results for area and volume elements derived in previous sections to compile a list of all the scale factors that we need.

Scale factors in some orthogonal coordinate systems

Polar coordinates (r, ϕ)	$h_r = 1,\ h_\phi = r$	(34)
Cylindrical coordinates (r, ϕ, z)	$h_r = 1,\ h_\phi = r,\ h_z = 1$	(35)
Spherical coordinates (r, θ, ϕ)	$h_r = 1,\ h_\theta = r,\ h_\phi = r\sin\theta$	(36)

The scale factors for polar coordinates correspond to the area element in Figure 37. For reference purposes, the volume elements in cylindrical and spherical coordinates are reproduced in Figure 39, and you can see that these correspond to the scale factors in the list above.

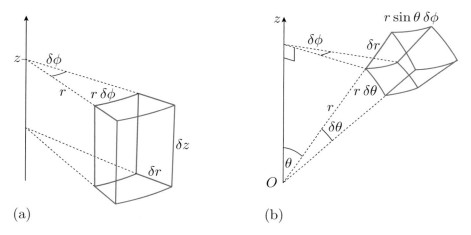

(a)   (b)

Figure 39   Volume elements in (a) cylindrical coordinates and (b) spherical coordinates

---

Exercise 23

Use the scale factors in equations (35) and (36) to write down formulas for volume elements in cylindrical and spherical coordinates.

Why should we bother with scale factors? The main reason is conceptual – they provide a unified language for discussing area and volume integrals.

Apart from this, the concepts of *orthogonal coordinate systems*, *coordinate lines* and *scale factors* are all used later in this book. They reappear in contexts other than integration, but the introduction given here provides a good foundation.

4.2   Another way of calculating scale factors

This subsection derives a neat formula (equation (39)) that can be used to find scale factors without drawing diagrams or using trigonometry. The formula is used later, but its derivation will not be assessed.

Suppose that we have a coordinate system (u, v, w), and we know the relationship between Cartesian coordinates (x, y, z) and (u, v, w). For example, in spherical coordinates (r, θ, ϕ), we know that

$$x = r \sin \theta \cos \phi, \quad y = r \sin \theta \sin \phi \quad \text{and} \quad z = r \cos \theta.$$

Then we can use this information directly to find the scale factors.

Figure 40 shows the effect of stepping out along the u-coordinate line by making a small increment $\delta u > 0$ in the coordinate u. We move from a point P with coordinates (u, v, w), to a point Q with coordinates $(u + \delta u, v, w)$. The displacement vector between P and Q is denoted by $\mathbf{a}$. The magnitude of this vector is the distance between P and Q, which, by definition, is equal to $h_u \, \delta u$. So we have

$$|\mathbf{a}| = h_u \, \delta u. \tag{37}$$

The displacement vector $\mathbf{a}$ can be written in Cartesian coordinates as

$$\mathbf{a} = \delta x \, \mathbf{i} + \delta y \, \mathbf{j} + \delta z \, \mathbf{k},$$

where δx, δy and δz are the changes in Cartesian coordinates between P and Q. However, the chain rule tells us how a small change in x is related to small changes in u, v and w:

$$\delta x = \frac{\partial x}{\partial u} \, \delta u + \frac{\partial x}{\partial v} \, \delta v + \frac{\partial x}{\partial w} \, \delta w = \frac{\partial x}{\partial u} \, \delta u,$$

where the last step follows because $\delta v = 0$ and $\delta w = 0$ along the u-coordinate line. Of course, there are similar expressions for δy and δz, so we conclude that

$$\mathbf{a} = \left(\frac{\partial x}{\partial u} \, \mathbf{i} + \frac{\partial y}{\partial u} \, \mathbf{j} + \frac{\partial z}{\partial u} \, \mathbf{k} \right) \delta u. \tag{38}$$

Since $\delta u > 0$, the magnitude of $\mathbf{a}$ is given by

$$|\mathbf{a}| = \sqrt{\left(\frac{\partial x}{\partial u} \right)^2 + \left(\frac{\partial y}{\partial u} \right)^2 + \left(\frac{\partial z}{\partial u} \right)^2} \, \delta u.$$

Comparing this with equation (37), we get the following general formula for the scale factor h_u.

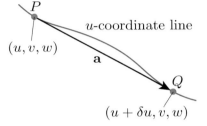

Figure 40   A small displacement along the u-coordinate line

This chain rule was introduced in equation (19) of Unit 7.

Formula for a scale factor

$$h_u = \sqrt{\left(\frac{\partial x}{\partial u}\right)^2 + \left(\frac{\partial y}{\partial u}\right)^2 + \left(\frac{\partial z}{\partial u}\right)^2}. \tag{39}$$

Similar formulas apply for h_v and h_w, but with partial derivatives taken with respect to v and w, respectively. For a two-dimensional coordinate system (u, v) in the xy-plane, we use essentially the same formula, but with the final term left out.

Example 11

Use equation (39) to find the scale factors for polar coordinates (r, ϕ), which are related to Cartesian coordinates by

$$x = r\cos\phi, \quad y = r\sin\phi.$$

Solution

Taking partial derivatives of x and y with respect to r and ϕ, we have

$$\frac{\partial x}{\partial r} = \cos\phi, \quad \frac{\partial y}{\partial r} = \sin\phi, \quad \frac{\partial x}{\partial \phi} = -r\sin\phi, \quad \frac{\partial y}{\partial \phi} = r\cos\phi.$$

Hence the scale factors are

$$h_r = \sqrt{\cos^2\phi + \sin^2\phi} = 1,$$
$$h_\phi = \sqrt{(-r\sin\phi)^2 + (r\cos\phi)^2} = r.$$

These values agree with those in equation (34).

Exercise 24

Use equation (39) to find the scale factors for spherical coordinates (r, θ, ϕ), which are related to Cartesian coordinates by

$$x = r\sin\theta\cos\phi, \quad y = r\sin\theta\sin\phi, \quad z = r\cos\theta.$$

5 Surface integrals

This section considers integrals over surfaces that are not flat. For example, we might know the *surface density* of paint at each point on the surface of a car. This surface density tells us the mass of paint per unit area in the vicinity of any given point on the surface of the car. If we integrate the surface density over the curved surface of the car, we will get the total mass of paint on the car. But how do we integrate over a *curved* surface?

5.1 The surface area of a sphere

As a simple example, consider the surface area of a sphere of radius R. You may know that this surface area is $4\pi R^2$, but it is worth seeing where this comes from.

We choose our origin to be at the centre of the sphere, and set up spherical coordinates (r, θ, ϕ). We need only two coordinates (θ, ϕ) to specify any point on the surface of the sphere (because all such points have $r = R$). We sometimes say that the surface of the sphere is *parametrised* by the coordinates θ and ϕ.

We can draw θ- and ϕ-coordinate lines on the surface of the sphere, and these subdivide the surface into a large number of surface elements (Figure 41). With a very fine subdivision, each tiny element can be approximated by a rectangle with sides of length $h_\theta \, \delta\theta$ and $h_\phi \, \delta\phi$, where $h_\theta = R$ and $h_\phi = R\sin\theta$ are the scale factors for spherical coordinates. Hence the area of an element centred on coordinates (θ, ϕ) is

$$\delta A = h_\theta h_\phi \, \delta\theta \, \delta\phi = R^2 \sin\theta \, \delta\theta \, \delta\phi. \tag{40}$$

Figure 41 The surface of a sphere is divided into surface elements by a grid formed by θ-coordinate lines (blue) and ϕ-coordinate lines (red)

To find the total surface area of the sphere, we must add the areas of all the surface elements. We do this in the limit of vanishingly small elements, so that the summation is achieved by integration. The values of θ and ϕ cover the ranges $0 \leq \theta \leq \pi$ and $0 \leq \phi \leq 2\pi$, so the total surface area of the sphere is

$$\text{surface area} = \int_{\phi=0}^{\phi=2\pi} \left(\int_{\theta=0}^{\theta=\pi} R^2 \sin\theta \, d\theta \right) d\phi$$

$$= R^2 \int_{\phi=0}^{\phi=2\pi} \left[-\cos\theta \right]_{\theta=0}^{\theta=\pi} d\phi$$

$$= R^2 \int_{\phi=0}^{\phi=2\pi} 2 \, d\phi = 4\pi R^2,$$

Remember that R is constant for a given spherical surface.

as expected.

This surface area is the integral over the spherical surface of the function $f = 1$. We can also integrate other functions over this surface. Suppose that the sphere is unevenly coated with a layer whose surface density (i.e. mass per unit area) is

$$f(\theta, \phi) = A\cos^2\theta,$$

where A is a positive constant. Then the total mass of the layer is

$$M = \int_{\phi=0}^{\phi=2\pi} \left(\int_{\theta=0}^{\theta=\pi} f(\theta, \phi) R^2 \sin\theta \, d\theta \right) d\phi$$

$$= AR^2 \int_{\phi=0}^{\phi=2\pi} \left(\int_{\theta=0}^{\theta=\pi} \cos^2\theta \sin\theta \, d\theta \right) d\phi.$$

The angular integrals over θ and ϕ were calculated in Example 10, and give factors of $\frac{2}{3}$ and 2π, respectively, so we get

$$M = AR^2 \times \tfrac{2}{3} \times 2\pi = \tfrac{4}{3}\pi AR^2.$$

Exercise 25

A sphere of radius R is centred on the origin. Find the surface area of the spherical cap formed by the portion of the sphere that has $z > R/2$.

5.2 A general method for surface integrals

In practice, scientists and engineers do not spend much time evaluating surface integrals. They either consider simple surfaces, such as spheres or cylinders, or use numerical methods.

The calculation of surface integrals on the surface of a sphere works well because points on the surface of a sphere can be labelled by the angular coordinates θ and ϕ of spherical coordinates. This coordinate system is orthogonal, so it generates area elements on the surface of the sphere that can be approximated by tiny rectangles. We know the relevant scale factors h_θ and h_ϕ in this case, so it is fairly easy to obtain equation (40) for an area element.

On a general surface, we have to work harder to get suitable expressions for the area elements. This final subsection develops a general method for doing this, summarised by equations (43) and (44) below. You may be asked to apply these results, but the arguments leading up to them will not be assessed.

Let us assume that the surface under investigation is parametrised by coordinates (u, v). This means that each allowed pair of values (u, v) labels a unique point on the surface. As u and v vary over their allowed ranges, the entire surface is mapped out. You have seen how this works for the surface of a sphere, which is parametrised by the coordinates θ and ϕ, with $0 \le \theta \le \pi$ and $0 \le \phi \le 2\pi$.

Each point on the surface can also be represented by Cartesian coordinates (x, y, z). So there must be some link between Cartesian coordinates and u and v. On the surface, x, y and z will be given by specific functions

$$x = x(u, v), \quad y = y(u, v), \quad z = z(u, v). \tag{41}$$

For example, in the case of a sphere of radius R, centred on the origin, and parametrised by $\theta = u$ and $\phi = v$, these equations take the form

$$x = R\sin\theta\cos\phi, \quad y = R\sin\theta\sin\phi, \quad z = R\cos\theta, \tag{42}$$

where R is a constant for a given sphere.

On an arbitrary surface, the u-coordinate lines intermesh with the v-coordinate lines to produce a grid of tiny surface elements (Figure 42).

Figure 42 A surface grid formed by intermeshing coordinate lines

In general, the u- and v-coordinate lines do not meet at right angles, and the surface elements are approximated by tiny flat parallelograms, rather than rectangles. We need to find the areas of these parallelograms, one of which is shown greatly enlarged in Figure 43.

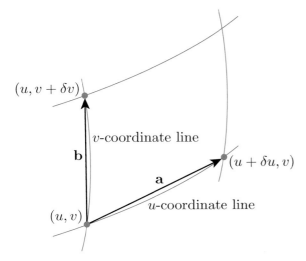

Figure 43   An area element can be approximated by a tiny parallelogram, shown greatly enlarged here

Using equation (34) from Unit 4, we have

$$\text{area of parallelogram} = |\mathbf{a} \times \mathbf{b}|,$$

where $\mathbf{a}$ and $\mathbf{b}$ are the displacement vectors shown in Figure 43. We also know from Unit 4 that the vector product $\mathbf{a} \times \mathbf{b}$ can be expressed as a determinant:

$$\mathbf{a} \times \mathbf{b} = \begin{vmatrix} \mathbf{i} & \mathbf{j} & \mathbf{k} \\ a_x & a_y & a_z \\ b_x & b_y & b_z \end{vmatrix}.$$

See Unit 4, equation (61).

However, we obtained an expression for the vector $\mathbf{a}$ in Subsection 4.2. Equation (38) tells us that

$$\mathbf{a} = (a_x, a_y, a_z) = \left(\frac{\partial x}{\partial u}, \frac{\partial y}{\partial u}, \frac{\partial z}{\partial u} \right) \delta u,$$

and by a similar argument,

$$\mathbf{b} = (b_x, b_y, b_z) = \left(\frac{\partial x}{\partial v}, \frac{\partial y}{\partial v}, \frac{\partial z}{\partial v} \right) \delta v.$$

Combining these results with the preceding equations, we obtain the following general result for the area of a surface element on a curved surface.

Area of a surface element on a curved surface

If a surface is parametrised by coordinates (u, v), where $x = x(u, v)$, $y = y(u, v)$ and $z = z(u, v)$, then the area of a surface element is given by

$$\delta A = |\mathbf{J}| \, \delta u \, \delta v, \tag{43}$$

Note that the vertical lines in equation (43) indicate the magnitude of a vector, while the vertical lines in equation (44) indicate a determinant.

where $|\mathbf{J}|$ is the magnitude of the vector

$$\mathbf{J} = \begin{vmatrix} \mathbf{i} & \mathbf{j} & \mathbf{k} \\ \dfrac{\partial x}{\partial u} & \dfrac{\partial y}{\partial u} & \dfrac{\partial z}{\partial u} \\ \dfrac{\partial x}{\partial v} & \dfrac{\partial y}{\partial v} & \dfrac{\partial z}{\partial v} \end{vmatrix}. \tag{44}$$

The vector $\mathbf{J}$ is sometimes called the **Jacobian vector**.

The magnitude of $\mathbf{J}$ determines the area of a surface element. The direction of $\mathbf{J}$ also has a simple interpretation. Because the vector product $\mathbf{a} \times \mathbf{b}$ is perpendicular to both $\mathbf{a}$ and $\mathbf{b}$, and because $\mathbf{a}$ and $\mathbf{b}$ in Figure 43 lie the plane of the surface, *the vector $\mathbf{J}$ is perpendicular to the surface.*

Before using equations (43) and (44) more generally, let us just check that they give the result obtained earlier for the surface element of a sphere, parametrised by θ and ϕ of spherical coordinates. In this case the relevant partial derivatives were calculated in Exercise 24. Setting $r = R$, we get

$$\mathbf{J} = \begin{vmatrix} \mathbf{i} & \mathbf{j} & \mathbf{k} \\ R\cos\theta\cos\phi & R\cos\theta\sin\phi & -R\sin\theta \\ -R\sin\theta\sin\phi & R\sin\theta\cos\phi & 0 \end{vmatrix}. \tag{45}$$

Exercise 26

You will need to use the identity $\cos^2 x + \sin^2 x = 1$.

Expand the determinant in equation (45), and hence confirm that the area of a surface element on a sphere is given by $\delta A = R^2 \sin\theta \, \delta\theta \, \delta\phi$.

Using the surface element $\delta A = |\mathbf{J}| \, \delta u \, \delta v$, it is easy to write down a general expression for a surface integral.

Surface integral over a curved surface

For a surface S parametrised by coordinates (u, v), the surface integral of a function $f(u, v)$ over S is given by

Equation (46) assumes that all the limits of integration are constants. This covers all the cases considered in this module.

$$\int_S f \, dA = \int_{v=v_1}^{v=v_2} \left(\int_{u=u_1}^{u=u_2} f(u, v) \, |\mathbf{J}| \, du \right) dv, \tag{46}$$

where the ranges $u_1 \leq u \leq u_2$ and $v_1 \leq v \leq u_2$ are chosen to cover the surface S exactly.

To find the area of a surface S, we use equation (46) with $f = 1$.

Example 12

A cone has height h and base radius a (see Figure 44). The sloping surface of this cone can be parametrised by two of the cylindrical coordinates, r and ϕ, with $0 \le r \le a$ and $0 \le \phi \le 2\pi$. In terms of these parameters, points on the sloping surface of the cone have Cartesian coordinates

$$x = r \cos\phi, \quad y = r \sin\phi, \quad z = h\left(1 - \frac{r}{a}\right).$$

Find the area of the sloping surface of the cone (not including its base).

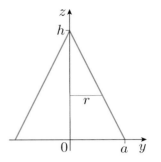

Figure 44   Cross-section through a cone

Solution

Taking partial derivatives of x, y and z with respect to our chosen parameters r and ϕ gives

$$\frac{\partial x}{\partial r} = \cos\phi, \quad \frac{\partial y}{\partial r} = \sin\phi, \quad \frac{\partial z}{\partial r} = -\frac{h}{a},$$

$$\frac{\partial x}{\partial \phi} = -r\sin\phi, \quad \frac{\partial y}{\partial \phi} = r\cos\phi, \quad \frac{\partial z}{\partial \phi} = 0.$$

Using these results in the expression for the Jacobian vector $\mathbf{J}$, we get

$$\mathbf{J} = \begin{vmatrix} \mathbf{i} & \mathbf{j} & \mathbf{k} \\ \cos\phi & \sin\phi & -h/a \\ -r\sin\phi & r\cos\phi & 0 \end{vmatrix}$$

$$= \frac{h}{a}r\cos\phi\,\mathbf{i} + \frac{h}{a}r\sin\phi\,\mathbf{j} + r(\cos^2\phi + \sin^2\phi)\,\mathbf{k}$$

$$= \frac{h}{a}r\cos\phi\,\mathbf{i} + \frac{h}{a}r\sin\phi\,\mathbf{j} + r\,\mathbf{k}.$$

The square of the magnitude of $\mathbf{J}$ is

$$|\mathbf{J}|^2 = \frac{h^2}{a^2}r^2(\cos^2\phi + \sin^2\phi) + r^2$$

$$= \left(1 + \frac{h^2}{a^2}\right)r^2,$$

so the area element is

$$\delta A = \left(1 + \frac{h^2}{a^2}\right)^{1/2} r\,\delta r\,\delta\phi.$$

Using this area element and integrating over the ranges of r and ϕ, we get

$$\text{area} = \left(1 + \frac{h^2}{a^2}\right)^{1/2} \int_{\phi=0}^{\phi=2\pi} \left(\int_{r=0}^{r=a} r\,dr\right) d\phi$$

$$= \left(1 + \frac{h^2}{a^2}\right)^{1/2} \times 2\pi \times \frac{a^2}{2}$$

$$= \pi a\sqrt{a^2 + h^2}.$$

A useful check is provided by letting h tend to zero. The surface area then tends to πa^2, which is the area of a circle, as expected.

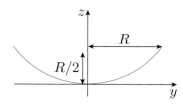

Exercise 27

The parabolic reflector dish shown in cross-section in the margin has radius R at its opening and axial depth $R/2$. Its surface can be parametrised by two of the cylindrical coordinates, r and ϕ, with $0 \le r \le R$ and $0 \le \phi \le 2\pi$. In terms of these parameters, points on the surface of the dish have Cartesian coordinates

$$x = r\cos\phi, \quad y = r\sin\phi, \quad z = \frac{r^2}{2R}.$$

Find the surface area of the outside of this dish.

Exercise 28

A certain surface S has parameters u and v, and extends over $0 \le u \le 1$ and $0 \le v \le 1$. In terms of these parameters, the Cartesian coordinates of points on S are

$$x = \tfrac{1}{2}(u^2 + v^2), \quad y = \tfrac{1}{2}(u^2 - v^2), \quad z = uv.$$

Find the surface area of S.

Learning outcomes

After studying this unit, you should be able to do the following.

- Evaluate area integrals over rectangular and non-rectangular regions of the xy-plane using Cartesian coordinates.

- Evaluate volume integrals over cuboid and non-cuboid regions using Cartesian coordinates.

- Evaluate area and volume integrals using polar, cylindrical and spherical coordinates.

- Define the terms orthogonal coordinate system, coordinate line, scale factor, Jacobian factor and Jacobian vector.

- Evaluate surface integrals over curved surfaces.

Solutions to exercises

Solution to Exercise 1

The integrand is a product of a function of x and a function of y, and the range of integration is a rectangle aligned with the coordinate axes, so we can evaluate the integral as the product of two definite integrals:

$$\int_S x^2 y^3 \, dA = \left(\int_{x=0}^{x=2} x^2 \, dx \right) \times \left(\int_{y=1}^{y=3} y^3 \, dy \right)$$

$$= \left[\tfrac{1}{3} x^3 \right]_{x=0}^{x=2} \times \left[\tfrac{1}{4} y^4 \right]_{y=1}^{y=3}$$

$$= \frac{8}{3} \times \frac{81 - 1}{4} = \frac{160}{3}.$$

Solution to Exercise 2

This integrand does *not* factorise into a function of x times a function of y, so we must evaluate it by two successive integrations. Because the limits for y involve a zero, it is slightly easier to integrate over y first. Remembering to treat x as a constant when we perform the y-integration, we get

$$\int_S (1 + x + y) \, dA = \int_{x=1}^{x=4} \left(\int_{y=0}^{y=3} (1 + x + y) \, dy \right) dx$$

$$= \int_{x=1}^{x=4} \left[y + xy + \tfrac{1}{2} y^2 \right]_{y=0}^{y=3} dx$$

$$= \int_{x=1}^{x=4} \left(\tfrac{15}{2} + 3x \right) dx.$$

Carrying out the remaining integration over x, we conclude that

$$\int_S (1 + x + y) \, dA = \left[\tfrac{15}{2} x + \tfrac{3}{2} x^2 \right]_{x=1}^{x=4}$$

$$= 30 + 24 - \tfrac{15}{2} - \tfrac{3}{2} = 45.$$

Solution to Exercise 3

The required area integral can be written as

$$I = \int_{y=0}^{y=\pi} \left(\int_{x=0}^{x=\pi} \cos(x + y) \, dx \right) dy.$$

Integrating with respect to x, with y held constant, we obtain

$$I = \int_{y=0}^{y=\pi} \left[\sin(x + y) \right]_{x=0}^{x=\pi} dy$$

$$= \int_{y=0}^{y=\pi} \left(\sin(\pi + y) - \sin(y) \right) dy.$$

The remaining integral over y gives

$$I = \left[-\cos(\pi + y) + \cos(y) \right]_{y=0}^{y=\pi}$$

$$= \left(-\cos(2\pi) + \cos(\pi) \right) - \left(-\cos(\pi) + \cos(0) \right) = -4.$$

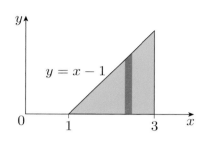

Solution to Exercise 4

The region of integration is shown in the diagram in the margin, with a typical strip parallel to the y-axis marked. It is clear that the lower y-limit is $y = 0$ and the upper y-limit is $y = x - 1$. These limits are the correct way round because $x - 1 > 0$ throughout the region of integration.

We can also immediately read off the lower and upper x-limits as $x = 1$ and $x = 3$, respectively. The required area integral is then given by

$$\int_S (x - y)\, dA = \int_{x=1}^{x=3} \left(\int_{y=0}^{y=x-1} (x - y)\, dy \right) dx.$$

Carrying out the inner integration over y first, we get

$$\int_S (x - y)\, dA = \int_{x=1}^{x=3} \left[xy - \tfrac{1}{2}y^2 \right]_{y=0}^{y=x-1} dx$$

$$= \int_{x=1}^{x=3} \left(x(x - 1) - \tfrac{1}{2}(x - 1)^2 \right) dx$$

$$= \int_{x=1}^{x=3} \left(\tfrac{1}{2}x^2 - \tfrac{1}{2} \right) dx.$$

Finally, the integral over x gives

$$\int_S (x - y)\, dA = \left[\tfrac{1}{6}x^3 - \tfrac{1}{2}x \right]_{x=1}^{x=3}$$

$$= \tfrac{27}{6} - \tfrac{3}{2} - \tfrac{1}{6} + \tfrac{1}{2}$$

$$= \tfrac{10}{3}.$$

Solution to Exercise 5

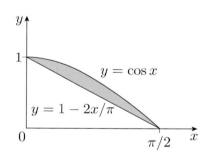

The figure in the margin shows the required region. We choose to integrate over y first, and so imagine dividing the region into thin vertical strips. The area is then given by

$$I = \int_{x=0}^{x=\pi/2} \left(\int_{y=1-2x/\pi}^{y=\cos x} 1\, dy \right) dx.$$

Carrying out the integrals, we get

$$I = \int_{x=0}^{x=\pi/2} \left[y \right]_{y=1-2x/\pi}^{y=\cos x} dx$$

$$= \int_{x=0}^{x=\pi/2} \left(\cos x - 1 + \frac{2x}{\pi} \right) dx$$

$$= \left[\sin x - x + \frac{x^2}{\pi} \right]_{x=0}^{x=\pi/2}$$

$$= \sin \left(\frac{\pi}{2} \right) - \frac{\pi}{2} + \frac{\pi}{4}$$

$$= 1 - \frac{\pi}{4}.$$

Solution to Exercise 6

(a) The first diagram in the margin shows the area of integration.

Using this diagram, the given area integral can be written as

$$\int_{y=0}^{y=1} \left(\int_{x=0}^{x=2y} f(x,y)\,dx \right) dy.$$

(b) The second diagram in the margin shows the area of integration.

Using this diagram, the given area integral can be written as

$$\int_{y=0}^{y=1} \left(\int_{x=2y}^{x=2} f(x,y)\,dx \right) dy.$$

Solution to Exercise 7

The diagram in the margin shows the given region. A typical narrow horizontal strip extends across this region from $x = 0$ to $x = 4 - y^2$. These are the lower and upper limits of the inner x-integration. The minimum and maximum values of y are $y = -2$ and $y = 2$, and these are the lower and upper limits of the y-integration. So using equations (11) and (12), the area is

$$\begin{aligned}
\text{area} &= \int_{y=-2}^{y=2} \left(\int_{x=0}^{x=4-y^2} 1\,dx \right) dy \\
&= \int_{y=-2}^{y=2} \left[x \right]_{x=0}^{x=4-y^2} dy \\
&= \int_{y=-2}^{y=2} (4 - y^2)\,dy = \left[4y - \tfrac{1}{3}y^3 \right]_{y=-2}^{y=2} = \tfrac{32}{3}.
\end{aligned}$$

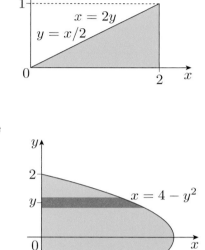

Solution to Exercise 8

Following the hint in the question, we integrate first over x, then over y. Considering a horizontal strip, the limits of the x-integration are $0 \le x \le \sqrt{1 - y^2}$, so the area integral is

$$\begin{aligned}
\int_S f(x,y)\,dA &= \int_{y=0}^{y=1} \left(\int_{x=0}^{x=\sqrt{1-y^2}} x\,dx \right) dy \\
&= \int_{y=0}^{y=1} \left[\tfrac{1}{2}x^2 \right]_{x=0}^{x=\sqrt{1-y^2}} dy \\
&= \int_{y=0}^{y=1} \tfrac{1}{2}(1 - y^2)\,dy \\
&= \left[\tfrac{1}{2}\left(y - \tfrac{1}{3}y^3 \right) \right]_{y=0}^{y=1} = \tfrac{1}{3}.
\end{aligned}$$

You can see *why* it is easier to do the integration in this order: integrating over x first leads to $\tfrac{1}{2}x^2$, and this allows us to avoid a tricky integral involving square roots. The ability to anticipate such things is a useful skill.

Solution to Exercise 9

Choosing to integrate first over y and then over x, the required area integral is

$$I = \int_{x=0}^{x=1} \left(\int_{y=0}^{y=x} \exp(x^2)\, dy \right) dx$$

$$= \int_{x=0}^{x=1} \left[y \exp(x^2) \right]_{y=0}^{y=x} dx$$

$$= \int_{x=0}^{x=1} x \exp(x^2)\, dx.$$

This tactic is chosen because the argument x^2 of $\exp(x^2)$ has derivative $2x$, which is proportional to the factor x in the integrand.

We make the substitution $u = x^2$. Then we have $du/dx = 2x$, and the lower and upper limits of integration become $u = 0$ and $u = 1$. Hence

$$I = \int_{x=0}^{x=1} \exp(u)\, \tfrac{1}{2} \frac{du}{dx}\, dx$$

$$= \tfrac{1}{2} \int_{u=0}^{u=1} \exp(u)\, du = \tfrac{1}{2} \left[\exp(u) \right]_{u=0}^{u=1} = \tfrac{1}{2}(e - 1) \simeq 0.859.$$

If we had tried to integrate first over x and then over y, the area integral would have been written as

$$I = \int_{y=0}^{y=1} \left(\int_{x=y}^{x=1} \exp(x^2)\, dx \right) dy.$$

This is correct, but frustrating, because the integration over x cannot be done using standard mathematical functions.

Solution to Exercise 10

The mass of the block is given by the volume integral

$$M = \int_R (x + y + z)\, dV$$

$$= \int_{x=0}^{x=2} \left(\int_{y=1}^{y=2} \left(\int_{z=2}^{z=5} (x + y + z)\, dz \right) dy \right) dx.$$

Evaluating the inner integral over z gives

$$M = \int_{x=0}^{x=2} \left(\int_{y=1}^{y=2} \left[xz + yz + \tfrac{1}{2}z^2 \right]_{z=2}^{z=5} dy \right) dx$$

$$= \int_{x=0}^{x=2} \left(\int_{y=1}^{y=2} \left(3x + 3y + \tfrac{21}{2} \right) dy \right) dx.$$

Evaluating the integral over y gives

$$M = \int_{x=0}^{x=2} \left[3xy + \tfrac{3}{2}y^2 + \tfrac{21}{2}y \right]_{y=1}^{y=2} dx$$

$$= \int_{x=0}^{x=2} \left((6x + 6 + 21) - \left(3x + \tfrac{3}{2} + \tfrac{21}{2} \right) \right) dx$$

$$= \int_{x=0}^{x=2} (3x + 15)\, dx.$$

Finally, the integral over x gives

$$M = \left[\tfrac{3}{2}x^2 + 15x\right]_{x=0}^{x=2} = 36.$$

So the mass of the block is 36 kilograms.

Solution to Exercise 11

We have

$$\begin{aligned}
f(x,y,z) &= xyz\, e^{-(x^2+y^2+z^2)} \\
&= xyz\, e^{-x^2} e^{-y^2} e^{-z^2} \\
&= xe^{-x^2} \times ye^{-y^2} \times ze^{-z^2},
\end{aligned}$$

which is a product of the form $u(x)\, v(y)\, w(z)$. The required volume integral over the cube therefore becomes

$$I = \int_{x=0}^{x=1} xe^{-x^2}\, dx \times \int_{y=0}^{y=1} ye^{-y^2}\, dy \times \int_{z=0}^{z=1} ze^{-z^2}\, dz.$$

The individual integrals are evaluated using a method similar to that used in Exercise 9. In the integral over x, for example, we substitute $u = x^2$. Then $du/dx = 2x$, and the limits $x = 0$ and $x = 1$ become $u = 0$ and $u = 1$, so

$$\begin{aligned}
\int_{x=0}^{x=1} xe^{-x^2}\, dx &= \int_{x=0}^{x=1} e^{-u}\, \tfrac{1}{2}\, \frac{du}{dx}\, dx \\
&= \int_{u=0}^{u=1} \tfrac{1}{2} e^{-u}\, du \\
&= \left[-\tfrac{1}{2} e^{-u}\right]_{u=0}^{u=1} = \tfrac{1}{2}(1 - e^{-1}).
\end{aligned}$$

Similar results apply to the y and z integrals, so the volume integral is

$$I = \tfrac{1}{8}(1 - e^{-1})^3 \simeq 0.0316.$$

Solution to Exercise 12

The required volume integral is

$$\int_R f(x,y,z)\, dV = \int_{z=0}^{z=1} \left(\int_{y=0}^{y=1-z} \left(\int_{x=0}^{x=1-y-z} z^2\, dx \right) dy \right) dz.$$

The inner integral is with respect to x, and we evaluate this first (holding y and z constant). We get

$$\begin{aligned}
\int_{x=0}^{x=1-y-z} z^2\, dx &= \left[z^2 x\right]_{x=0}^{x=1-y-z} \\
&= z^2(1 - y - z) = z^2(1 - z) - z^2 y.
\end{aligned}$$

The middle integral is with respect to y. Evaluating this (with z held constant), we obtain

$$\begin{aligned}
\int_{y=0}^{y=1-z} \left(z^2(1 - z) - z^2 y\right) dy &= \left[z^2(1-z)y - \tfrac{1}{2}z^2 y^2\right]_{y=0}^{y=1-z} \\
&= \tfrac{1}{2} z^2 (1 - z)^2 \\
&= \tfrac{1}{2} z^2 - z^3 + \tfrac{1}{2} z^4.
\end{aligned}$$

Finally, we integrate over z to obtain

$$\int_R f(x,y,z)\,dV = \int_{z=0}^{z=1} \left(\tfrac{1}{2}z^2 - z^3 + \tfrac{1}{2}z^4\right) dz$$

$$= \left[\tfrac{1}{6}z^3 - \tfrac{1}{4}z^4 + \tfrac{1}{10}z^5\right]_{z=0}^{z=1}$$

$$= \tfrac{1}{6} - \tfrac{1}{4} + \tfrac{1}{10} = \tfrac{1}{60},$$

which does agree with Example 4.

Solution to Exercise 13

The region R and its projection onto the xy-plane are shown in the figure below.

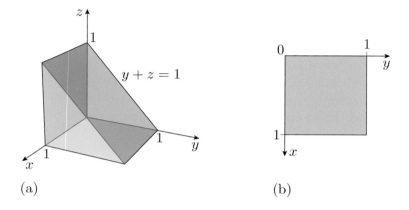

(a)   (b)

The required volume integral is

$$\int_R f(x,y,z)\,dV = \int_{x=0}^{x=1} \left(\int_{y=0}^{y=1} \left(\int_{z=0}^{z=1-y} x^2 yz\,dz \right) dy \right) dx.$$

Although the integrand is a product function, this volume integral cannot be expressed as the product of three ordinary integrals because the limits of integration are not all constants.

The integral over z gives

$$\int_{z=0}^{z=1-y} x^2 yz\,dz = \left[\tfrac{1}{2}x^2 yz^2\right]_{z=0}^{z=1-y}$$

$$= \tfrac{1}{2}x^2 y(1-y)^2 = \tfrac{1}{2}x^2(y - 2y^2 + y^3).$$

The integral over y then gives

$$\int_{y=0}^{y=1} \tfrac{1}{2}x^2(y - 2y^2 + y^3)\,dy = \left[\tfrac{1}{2}x^2 \left(\tfrac{1}{2}y^2 - \tfrac{2}{3}y^3 + \tfrac{1}{4}y^4\right)\right]_{y=0}^{y=1}$$

$$= \tfrac{1}{24}x^2.$$

Finally, integrating over x gives

$$\int_R f(x,y,z)\,dV = \int_{x=0}^{x=1} \tfrac{1}{24}x^2\,dx = \left[\tfrac{1}{72}x^3\right]_{x=0}^{x=1} = \tfrac{1}{72}.$$

Solution to Exercise 14

There is no need to draw diagrams in this case because the limits are given in the question. However, we need to ensure that the integrals are nested in the right way. The required volume is

$$V = \int_{z=0}^{z=1} \left(\int_{y=0}^{y=z} \left(\int_{x=0}^{x=y^2+z^2} 1 \, dx \right) dy \right) dz.$$

The integral over x is chosen as the innermost integral because its limits depend on the other two variables of integration, y and z. The integral over y is done next because its limits depend on z. The integral over z is chosen as the outermost integral because its limits are constants.

Carrying out the integrals, we obtain

$$V = \int_{z=0}^{z=1} \left(\int_{y=0}^{y=z} (y^2 + z^2) \, dy \right) dz$$

$$= \int_{z=0}^{z=1} \left[\tfrac{1}{3}y^3 + z^2 y \right]_{y=0}^{y=z} dz$$

$$= \int_{z=0}^{z=1} \tfrac{4}{3}z^3 \, dz$$

$$= \left[\tfrac{1}{3}z^4 \right]_{z=0}^{z=1} = \tfrac{1}{3} \simeq 0.33.$$

Since the lengths are measured in metres, the volume is $0.33 \, \mathrm{m}^3$.

Solution to Exercise 15

Recognising that $x^2 + y^2 = r^2$, the surface density function becomes

$$f(r, \phi) = \frac{C}{R^4}(2R^2 - r^2)$$

in polar coordinates. Note that we continue to use the symbol f for this function even though it is now expressed in terms of new variables. This convention was discussed at the start of this book.

The total number of bacteria on the dish is given by the area integral

$$N = \int_{\phi=0}^{\phi=2\pi} \left(\int_{r=0}^{r=R} f(r, \phi) \, r \, dr \right) d\phi$$

$$= \frac{C}{R^4} \int_{\phi=0}^{\phi=2\pi} \left(\int_{r=0}^{r=R} (2R^2 r - r^3) \, dr \right) d\phi.$$

Carrying out the integral over r first gives

$$N = \frac{C}{R^4} \int_{\phi=0}^{\phi=2\pi} \left[R^2 r^2 - \tfrac{1}{4}r^4 \right]_{r=0}^{r=R} d\phi$$

$$= \frac{C}{R^4} \int_{\phi=0}^{\phi=2\pi} \tfrac{3}{4}R^4 \, d\phi.$$

The final integral over ϕ is trivial, giving the answer

$$N = \frac{C}{R^4} \times 2\pi \times \tfrac{3}{4}R^4 = \tfrac{3}{2}\pi C.$$

Solution to Exercise 16

The semicircular region S is defined by $0 \leq r \leq R$ and $0 \leq \phi \leq \pi$. Recalling that $x = r \cos \phi$ and including the factor r required by the area element in polar coordinates, we obtain

$$\int_S x \, dA = \int_{\phi=0}^{\phi=\pi} \left(\int_{r=0}^{r=R} (r \cos \phi) \, r \, dr \right) d\phi.$$

The integrand is the product of a function of r and a function of ϕ, and the limits of integration are all constants. This allows us to write the area integral as a product of two ordinary integrals. Hence

$$\int_S x \, dA = \int_{r=0}^{r=R} r^2 \, dr \times \int_{\phi=0}^{\phi=\pi} \cos \phi \, d\phi$$

$$= \tfrac{1}{3} R^3 \times \left[\sin \phi \right]_{\phi=0}^{\phi=\pi} = 0.$$

This answer is not surprising: the region of integration is symmetrical about the y-axis, but the integrand is an odd function of x, so contributions from $x < 0$ cancel those from $x > 0$.

A similar calculation for $y = r \sin \phi$ gives

$$\int_S y \, dA = \int_{r=0}^{r=R} r^2 \, dr \times \int_{\phi=0}^{\phi=\pi} \sin \phi \, d\phi$$

$$= \tfrac{1}{3} R^3 \times \left[- \cos \phi \right]_{\phi=0}^{\phi=\pi} = \tfrac{2}{3} R^3.$$

Solution to Exercise 17

The area integral of e^{-r^2} over the entire xy-plane is

$$I = \int_{\phi=0}^{\phi=2\pi} \left(\int_{r=0}^{r=\infty} e^{-r^2} \, r \, dr \right) d\phi.$$

The integrand is a function of r only. This can be regarded as a product function where the function of ϕ is equal to 1. Also, the limits of integration are all constants. We can therefore write the area integral as the product of two ordinary integrals:

$$I = \int_{\phi=0}^{\phi=2\pi} 1 \, d\phi \times \int_{r=0}^{r=\infty} e^{-r^2} \, r \, dr = 2\pi \int_{r=0}^{r=\infty} e^{-r^2} \, r \, dr.$$

This tactic works because r^2 in $\exp(-r^2)$ has a derivative that is proportional to the factor r in the integrand.

We make the substitution $u = r^2$. Then $du/dr = 2r$, and the new limits of integration are $u = 0$ and $u = \infty$. Hence

$$I = 2\pi \int_{r=0}^{r=\infty} e^{-u} \, \tfrac{1}{2} \frac{du}{dr} \, dr$$

$$= \pi \int_{u=0}^{u=\infty} e^{-u} \, du$$

$$= \pi \left[-e^{-u} \right]_{u=0}^{u=\infty} = \pi \left(-e^{-\infty} + e^0 \right) = \pi,$$

where we have interpreted $e^{-\infty}$ as being equal to zero. This is appropriate because e^{-x} tends to zero as x tends to infinity.

Solution to Exercise 18

The region of integration corresponds to $2 \le r \le 5$, $0 \le \phi \le 2\pi$ and $-1 \le z \le 1$, so the required volume integral of rz^2 is

$$I = \int_{z=-1}^{z=1} \left(\int_{\phi=0}^{\phi=2\pi} \left(\int_{r=2}^{r=5} r^2 z^2 \, dr \right) d\phi \right) dz,$$

where the extra factor of r in the integrand comes from the volume element in cylindrical coordinates.

In an integral such as this, where the integrand is a product of a function of r and a function of z, and the limits of integration are all constants, we can write the integral as a product of three ordinary integrals:

$$I = \int_{z=-1}^{z=1} z^2 \, dz \times \int_{\phi=0}^{\phi=2\pi} 1 \, d\phi \times \int_{r=2}^{r=5} r^2 \, dr$$

$$= \left[\tfrac{1}{3} z^3 \right]_{z=-1}^{z=1} \times 2\pi \times \left[\tfrac{1}{3} r^3 \right]_{r=2}^{r=5}$$

$$= \tfrac{2}{3} \times 2\pi \times \tfrac{117}{3}$$

$$= 52\pi.$$

Solution to Exercise 19

Using equation (27), the volume of the rugby ball is

$$V = \pi \int_{z=-b}^{z=b} a^2 \left(1 - \frac{z^2}{b^2} \right) dz$$

$$= \pi a^2 \left[z - \frac{z^3}{3b^2} \right]_{z=-b}^{z=b}$$

$$= \tfrac{4}{3} \pi a^2 b.$$

Check: When $a = b = R$, the rugby ball becomes a sphere of radius R, and the volume becomes $4\pi R^3 / 3$, as expected.

Solution to Exercise 20

The figure in the margin shows a cross-section through the spherical cap (shaded). At a given value of z, the surface of the cap has cylindrical radial coordinate

$$r = r_{\max}(z) = \sqrt{R^2 - z^2}.$$

The spherical cap has $R/2 \le z \le R$, so its volume is

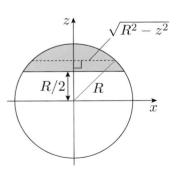

$$V = \pi \int_{z=R/2}^{z=R} \left(R^2 - z^2 \right) dz$$

$$= \pi \left[R^2 z - \tfrac{1}{3} z^3 \right]_{z=R/2}^{z=R}$$

$$= \pi R^3 \left(1 - \tfrac{1}{3} - \tfrac{1}{2} + \tfrac{1}{24} \right)$$

$$= \tfrac{5}{24} \pi R^3.$$

Solution to Exercise 21

The required volume integral is

$$I = \int_{\phi=0}^{\phi=2\pi} \left(\int_{\theta=0}^{\theta=\pi} \left(\int_{r=1}^{r=2} \frac{\sin\theta}{r}\, r^2 \sin\theta\, dr \right) d\theta \right) d\phi.$$

The integrand is a product function, and the limits of integration are all constants, so the volume integral can be written as

$$I = \int_{\phi=0}^{\phi=2\pi} 1\, d\phi \times \int_{\theta=0}^{\theta=\pi} \sin^2\theta\, d\theta \times \int_{r=1}^{r=2} r\, dr.$$

Using the trigonometric identity $\sin^2\theta = \frac{1}{2}\left(1 - \cos(2\theta)\right)$, we get

$$\int_{\theta=0}^{\theta=\pi} \sin^2\theta\, d\theta = \frac{1}{2}\int_{\theta=0}^{\theta=\pi} \left(1 - \cos(2\theta)\right) d\theta = \frac{1}{2}\left[\theta - \frac{1}{2}\sin(2\theta)\right]_{\theta=0}^{\theta=\pi} = \frac{1}{2}\pi.$$

So the required volume integral is

$$I = 2\pi \times \tfrac{1}{2}\pi \times \left[\tfrac{1}{2}r^2\right]_{r=1}^{r=2} = \tfrac{3}{2}\pi^2.$$

Solution to Exercise 22

(a) The variable r is the radial coordinate of spherical coordinates, so the volume integral is

$$\int_{\text{sphere}} f\, dV = \int_{\phi=0}^{\phi=2\pi} \left(\int_{\theta=0}^{\theta=\pi} \left(\int_{r=0}^{r=R} f(r)\, r^2 \sin\theta\, dr \right) d\theta \right) d\phi.$$

The integrand is a product function, and the limits of integration are all constants, so the volume integral can be split into the product of three ordinary integrals:

$$\int_{\text{sphere}} f\, dV = \int_{\phi=0}^{\phi=2\pi} 1\, d\phi \times \int_{\theta=0}^{\theta=\pi} \sin\theta\, d\theta \times \int_0^R f(r)\, r^2\, dr$$

$$= 2\pi \times \left[-\cos\theta\right]_{\theta=0}^{\theta=\pi} \times \int_0^R f(r)\, r^2\, dr$$

$$= 4\pi \int_0^R f(r)\, r^2\, dr,$$

as required.

(b) The quantity $\sqrt{x^2 + y^2 + z^2}$ is the distance of a point from the origin, which is equal to the radial coordinate r in spherical coordinates. This can be established more formally using equations (28), which give

$$x^2 + y^2 + z^2 = r^2 \sin^2\theta \cos^2\phi + r^2 \sin^2\theta \sin^2\phi + r^2 \cos^2\theta$$

$$= r^2 \sin^2\theta \left(\cos^2\phi + \sin^2\phi\right) + r^2 \cos^2\theta$$

$$= r^2(\sin^2\theta + \cos^2\theta) = r^2.$$

Hence the result of part (a) gives

$$\int_{\text{sphere}} \sqrt{x^2 + y^2 + z^2}\, dV = 4\pi \int_0^R r^3\, dr = \pi R^4.$$

Solution to Exercise 23

Using equation (33), we get the following results. In cylindrical coordinates,

$$\delta V = 1 \times r \times 1 \, \delta r \, \delta \phi \, \delta z = r \, \delta r \, \delta \phi \, \delta z,$$

and in spherical coordinates,

$$\delta V = 1 \times r \times r \sin \theta \, \delta r \, \delta \theta \, \delta \phi = r^2 \sin \theta \, \delta r \, \delta \theta \, \delta \phi.$$

Both of these expressions agree with our previous results.

Solution to Exercise 24

Taking partial derivatives of x, y and z with respect to r, θ and ϕ, we have

$$\frac{\partial x}{\partial r} = \sin \theta \cos \phi, \quad \frac{\partial y}{\partial r} = \sin \theta \sin \phi, \quad \frac{\partial z}{\partial r} = \cos \theta,$$

$$\frac{\partial x}{\partial \theta} = r \cos \theta \cos \phi, \quad \frac{\partial y}{\partial \theta} = r \cos \theta \sin \phi, \quad \frac{\partial z}{\partial \theta} = -r \sin \theta,$$

$$\frac{\partial x}{\partial \phi} = -r \sin \theta \sin \phi, \quad \frac{\partial y}{\partial \phi} = r \sin \theta \cos \phi, \quad \frac{\partial z}{\partial \phi} = 0.$$

Hence the scale factors are

$$
\begin{aligned}
h_r &= \sqrt{\sin^2 \theta \cos^2 \phi + \sin^2 \theta \sin^2 \phi + \cos^2 \theta} \\
&= \sqrt{\sin^2 \theta (\cos^2 \phi + \sin^2 \phi) + \cos^2 \theta} \\
&= 1, \\
h_\theta &= \sqrt{r^2 \cos^2 \theta \cos^2 \phi + r^2 \cos^2 \theta \sin^2 \phi + r^2 \sin^2 \theta} \\
&= \sqrt{r^2 (\cos^2 \theta (\cos^2 \phi + \sin^2 \phi) + \sin^2 \theta)} \\
&= r, \\
h_\phi &= \sqrt{r^2 \sin^2 \theta \sin^2 \phi + r^2 \sin^2 \theta \cos^2 \phi + 0} \\
&= \sqrt{r^2 \sin^2 \theta (\sin^2 \phi + \cos^2 \phi)} \\
&= r \sin \theta,
\end{aligned}
$$

where the square roots have been taken in the knowledge that $r \geq 0$ and $\sin \theta \geq 0$ for spherical coordinates. Our answers agree with equation (36).

Solution to Exercise 25

The cross-section in the figure shows that the spherical cap (shaded) extends from $\theta = 0$ to $\theta = \alpha$, where $\cos \alpha = (\frac{1}{2}R)/R = \frac{1}{2}$.

Using the area element in equation (40), we get

$$
\begin{aligned}
\text{area of cap} &= \int_{\phi=0}^{\phi=2\pi} \left(\int_{\theta=0}^{\theta=\alpha} R^2 \sin \theta \, d\theta \right) d\phi \\
&= R^2 \int_{\phi=0}^{\phi=2\pi} \left[-\cos \theta \right]_{\theta=0}^{\theta=\alpha} d\phi \\
&= 2\pi R^2 (1 - \cos \alpha).
\end{aligned}
$$

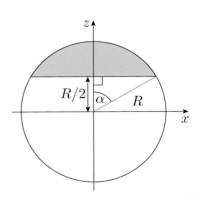

In the present case, $\cos \alpha = 1/2$, so the area of the cap is πR^2. For the (practically) spherical surface of the Earth, this means that there is the same amount of area north of latitude $30°$ (the latitude of Cairo) as there is between latitude $30°$ and the Equator.

Note: This calculation works very well in spherical coordinates. By contrast, finding the *volume* of a spherical cap works better in cylindrical coordinates (see Exercise 20). In the volume integral the flat base of the spherical cap must be taken into account, and this is more simply described in cylindrical, rather than spherical, coordinates.

Solution to Exercise 26

Expanding the determinant, we obtain

$$\begin{aligned}
\mathbf{J} &= R^2 \sin^2 \theta \cos \phi \, \mathbf{i} + R^2 \sin^2 \theta \sin \phi \, \mathbf{j} + R^2 \cos \theta \sin \theta (\cos^2 \phi + \sin^2 \phi) \, \mathbf{k} \\
&= R^2 \sin^2 \theta \cos \phi \, \mathbf{i} + R^2 \sin^2 \theta \sin \phi \, \mathbf{j} + R^2 \cos \theta \sin \theta \, \mathbf{k} \\
&= R^2 \sin \theta (\sin \theta \cos \phi \, \mathbf{i} + \sin \theta \sin \phi \, \mathbf{j} + \cos \theta \, \mathbf{k}).
\end{aligned}$$

The square of the magnitude of this vector is

$$\begin{aligned}
|\mathbf{J}|^2 &= R^4 \sin^2 \theta \left(\sin^2 \theta \left(\cos^2 \phi + \sin^2 \phi \right) + \cos^2 \theta \right) \\
&= R^4 \sin^2 \theta \left(\sin^2 \theta + \cos^2 \theta \right) \\
&= R^4 \sin^2 \theta.
\end{aligned}$$

We have $R > 0$ and $0 \le \theta \le \pi$, so $R^2 \sin \theta \ge 0$. Hence $|\mathbf{J}| = R^2 \sin \theta$, and the area of a surface element is

$$\delta A = |\mathbf{J}| \, \delta\theta \, \delta\phi = R^2 \sin \theta \, \delta\theta \, \delta\phi.$$

Solution to Exercise 27

Differentiating the functions for x, y and z with respect to r and ϕ, we get

$$\frac{\partial x}{\partial r} = \cos \phi, \quad \frac{\partial y}{\partial r} = \sin \phi, \quad \frac{\partial z}{\partial r} = \frac{r}{R},$$

$$\frac{\partial x}{\partial \phi} = -r \sin \phi, \quad \frac{\partial y}{\partial \phi} = r \cos \phi, \quad \frac{\partial z}{\partial \phi} = 0,$$

so the Jacobian vector is

$$\begin{aligned}
\mathbf{J} &= \begin{vmatrix} \mathbf{i} & \mathbf{j} & \mathbf{k} \\ \cos \phi & \sin \phi & r/R \\ -r \sin \phi & r \cos \phi & 0 \end{vmatrix} \\
&= -\frac{r^2}{R} \cos \phi \, \mathbf{i} - \frac{r^2}{R} \sin \phi \, \mathbf{j} + r(\cos^2 \phi + \sin^2 \phi) \, \mathbf{k} \\
&= -\frac{r^2}{R} \cos \phi \, \mathbf{i} - \frac{r^2}{R} \sin \phi \, \mathbf{j} + r \, \mathbf{k}.
\end{aligned}$$

Hence

$$|\mathbf{J}|^2 = \frac{r^4}{R^2}(\cos^2 \phi + \sin^2 \phi) + r^2 = r^2 \left(1 + \frac{r^2}{R^2} \right).$$

The area element is therefore

$$\delta A = |\mathbf{J}|\,\delta r\,\delta\phi = \left(1 + \frac{r^2}{R^2}\right)^{1/2} r\,\delta r\,\delta\phi,$$

and the surface area of the dish is

$$\text{surface area} = \int_{\phi=0}^{\phi=2\pi} \left(\int_{r=0}^{r=R} \left(1 + \frac{r^2}{R^2}\right)^{1/2} r\,dr \right) d\phi.$$

To evaluate the integral over r, we make the substitution $u = 1 + r^2/R^2$. Then $du/dr = 2r/R^2$, and the lower and upper limits of integration become $u = 1$ and $u = 2$. So we get

$$\text{surface area} = \int_{\phi=0}^{\phi=2\pi} \left(\int_{r=0}^{r=R} u^{1/2} \times \tfrac{1}{2}R^2 \frac{du}{dr}\,dr \right) d\phi$$

$$= \tfrac{1}{2}R^2 \int_{\phi=0}^{\phi=2\pi} \left(\int_{u=1}^{u=2} u^{1/2}\,du \right) d\phi$$

$$= \tfrac{1}{2}R^2 \int_{\phi=0}^{\phi=2\pi} \left[\tfrac{2}{3}u^{3/2} \right]_{u=1}^{u=2} d\phi$$

$$= \tfrac{1}{2}R^2 \tfrac{2}{3} \int_{\phi=0}^{\phi=2\pi} (\sqrt{8} - 1)\,d\phi = \tfrac{2}{3}\pi(\sqrt{8} - 1)R^2.$$

Solution to Exercise 28

Taking partial derivatives of x, y and z with respect to u and v, we get

$$\frac{\partial x}{\partial u} = u, \quad \frac{\partial y}{\partial u} = u, \quad \frac{\partial z}{\partial u} = v,$$

$$\frac{\partial x}{\partial v} = v, \quad \frac{\partial y}{\partial v} = -v, \quad \frac{\partial z}{\partial v} = u.$$

Hence

$$\mathbf{J} = \begin{vmatrix} \mathbf{i} & \mathbf{j} & \mathbf{k} \\ u & u & v \\ v & -v & u \end{vmatrix} = (u^2 + v^2)\,\mathbf{i} - (u^2 - v^2)\,\mathbf{j} - 2uv\,\mathbf{k},$$

and

$$|\mathbf{J}|^2 = (u^4 + 2u^2v^2 + v^4) + (u^4 - 2u^2v^2 + v^4) + 4u^2v^2$$

$$= 2(u^4 + 2u^2v^2 + v^4)$$

$$= 2(u^2 + v^2)^2.$$

The required surface area is

$$\text{surface area} = \int_{v=0}^{v=1} \left(\int_{u=0}^{u=1} \sqrt{2}(u^2 + v^2)\,du \right) dv$$

$$= \sqrt{2} \int_{v=0}^{v=1} \left[\tfrac{1}{3}u^3 + uv^2 \right]_{u=0}^{u=1} dv$$

$$= \sqrt{2} \int_{v=0}^{v=1} \left(\tfrac{1}{3} + v^2 \right) dv = \sqrt{2} \left[\tfrac{1}{3}v + \tfrac{1}{3}v^3 \right]_{v=0}^{v=1} = \tfrac{2\sqrt{2}}{3}.$$

Acknowledgements

Grateful acknowledgement is made to the following source:

Figure 4: NASA.

Every effort has been made to contact copyright holders. If any have been inadvertently overlooked, the publishers will be pleased to make the necessary arrangements at the first opportunity.

Unit 9

Differentiating scalar and vector fields

Introduction

This unit investigates fields and explains what can be learned by differentiating them.

Roughly speaking, a **field** is a physical quantity that has definite values at points throughout a region of space. For example, at a given instant, each point in a room has a particular temperature. Near a radiator, the temperature may be 40°C, but near an open door it may be only 10°C. We cannot say that the room has a single temperature, but each point in the room does have a definite temperature, and the distribution of temperatures throughout the room is described by a *temperature field*.

If the room is a cuboid of dimensions $a \times b \times c$, we can choose a Cartesian coordinate system with its origin at one corner and its axes running along three adjacent edges of the cuboid. Then each point in the room can be represented by a triplet of coordinates (x, y, z), and the temperature field can be represented by a function

$$T = T(x, y, z) \quad (0 \le x \le a,\ 0 \le y \le b,\ 0 \le z \le c),$$

where the conditions in parentheses specify the domain of the function, which corresponds to the region inside the room.

A second example is provided by wind velocity in a given region of the atmosphere. This would be of keen interest to anyone living close to the track of a tornado, for example! We focus on a cubic volume that is fixed relative to the ground, with sides of length 1 kilometre, and arrange the axes of a Cartesian coordinate system to run along three adjacent edges of this cube. At a given instant, the wind velocity may vary throughout the cube, but at each point it has a definite velocity, described by a velocity vector **v**. The distribution of wind velocities within the cube is described by a *velocity field*, and is represented by a function

$$\mathbf{v} = \mathbf{v}(x, y, z) \quad (0 \le x \le 1000,\ 0 \le y \le 1000,\ 0 \le z \le 1000),$$

where x, y and z are the coordinates of a point (measured in metres), and the conditions in parentheses restrict attention to the region inside the cube, which is the domain of the function.

At each point (x, y, z) in its domain, the function $\mathbf{v}(x, y, z)$ specifies a vector – the wind velocity at that point. A velocity vector **v** can be written in component form as

$$\mathbf{v} = v_x\,\mathbf{i} + v_y\,\mathbf{j} + v_z\,\mathbf{k},$$

where **i**, **j** and **k** are Cartesian unit vectors, and v_x, v_y and v_z are the corresponding Cartesian components. So the wind velocity field can be written as

$$\mathbf{v}(x, y, z) = v_x(x, y, z)\,\mathbf{i} + v_y(x, y, z)\,\mathbf{j} + v_z(x, y, z)\,\mathbf{k},$$

which involves three functions $v_x(x, y, z)$, $v_y(x, y, z)$ and $v_z(x, y, z)$. Each of these functions has the domain $0 \le x \le 1000$, $0 \le y \le 1000$, $0 \le z \le 1000$, corresponding to the cubic region of interest.

Fields are classified according to the nature of the physical quantity that they describe. In this module we consider two types of field:

- **scalar fields** describe the distribution of a scalar quantity (such as temperature) throughout a region
- **vector fields** describe the distribution of a vector quantity (such as velocity) throughout a region.

Fields are everywhere

The example of a temperature field arises naturally in the context of heating a room, and the example of a wind velocity field is clearly important for weather forecasters. However, the full importance of the field concept goes beyond what these examples suggest.

One of the first people to suspect this was Michael Faraday (Figure 1), an extraordinary genius who had only a rudimentary education but gained entry into the scientific world by taking notes in public lectures, presenting a bound copy to the lecturer, and asking if he could help with experiments. As Faraday became more independent, he made revolutionary discoveries about electricity and magnetism.

Mulling over his observations, Faraday became convinced that magnets and electric currents produce magnetic fields in the space around them, and that other magnets and electric currents respond to the magnetic fields that they encounter. Before long, it was realised that electrical and magnetic phenomena were best described using two vector fields: the *electric field* and the *magnetic field*. Faraday was not a mathematician and could not develop his ideas in terms of equations, but he highlighted the importance of the field concept, and the urgent need to develop a *calculus of fields* became clear.

At first, physicists thought that electric and magnetic fields must describe distortions in a mysterious medium, which they called the *ether*. However, this is not the modern view: electric and magnetic fields (along with gravitational fields) are now regarded as part of the fabric of the Universe. Since the 1930s, this view has been extended to matter, as *quantum field theories* treat fundamental particles such as electrons or quarks as states of excitation of various fields. In 1964, Peter Higgs (Figure 2) and others predicted a new type of scalar field called the *Higgs field*. Nearly 50 years later, the existence of this field was confirmed by the Large Hadron Collider near Geneva, and Higgs shared the Nobel Prize for Physics in 2013.

Figure 1   Michael Faraday (1791–1867)

Figure 2   Peter Higgs (1929–)

Study guide

This unit is concerned with the description of fields and, in particular, with ways of characterising them by their rates of change with respect to position. These rates of change are expressed in terms of partial derivatives with respect to the coordinates. You will therefore need to be familiar with partial differentiation, as covered in Unit 7.

One of the themes of the preceding unit on multiple integration was the use of different types of coordinate system. You saw, for example, that a volume integral over a spherical region is simplified by using spherical coordinates. A similar situation applies to fields. Many of the situations considered by scientists involve fields with cylindrical or spherical symmetry, and it is then a great advantage to use cylindrical or spherical coordinates. You will therefore need to be familiar with the coordinate systems introduced in Unit 8: in particular, you will need to be familiar with the concept of a scale factor, as outlined in Section 4 of Unit 8.

The unit is organised as follows. Section 1 gives essential background for the main topics that follow. It defines scalar and vector fields, and describes ways of representing them, both visually and in terms of equations. Section 2 defines the gradient of a scalar field. You met gradients in Unit 7, so part of this section is a review. However, we will go beyond the material in Unit 7 and show how gradients are represented in non-Cartesian coordinate systems. In the process, we will introduce the important concept of the *del operator*, denoted by ∇.

The rest of the unit is concerned with the spatial derivatives of vector fields. In three dimensions, a vector field has three components, each of which may depend on three position coordinates, so there are nine partial derivatives that describe how rapidly a vector field varies with position. Three of these partial derivatives can be grouped together to define a scalar quantity called the *divergence*, and the other six can be grouped together to form a vector quantity called the *curl*. As their names suggest, divergence and curl have direct physical interpretations, which will be explored in this unit and the next. Section 3 discusses divergence, and Section 4 discusses curl. As in the rest of the unit, these quantities will be described in a variety of coordinate systems.

1   Scalar and vector fields

1.1   Preliminary remarks on scalar and vector fields

The Introduction described a field as a physical quantity with definite values at points throughout a region of space. This is a fair description, but some clarification is needed.

- In practice, fields are used to describe physical quantities, and it is generally helpful to keep real examples in mind. Physicists use many different types of field, but in this unit we focus on examples such as temperature and velocity fields that require a minimum of background knowledge.

- Fields are classified according to the type of quantity involved. This module discusses *scalar fields* and *vector fields*. Other types of field exist as well – for example, elastic stress at each point in a solid is best described by a square matrix – but scalar and vector fields are by far the most important in physical applications.

- In this unit we are especially interested in differentiating fields, so we assume that they vary smoothly from point to point. In particular, we assume that all the required partial derivatives exist.

One other aspect of fields must be discussed. In the case of a *scalar field*, such as temperature, the value of the field at a given point is independent of the orientation of the coordinate system used to label the point. For example, in Figure 3, the blue and red coordinate systems are at 45° to one another. However, the temperature at P is 30°C whether we describe that point by the coordinates $x = 1$, $y = 1$ in the blue coordinate system or by the coordinates $X = \sqrt{2}$, $Y = 0$ in the red coordinate system. Such **invariance in value** is taken as a defining property of a scalar field.

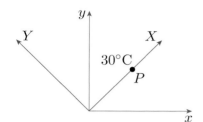

Figure 3   The temperature at P has a definite value, no matter what the orientation of the coordinate system

In the case of a *vector field*, such as wind velocity, similar ideas apply but the details play out differently. At a given point P, a vector field has a definite magnitude and a definite direction in space, irrespective of the orientation of our coordinate system. For example, in Figure 4 the velocity field at P has a magnitude of 5 metres per second and points in a northward direction. We require that this meaning is preserved no matter what the orientation of the coordinate system. Such **invariance in magnitude and direction** is taken as a defining property of a vector field. Let us explore further what this means.

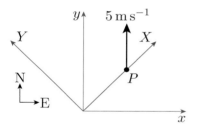

Figure 4   The velocity vector at P has a definite magnitude and direction, but its components depend on the orientation of the coordinate system

In Figure 4, the bold arrow indicates the velocity vector at P (5 metres per second in a northward direction). If we describe this vector in the blue coordinate system, we get components $v_x = 0$ and $v_y = 5$ (in metres per second). But if we describe the same vector in the red coordinate system, the components have different values: $v_X = 5/\sqrt{2}$ and $v_Y = 5/\sqrt{2}$. So the components of the vector depend on the orientation of the coordinate system. Nevertheless, these are just different descriptions of the *same* vector – the vector itself does not depend on the orientation of the coordinate system.

Notice, by the way, that it would be incorrect to describe the components of a vector field as scalar fields. This is because the components of a vector field depend on the orientation of the coordinate system but, by definition, scalar fields do not.

In any given coordinate system, fields are described by functions of several variables (the coordinates of points). This unit and the next will describe the differentiation and integration of fields, and you might wonder whether there will be anything new to say, beyond the topics already covered in Units 7 and 8. Indeed there is, and the fundamental reason for this is that scalar and vector fields have properties that transcend the choice of coordinate system. This gives us a richer structure to explore – and one that is directly relevant to descriptions of the physical world.

1.2   Describing scalar fields

In a given Cartesian coordinate system, a scalar field is described by a single function. For example, a temperature field may be described in two dimensions by a function $T(x, y)$, and in three dimensions by a function $T(x, y, z)$. This idea was discussed in the Introduction of Unit 7, but we give a brief review here.

Suppose that the temperature field on the surface of a circular disc of radius 1 metre is given by the function

$$T(x, y) = 100\, e^{-(x^2+y^2)} \quad (\sqrt{x^2 + y^2} \leq 1), \tag{1}$$

where T is the temperature in degrees Celsius, x and y are Cartesian coordinates for points on the surface of the disc (measured in metres), and the origin is at the centre of the disc. The condition in parentheses gives the domain of the function, which is the surface of the disc. Clearly, the centre of the disc has temperature $T(0, 0) = 100$, and a point on the edge of the disc has temperature $T(1, 0) = 100\, e^{-1} \simeq 37$ (in degrees Celsius).

There are a number of ways of representing this situation graphically. Figure 5(a) shows a three-dimensional diagram of the temperature on the surface of the disc, with x and y plotted horizontally and T plotted vertically. Figure 5(b) shows a slice through this surface at $y = 0$, which gives a graph of T against x when $y = 0$.

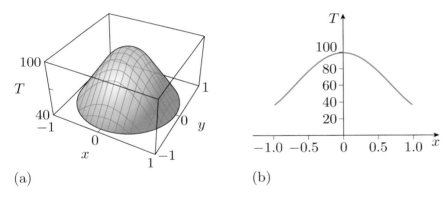

(a)   (b)

Figure 5   Visualisation of the temperature field $T(x, y)$ in equation (1), with values in degrees Celsius: (a) a perspective view with T plotted vertically; (b) a graph of T against x for a slice with $y = 0$

While both of these representations are useful, they are somewhat limited. The perspective view gives a good overall impression, but we cannot read values accurately from its scales. The graph in Figure 5(b) is quantitative, but it does not tell us about the behaviour for other slices (such as a slice with $y = 0.1$).

Perhaps the best tool for visualising a scalar field in two dimensions is to draw a **contour map**. Figure 6 shows a contour map for the temperature field described by equation (1). The orange curves are **contour lines**. Each contour line joins neighbouring points where the temperature has a fixed value, marked next to the contour line.

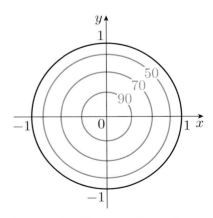

Figure 6   Contour lines (in orange) for equation (1), with values in degrees Celsius

135

For particular scalar fields, contour lines are sometimes given special names. For example, lines joining points of equal temperature are called *isotherms*, and lines joining points of equal pressure are called *isobars*. We will not bother with these terms here because, from the point of view of mathematics, they are all the same idea.

By studying a contour map, we can get a good idea of the form of a scalar field. In Figure 6, the contours corresponding to higher temperatures are closer to the centre of the disc, so the temperature falls as we move outwards. It is significant that the contour lines are circles around the centre of the disc. This shows that the temperature falls equally in all outward radial directions.

These ideas can be extended to three dimensions. For example, the temperature field throughout a sphere of radius 1 metre could be given by the function

$$T(x, y, z) = 100 \, e^{-(x^2 + y^2 + z^2)} \quad (\sqrt{x^2 + y^2 + z^2} \le 1), \tag{2}$$

where T is the temperature in degrees Celsius, x, y and z (in metres) are Cartesian coordinates, and the origin is at the centre of the sphere. The domain of the function is given in parentheses: this is the region occupied by the sphere.

In this case, rather than contour lines, there are **contour surfaces** joining neighbouring points where the temperature has a fixed value. A series of contour surfaces can be imagined at equally-spaced values of temperature. For the field specified in equation (2), these would be concentric spherical surfaces centred on the origin, and a cross-section through these surfaces at $z = 0$ would look exactly like Figure 6. We inevitably struggle to give an accurate impression of contour surfaces using a two-dimensional sketch, and it is generally necessary to show a cross-sectional view.

Scalar fields in polar coordinates

One of the themes that emerged from our study of multiple integrals was the importance of choosing a suitable coordinate system. Apart from Cartesian coordinates, three coordinate systems are of special importance in this module (and in physics and applied mathematics more generally). They are *polar coordinates*, *cylindrical coordinates* and *spherical coordinates*. It is a straightforward task to represent scalar fields in terms of these coordinates. We begin with polar coordinates.

As shown in Figure 7, points in the xy-plane can be labelled by **polar coordinates** (r, ϕ), which are related to Cartesian coordinates (x, y) by the equations

$$x = r \cos \phi, \quad y = r \sin \phi. \tag{3}$$

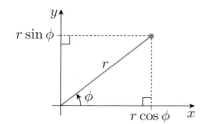

Figure 7 Polar coordinates

If a two-dimensional scalar field is expressed in Cartesian coordinates as $V(x, y)$, it is easy to express it in polar coordinates: we just replace x and y by r and ϕ using equations (3). This substitution ensures that the scalar field has a definite value at a given point (regardless of the coordinate system used to label it).

For example, to express the two-dimensional temperature field of equation (1) in polar coordinates, we note that

$$\begin{aligned} x^2 + y^2 &= (r\cos\phi)^2 + (r\sin\phi)^2 \\ &= r^2(\cos^2\phi + \sin^2\phi) \\ &= r^2, \end{aligned}$$

The relationship $x^2 + y^2 = r^2$ is worth remembering; it is a consequence of Pythagoras's theorem in Figure 7.

so

$$T(r, \phi) = 100\, e^{-r^2} \quad (r \le 1). \tag{4}$$

Notice that we have used the symbols $T(x, y)$ and $T(r, \phi)$ to represent the temperature field in Cartesian and polar coordinates, even through these are different mathematical functions. The arguments of the function – (x, y) or (r, ϕ) – indicate whether we intend the function of equation (1) or the function of equation (4). This follows our usual convention, used many times previously in this module, and for good reason: it would be impractical to invent new symbols for temperature (or any other physical quantity) every time we change coordinates.

Notice also that equation (4) is simpler than equation (1) because it depends on just one variable, r. This is an important point. A two-dimensional scalar field that is unchanged by any rotation around the origin is said to be **rotationally symmetric**. It is generally wise to describe such a field in polar coordinates.

Exercise 1

Each of the following expressions represents a two-dimensional scalar field expressed in Cartesian coordinates. Find expressions for these fields in polar coordinates.

(a) $U(x, y) = x^2 - y^2$

(b) $V(x, y) = 2xy$

(c) $W(x, y) = \dfrac{1}{\sqrt{x^2 + y^2}} \quad ((x, y) \ne (0, 0))$

Scalar fields in cylindrical coordinates

For three-dimensional fields, the most commonly used non-Cartesian coordinate systems are cylindrical and spherical. Figure 8(a) illustrates a **cylindrical coordinate system** (r, ϕ, z).

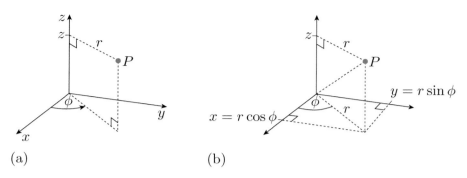

(a)   (b)

Figure 8   A cylindrical coordinate system: (a) the coordinates (r, ϕ, z); (b) relationship to Cartesian coordinates

The relationship with Cartesian coordinates can be found using trigonometry in Figure 8(b). We get

$$x = r \cos \phi, \quad y = r \sin \phi, \quad z = z, \tag{5}$$

where

$$r = \sqrt{x^2 + y^2} \tag{6}$$

is the distance from the z-axis. The first two equations in (5) are the same as for two-dimensional polar coordinates, while the third equation, $z = z$, shows that the z-coordinates of cylindrical and Cartesian coordinates are identical.

Recall: in cylindrical coordinates, r is not the distance from the origin.

If a scalar field is a known function of x, y and z, we can use equations (5) to express it in terms of cylindrical coordinates. For example, the scalar field

$$U(x, y, z) = x^2 + y^2 + 2z^2$$

is expressed in Cartesian coordinates. In cylindrical coordinates, it is

$$\begin{aligned} U(r, \phi, z) &= r^2 \cos^2 \phi + r^2 \sin^2 \phi + 2z^2 \\ &= r^2 + 2z^2, \end{aligned}$$

and this is a simpler description because it depends on two coordinates rather than three. Any three-dimensional scalar field that is independent of the ϕ-coordinate of cylindrical coordinates is said to be **axially symmetric**. It is usually better to describe such fields in cylindrical coordinates rather than Cartesian coordinates.

Exercise 2

A temperature field (in degrees Celsius) is specified in Cartesian coordinates by

$$T(x, y, z) = 100 \, e^{-(x^2 + y^2 + z^2)} \quad (x^2 + y^2 + z^2 \leq 1).$$

Express this field in cylindrical coordinates, and find the temperature at a point with cylindrical coordinates $(r, \phi, z) = (0.5, 0, 0.5)$.

Scalar fields in spherical coordinates

Figure 9(a) shows a **spherical coordinate system** (r, θ, ϕ).

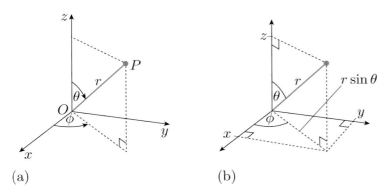

(a)   (b)

Figure 9   A spherical coordinate system: (a) the coordinates (r, θ, ϕ); (b) relationship to Cartesian coordinates

The relationship with Cartesian coordinates can be found using trigonometry in the right-angled triangles shown in Figure 9(b). We get

$$x = r \sin \theta \cos \phi, \quad y = r \sin \theta \sin \phi, \quad z = r \cos \theta, \tag{7}$$

where

$$r = \sqrt{x^2 + y^2 + z^2} \tag{8}$$

is the distance from the origin. We can check that this is consistent with the sum of the squares of x, y and z in equations (7):

$$\begin{aligned} x^2 + y^2 + z^2 &= r^2 \sin^2 \theta \cos^2 \phi + r^2 \sin^2 \theta \sin^2 \phi + r^2 \cos^2 \theta \\ &= r^2 \sin^2 \theta (\cos^2 \phi + \sin^2 \phi) + r^2 \cos^2 \theta \\ &= r^2 (\sin^2 \theta + \cos^2 \theta) \\ &= r^2. \end{aligned}$$

Using this expression, the three-dimensional temperature field in equation (2) and Exercise 2 can be expressed in spherical coordinates as

$$T(r, \theta, \phi) = 100 \, e^{-r^2} \quad (r \leq 1).$$

This is simpler than the Cartesian or cylindrical descriptions because it depends on one coordinate rather than three or two. Any three-dimensional scalar field that is independent of the θ- and ϕ-coordinates of spherical coordinates is said to be **spherically symmetric**. It is generally advisable to describe such fields in spherical coordinates.

Exercise 3

Express the scalar field

$$U(x, y, z) = \frac{z}{(x^2 + y^2 + z^2)^{1/2}}$$

in terms of:

(a) cylindrical coordinates,

(b) spherical coordinates.

1.3   Describing vector fields

You have seen that a vector field is a function that associates a vector with each point in a given region. For example, if the surface of a river is treated as being flat, the velocity of water flowing on this surface can be represented by a function of the form

$$\mathbf{v}(x, y) = v_x(x, y)\,\mathbf{i} + v_y(x, y)\,\mathbf{j},$$

where the Cartesian coordinates x and y label points on the river's surface, and the unit vectors $\mathbf{i}$ and $\mathbf{j}$ point in the directions of increasing x and increasing y. The domain of $\mathbf{v}(x, y)$ is the river's surface, and within this domain, the functions $v_x(x, y)$ and $v_y(x, y)$ give the x- and y-components of the water's velocity at any point (x, y). This is a two-dimensional vector field.

To take a specific case, suppose that a river has a straight stretch between $x = 0$ and $x = 100$, with its banks at $y = 0$ and $y = 10$ (all measured in metres). Then the flow of water (in metres per second) might be described by the function

$$\mathbf{v}(x, y) = \tfrac{1}{10}\,y(10 - y)\,\mathbf{i} \quad (0 \le x \le 100,\ 0 \le y \le 10). \tag{9}$$

In this simple model, all the water flows in the direction of $\mathbf{i}$ (the x-direction). The rate of flow does not depend on the downstream distance x, but is fastest in the middle of the river ($y = 5$), and drops to zero at either bank (at $y = 0$ and $y = 10$).

A good way of visualising a two-dimensional vector field is to draw an **arrow map**. For a vector field in the xy-plane, this is done by choosing a selection of points in the xy-plane and drawing an arrow at each point. Each arrow points in the direction of the vector field, and has a length proportional to the magnitude of the field. For example, the arrow map in Figure 10 illustrates the velocity vector field in equation (9). The arrows all point in the x-direction (downstream) and are longer in the middle of the river where the flow is fastest.

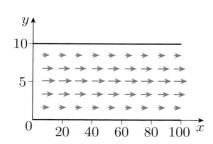

Figure 10 An arrow map for the velocity vector field in equation (9)

Another example of a vector field is provided by the **gravitational field** around a star. The gravitational field at a point P is defined to be the *gravitational force per unit mass* experienced by a small body placed at P. Gravity is an attractive force, and the gravitational field due to the star points inwards, towards the centre of the star. The gravitational influence of the star decreases as we move away from it, and the magnitude of the gravitational field outside the star turns out to be proportional to $1/r^2$, where r is the distance from the centre of the star.

The gravitational field of a star is three-dimensional, so it cannot be captured on a two-dimensional arrow map. But we can show a cross-section of the field in the xy-plane, as in Figure 11. As you would expect, all the arrows point towards the centre of the star, and their length increases they get closer to the star.

An alternative graphical way of depicting vector fields is to sketch a **field line map**. Instead of drawing arrows at a set of discrete points, we draw continuous directed lines called **field lines**. At each point along its path, the direction of a field line is the direction of the vector field, and this is indicated by placing one or more arrows on the field line. Vector fields generally vary smoothly in space, so the field lines are generally continuous curves. They tell us the direction of the vector field but they do not, by themselves, reveal the relative magnitudes of the field at different points. Figure 12(a) shows field lines for the velocity vector field of equation (9), and Figure 12(b) shows the field lines for the gravitational field around a star.

This is Newton's celebrated inverse square law of gravity.

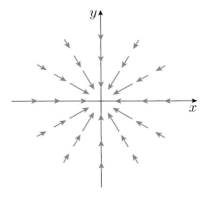

Figure 11 An arrow map for the gravitational field in the xy-plane due to a star at the origin

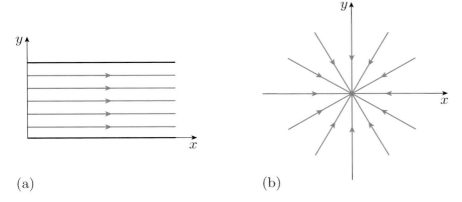

(a)   (b)

Figure 12 Field line maps for vector fields: (a) the velocity vector field of equation (9); (b) the gravitational field due to a star

So far, we have described vector fields in Cartesian coordinates and Cartesian unit vectors. But for vector fields with axial or spherical symmetry, it is often better to use non-Cartesian coordinates and non-Cartesian unit vectors. We briefly survey how these descriptions work in polar, cylindrical and spherical coordinates before looking more closely at the details.

Vector fields in polar coordinates

When a two-dimensional vector field $\mathbf{v}$ is described in a given Cartesian coordinate system, it takes the form

$$\mathbf{v}(x, y) = v_x(x, y)\,\mathbf{i} + v_y(x, y)\,\mathbf{j}.$$

It is worth noting that the unit vectors **i** and **j** are an important part of this description – as essential as the components v_x and v_y. If we were to choose a different set of Cartesian unit vectors, pointing in different directions, we would have a different set of components.

When we represent a vector field in a given coordinate system, the first step is to define suitable unit vectors. Let us recall how this is done in a two-dimensional Cartesian coordinate system. In this case, the unit vector **i** is a vector of unit magnitude that points in the direction of increasing x, with y held constant. Similarly, the unit vector **j** is a vector of unit magnitude that points in the direction of increasing y, with x held constant. These unit vectors point in fixed directions, perpendicular to one another.

Now consider polar coordinates (r, ϕ) in a plane (shown again in Figure 13). These are related to Cartesian coordinates by the equations

$$x = r \cos \phi, \quad y = r \sin \phi. \tag{10}$$

Based on these coordinates, at any given point P, we can introduce two unit vectors $\mathbf{e}_r$ and $\mathbf{e}_\phi$, as shown in Figure 14.

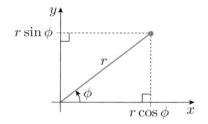

Figure 13 The polar coordinate system

- $\mathbf{e}_r$ is a vector of unit magnitude pointing in the direction of increasing r, with ϕ held constant.

- $\mathbf{e}_\phi$ is a vector of unit magnitude pointing in the direction of increasing ϕ, with r held constant.

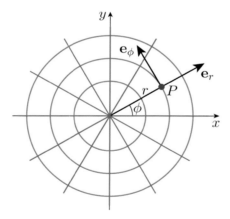

Figure 14   Unit vectors and coordinate lines in polar coordinates: r-coordinate lines in blue, ϕ-coordinate lines in orange

These unit vectors are related to the coordinate lines marked in Figure 14. The r-coordinate lines (in blue) are radial paths along which r increases while ϕ remains constant, while the ϕ-coordinate lines (in orange) are circular paths along which ϕ increases while r remains constant. At any point P, $\mathbf{e}_r$ is tangential to the r-coordinate line through P, and $\mathbf{e}_\phi$ is tangential to the ϕ-coordinate line through P. Because the radial paths meet the circles at right angles, the unit vectors $\mathbf{e}_r$ and $\mathbf{e}_\phi$ are mutually orthogonal.

Using trigonometry in Figure 15, we can resolve $\mathbf{e}_r$ and $\mathbf{e}_\phi$ along the directions $\mathbf{i}$ and $\mathbf{j}$ to get the following useful formulas.

$$\left.\begin{array}{l} \mathbf{e}_r = \cos\phi\,\mathbf{i} + \sin\phi\,\mathbf{j}, \\ \mathbf{e}_\phi = -\sin\phi\,\mathbf{i} + \cos\phi\,\mathbf{j}. \end{array}\right\} \tag{11}$$

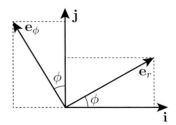

Figure 15 Relating polar unit vectors to Cartesian unit vectors

Exercise 4

Show that the vectors given in equations (11) are unit vectors that are orthogonal to one another.

The Cartesian unit vectors $\mathbf{i}$ and $\mathbf{j}$ are constant vectors – they remain the same, no matter which point (x, y) is being described. But the same is not true for the polar unit vectors $\mathbf{e}_r$ and $\mathbf{e}_\phi$. This is implicit in equations (11) and is illustrated in Figure 16. At point P, the radial unit vector $\mathbf{e}_r$ points directly away from the origin in the direction OP; at another point Q, it points in the direction OQ. The 'transverse' unit vector $\mathbf{e}_\phi$, which is always perpendicular to $\mathbf{e}_r$, also varies with position.

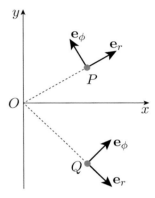

Figure 16 The polar unit vectors vary from one point to another

At first sight, this may seem to be an unwelcome complication, but in many cases it gives us the freedom to replace a complicated description in Cartesian coordinates by a simpler description in polar coordinates. The vectors $\mathbf{e}_r$ and $\mathbf{e}_\phi$ tell us the *local* radial and transverse directions at a given point, and these are sometimes very significant. For example, a mass at the origin produces an inward radial gravitational field, which is best described using radial unit vectors – this is more natural and simpler than introducing Cartesian unit vectors, which point in arbitrary directions unrelated to the direction of the gravitational field.

An example of a two-dimensional vector field expressed in polar coordinates is provided by

$$\mathbf{v}(r, \phi) = 2r\,\mathbf{e}_r. \tag{12}$$

At each point, this field points radially outwards, and its magnitude is proportional to the distance from the origin. The corresponding arrow map is shown in Figure 17, where you should note that the arrows point radially away from the origin, and have a length that increases steadily as we move further away from the origin.

The vector field given in equation (12) can be converted to Cartesian coordinates by using equations (10) and (11). At a point with coordinates (x, y) we get

$$\mathbf{v}(x, y) = 2r(\cos\phi\,\mathbf{i} + \sin\phi\,\mathbf{j}) = 2x\,\mathbf{i} + 2y\,\mathbf{j}.$$

This description is entirely equivalent to equation (12), but the link to Figure 17 is a little less obvious. In this case, polar coordinates provide the simplest and most transparent description of the field.

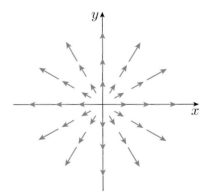

Figure 17 An arrow map for the vector field in equation (12)

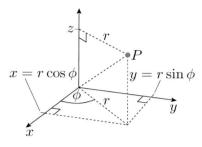

Figure 18   The cylindrical coordinate system

Vector fields in cylindrical coordinates

Three-dimensional vector fields can also be described in non-Cartesian coordinates. Cylindrical coordinates (r, ϕ, z) are shown again in Figure 18. They are related to Cartesian coordinates by the equations

$$x = r \cos \phi, \quad y = r \sin \phi, \quad z = z, \tag{13}$$

where $r = \sqrt{x^2 + y^2}$ is the distance from the z-axis (*not* the distance from the origin) in this coordinate system.

At any given point P, we can introduce three unit vectors $\mathbf{e}_r$, $\mathbf{e}_\phi$ and $\mathbf{e}_z$, based on cylindrical coordinates. These are illustrated in Figure 19 and defined as follows.

- $\mathbf{e}_r$ points in the direction of increasing r, with ϕ and z held constant.

- $\mathbf{e}_\phi$ points in the direction of increasing ϕ, with r and z held constant.

- $\mathbf{e}_z$ points in the direction of increasing z, with r and ϕ held constant.

Each of these unit vectors is tangential to a particular coordinate line along which just one of the cylindrical coordinates (r, ϕ or z) increases while the other two remain fixed.

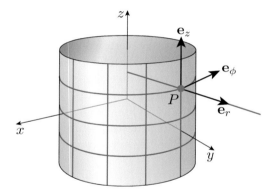

Figure 19   Unit vectors and coordinate lines in cylindrical coordinates: r-coordinate lines are shown in green, ϕ-coordinate lines in red and z-coordinate lines in blue

The unit vectors $\mathbf{e}_r$ and $\mathbf{e}_\phi$ lie in a plane parallel to the xy-plane and are identical to the polar unit vectors, while the unit vector $\mathbf{e}_z$ points in the z-direction and is identical to the unit vector $\mathbf{k}$ of Cartesian coordinates. Hence equations (11) still apply for $\mathbf{e}_r$ and $\mathbf{e}_\phi$, and we have the following results.

$$\left. \begin{array}{l} \mathbf{e}_r = \cos \phi \, \mathbf{i} + \sin \phi \, \mathbf{j}, \\ \mathbf{e}_\phi = -\sin \phi \, \mathbf{i} + \cos \phi \, \mathbf{j}, \\ \mathbf{e}_z = \mathbf{k}. \end{array} \right\} \tag{14}$$

These equations show that the unit vectors $\mathbf{e}_r$ and $\mathbf{e}_\phi$ depend on position, but $\mathbf{e}_z$ remains constant, being equal to the Cartesian unit vector $\mathbf{k}$.

An example of a vector field expressed in cylindrical coordinates is given by

$$\mathbf{v}(r, \phi, z) = r\, \mathbf{e}_\phi. \tag{15}$$

The field lines for this field are circles around the z-axis, as shown in Figure 20.

Vector fields in spherical coordinates

Spherical coordinates (r, θ, ϕ) are shown again in Figure 21. They are related to Cartesian coordinates by the equations

$$x = r\sin\theta\cos\phi, \quad y = r\sin\theta\sin\phi, \quad z = r\cos\theta, \tag{16}$$

where $r = \sqrt{x^2 + y^2 + z^2}$ is the distance from the origin.

At any given point, we can introduce three unit vectors $\mathbf{e}_r$, $\mathbf{e}_\theta$ and $\mathbf{e}_\phi$. These are illustrated in Figure 22 and defined as follows.

- $\mathbf{e}_r$ points in the direction of increasing r, with θ and ϕ held constant.
- $\mathbf{e}_\theta$ points in the direction of increasing θ, with r and ϕ held constant.
- $\mathbf{e}_\phi$ points in the direction of increasing ϕ, with r and θ held constant.

Each of these unit vectors is tangential to a coordinate line along which just one of the coordinates (r, θ or ϕ) increases while the other two remain fixed.

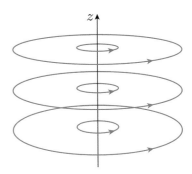

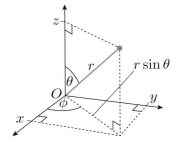

Figure 20 Field lines for the vector field in equation (15)

Figure 21 The spherical coordinate system

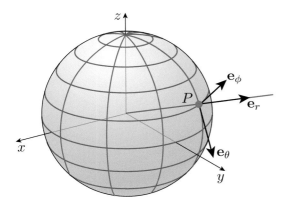

Figure 22 Unit vectors and coordinate lines in spherical coordinates: r-coordinate lines are shown in green, θ-coordinate lines in blue and ϕ-coordinate lines in red

The spherical unit vectors can be visualised as follows. Imagine a spherical coordinate system with its origin at the Earth's centre, and a positive z-axis that points from the origin through the North Pole. Then at a typical point on the Earth's surface, the vector $\mathbf{e}_r$ points vertically upwards, the vector $\mathbf{e}_\theta$ points southwards, and the vector $\mathbf{e}_\phi$ points eastwards. Obviously, these three unit vectors are mutually orthogonal.

There is no unique southward direction at the North or South Pole, but such isolated exceptions can be safely ignored in this module.

Note carefully that $\mathbf{e}_r$ points radially away from the origin in spherical coordinates. This is not the same as the direction of $\mathbf{e}_r$ in cylindrical coordinates (which points radially away from the z-axis). For this reason, it is always important to state clearly which coordinate system is being used. You cannot assume that the symbols speak for themselves.

While the meanings of the spherical unit vectors are clear, the three-dimensional trigonometry needed to express $\mathbf{e}_r$, $\mathbf{e}_\theta$ and $\mathbf{e}_\phi$ in terms of the Cartesian unit vectors $\mathbf{i}$, $\mathbf{j}$ and $\mathbf{k}$ is rather cumbersome. For the moment, we just quote the results.

$$\left. \begin{aligned} \mathbf{e}_r &= \sin\theta\cos\phi\,\mathbf{i} + \sin\theta\sin\phi\,\mathbf{j} + \cos\theta\,\mathbf{k}, \\ \mathbf{e}_\theta &= \cos\theta\cos\phi\,\mathbf{i} + \cos\theta\sin\phi\,\mathbf{j} - \sin\theta\,\mathbf{k}, \\ \mathbf{e}_\phi &= -\sin\phi\,\mathbf{i} + \cos\phi\,\mathbf{j}. \end{aligned} \right\} \qquad (17)$$

You should take these equations on trust for the moment; in Subsection 1.5 we will derive them using an alternative (non-geometric) route.

An example of a vector field that is conveniently described in spherical coordinates is the gravitational field around a star. With a spherical coordinate system centred on the star, this field is

g is the gravitational force per unit mass experienced by a body in the vicinity of the star.

$$\mathbf{g}(r,\theta,\phi) = -\frac{GM}{r^2}\,\mathbf{e}_r \quad (r > 0), \qquad (18)$$

where G is a positive constant (called the constant of gravitation) and M is the mass of the star.

Since M, G and r are all positive, the minus sign on the right-hand side of equation (18) implies that the gravitational field vector $\mathbf{g}$ points in the opposite direction to $\mathbf{e}_r$. In other words, it points radially inwards, *towards* the star, corresponding to gravitational *attraction*. You can also see from equation (18) that the magnitude of $\mathbf{g}$ is independent of θ and ϕ, and decreases as $1/r^2$ as the distance r from the star increases. The ability to read the meaning of equations in this way is a valuable skill for scientists, engineers and all who need to relate equations to the real world.

1.4   Vector field conversions

In principle, you are free to choose whichever coordinate system you like, but the physical situation often singles out a preferred coordinate system – one that makes calculations easier. For all their apparent simplicity, Cartesian coordinates are not always the best choice. For example, the gravitational field of a star has spherical symmetry, and is best described in spherical coordinates, as in equation (18).

We may be given a vector field in one coordinate system, and wish to express it in another coordinate system.

As an example, suppose that we are given a vector field

$$\mathbf{v}(x, y) = v_x(x, y)\,\mathbf{i} + v_y(x, y)\,\mathbf{j} \tag{19}$$

in Cartesian coordinates, and we want to express it in polar coordinates, that is, in the form

$$\mathbf{v}(r, \phi) = v_r(r, \phi)\,\mathbf{e}_r + v_\phi(r, \phi)\,\mathbf{e}_\phi. \tag{20}$$

We need to find the functions $v_r(r, \phi)$ and $v_\phi(r, \phi)$ that describe how the polar components of the given field vary from point to point.

A vector field does not depend on the orientation of the coordinate system used to describe it. So if a particular point has Cartesian coordinates (x, y) and polar coordinates (r, ϕ), we must have

$$\mathbf{v}(x, y) = \mathbf{v}(r, \phi). \tag{21}$$

On the understanding that equations (19) and (20) refer to the same point, we can simplify our notation by omitting the arguments (x, y) and (r, ϕ). We write

$$\mathbf{v} = v_x\,\mathbf{i} + v_y\,\mathbf{j}, \tag{22}$$
$$\mathbf{v} = v_r\,\mathbf{e}_r + v_\phi\,\mathbf{e}_\phi. \tag{23}$$

Both of these equations refer to the *same* vector $\mathbf{v}$, expressed in different coordinate systems.

The key to finding an expression for v_r is to note that $\mathbf{e}_r$ and $\mathbf{e}_\phi$ are orthogonal and of unit magnitude, so $\mathbf{e}_r \cdot \mathbf{e}_\phi = 0$ and $\mathbf{e}_r \cdot \mathbf{e_r} = 1$. Taking the scalar product of both sides of equation (23) with $\mathbf{e}_r$ then gives

$$\mathbf{e}_r \cdot \mathbf{v} = v_r\,\mathbf{e}_r \cdot \mathbf{e}_r + v_\phi\,\mathbf{e}_r \cdot \mathbf{e}_\phi = v_r.$$

So

$$v_r = \mathbf{e}_r \cdot \mathbf{v}.$$

The scalar product on the right-hand side of this equation can be expressed in Cartesian coordinates by taking $\mathbf{e}_r$ from equations (11) and $\mathbf{v}$ from equation (22). We get

$$v_r = (\cos\phi\,\mathbf{i} + \sin\phi\,\mathbf{j}) \cdot (v_x\,\mathbf{i} + v_y\,\mathbf{j}) = \cos\phi\,v_x + \sin\phi\,v_y.$$

An expression for v_y can be found in a similar way. In this case, taking the scalar product of both sides of equation (23) with $\mathbf{e}_\phi$ gives

$$\mathbf{e}_\phi \cdot \mathbf{v} = v_r\,\mathbf{e}_\phi \cdot \mathbf{e}_r + v_\phi\,\mathbf{e}_\phi \cdot \mathbf{e}_\phi = v_\phi.$$

So

$$v_\phi = \mathbf{e}_\phi \cdot \mathbf{v}.$$

Using equations (11) and (22) to expand the scalar product then gives

$$v_\phi = (-\sin\phi\,\mathbf{i} + \cos\phi\,\mathbf{j}) \cdot (v_x\,\mathbf{i} + v_y\,\mathbf{j}) = -\sin\phi\,v_x + \cos\phi\,v_y.$$

Example 1

A field like this could describe the velocity at points on a steadily rotating turntable.

A two-dimensional vector field is expressed in Cartesian coordinates as

$$\mathbf{v}(x, y) = -y\,\mathbf{i} + x\,\mathbf{j}.$$

Express this field in polar coordinates (r, ϕ).

Solution

In polar coordinates, the field is expressed as

$$\mathbf{v}(r, \phi) = v_r\,\mathbf{e}_r + v_\phi\,\mathbf{e}_\phi.$$

We have

$$
\begin{aligned}
v_r &= \mathbf{e}_r \cdot \mathbf{v} \\
&= (\cos\phi\,\mathbf{i} + \sin\phi\,\mathbf{j}) \cdot (-y\,\mathbf{i} + x\,\mathbf{j}) \\
&= -y\cos\phi + x\sin\phi.
\end{aligned}
$$

Similarly,

$$
\begin{aligned}
v_\phi &= \mathbf{e}_\phi \cdot \mathbf{v} \\
&= (-\sin\phi\,\mathbf{i} + \cos\phi\,\mathbf{j}) \cdot (-y\,\mathbf{i} + x\,\mathbf{j}) \\
&= y\sin\phi + x\cos\phi.
\end{aligned}
$$

The coordinate transformation equations for polar coordinates are $x = r\cos\phi$ and $y = r\sin\phi$. Using these, we get

$$v_r = -(r\sin\phi)\cos\phi + (r\cos\phi)\sin\phi = 0,$$
$$v_\phi = (r\sin\phi)\sin\phi + (r\cos\phi)\cos\phi = r(\sin^2\phi + \cos^2\phi) = r,$$

So in polar coordinates,

$$\mathbf{v}(r, \phi) = r\,\mathbf{e}_\phi.$$

The method that we have just used to convert a vector field expressed in Cartesian form into polar coordinates can be extended. It relies on the fact that the polar unit vectors $\mathbf{e}_r$ and $\mathbf{e}_\phi$ are orthogonal. A similar method works in cylindrical and spherical coordinates, and all other orthogonal coordinate systems.

To take a general three-dimensional case, suppose that we are given a vector field $\mathbf{F}$ in Cartesian coordinates,

$$\mathbf{F} = F_x\,\mathbf{i} + F_y\,\mathbf{j} + F_z\,\mathbf{k},$$

and we wish to express it in an orthogonal coordinate system (u, v, w), with orthogonal unit vectors $\mathbf{e}_u$, $\mathbf{e}_v$ and $\mathbf{e}_w$. Then we write

$$\mathbf{F} = F_u\,\mathbf{e}_u + F_v\,\mathbf{e}_v + F_w\,\mathbf{e}_w,$$

where the components F_u, F_v and F_w are unknown functions of (u, v, w).

These functions can be found using the following procedure.

Procedure 1   Finding components in orthogonal coordinates

For a vector field $\mathbf{F}$ in an orthogonal coordinate system (u, v, w), the component F_u in the direction of $\mathbf{e}_u$ is found as follows.

1. Write down

    $$F_u = \mathbf{e}_u \cdot \mathbf{F},$$

    and expand the scalar product on the right-hand side using Cartesian expressions for $\mathbf{e}_u$ and $\mathbf{F}$ (involving $\mathbf{i}$, $\mathbf{j}$ and $\mathbf{k}$).

2. The resulting expression generally depends on (x, y, z). Use coordinate transformation equations of the form

    $$x = x(u, v, w), \quad y = y(u, v, w), \quad z = z(u, v, w),$$

    to obtain an expression for F_u solely in terms of u, v and w.

The following example illustrates how this procedure is used.

Example 2

In Cartesian coordinates, a vector field takes the form

$$\mathbf{B}(x, y, z) = yz\,\mathbf{i} - xz\,\mathbf{j} + 2xy\,\mathbf{k}.$$

Express this field in cylindrical coordinates (r, ϕ, z).

Solution

We write the field as

$$\mathbf{B}(r, \phi, z) = B_r\,\mathbf{e}_r + B_\phi\,\mathbf{e}_\phi + B_z\,\mathbf{e}_z,$$

where the cylindrical unit vectors are given by equations (14):

$$\mathbf{e}_r = \cos\phi\,\mathbf{i} + \sin\phi\,\mathbf{j}, \quad \mathbf{e}_\phi = -\sin\phi\,\mathbf{i} + \cos\phi\,\mathbf{j}, \quad \mathbf{e}_z = \mathbf{k}.$$

Using Procedure 1, we get

$$\begin{aligned}
B_r &= \mathbf{e}_r \cdot \mathbf{B} = (\cos\phi\,\mathbf{i} + \sin\phi\,\mathbf{j}) \cdot (yz\,\mathbf{i} - xz\,\mathbf{j} + 2xy\,\mathbf{k}) \\
&= yz\cos\phi - xz\sin\phi,
\end{aligned}$$

$$\begin{aligned}
B_\phi &= \mathbf{e}_\phi \cdot \mathbf{B} = (-\sin\phi\,\mathbf{i} + \cos\phi\,\mathbf{j}) \cdot (yz\,\mathbf{i} - xz\,\mathbf{j} + 2xy\,\mathbf{k}) \\
&= -yz\sin\phi - xz\cos\phi,
\end{aligned}$$

$$B_z = \mathbf{e}_z \cdot \mathbf{B} = \mathbf{k} \cdot (yz\,\mathbf{i} - xz\,\mathbf{j} + 2xy\,\mathbf{k}) = 2xy.$$

These expressions still involve (x, y, z), but in cylindrical coordinates

$$x = r\cos\phi, \quad y = r\sin\phi, \quad z = z,$$

so we get

$$B_r = (r\sin\phi)z\cos\phi - (r\cos\phi)z\sin\phi = 0,$$

$$B_\phi = -(r\sin\phi)z\sin\phi - (r\cos\phi)z\cos\phi = -rz(\sin^2\phi + \cos^2\phi) = -rz,$$

$$B_z = 2r^2\cos\phi\sin\phi = r^2\sin(2\phi).$$

Hence in cylindrical coordinates,

$$\mathbf{B}(r, \phi, z) = -rz\,\mathbf{e}_\phi + r^2\sin(2\phi)\,\mathbf{e}_z.$$

Exercise 5

In Cartesian coordinates, a vector field takes the form

$$\mathbf{F}(x, y, z) = (x + y)\,\mathbf{i} + (y - x)\,\mathbf{j} + 3z\,\mathbf{k}.$$

Express this field in cylindrical coordinates (r, ϕ, z).

Exercise 6

In Cartesian coordinates, a vector field takes the form

$$\mathbf{F}(x, y, z) = z\,\mathbf{k}.$$

Use equations (17) to express this field in spherical coordinates (r, θ, ϕ).

You have seen how to convert a vector field from Cartesian coordinates to non-Cartesian orthogonal coordinates. We sometimes need the opposite conversion, from non-Cartesian to Cartesian coordinates. For example, a vector field may be given in spherical coordinates as

$$\mathbf{F} = \frac{1}{r^2}\,\mathbf{e}_r.$$

To express this field in Cartesian coordinates, we begin by using equations (17) to express $\mathbf{e}_r$ in terms of $\mathbf{i}$, $\mathbf{j}$ and $\mathbf{k}$. This gives

$$\mathbf{F} = \frac{1}{r^2}\,(\sin\theta\cos\phi\,\mathbf{i} + \sin\theta\sin\phi\,\mathbf{j} + \cos\theta\,\mathbf{k}).$$

The remaining task is to express the quantities involving r, θ and ϕ in terms of x, y and z. This can often be done by inspection. In the present case, the coordinate transformation equations

$$x = r\sin\theta\cos\phi, \quad y = r\sin\theta\sin\phi, \quad z = r\cos\theta$$

give

$$\sin\theta\cos\phi = \frac{x}{r}, \quad \sin\theta\sin\phi = \frac{y}{r}, \quad \cos\theta = \frac{z}{r}.$$

Also, it is clear from geometry (and equation (8)) that the distance from the origin is $r = (x^2 + y^2 + z^2)^{1/2}$. Hence the vector field can be expressed as

$$\mathbf{F} = \frac{1}{r^2}\left(\frac{x}{r}\,\mathbf{i} + \frac{y}{r}\,\mathbf{j} + \frac{z}{r}\,\mathbf{k}\right)$$

$$= \frac{x\,\mathbf{i} + y\,\mathbf{j} + z\,\mathbf{k}}{(x^2 + y^2 + z^2)^{3/2}}.$$

Exercise 7

In spherical coordinates, a vector field takes the form

$$\mathbf{F}(r, \theta, \phi) = \cos\theta\,\mathbf{e}_r - \sin\theta\,\mathbf{e}_\theta.$$

Express this field in Cartesian coordinates.

1.5   Unit vectors and scale factors

This subsection develops the theme of scale factors introduced in Unit 8. It shows that unit vectors in all coordinate systems can be obtained from a single formula (equation (27)). This useful formula allows us to avoid elaborate geometric arguments in three dimensions. It will be used later on, but its derivation is not assessed.

To take a unified view, we consider any three-dimensional coordinate system with coordinates (u, v, w). The coordinates u, v and w are related to Cartesian coordinates by equations of the type

$$x = x(u, v, w), \quad y = y(u, v, w), \quad z = z(u, v, w).$$

In spherical coordinates, for example, $(u, v, w) = (r, \theta, \phi)$, and these equations take the form

$$x = r\sin\theta\cos\phi, \quad y = r\sin\theta\sin\phi, \quad z = r\cos\theta.$$

We can define coordinate lines along which just one coordinate increases while the other two remain fixed. Along a u-coordinate line, for example, u increases while v and w have fixed values. Then we can imagine taking a small step along a u-coordinate line. In general, the chain rule tells us that

$$\delta x = \frac{\partial x}{\partial u}\,\delta u + \frac{\partial x}{\partial v}\,\delta v + \frac{\partial x}{\partial w}\,\delta w.$$

But along a u-coordinate line, v and w are held constant, so $\delta v = 0$ and $\delta w = 0$, giving

$$\delta x = \frac{\partial x}{\partial u}\,\delta u.$$

Similarly,

$$\delta y = \frac{\partial y}{\partial u}\,\delta u \quad \text{and} \quad \delta z = \frac{\partial z}{\partial u}\,\delta u.$$

The displacement along the u-coordinate line produced by a small increase in u is therefore given by the vector

Unit 8, Subsection 4.2 gave a similar argument.

$$\delta x\,\mathbf{i} + \delta y\,\mathbf{j} + \delta z\,\mathbf{k} = \left(\frac{\partial x}{\partial u}\,\mathbf{i} + \frac{\partial y}{\partial u}\,\mathbf{j} + \frac{\partial z}{\partial u}\,\mathbf{k}\right)\delta u. \tag{24}$$

This vector describes a tiny displacement along the u-coordinate line in the direction of increasing u. The crucial point is that this is just the direction of the required unit vector $\mathbf{e}_u$. The factor δu in equation (24) simply scales the vector in brackets without changing its direction. We can therefore concentrate on the vector in brackets, which is denoted by

$$\mathbf{T}_u = \frac{\partial x}{\partial u}\,\mathbf{i} + \frac{\partial y}{\partial u}\,\mathbf{j} + \frac{\partial z}{\partial u}\,\mathbf{k}. \tag{25}$$

Because this vector is tangential to the u-coordinate line, it is called a **tangent vector**.

To obtain the unit vector $\mathbf{e}_u$, we just need to scale $\mathbf{T}_u$ by $1/|\mathbf{T}_u|$. So we get

$$\mathbf{e}_u = \frac{1}{|\mathbf{T}_u|}\,\mathbf{T}_u, \tag{26}$$

where

$$|\mathbf{T}_u| = \sqrt{\left(\frac{\partial x}{\partial u}\right)^2 + \left(\frac{\partial y}{\partial u}\right)^2 + \left(\frac{\partial z}{\partial u}\right)^2}.$$

Referring back to Unit 8, Section 4, you can see that $|\mathbf{T}_u|$ is just the **scale factor** h_u for the u-coordinate. We have therefore derived the following result for any unit vector.

> ### Calculating unit vectors
>
> In any orthogonal coordinate system (u, v, w) with
>
> $$x = x(u, v, w), \quad y = y(u, v, w), \quad z = z(u, v, w),$$
>
> the unit vector $\mathbf{e}_u$ in the direction of the u-coordinate line is related to the Cartesian unit vectors by
>
> $$\mathbf{e}_u = \frac{1}{h_u}\left(\frac{\partial x}{\partial u}\,\mathbf{i} + \frac{\partial y}{\partial u}\,\mathbf{j} + \frac{\partial z}{\partial u}\,\mathbf{k}\right), \tag{27}$$
>
> where h_u is the scale factor
>
> $$h_u = \sqrt{\left(\frac{\partial x}{\partial u}\right)^2 + \left(\frac{\partial y}{\partial u}\right)^2 + \left(\frac{\partial z}{\partial u}\right)^2}. \tag{28}$$

Of course, similar equations apply for two-dimensional coordinate systems in the xy-plane, but without the terms involving z and $\mathbf{k}$.

The geometric relationship between tangent vectors, unit vectors and scale factors is illustrated in Figure 23.

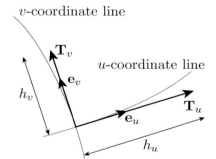

Figure 23 Tangent vectors, unit vectors and scale factors

Example 3

Use tangent vectors to derive expressions for the unit vectors $\mathbf{e}_r$ and $\mathbf{e}_\phi$ of polar coordinates.

Solution

In polar coordinates we have $x = r\cos\phi$ and $y = r\sin\phi$. So the tangent vectors in the r- and ϕ-directions are

$$\mathbf{T}_r = \frac{\partial x}{\partial r}\mathbf{i} + \frac{\partial y}{\partial r}\mathbf{j} = \cos\phi\,\mathbf{i} + \sin\phi\,\mathbf{j},$$
$$\mathbf{T}_\phi = \frac{\partial x}{\partial \phi}\mathbf{i} + \frac{\partial y}{\partial \phi}\mathbf{j} = -r\sin\phi\,\mathbf{i} + r\cos\phi\,\mathbf{j}.$$

These vectors have magnitudes

$$h_r = \sqrt{\cos^2\phi + \sin^2\phi} = 1,$$
$$h_\phi = \sqrt{(-r\sin\phi)^2 + (r\cos\phi)^2} = r,$$

which are the familiar scale factors of polar coordinates. So the unit vectors are

$$\mathbf{e}_r = \frac{1}{h_r}\mathbf{T}_r = \cos\phi\,\mathbf{i} + \sin\phi\,\mathbf{j},$$
$$\mathbf{e}_\phi = \frac{1}{h_\phi}\mathbf{T}_\phi = -\sin\phi\,\mathbf{i} + \cos\phi\,\mathbf{j},$$

in agreement with equations (11).

Exercise 8

Use tangent vectors to derive expressions for the unit vectors $\mathbf{e}_r$, $\mathbf{e}_\theta$ and $\mathbf{e}_\phi$ of spherical coordinates.

2 The gradient of a scalar field

We can now discuss the main topic of this unit – describing how rapidly fields change in space. This section describes the spatial rates of change of *scalar fields*, while Sections 3 and 4 describe spatial rates of change of *vector fields*.

The spatial rates of change of a scalar field $V(x, y, z)$ can be described using three partial derivatives: $\partial V/\partial x$, $\partial V/\partial y$ and $\partial V/\partial z$. An important quantity can be constructed from these – the *gradient vector*, which you met in Unit 7. Subsection 2.1 gives a brief review of the gradient vector in Cartesian coordinates, covering much the same ground as in Unit 7. In Subsection 2.2 we go further and explain how the gradient vector is calculated in non-Cartesian coordinates.

2.1   Gradients in Cartesian coordinates

Suppose that $V(x, y, z)$ is a three-dimensional scalar field expressed in Cartesian coordinates. Then you know how to find the gradient of this field. According to Unit 7,

$$\mathbf{grad}\, V = \frac{\partial V}{\partial x}\mathbf{i} + \frac{\partial V}{\partial y}\mathbf{j} + \frac{\partial V}{\partial z}\mathbf{k}. \tag{29}$$

The symbol $\boldsymbol{\nabla}$ is read as 'del' or 'nabla'.

This is often written in a different notation, using the symbol $\boldsymbol{\nabla}$ instead of **grad**. In this notation, the gradient of $V(x, y, z)$ is

$$\boldsymbol{\nabla} V = \frac{\partial V}{\partial x}\mathbf{i} + \frac{\partial V}{\partial y}\mathbf{j} + \frac{\partial V}{\partial z}\mathbf{k}. \tag{30}$$

Because $\boldsymbol{\nabla} V$ is a vector, the symbol $\boldsymbol{\nabla}$ is printed in bold type, and should be underlined in handwriting. We will use the notations $\mathbf{grad}\, V$ and $\boldsymbol{\nabla} V$ interchangeably.

For a two-dimensional scalar field $V(x, y)$, the gradient is

$$\mathbf{grad}\, V = \boldsymbol{\nabla} V = \frac{\partial V}{\partial x}\mathbf{i} + \frac{\partial V}{\partial y}\mathbf{j}. \tag{31}$$

Example 4

Calculate the gradient of $V(x, y, z) = xy^2 z^3$.

Solution

Using equation (29), the gradient is

$$\mathbf{grad}\, V = \frac{\partial V}{\partial x}\mathbf{i} + \frac{\partial V}{\partial y}\mathbf{j} + \frac{\partial V}{\partial z}\mathbf{k}$$
$$= y^2 z^3\,\mathbf{i} + 2xyz^3\,\mathbf{j} + 3xy^2 z^2\,\mathbf{k}.$$

In the alternative $\boldsymbol{\nabla}$ notation, this is written as

$$\boldsymbol{\nabla} V = y^2 z^3\,\mathbf{i} + 2xyz^3\,\mathbf{j} + 3xy^2 z^2\,\mathbf{k}.$$

Exercise 9

Find the gradients of the following functions.

(a) $V(x, y) = e^{x^2 + y^2}$

(b) $V(x, y, z) = e^{x^2 + y^2 + z^2}$

Properties of gradient

The properties of the gradient vector were outlined in Unit 7, mainly for functions of two variables. Given a function $V(x, y)$, the gradient vector **grad** V at any given point P is a vector in the xy-plane. This vector satisfies the following properties.

Have another look at Unit 7 if you need to refresh your memory.

- Its direction is that in which V increases most rapidly. This direction is perpendicular to the contour lines of $V(x, y)$.

- Its magnitude is the maximum rate of increase of V with respect to distance travelled in the xy-plane.

Exercise 10

The figure in the margin shows a contour map of a two-dimensional scalar field V. Use arrows to indicate the directions and relative magnitudes of **grad** V at points A, B and C. You should use the convention that an arrow represents the value of **grad** V at its own tail. The absolute lengths of the arrows are arbitrary, but you should choose their relative lengths appropriately.

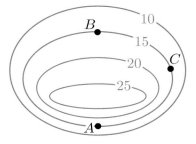

Exercise 11

A two-dimensional scalar field is given by

$$V(x, y) = \ln(\sqrt{x^2 + y^2}) \quad ((x, y) \neq (0, 0)).$$

Find the gradient of this field, and draw a sketch showing the contour line of V through $(1, 1)$ and an arrow representing $\boldsymbol{\nabla} V$ at this point.

Most of the scalar fields met in science vary in three-dimensional space. The properties of gradient in three dimensions are natural extensions of those in two dimensions.

Properties of gradient in three dimensions

Given a function $V(x, y, z)$, at any given point **grad** V is a vector in three-dimensional space.

- Its direction is that in which V increases most rapidly. This direction is perpendicular to the contour surfaces of V.

- Its magnitude is the maximum rate of increase of V with respect to distance travelled in three-dimensional space.

All these properties of gradient, in two and three dimensions, are taken as known facts in the context of this unit. For *scalar fields*, however, we can take things a step further.

Remember that, by definition, the values of a scalar field V do not depend on the orientation of the coordinate system. It follows that at any given point, the direction and magnitude of steepest increase of V, and hence the direction and magnitude of **grad** V, do not depend on the orientation of the coordinate system. This means that **grad** V is a vector field in the full sense of the term, as defined in Subsection 1.1.

We will use the terms gradient, gradient vector and gradient vector field interchangeably.

The gradient of a scalar field is a *vector field*: at each point, **grad** V has a definite magnitude and a definite direction in space that do not depend on the orientation of the coordinate system.

This conclusion is a deep one. Suppose that a Cartesian coordinate system has coordinates (x, y, z) and unit vectors $\mathbf{i}$, $\mathbf{j}$ and $\mathbf{k}$, and that it is rotated to create another Cartesian coordinate system with coordinates (X, Y, Z) and unit vectors $\mathbf{I}$, $\mathbf{J}$ and $\mathbf{K}$. Then a scalar field

Following our usual convention, f labels two *different* functions: $f(x, y, z)$ and $f(X, Y, Z)$.

$$f(x, y, z) = f(X, Y, Z)$$

has gradient

$$\mathbf{grad}\, f = \frac{\partial f}{\partial x}\,\mathbf{i} + \frac{\partial f}{\partial y}\,\mathbf{j} + \frac{\partial f}{\partial z}\,\mathbf{k} = \frac{\partial f}{\partial X}\,\mathbf{I} + \frac{\partial f}{\partial Y}\,\mathbf{J} + \frac{\partial f}{\partial Z}\,\mathbf{K}.$$

The equality of the two expressions on the right is not a trivial fact, but is guaranteed because **grad** f is a *vector field* and therefore cannot depend on the orientation of the coordinate system used to describe it.

Exercise 12

A three-dimensional scalar field is given by

$$V(x, y, z) = \frac{1}{(x^2 + y^2 + z^2)^{3/2}} \quad ((x, y, z) \neq (0, 0, 0)).$$

Calculate the gradient of this field.

Exercise 13

The temperature (in degrees Celsius) in a certain region of space is given by the scalar field

$$T(x, y, z) = 1000\,\exp(-(x^2 + 2y^2 + 2z^2)),$$

where x, y and z are measured in metres.

(a) Calculate the gradient of this scalar field at the point $(1, 1, 1)$.

(b) Specify a unit vector $\hat{\mathbf{n}}$ that gives the direction of the most rapid increase in temperature on moving away from $(1, 1, 1)$.

Gradients and small changes

The components of $\boldsymbol{\nabla} V$ are $\partial V/\partial x$, $\partial V/\partial y$ and $\partial V/\partial z$, which are the rates of change of V in the x-, y- and z-directions. However, if we know $\boldsymbol{\nabla} V$, we can also deduce how V changes in any other direction.

Suppose that we make a tiny displacement from a point (x, y, z) to a neighbouring point $(x + \delta x, y + \delta y, z + \delta z)$. As a result of this displacement, a scalar field $V(x, y, z)$ changes by

$$\delta V = V(x + \delta x, y + \delta y, z + \delta z) - V(x, y, z),$$

and the chain rule tells us that

$$\delta V \simeq \frac{\partial V}{\partial x}\,\delta x + \frac{\partial V}{\partial y}\,\delta y + \frac{\partial V}{\partial z}\,\delta z.$$

Now, the right-hand side of this equation can be rewritten as a scalar product:

$$\delta V \simeq \left(\frac{\partial V}{\partial x}\,\mathbf{i} + \frac{\partial V}{\partial y}\,\mathbf{j} + \frac{\partial V}{\partial z}\,\mathbf{k}\right) \cdot (\delta x\,\mathbf{i} + \delta y\,\mathbf{j} + \delta z\,\mathbf{k}).$$

But

$$\frac{\partial V}{\partial x}\,\mathbf{i} + \frac{\partial V}{\partial y}\,\mathbf{j} + \frac{\partial V}{\partial z}\,\mathbf{k} = \boldsymbol{\nabla} V$$

is the gradient of V, and

$$\delta x\,\mathbf{i} + \delta y\,\mathbf{j} + \delta z\,\mathbf{k} = \delta\mathbf{s}$$

is the displacement vector, so we reach the following conclusion.

The small change in a scalar field V due to a small displacement $\delta\mathbf{s}$ is

$$\delta V \simeq \boldsymbol{\nabla} V \cdot \delta\mathbf{s}. \tag{32}$$

If we know the gradient of a scalar field at a given point, we can use equation (32) to estimate the change in V that occurs when we make a small displacement $\delta\mathbf{s}$ away from that point.

If the tiny displacement vector $\delta\mathbf{s}$ covers a distance δs in the direction of the unit vector $\widehat{\mathbf{n}}$, we can write $\delta\mathbf{s} = \widehat{\mathbf{n}}\,\delta s$, so

$$\delta V \simeq (\boldsymbol{\nabla} V \cdot \widehat{\mathbf{n}})\,\delta s.$$

Then dividing both sides by δs and taking the limit as the distance δs tends to zero, we see that

In the limit where δs tends to zero, our approximations become exact.

$$\frac{dV}{ds} = \boldsymbol{\nabla} V \cdot \widehat{\mathbf{n}}. \tag{33}$$

The rate of change of V with distance in the direction of the unit vector $\widehat{\mathbf{n}}$ is the *component* of the gradient vector $\boldsymbol{\nabla} V$ in the direction of $\widehat{\mathbf{n}}$.

Exercise 14

A scalar field takes the form $V(x, y, z) = (x^2 + y^2 + z^2)^{3/2}$.

(a) Estimate the change in V between the points $(1, 2, 2)$ and $(0.98, 1.99, 2.01)$.

(b) Find the rate of change of V at the point $(1, 2, 2)$ in the direction of the unit vector $\widehat{\mathbf{n}} = (3\,\mathbf{i} + 4\,\mathbf{k})/5$.

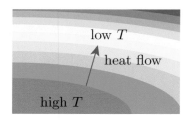

Figure 24 Heat flows in the opposite direction to the gradient of temperature

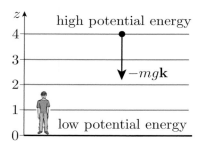

Figure 25 The gravitational force acts downwards, in the opposite direction to the gradient of potential energy

Gradients of scalar fields in the real world

Gradients often appear in mathematical descriptions of physical systems. You know that heat flows from the hot ring of an electric stove to a colder saucepan, warming its contents. In general, heat flows from regions of high temperature to regions of low temperature, a process that tends to reduce spatial variations in temperature.

For any temperature field $T(x, y, z)$, the temperature gradient $\mathbf{grad}\, T$ plays a vital role in determining how heat is conducted.

As indicated in Figure 24, heat flows in the direction in which temperature decreases most rapidly, which is the direction of $-\mathbf{grad}\, T$. Moreover, the rate of flow of heat at each point is proportional to the magnitude of $\mathbf{grad}\, T$. We can therefore say that

$$\text{heat flow} \propto -\mathbf{grad}\, T.$$

Similar results apply when pressure P or molecular concentration C vary in space. Again, flows arise that tend to reduce these spatial variations, and which are proportional to $-\mathbf{grad}\, P$ and $-\mathbf{grad}\, C$.

Gradients are also important in mechanics. Physicists use a concept called *potential energy*. For example, close to the Earth's surface, the gravitational potential energy of an object of mass m is $V = mgz$, where g is a constant and z is the object's height above the ground. Whenever we are given a potential energy field $V(x, y, z)$, we can deduce the corresponding force by taking minus its gradient. In the case of terrestrial gravity,

$$\mathbf{F} = -\mathbf{grad}\,(mgz) = -mg\,\mathbf{k},$$

which is a constant force that acts vertically downwards (Figure 25).

2.2 Gradients in non-Cartesian coordinates

In situations where there is axial or spherical symmetry it is usually best to describe a scalar field in polar, cylindrical or spherical coordinates. In this subsection we explain how to derive the corresponding gradient vector fields, also in polar, cylindrical or spherical coordinates.

We therefore consider a general three-dimensional coordinate system with coordinates (u, v, w) and corresponding unit vectors $\mathbf{e}_u$, $\mathbf{e}_v$ and $\mathbf{e}_w$. We assume that the coordinate system is orthogonal, which means that these three unit vectors are mutually orthogonal. If you want to keep a specific example in mind, you can imagine that (u, v, w) stand for (r, θ, ϕ) of spherical coordinates, but the strength of our argument is that (u, v, w) can represent any orthogonal coordinate system.

If we are given a scalar field V, this can be expressed either in Cartesian coordinates or in the (u, v, w) coordinate system. If (x, y, z) and (u, v, w)

label the same point, we can write

$$V(x, y, z) = V(u, v, w).$$

The gradient of V is a vector field, which can be expressed in Cartesian coordinates as

$$\nabla V = \frac{\partial V}{\partial x}\mathbf{i} + \frac{\partial V}{\partial y}\mathbf{j} + \frac{\partial V}{\partial z}\mathbf{k}. \tag{34}$$

The same vector field can also be expressed in the (u, v, w) coordinate system. We do not know the components of ∇V in this system, but we can write

$$\nabla V = g_u\, \mathbf{e}_u + g_v\, \mathbf{e}_v + g_w\, \mathbf{e}_w,$$

where the components g_u, g_v and g_w remain to be determined.

Now, the crucial step is to recall that the gradient of a *scalar field* is a *vector field* – a field whose vector values at each point are independent of the orientation of the coordinate system. This means that we can use Procedure 1 to write, for example,

$$g_u = \mathbf{e}_u \cdot \nabla V.$$

We then evaluate this scalar product using Cartesian expressions for $\mathbf{e}_u$ and ∇V. In Subsection 1.5 you saw that there is a general expression for $\mathbf{e}_u$. According to equation (27),

$$\mathbf{e}_u = \frac{1}{h_u}\left(\frac{\partial x}{\partial u}\mathbf{i} + \frac{\partial y}{\partial u}\mathbf{j} + \frac{\partial z}{\partial u}\mathbf{k}\right),$$

where h_u is the scale factor for the u-coordinate. Combining this with the Cartesian expression for ∇V given in equation (34), we get

$$g_u = \frac{1}{h_u}\left(\frac{\partial x}{\partial u}\mathbf{i} + \frac{\partial y}{\partial u}\mathbf{j} + \frac{\partial z}{\partial u}\mathbf{k}\right) \cdot \left(\frac{\partial V}{\partial x}\mathbf{i} + \frac{\partial V}{\partial y}\mathbf{j} + \frac{\partial V}{\partial z}\mathbf{k}\right)$$

$$= \frac{1}{h_u}\left(\frac{\partial V}{\partial x}\frac{\partial x}{\partial u} + \frac{\partial V}{\partial y}\frac{\partial y}{\partial u} + \frac{\partial V}{\partial z}\frac{\partial z}{\partial u}\right).$$

Finally, the term in brackets can now be simplified using a version of the chain rule (given in Unit 7, equation (24)). We conclude that

$$g_u = \frac{1}{h_u}\frac{\partial V}{\partial u},$$

and there are similar results for the other two components, g_v and g_w. We therefore reach the following very useful conclusion.

Gradient in a general orthogonal coordinate system

Given an orthogonal coordinate system (u, v, w) with unit vectors $\mathbf{e}_u$, $\mathbf{e}_v$ and $\mathbf{e}_w$, and scale factors h_u, h_v and h_w, the gradient of a scalar field $V(u, v, w)$ is

$$\nabla V = \frac{1}{h_u}\frac{\partial V}{\partial u}\mathbf{e}_u + \frac{1}{h_v}\frac{\partial V}{\partial v}\mathbf{e}_v + \frac{1}{h_w}\frac{\partial V}{\partial w}\mathbf{e}_w. \tag{35}$$

For a scalar field $V(u, v)$ in two dimensions, the same formula applies, but with the last term (involving $\mathbf{e}_w$) omitted.

This remarkable result applies in all orthogonal coordinate systems. This includes the Cartesian, polar, cylindrical and spherical coordinates studied in this module, as well as other orthogonal coordinate systems that are in occasional use.

In two- and three-dimensional Cartesian coordinate systems, the scale factors are all equal to 1, and equation (35) gives

$$\nabla V = \frac{\partial V}{\partial x}\,\mathbf{e}_x + \frac{\partial V}{\partial y}\,\mathbf{e}_y \quad \text{in two dimensions,}$$

$$\nabla V = \frac{\partial V}{\partial x}\,\mathbf{e}_x + \frac{\partial V}{\partial y}\,\mathbf{e}_y + \frac{\partial V}{\partial z}\,\mathbf{e}_z \quad \text{in three dimensions.}$$

Here, of course, $\mathbf{e}_x$, $\mathbf{e}_y$ and $\mathbf{e}_z$ are Cartesian unit vectors in the x-, y- and z-directions, more usually written as $\mathbf{i}$, $\mathbf{j}$ and $\mathbf{k}$. So we recover the definition of gradient in Cartesian coordinates in equations (30) and (31).

In polar, cylindrical or spherical coordinates, the key to using equation (35) is to know the appropriate scale factors. These were given in Unit 8 in the context of finding area or volume elements for multiple integrals. For ease of reference, the results are summarised below.

Table 1   Scale factors of common coordinate systems

Coordinate system		Scale factors
Polar coordinates	(r, ϕ)	$h_r = 1,\ h_\phi = r$
Cylindrical coordinates	(r, ϕ, z)	$h_r = 1,\ h_\phi = r,\ h_z = 1$
Spherical coordinates	(r, θ, ϕ)	$h_r = 1,\ h_\theta = r,\ h_\phi = r\sin\theta$

Using Table 1 and equation (35), we can immediately write down the expression for gradient in polar coordinates. With $h_r = 1$ and $h_\phi = r$, we get

$$\nabla V = \frac{\partial V}{\partial r}\,\mathbf{e}_r + \frac{1}{r}\frac{\partial V}{\partial \phi}\,\mathbf{e}_\phi. \tag{36}$$

You can use this formula to find the gradient of any scalar field given in polar coordinates.

Example 5

The domains of V and ∇V exclude the origin $r = 0$.

Exercise 11 considered the scalar field $V(x, y) = \ln(\sqrt{x^2 + y^2})$ in Cartesian coordinates. In polar coordinates, this field takes the form $V(r, \phi) = \ln(r)$. Find the gradient of $V(r, \phi)$ in polar coordinates.

Solution

The partial derivatives of $V(r, \phi) = \ln(r)$ are

$$\frac{\partial V}{\partial r} = \frac{1}{r} \quad \text{and} \quad \frac{\partial V}{\partial \phi} = 0,$$

so for this scalar field,

$$\boldsymbol{\nabla} V = \frac{1}{r}\,\mathbf{e}_r + \frac{1}{r}\,0\,\mathbf{e}_\phi = \frac{1}{r}\,\mathbf{e}_r \quad (r \neq 0).$$

This gradient field has magnitude $1/r$ and points radially outwards, away from the origin. This answer agrees with that of Exercise 11, but has been obtained more efficiently.

Using Table 1 and equation (35), we can also find expressions for gradient in cylindrical coordinates and spherical coordinates.

In *cylindrical coordinates*, the scale factors are $h_r = 1$, $h_\phi = r$ and $h_z = 1$, so

$$\boldsymbol{\nabla} V = \frac{\partial V}{\partial r}\,\mathbf{e}_r + \frac{1}{r}\frac{\partial V}{\partial \phi}\,\mathbf{e}_\phi + \frac{\partial V}{\partial z}\,\mathbf{e}_z. \tag{37}$$

In *spherical coordinates*, the scale factors are $h_r = 1$, $h_\theta = r$ and $h_\phi = r\sin\theta$, so

$$\boldsymbol{\nabla} V = \frac{\partial V}{\partial r}\,\mathbf{e}_r + \frac{1}{r}\frac{\partial V}{\partial \theta}\,\mathbf{e}_\theta + \frac{1}{r\sin\theta}\frac{\partial V}{\partial \phi}\,\mathbf{e}_\phi. \tag{38}$$

You should not bother to memorise these results, as it is easier to recall the general shape of equation (35) and the relevant scale factors.

Exercise 15

Exercise 12 considered the scalar field $V(x, y, z) = 1/(x^2 + y^2 + z^2)^{3/2}$ in Cartesian coordinates. In spherical coordinates, this field takes the form

The domains of V and $\boldsymbol{\nabla} V$ exclude the origin $r = 0$.

$$V(r, \theta, \phi) = \frac{1}{r^3}.$$

Calculate the gradient of $V(r, \theta, \phi)$ in spherical coordinates.

Exercise 16

In cylindrical coordinates, a scalar field takes the form

$$f(r, \phi, z) = r^2 \sin(2\phi) + z^2.$$

Calculate the gradient $\boldsymbol{\nabla} f$, and hence find the magnitude of the gradient at any point.

Exercise 17

In spherical coordinates, a scalar field takes the form

$$T(r, \theta, \phi) = r \sin\theta.$$

(a) Find the corresponding gradient vector field.

(b) Find the rate of change of T with distance in the direction of the unit vector $\hat{\mathbf{n}} = (\mathbf{e}_\theta + \mathbf{e}_\phi)/\sqrt{2}$.

2.3 The del operator

The process that leads from a scalar field to a gradient field can be described using a concept called the *del operator*. For the moment, this just repackages what you already know, but you will soon see that the del operator is useful in other contexts.

Essentially, an *operator* is something that 'acts on things to produce other things'. For example, a particular rotation operator may represent a rotation by $30°$ about the z-axis; when this operator acts on any position vector, it produces another position vector.

We are interested in operators that act on functions to produce other functions. An example is the differentiation operator d/dx. This acts on any differentiable function $f(x)$ to produce another function, $f'(x)$.

In Cartesian coordinates, the **del operator** is defined by

$$\boldsymbol{\nabla} = \frac{\partial}{\partial x}\,\mathbf{i} + \frac{\partial}{\partial y}\,\mathbf{j} + \frac{\partial}{\partial z}\,\mathbf{k}. \tag{39}$$

When this operator acts on a scalar field $V(x, y, x)$ expressed in Cartesian coordinates, it produces the gradient vector field

$$\boldsymbol{\nabla}V = \frac{\partial V}{\partial x}\,\mathbf{i} + \frac{\partial V}{\partial y}\,\mathbf{j} + \frac{\partial V}{\partial z}\,\mathbf{k},$$

in agreement with equation (30).

When the del operator acts on a given scalar field, it produces a definite gradient vector field. However, the scalar field and the resulting gradient vector field can be described in various coordinate systems. The form chosen to represent the del operator also depends on the coordinate system used. In an orthogonal coordinate system (u, v, w) with unit vectors $\mathbf{e}_u$, $\mathbf{e}_v$, $\mathbf{e}_w$ and scale factors h_u, h_v, h_w, the del operator is given by

$$\boldsymbol{\nabla} = \mathbf{e}_u\,\frac{1}{h_u}\,\frac{\partial}{\partial u} + \mathbf{e}_v\,\frac{1}{h_v}\,\frac{\partial}{\partial v} + \mathbf{e}_w\,\frac{1}{h_w}\,\frac{\partial}{\partial w}. \tag{40}$$

When this operator acts on a scalar field $V(u, v, w)$ expressed in (u, v, w) coordinates, it produces the gradient vector field

$$\boldsymbol{\nabla}V = \mathbf{e}_u\,\frac{1}{h_u}\,\frac{\partial V}{\partial u} + \mathbf{e}_v\,\frac{1}{h_v}\,\frac{\partial V}{\partial v} + \mathbf{e}_w\,\frac{1}{h_w}\,\frac{\partial V}{\partial w},$$

in agreement with equation (35).

Notice that the unit vectors in equation (40) have been placed to the left of the partial derivative operators $\partial/\partial u$, $\partial/\partial v$ and $\partial/\partial w$. This is a necessary precaution because the unit vectors generally depend on the coordinates (u, v, w). If they were placed to the right of the partial derivative operators, we would need to differentiate them, and this would not give the correct gradient vector field. Cartesian coordinates are a special case because the unit vectors $\mathbf{i}$, $\mathbf{j}$ and $\mathbf{k}$ are all constant vectors, so they can be placed either to the left or to the right of $\partial/\partial x$, $\partial/\partial y$ and $\partial/\partial z$.

Because the del operator contains unit vectors, it should be thought of as having a vectorial (rather than scalar) character. It is sometimes described as being a *vector differential operator*. That is why it is printed in bold. In written work, you should underline it with a wavy or straight line.

Exercise 18

Use equation (40) and the scale factors of Table 1 to express the del operator in polar coordinates, cylindrical coordinates and spherical coordinates.

3   The divergence of a vector field

For a scalar field $V(x, y, z)$, the three partial derivatives

$$\frac{\partial V}{\partial x}, \quad \frac{\partial V}{\partial y}, \quad \frac{\partial V}{\partial z}$$

describe its spatial rates of change in the x-, y- and z-directions. However, you have seen that it is useful to group these three partial derivatives together to form the gradient field ∇V. Rather than thinking about the separate partial derivatives, we can think about the gradient field, which has a magnitude and direction at each point. This is a powerful idea – you have seen that the gradient field allows us to calculate the spatial rate of change of V in *any* direction (not just the coordinate directions).

The rest of this unit discusses the spatial rates of change of *vector fields*. A three-dimensional vector field $\mathbf{F}(x, y, z)$ has three components, F_x, F_y and F_z, so there are nine partial derivatives to consider at each point:

$$\frac{\partial F_x}{\partial x}, \frac{\partial F_x}{\partial y}, \frac{\partial F_x}{\partial z}, \quad \frac{\partial F_y}{\partial x}, \frac{\partial F_y}{\partial y}, \frac{\partial F_y}{\partial z}, \quad \frac{\partial F_z}{\partial x}, \frac{\partial F_z}{\partial y}, \frac{\partial F_z}{\partial z}.$$

This is a great deal of information, making it hard to visualise what is going on. Fortunately, the nine partial derivatives can be grouped into two significant quantities – called the *divergence* and the *curl* of the vector field. In most cases, these two quantities tell us all we need to know about the spatial rates of change of a vector field.

The fact that the del operator ∇ has a vectorial character suggests two ways of grouping the partial derivatives. Given two vectors $\mathbf{a}$ and $\mathbf{b}$, we can define two different types of product. The scalar product is

$$\mathbf{a} \cdot \mathbf{b} = a_x b_x + a_y b_y + a_z b_z,$$

and the vector product is

$$\mathbf{a} \times \mathbf{b} = (a_y b_z - a_z b_y)\, \mathbf{i} + (a_z b_x - a_x b_z)\, \mathbf{j} + (a_x b_y - a_y b_x)\, \mathbf{k}.$$

For the del operator $\boldsymbol{\nabla}$ acting on a vector field $\mathbf{F}(x, y, z)$, we can introduce the corresponding combinations

$$\boldsymbol{\nabla} \cdot \mathbf{F} = \frac{\partial F_x}{\partial x} + \frac{\partial F_y}{\partial y} + \frac{\partial F_z}{\partial z}$$

and

$$\boldsymbol{\nabla} \times \mathbf{F} = \left(\frac{\partial F_z}{\partial y} - \frac{\partial F_y}{\partial z} \right) \mathbf{i} + \left(\frac{\partial F_x}{\partial z} - \frac{\partial F_z}{\partial x} \right) \mathbf{j} + \left(\frac{\partial F_y}{\partial x} - \frac{\partial F_x}{\partial y} \right) \mathbf{k}.$$

It turns out that these are precisely the combinations that we need: $\boldsymbol{\nabla} \cdot \mathbf{F}$ is called the **divergence** of $\mathbf{F}$, and $\boldsymbol{\nabla} \times \mathbf{F}$ is called the **curl** of $\mathbf{F}$. This section discusses divergence, while Section 4 discusses curl.

3.1   Divergence in Cartesian coordinates

The above discussion gave a broad overview. Here we begin afresh with the basic definition of divergence in Cartesian coordinates.

> **Divergence of a vector field in Cartesian coordinates**
>
> Suppose that a vector field $\mathbf{F}$ is expressed in Cartesian coordinates as
>
> $$\mathbf{F} = F_x \mathbf{i} + F_y \mathbf{j} + F_z \mathbf{k}.$$
>
> Then the divergence of $\mathbf{F}$ is defined as
>
> $$\boldsymbol{\nabla} \cdot \mathbf{F} = \frac{\partial F_x}{\partial x} + \frac{\partial F_y}{\partial y} + \frac{\partial F_z}{\partial z}. \tag{41}$$
>
> The alternative notation $\operatorname{div} \mathbf{F}$ is sometimes used for divergence, so we can also write
>
> $$\operatorname{div} \mathbf{F} = \frac{\partial F_x}{\partial x} + \frac{\partial F_y}{\partial y} + \frac{\partial F_z}{\partial z}. \tag{42}$$

Two questions naturally arise: how is divergence calculated, and what does divergence tell us? We begin with the calculations, and then discuss the interpretation.

Calculating divergence

It is easy to calculate the divergence of a vector field $\mathbf{F}$ in Cartesian coordinates. All you need to do is to identify the Cartesian components F_x, F_y and F_z of the field, find their partial derivatives with respect to the corresponding coordinates x, y and z, and add the results together.

We begin with two-dimensional vector fields because they are simpler to visualise.

Example 6

Find the divergence of each of the following vector fields:

$$\mathbf{A} = 3\mathbf{i} + 2\mathbf{j}, \quad \mathbf{B} = y\mathbf{i} - x\mathbf{j}, \quad \mathbf{C} = x\mathbf{i} + y\mathbf{j}, \quad \mathbf{D} = x^2\mathbf{i} - y^2\mathbf{j}.$$

Solution

Using the definition of divergence (equation (41)), we get

$$\boldsymbol{\nabla}\cdot\mathbf{A} = \frac{\partial(3)}{\partial x} + \frac{\partial(2)}{\partial y} + \frac{\partial(0)}{\partial z} = 0,$$

$$\boldsymbol{\nabla}\cdot\mathbf{B} = \frac{\partial(y)}{\partial x} + \frac{\partial(-x)}{\partial y} + \frac{\partial(0)}{\partial z} = 0,$$

$$\boldsymbol{\nabla}\cdot\mathbf{C} = \frac{\partial(x)}{\partial x} + \frac{\partial(y)}{\partial y} + \frac{\partial(0)}{\partial z} = 2,$$

$$\boldsymbol{\nabla}\cdot\mathbf{D} = \frac{\partial(x^2)}{\partial x} + \frac{\partial(-y^2)}{\partial y} + \frac{\partial(0)}{\partial z} = 2(x-y).$$

This example illustrates some cases that can arise. For vector fields $\mathbf{A}$ and $\mathbf{B}$, the divergence is equal to zero everywhere. The vector field $\mathbf{C}$ has a constant non-zero divergence, and $\mathbf{D}$ has a divergence that varies with position, which is the most usual situation. The divergence is always a scalar function of position (which may be a constant or zero).

It is important to understand the distinction between gradient and divergence. Given a scalar field V, we can construct its gradient $\boldsymbol{\nabla}V$, which has vector values:

$$\boldsymbol{\nabla}V = \frac{\partial V}{\partial x}\mathbf{i} + \frac{\partial V}{\partial y}\mathbf{j} + \frac{\partial V}{\partial z}\mathbf{k}.$$

Given a vector field $\mathbf{F}$, we can construct its divergence $\boldsymbol{\nabla}\cdot\mathbf{F}$, which has scalar values:

$$\boldsymbol{\nabla}\cdot\mathbf{F} = \frac{\partial F_x}{\partial x} + \frac{\partial F_y}{\partial y} + \frac{\partial F_z}{\partial z}.$$

The gradient is a vector, so its expression involves unit vectors. By contrast, divergence is a scalar, and its expression is just a sum of derivatives with no unit vectors. When you specify $\boldsymbol{\nabla}\cdot\mathbf{F}$ in handwriting, you must underline both $\boldsymbol{\nabla}$ and $\mathbf{F}$ *and* include a dot between them – otherwise your reader may think that you are referring to the gradient of a scalar field F.

Exercise 19

Calculate the divergence of each of the following vector fields.

(a) $\mathbf{F}(x,y,z) = x^2 y\,\mathbf{i} + y^2 z\,\mathbf{j} - yz^2\,\mathbf{k}$

(b) $\mathbf{G}(x,y,z) = (x+y)^2\,\mathbf{i} + (y+z)^2\,\mathbf{j} + (x+z)^2\,\mathbf{k}$

Exercise 20

A scalar field V takes the form $V = x^4 + y^4 + z^4$.

(a) Would it make sense to take the divergence of this field?

(b) Find the gradient field $\boldsymbol{\nabla}V$, and calculate its divergence, $\boldsymbol{\nabla}\cdot(\boldsymbol{\nabla}V)$.

Interpreting divergence

At any given point (x, y, z), the divergence of a vector field has a definite scalar value. In fact, we can go further.

> It turns out that the divergence of a vector field is a *scalar field*.

This is a important fact. Recalling the definition of a scalar field given in Subsection 1.1, it means that the value of the divergence at any given point is *independent of the orientation of the coordinate system*. This suggests that the divergence of a vector field might describe some significant property of the vector field. Indeed it does, and the name *divergence* provides a clue.

> **Intuitive meaning of divergence**
>
> The divergence of a vector field $\mathbf{F}$ describes the extent to which $\mathbf{F}$ flows outwards or diverges from each point.

This statement is not precise. Deciding how to quantify the 'extent of outward flow' and linking this to the definition of divergence in equation (41) involves a lengthy discussion, and the details are left for the next unit. For the moment, we just consider a few typical examples. The aim is to give you an intuitive feeling for divergence so that you can interpret the results of your calculations.

In fact, $\mathbf{J}$ is the fluid density times the fluid velocity at each point. In this context, $\mathbf{J}$ is not the Jacobian vector of Unit 8.

Consider a vector field $\mathbf{J}(x, y, z)$ that describes the flow of mass in a fluid. The fluid could be water or air, and it may have a fixed or variable density. The precise definition of $\mathbf{J}$ is not needed in this informal discussion.

The cube should be tiny: strictly speaking, we are interested in the limiting case where its size tends to zero.

At a point P, the value of $\boldsymbol{\nabla} \cdot \mathbf{J}$ tells us about the net flow of fluid towards or away from P. If we draw a tiny cube around P, then the divergence of $\mathbf{J}$ at P is:

- positive if more fluid leaves the cube than enters it
- negative if more fluid enters the cube than leaves it
- equal to zero if the outflow exactly matches the inflow.

Similar remarks apply to two-dimensional velocity fields, but with the cube replaced by a square.

These ideas can be illustrated with the vector fields of Example 6. Arrow maps for the fields $\mathbf{A} = 3\mathbf{i} + 2\mathbf{j}$ and $\mathbf{B} = y\mathbf{i} - x\mathbf{j}$ are shown in Figure 26, with selected points indicated by blue dots and small blue squares drawn around them. Example 6 showed that these fields have zero divergence everywhere. So according to our interpretation of divergence, there should be no net flow into or out of these squares. So far as it is possible to tell, the arrow maps confirm this interpretation.

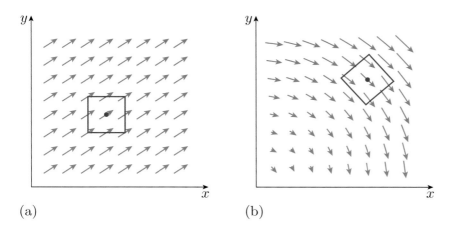

(a)   (b)

Figure 26   Arrow maps for the vector fields **A** and **B** of Example 6

Arrow maps for the vector fields $\mathbf{C} = x\,\mathbf{i} + y\,\mathbf{j}$ and $\mathbf{D} = x^2\,\mathbf{i} - y^2\,\mathbf{j}$ of Example 6 are shown in Figure 27. Example 6 showed that **C** has a divergence that is equal to 2 everywhere. This positive divergence corresponds to the fact that there is a net flow out of the blue square in Figure 27(a). The vector field **D** has a divergence equal to $2(x - y)$, which is positive for $x > y$ and negative for $x < y$. Our interpretation of divergence is supported by Figure 27(b), which shows a net flow out of the lower square, and a net flow into the upper square.

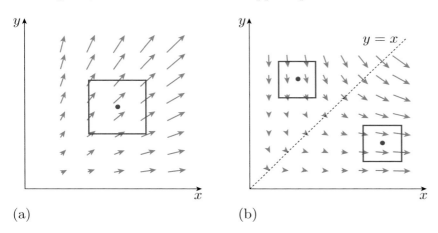

(a)   (b)

Figure 27   Arrow maps for the vector fields **C** and **D** of Example 6

Exercise 21

(a) Calculate the divergence of the vector field

$$\mathbf{F} = \frac{x}{\sqrt{x^2 + y^2}}\,\mathbf{i} + \frac{y}{\sqrt{x^2 + y^2}}\,\mathbf{j} \quad ((x, y) \neq (0, 0)).$$

(b) The arrow map for **F** is shown in the margin. Use the square $ABCD$ to show that this diagram supports our interpretation of divergence.

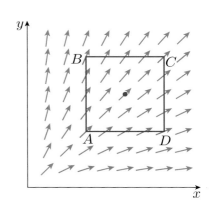

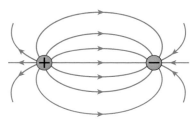

Figure 28   The electric field around positive and negative charge distributions

Divergences of vector fields in the real world

Not all vector fields describe flows. A *gravitational field*, for example, quantifies the gravitational influence of massive objects. The divergence of a gravitational field turns out to be negative at points occupied by matter (inside the Earth, for example, or inside the Sun). In empty space, the divergence of a gravitational field is equal to zero.

A similar situation applies to *electric fields* (Figure 28). The divergence of an electric field is positive at points where there is positive charge, and negative at points where there is negative charge. In empty space, the divergence of an electric field is equal to zero.

Magnetic fields are unusual: so far as we know, the divergence of any magnetic field is equal to zero everywhere.

3.2   Divergence in non-Cartesian coordinates

You have seen that some vector fields are best described in non-Cartesian coordinate systems. For example, the gravitational field around the Sun points radially inwards towards the Sun, and is most naturally described in spherical coordinates. We often have to calculate the divergence of such vector fields, so we need to know how to calculate divergence in non-Cartesian coordinates. Polar, cylindrical and spherical coordinates are all important in applications. All of these are orthogonal coordinate systems.

In an orthogonal system of coordinates (u, v, w) with unit vectors $\mathbf{e}_u$, $\mathbf{e}_v$ and $\mathbf{e}_w$, a vector field $\mathbf{F}$ can be expressed as

$$\mathbf{F} = F_u\,\mathbf{e}_u + F_v\,\mathbf{e}_v + F_w\,\mathbf{e}_w,$$

and the del operator is given by

$$\boldsymbol{\nabla} = \mathbf{e}_u\,\frac{1}{h_u}\,\frac{\partial}{\partial u} + \mathbf{e}_v\,\frac{1}{h_v}\,\frac{\partial}{\partial v} + \mathbf{e}_w\,\frac{1}{h_w}\,\frac{\partial}{\partial w}.$$

It follows that the divergence of $\mathbf{F}$ in the (u, v, w) coordinate system is

$$\boldsymbol{\nabla} \cdot \mathbf{F} = \left(\mathbf{e}_u\,\frac{1}{h_u}\,\frac{\partial}{\partial u} + \mathbf{e}_v\,\frac{1}{h_v}\,\frac{\partial}{\partial v} + \mathbf{e}_w\,\frac{1}{h_w}\,\frac{\partial}{\partial w} \right) \cdot (F_u\,\mathbf{e}_u + F_v\,\mathbf{e}_v + F_w\,\mathbf{e}_w).$$

This formula is correct, but is not immediately useful because there are still partial derivatives and scalar products to evaluate. The situation is complicated by the fact that unit vectors such as $\mathbf{e}_u$ may depend on the coordinates (u, v, w). So when the partial differentials act on the right-hand bracket, the unit vectors $\mathbf{e}_u$, $\mathbf{e}_v$ and $\mathbf{e}_w$ must be differentiated as well as the components F_u, F_v and F_w. The calculations get very messy!

In practice, scientists and mathematicians do not spend time deriving general formulas for divergence in non-Cartesian coordinates. Life is too short, so they simply look up the results they need in reference works.

We take a similar attitude. The Appendix to this unit justifies the expressions that we will use, but this is optional material, and will not be assessed or examined. We focus here on the more important (and more straightforward) task of stating and applying standard formulas.

Equation (35) gave a general formula for the gradient of a scalar field in any orthogonal coordinate system. Rather wonderfully, in spite of the complications noted above, there is a corresponding formula for the divergence of a vector field in any orthogonal coordinate system.

Divergence of a vector field in orthogonal coordinates

In any orthogonal coordinate system (u, v, w) with scale factors h_u, h_v and h_w, a vector field $\mathbf{F}$ has divergence

$$\mathbf{\nabla} \cdot \mathbf{F} = \frac{1}{J} \left[\frac{\partial}{\partial u} \left(\frac{J F_u}{h_u} \right) + \frac{\partial}{\partial v} \left(\frac{J F_v}{h_v} \right) + \frac{\partial}{\partial w} \left(\frac{J F_w}{h_w} \right) \right], \quad (43)$$

where

$$J = h_u h_v h_w$$

is the product of the scale factors, called the **Jacobian factor**.

In a two-dimensional orthogonal system (u, v), the same formula applies, but with the last term omitted, and $J = h_u h_v$.

J also appeared in Unit 8 in the context of volume integrals.

It is easy to check that this formula gives the correct result in Cartesian coordinates $(u, v, w) = (x, y, z)$. In this case, all the scale factors are equal to 1, so $J = 1$ and equation (43) reduces to

$$\mathbf{\nabla} \cdot \mathbf{F} = \frac{\partial F_x}{\partial x} + \frac{\partial F_y}{\partial y} + \frac{\partial F_z}{\partial z},$$

as expected.

In polar coordinates $(u, v) = (r, \phi)$, the scale factors are $h_r = 1$ and $h_\phi = r$, so $J = r$. In this case, equation (43) gives the following formula.

These scale factors are given in Table 1.

Divergence in polar coordinates

$$\mathbf{\nabla} \cdot \mathbf{F} = \frac{1}{r} \frac{\partial (r F_r)}{\partial r} + \frac{1}{r} \frac{\partial F_\phi}{\partial \phi}. \quad (44)$$

When there is rotational symmetry, it is often best to specify two-dimensional vector fields in polar coordinates, and to calculate their divergences using equation (44).

Example 7

Find the divergences of the following two-dimensional vector fields, expressed in polar coordinates.

(a) $\mathbf{F}(r, \phi) = \mathbf{e}_r \ (r \neq 0)$

(b) $\mathbf{G}(r, \phi) = r\,\mathbf{e}_r + r \sin \phi\,\mathbf{e}_\phi$

Solution

(a) The polar components of **F** are $F_r = 1$ and $F_\phi = 0$, so

$$\nabla \cdot \mathbf{F} = \frac{1}{r}\frac{\partial(r)}{\partial r} = \frac{1}{r} \quad (r \neq 0).$$

This is the same field as that in Exercise 21. The calculation is much easier in polar, rather than Cartesian coordinates!

(b) The polar components of **G** are $G_r = r$ and $G_\phi = r \sin\phi$, so

$$\nabla \cdot \mathbf{G} = \frac{1}{r}\frac{\partial(r^2)}{\partial r} + \frac{1}{r}\frac{\partial(r \sin\phi)}{\partial \phi} = 2 + \cos\phi.$$

Similar methods apply in three dimensions. In *cylindrical coordinates* $(u, v, w) = (r, \phi, z)$, the scale factors are $h_r = 1$, $h_\phi = r$ and $h_z = 1$, so $J = r$. In this case, equation (43) gives

$$\nabla \cdot \mathbf{F} = \frac{1}{r}\left(\frac{\partial(r F_r)}{\partial r} + \frac{\partial F_\phi}{\partial \phi} + \frac{\partial(r F_z)}{\partial z}\right).$$

Since r is treated as a constant when partially differentiating with respect to z, we have the following result.

Divergence in cylindrical coordinates

$$\nabla \cdot \mathbf{F} = \frac{1}{r}\frac{\partial(r F_r)}{\partial r} + \frac{1}{r}\frac{\partial F_\phi}{\partial \phi} + \frac{\partial F_z}{\partial z}. \tag{45}$$

Not surprisingly, this is similar to the expression for divergence in polar coordinates, but with an additional term, $\partial F_z / \partial z$.

In *spherical coordinates*, the scale factors are $h_r = 1$, $h_\theta = r$ and $h_\phi = r \sin\theta$, so $J = r^2 \sin\theta$. Hence

$$\nabla \cdot \mathbf{F} = \frac{1}{r^2 \sin\theta}\left(\frac{\partial(r^2 \sin\theta \, F_r)}{\partial r} + \frac{\partial(r \sin\theta \, F_\theta)}{\partial \theta} + \frac{\partial(r F_\phi)}{\partial \phi}\right).$$

Remembering that functions of one variable are treated as constants when partially differentiating with respect to another variable, we get the following formula.

Divergence in spherical coordinates

$$\nabla \cdot \mathbf{F} = \frac{1}{r^2}\frac{\partial(r^2 F_r)}{\partial r} + \frac{1}{r \sin\theta}\frac{\partial(\sin\theta \, F_\theta)}{\partial \theta} + \frac{1}{r \sin\theta}\frac{\partial F_\phi}{\partial \phi}. \tag{46}$$

You can take all these results on trust. Equations (44)–(46) are all listed in the Handbook, so you need not memorise them for the exam. For more general purposes, it is worth trying to remember equation (43), which has a more symmetrical shape than the others, and can be used to construct them all.

The focus here is on *using* equations (44)–(46) to find the divergences of given vector fields. You will generally be told which coordinate system is used, so you just need to select the appropriate formula for divergence, carry out the partial differentiations, and simplify the result if possible.

Exercise 22

The following fields are in cylindrical coordinates. Find their divergences.

(a) $\mathbf{F}(r, \phi, z) = 4r^3 \, \mathbf{e}_r$ (b) $\mathbf{G}(r, \phi, z) = r^2 \sin \phi \, \mathbf{e}_r + z^2 \, \mathbf{e}_z$

It is essential to state which coordinate system is used because the coordinate r has different meanings in the cylindrical and spherical systems.

Exercise 23

The following fields are in spherical coordinates. Find their divergences.

(a) $\mathbf{F}(r, \theta, \phi) = 4r^3 \, \mathbf{e}_r$ (b) $\mathbf{G}(r, \theta, \phi) = r \sin^2 \theta \, \mathbf{e}_\theta + r \cos \theta \cos \phi \, \mathbf{e}_\phi$

Exercise 24

In spherical coordinates, a vector field $\mathbf{F}$ takes the form $\mathbf{F} = f(r) \, \mathbf{e}_r$, where $f(r)$ depends only on r, the distance from the origin. If div $\mathbf{F} = 0$ at all points except the origin, show that $f(r)$ is proportional to $1/r^2$.

---

4   The curl of a vector field

The second important quantity describing the spatial rate of change of a vector field $\mathbf{F}$ is its curl. In this section, we introduce curl in Cartesian coordinates and illustrate its physical meaning with some typical vector fields. We also show how curl is calculated in non-Cartesian orthogonal coordinate systems.

4.1   Curl in Cartesian coordinates

We briefly mentioned curl when considering ways in which the operator ∇ can act on vector fields. Here we begin afresh with the basic definition.

Curl of a vector field in Cartesian coordinates

Suppose that a vector field $\mathbf{F}$ is expressed in Cartesian coordinates as

$$\mathbf{F} = F_x \, \mathbf{i} + F_y \, \mathbf{j} + F_z \, \mathbf{k}.$$

Then the curl of $\mathbf{F}$ is defined as

$$\nabla \times \mathbf{F} = \begin{vmatrix} \mathbf{i} & \mathbf{j} & \mathbf{k} \\ \dfrac{\partial}{\partial x} & \dfrac{\partial}{\partial y} & \dfrac{\partial}{\partial z} \\ F_x & F_y & F_z \end{vmatrix}. \tag{47}$$

The alternative notation **curl F** is commonly used.

As always when dealing with vector products, we assume that the coordinate system is right-handed.

In this definition, the partial derivative operators in the second row act on the components in the third row. The determinant can then be expanded in the usual way. For example, the term involving **i** is

$$\mathbf{i}\left(\frac{\partial}{\partial y}F_z - \frac{\partial}{\partial z}F_y\right) = \left(\frac{\partial F_z}{\partial y} - \frac{\partial F_y}{\partial z}\right)\mathbf{i}.$$

The complete expansion gives the vector quantity

$$\nabla \times \mathbf{F} = \left(\frac{\partial F_z}{\partial y} - \frac{\partial F_y}{\partial z}\right)\mathbf{i} + \left(\frac{\partial F_x}{\partial z} - \frac{\partial F_z}{\partial x}\right)\mathbf{j} + \left(\frac{\partial F_y}{\partial x} - \frac{\partial F_x}{\partial y}\right)\mathbf{k}. \quad (48)$$

It is worth comparing the definitions of divergence and curl in equations (41) and (48). The derivatives that occur in divergence may be said to 'go with the components' – for example, $\partial/\partial x$ acts on F_x, and so on. Curl is quite different: it is built up of partial derivatives such as $\partial F_x/\partial y$ and $\partial F_y/\partial x$ that describe how rapidly a component in one direction changes when we move in a *perpendicular* direction. In three dimensions, there are six such derivatives, and these are arranged in pairs to give the components of $\nabla \times \mathbf{F}$ shown in equation (48).

We will calculate curls shortly. This is a straightforward task – we just need to calculate and combine the appropriate partial derivatives. Before doing this, let us see what curl means. Clearly, at any given point, $\nabla \times \mathbf{F}$ has a definite value. In fact, we can go further.

By contrast, the divergence of a vector field is a scalar field.

It turns out that the curl of a vector field is another *vector field*.

From the definition of a vector field (see Subsection 1.1), this implies that at any given point, the magnitude and direction of $\nabla \times \mathbf{F}$ are *independent of the orientation of the coordinate system*. This suggests that $\nabla \times \mathbf{F}$ might have some significant physical meaning. This is indeed the case, and the name *curl* provides a good clue.

Intuitive meaning of curl

The curl of a vector field **F** describes the extent to which **F** rotates or swirls locally about each point.

In three-dimensional space, rotation involves an axis of rotation and a sense of rotation about that axis. Taking the coordinate system to be right-handed, these features are related to curl in a simple and direct way.

- The axis of local rotation is along the direction of the curl vector.
- The sense of rotation around this axis is found by the **right-hand grip rule** illustrated in Figure 29. With the thumb of your right hand pointing in the direction of $\nabla \times \mathbf{F}$, the fingers of your closed right hand indicate the sense of rotation associated with **F**.

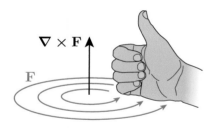

Figure 29   The right-hand grip rule

Establishing a precise link between the concept of 'local rotation' and the definition of curl is left for the next unit. For the moment, we just consider a few typical examples. The aim is to give you an intuitive feeling for curl so that you can interpret the results of your calculations.

First, we consider two-dimensional vector fields. A vector field in the xy-plane takes the form

$$\mathbf{V} = V_x(x, y)\,\mathbf{i} + V_y(x, y)\,\mathbf{j}.$$

In this case, $V_z = 0$, $\partial V_x/\partial z = 0$ and $\partial V_y/\partial z = 0$. Substituting into equation (48), we see that the curl of $\mathbf{V}$ has only one component:

$$\nabla \times \mathbf{V} = \left(\frac{\partial V_y}{\partial x} - \frac{\partial V_x}{\partial y}\right)\mathbf{k}. \tag{49}$$

One way of interpreting such a curl is to suppose that $\mathbf{V}$ describes the velocity of water on the surface of a river. Imagine a tiny circular disc floating on the water. The disc will be carried downstream following the direction of flow, but it may also rotate about a vertical axis as it drifts. The curl of $\mathbf{V}$ is proportional to the rate of rotation of the disc. Of course, the disc just serves as a marker making the curl of the underlying vector field visible – we are not really interested in the disc itself.

To take a specific example, Figure 30 shows a straight stretch of river with its banks at $y = -4$ and $y = 4$ (in metres), with water flowing in the x-direction. Suppose that the velocity of water on the surface of this river (in metres per second) is given by the vector field

$$\mathbf{V} = (16 - y^2)\,\mathbf{i} \quad (-4 \le y \le 4). \tag{50}$$

Then the curl of this vector field is

$$\mathbf{curl\,V} = \left(\frac{\partial V_y}{\partial x} - \frac{\partial V_x}{\partial y}\right)\mathbf{k} = 2y\,\mathbf{k}, \tag{51}$$

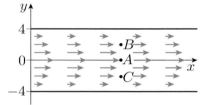

Figure 30   The flow of water in a river

which varies from point to point. Remember that our conventions require us to use right-handed coordinate systems, so with the x- and y-axes as shown in Figure 30, the z-axis points out of the page, towards you. Bearing this in mind, the interpretation of curl can be checked as follows.

Suppose that a disc is placed at point A in Figure 30, equidistant from either bank. At this point $y = 0$, and equation (51) gives zero curl. This makes good sense because water flows symmetrically around the disc, producing no tendency to rotate one way or another: the disc drifts downstream without rotating.

At point B, $y = 2$ and the calculated curl points along the positive z-axis. Using the right-hand grip rule, this is associated with a rotation about a vertical axis in an anticlockwise sense when viewed from above the river. This correctly describes how the disc revolves in response to a current that is stronger at the centre of the river than near its banks. At point C, $y = -2$ and this conclusion is reversed. The curl now points along the negative z-axis, corresponding to a clockwise rotation of the disc when seen from above, which is again what we should expect.

Even a straight-line flow may be associated with rotation and curl.

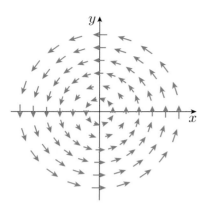

Figure 31 A swirling flow

A good example of a swirling flow is given by the vector field

$$\mathbf{V} = -y\,\mathbf{i} + x\,\mathbf{j},$$

whose arrow map is shown in Figure 31. We have

$$\mathbf{curl\,V} = \left(\frac{\partial(x)}{\partial x} - \frac{\partial(-y)}{\partial y} \right)\mathbf{k} = 2\,\mathbf{k},$$

which is in the positive z-direction (i.e. out of the page towards you).

The result can be interpreted using the right-hand grip rule. With the outstretched thumb of your right hand pointing in the z-direction, your fingers wrap in an anticlockwise sense. This is as expected: if Figure 31 represents a flow of water, then a float placed in the centre of this flow would certainly revolve anticlockwise. In fact, **curl V** is a constant in this case, so the float would revolve anticlockwise, at the same rate, no matter where it was placed in the flow. This happens because water flows unsymmetrically around the float, producing an effect similar to that already described for the straight-flowing river of Figure 30.

It may be tempting to suppose that any vector field with field lines that are closed loops has a non-zero curl. This is not true, as the following exercise shows.

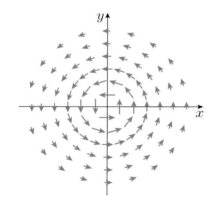

Exercise 25

The vector field

$$\mathbf{V} = -\frac{y}{x^2 + y^2}\,\mathbf{i} + \frac{x}{x^2 + y^2}\,\mathbf{j} \quad ((x,y) \neq (0,0))$$

has the arrow map sketched in the margin. Show that the curl of **V** is equal to the zero vector at all points in the domain of **V**.

The result of this exercise does not contradict our statement that curl describes the local rotation of a vector field. The important word here is *local*. If the field in Exercise 25 describes the two-dimensional flow of water, and a tiny disc is placed on the surface of the water, then the disc will travel around the origin in circles, following the circular field lines. However, for this particular flow, the disc does not rotate *locally*. If the disc is marked with an arrow that initially points East, the arrow continues to point East as the disc drifts in the current, as shown in Figure 32. This absence of *local* rotation agrees with the calculation of zero curl.

Curl in three dimensions

So far we have considered the curls of two-dimensional vector fields. More usually, we need to find the curl of a three-dimensional vector field. The interpretation is essentially the same. If a fluid has a velocity field **V**, then a sphere immersed in the fluid revolves about an axis aligned with the curl of **V**, and the sense of rotation is given by the right-hand grip rule.

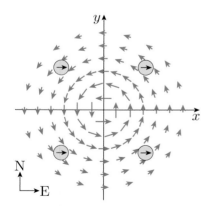

Figure 32 An arrow on a very small disc points in a fixed direction as the disc drifts in the flow of Exercise 25

To calculate the curl of any three-dimensional vector field **F**, we start from the definition:

$$\nabla \times \mathbf{F} = \begin{vmatrix} \mathbf{i} & \mathbf{j} & \mathbf{k} \\ \dfrac{\partial}{\partial x} & \dfrac{\partial}{\partial y} & \dfrac{\partial}{\partial z} \\ F_x & F_y & F_z \end{vmatrix}.$$

It is a good idea to write down this equation at the start of any calculation of curl in three dimensions. The alternative is to write down the expanded version of the determinant,

$$\nabla \times \mathbf{F} = \left(\frac{\partial F_z}{\partial y} - \frac{\partial F_y}{\partial z} \right) \mathbf{i} + \left(\frac{\partial F_x}{\partial z} - \frac{\partial F_z}{\partial x} \right) \mathbf{j} + \left(\frac{\partial F_y}{\partial x} - \frac{\partial F_x}{\partial y} \right) \mathbf{k},$$

but this equation is harder to remember. If you want to use it as your starting point, it is helpful to note that it contains a strong pattern, based on the cyclic ordering shown in Figure 33.

- The x-component is obtained by acting with $\partial/\partial y$ on F_z (note the order $x \to y \to z$); a term with y and z interchanged is then subtracted.

- The y-component is obtained by acting with $\partial/\partial z$ on F_x (note the order $y \to z \to x$); a term with z and x interchanged is then subtracted.

- The z-component is obtained by acting with $\partial/\partial x$ on F_y (note the order $z \to x \to y$); a term with x and y interchanged is then subtracted.

Figure 33 A cyclic ordering of x, y and z underlies the formula for curl in Cartesian coordinates

Exercise 26

Find the curls of the following vector fields.

(a) $\mathbf{F} = (z - y)\,\mathbf{i} + (x - z)\,\mathbf{j} + (y - x)\,\mathbf{k}$ (b) $\mathbf{G} = zy^2\,\mathbf{i} + xz^2\,\mathbf{j} + yx^2\,\mathbf{k}$

Exercise 27

Given a scalar field $U(x, y, z)$, the corresponding gradient vector field is

$$\nabla U = \frac{\partial U}{\partial x}\,\mathbf{i} + \frac{\partial U}{\partial y}\,\mathbf{j} + \frac{\partial U}{\partial z}\,\mathbf{k}.$$

Show that the curl of this gradient vector field vanishes everywhere.

You may assume that U varies smoothly enough to obey the mixed partial derivative theorem of Unit 7.

Curls of vector fields in the real world

Many fluid flows have a swirling motion, known as a vortex. Very often, the curl of the velocity is small over large regions, and is significant only in a small central region called the *vortex core*.

An aircraft in flight continually generates a vortex from each of its wing tips, as illustrated in Figure 34. This is an inevitable consequence of the air flows that generate lift, but introduces unwelcome drag. To improve fuel economy, wings are designed to minimise the energy that is wasted by generating such vortices.

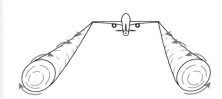

Figure 34 Vortices shed from an aeroplane's wing tips

Figure 35   Migrating geese maintain a V-formation

You may have seen birds such as geese flying in a V-formation (Figure 35). This is also an adaptation to the generation of vortices at wing tips, because the lagging birds benefit from the upward-flowing air in vortices generated by the leading bird. Fair play is observed, as the birds regularly switch positions in the formation.

Electric and magnetic fields can also have curl, and this is vital for many phenomena. A magnetic field that changes with time produces an electric field with a non-zero curl, and this lies behind the functioning of electricity generators. Moreover, an electric field that changes with time produces a magnetic field with a non-zero curl. These facts underpin the interpretation of light as a travelling disturbance of electric and magnetic fields.

4.2   Curl in non-Cartesian coordinates

You have seen that some vector fields are best described in non-Cartesian coordinate systems. This subsection explains how to calculate the curl of a vector field expressed in any orthogonal coordinate system.

In an orthogonal system of coordinates (u, v, w) with unit vectors $\mathbf{e}_u$, $\mathbf{e}_v$ and $\mathbf{e}_w$, a vector field $\mathbf{F}$ can be expressed as

$$\mathbf{F} = F_u \, \mathbf{e}_u + F_v \, \mathbf{e}_v + F_w \, \mathbf{e}_w,$$

and we know that the del operator can be written as

$$\boldsymbol{\nabla} = \mathbf{e}_u \, \frac{1}{h_u} \, \frac{\partial}{\partial u} + \mathbf{e}_v \, \frac{1}{h_v} \, \frac{\partial}{\partial v} + \mathbf{e}_w \, \frac{1}{h_w} \, \frac{\partial}{\partial w}.$$

It follows that the curl of $\mathbf{F}$ in the (u, v, w) coordinate system is

$$\boldsymbol{\nabla} \times \mathbf{F} = \left(\mathbf{e}_u \, \frac{1}{h_u} \, \frac{\partial}{\partial u} + \mathbf{e}_v \, \frac{1}{h_v} \, \frac{\partial}{\partial v} + \mathbf{e}_w \, \frac{1}{h_w} \, \frac{\partial}{\partial w} \right) \times (F_u \, \mathbf{e}_u + F_v \, \mathbf{e}_v + F_w \, \mathbf{e}_w).$$

This equation is correct, but is not immediately useful because there are still differentiations and vector products to carry out. We take a similar approach to that adopted earlier for divergence. The optional Appendix justifies the expressions that we use, but we just state the standard formulas here. Your task is to apply these formulas to specific vector fields.

Curl of a vector field in orthogonal coordinates

In any orthogonal right-handed system of coordinates (u, v, w) with scale factors h_u, h_v and h_w, a vector field

$$\mathbf{F} = F_u \, \mathbf{e}_u + F_v \, \mathbf{e}_v + F_w \, \mathbf{e}_w$$

has curl

$$\boldsymbol{\nabla} \times \mathbf{F} = \frac{1}{J} \begin{vmatrix} h_u\,\mathbf{e}_u & h_v\,\mathbf{e}_v & h_w\,\mathbf{e}_w \\ \dfrac{\partial}{\partial u} & \dfrac{\partial}{\partial v} & \dfrac{\partial}{\partial w} \\ h_u F_u & h_v F_v & h_w F_w \end{vmatrix}, \tag{52}$$

where $J = h_u h_v h_w$ is the Jacobian factor.

When the determinant is expanded, partial derivative operators in the second row act on elements in the third row.

The requirement for the coordinate system to be orthogonal *and* *right-handed* implies, for example, that $\mathbf{e}_u \times \mathbf{e}_v = \mathbf{e}_w$ (rather than $-\mathbf{e}_w$). All the coordinate systems (u, v, w) used in this module are right-handed. For example, in spherical coordinates (r, θ, ϕ), we have $\mathbf{e}_r \times \mathbf{e}_\theta = \mathbf{e}_\phi$.

It is easy to check that equation (52) works in Cartesian coordinates. In this system, all the scale factors are equal to 1, so $J = 1$. Moreover, $\mathbf{e}_x = \mathbf{i}$, $\mathbf{e}_y = \mathbf{j}$ and $\mathbf{e}_z = \mathbf{k}$, so we recover

$$\boldsymbol{\nabla} \times \mathbf{F} = \begin{vmatrix} \mathbf{i} & \mathbf{j} & \mathbf{k} \\ \dfrac{\partial}{\partial x} & \dfrac{\partial}{\partial y} & \dfrac{\partial}{\partial z} \\ F_x & F_y & F_z \end{vmatrix}.$$

In cylindrical coordinates (r, ϕ, z), the scale factors are $h_r = 1$, $h_\phi = r$ and $h_z = 1$, so $J = r$. We therefore obtain the following result.

Curl in cylindrical coordinates

$$\boldsymbol{\nabla} \times \mathbf{F} = \frac{1}{r} \begin{vmatrix} \mathbf{e}_r & r\,\mathbf{e}_\phi & \mathbf{e}_z \\ \dfrac{\partial}{\partial r} & \dfrac{\partial}{\partial \phi} & \dfrac{\partial}{\partial z} \\ F_r & r F_\phi & F_z \end{vmatrix}. \tag{53}$$

Note that the scale factors accompany the unit vectors in row 1 *and* the components in row 3. Also, take care to include the overall factor $1/J$, i.e. $1/r$ in this case.

Example 8

The vector field $\mathbf{F} = r^2\,\mathbf{e}_\phi$ is in cylindrical coordinates. Find its curl.

Solution

The field $\mathbf{F}$ has cylindrical components $F_r = 0$, $F_\phi = r^2$, $F_z = 0$, so

$$\boldsymbol{\nabla} \times \mathbf{F} = \frac{1}{r} \begin{vmatrix} \mathbf{e}_r & r\,\mathbf{e}_\phi & \mathbf{e}_z \\ \dfrac{\partial}{\partial r} & \dfrac{\partial}{\partial \phi} & \dfrac{\partial}{\partial z} \\ 0 & r^3 & 0 \end{vmatrix}$$

$$= \frac{1}{r}\left(\mathbf{e}_r\,(0) - r\,\mathbf{e}_\phi\,(0) + \mathbf{e}_z\,(3r^2)\right) = 3r\,\mathbf{e}_z.$$

Exercise 28

The following vector fields are in cylindrical coordinates. Find their curls.

(a) $\mathbf{F} = r^2\,\mathbf{e}_z$ (b) $\mathbf{G} = rz\,\mathbf{e}_\phi$ (c) $\mathbf{H} = rz\sin\phi\,\mathbf{e}_r$

In two dimensions, polar coordinates are similar to cylindrical coordinates, but there is no z-dependence. This means that we can get the expression for curl in polar coordinates by expanding equation (53), bearing in mind that $F_z = 0$, and F_r and F_ϕ are independent of z. Setting $F_z = 0$ gives

$$\nabla \times \mathbf{F} = \frac{1}{r}\begin{vmatrix} \mathbf{e}_r & r\,\mathbf{e}_\phi & \mathbf{e}_z \\ \dfrac{\partial}{\partial r} & \dfrac{\partial}{\partial \phi} & \dfrac{\partial}{\partial z} \\ F_r & rF_\phi & 0 \end{vmatrix}.$$

Then, using $\partial F_r/\partial z = 0$ and $\partial F_\phi/\partial z = 0$, we get the following result.

Curl in polar coordinates

$$\nabla \times \mathbf{F} = \frac{1}{r}\left(\frac{\partial(rF_\phi)}{\partial r} - \frac{\partial F_r}{\partial \phi}\right)\mathbf{e}_z. \tag{54}$$

Exercise 29

In polar coordinates, the vector field in Exercise 25 can be expressed as

$$\mathbf{F} = \frac{1}{r}\,\mathbf{e}_\phi \quad (r \neq 0).$$

Use equation (54) to confirm that the curl of this field is equal to the zero vector.

The final coordinate system that we need to consider is spherical coordinates (r, θ, ϕ). In this case, the scale factors are $h_r = 1$, $h_\theta = r$ and $h_\phi = r\sin\theta$, so $J = r^2\sin\theta$, leading to the following result.

Curl in spherical coordinates

$$\nabla \times \mathbf{F} = \frac{1}{r^2\sin\theta}\begin{vmatrix} \mathbf{e}_r & r\,\mathbf{e}_\theta & r\sin\theta\,\mathbf{e}_\phi \\ \dfrac{\partial}{\partial r} & \dfrac{\partial}{\partial \theta} & \dfrac{\partial}{\partial \phi} \\ F_r & rF_\theta & r\sin\theta\,F_\phi \end{vmatrix}. \tag{55}$$

Exercise 30

The following vector fields are in spherical coordinates. Find their curls.

(a) $\mathbf{F} = r\,\mathbf{e}_\theta$ (b) $\mathbf{G} = r\sin\theta\,\mathbf{e}_\phi$ (c) $\mathbf{H} = r^2\,\mathbf{e}_r$

Learning outcomes

After studying this unit, you should be able to do the following.

- Define the terms scalar field and vector field.
- Interpret contour maps of scalar fields, and interpret arrow maps and field line maps of vector fields.
- Convert a scalar or vector field expressed in Cartesian coordinates into polar, cylindrical or spherical coordinates.
- Given a scalar field, calculate its gradient field in Cartesian, polar, cylindrical or spherical coordinates.
- State and apply the properties of gradient fields.
- Given a vector field, calculate its divergence in Cartesian, polar, cylindrical or spherical coordinates.
- Given a vector field, calculate its curl in Cartesian, polar, cylindrical or spherical coordinates.
- Relate arrow maps of vector fields to their divergences and curls.

Appendix: proofs of results for div and curl

This optional Appendix is neither assessable nor examinable. Its aim is to justify the general formulas for divergence and curl in orthogonal coordinates given in equations (43) and (52). Because these proofs are difficult to find elsewhere, we include them for reference purposes and general interest. However, this material is more demanding than the general level of this module, so do not be dismayed if you find it hard.

Do not study this Appendix at the expense of other units. It can be read for interest when you have the time (perhaps after completing the module).

Consider a general orthogonal coordinate system with coordinates (u, v, w), unit vectors $\mathbf{e}_u$, $\mathbf{e}_v$ and $\mathbf{e}_w$, and scale factors h_u, h_v and h_w. In such a system, a vector field $\mathbf{F}$ is written as

$$\mathbf{F} = F_u\,\mathbf{e}_u + F_v\,\mathbf{e}_v + F_w\,\mathbf{e}_w,$$

and the del operator is

$$\boldsymbol{\nabla} = \mathbf{e}_u\,\frac{1}{h_u}\,\frac{\partial}{\partial u} + \mathbf{e}_v\,\frac{1}{h_v}\,\frac{\partial}{\partial v} + \mathbf{e}_w\,\frac{1}{h_w}\,\frac{\partial}{\partial w}.$$

Using these expressions, we can construct the divergence and curl in the usual way:

$$\operatorname{div}\mathbf{F} = \boldsymbol{\nabla} \cdot \mathbf{F} \quad \text{and} \quad \operatorname{\mathbf{curl}}\mathbf{F} = \boldsymbol{\nabla} \times \mathbf{F}.$$

In practice, however, these expressions need to be unpacked. The unit vectors may vary from point to point, and the effect of partial derivative operators such as $\partial/\partial u$ on the components and the unit vectors of $\mathbf{F}$ must be worked out. The main text skipped directly to the final results, namely equations (43) and (52), but no proofs were given. The missing proofs are contained in this Appendix.

Divergence and curl in polar coordinates

Before looking at the general problem, it is helpful to consider a specific case: the expressions for the divergence and curl of a two-dimensional vector field in polar coordinates (r, ϕ). In this case, the scale factors are $h_r = 1$ and $h_\phi = r$, and the divergence is

$$\nabla \cdot \mathbf{F} = \left(\mathbf{e}_r \frac{\partial}{\partial r} + \frac{1}{r} \mathbf{e}_\phi \frac{\partial}{\partial \phi} \right) \cdot (F_r \, \mathbf{e}_r + F_\phi \, \mathbf{e}_\phi). \tag{56}$$

The first task is to carry out the partial differentiations. One very important fact must be understood: the unit vectors $\mathbf{e}_r$ and $\mathbf{e}_\phi$ are not fixed, but vary with position. In fact, you saw in equations (11) that

$$\mathbf{e}_r = \cos\phi \, \mathbf{i} + \sin\phi \, \mathbf{j},$$
$$\mathbf{e}_\phi = -\sin\phi \, \mathbf{i} + \cos\phi \, \mathbf{j}.$$

Partially differentiating these equations with respect to ϕ, we obtain

$$\frac{\partial \mathbf{e}_r}{\partial \phi} = -\sin\phi \, \mathbf{i} + \cos\phi \, \mathbf{j} = \mathbf{e}_\phi,$$

$$\frac{\partial \mathbf{e}_\phi}{\partial \phi} = -\cos\phi \, \mathbf{i} - \sin\phi \, \mathbf{j} = -\mathbf{e}_r.$$

Using these results, and noting that the unit vectors do not depend on r, the derivatives that appear in equation (56) can be evaluated as follows:

$$\frac{\partial}{\partial r}(F_r \, \mathbf{e}_r + F_\phi \, \mathbf{e}_\phi) = \frac{\partial F_r}{\partial r} \mathbf{e}_r + \frac{\partial F_\phi}{\partial r} \mathbf{e}_\phi, \tag{57}$$

$$\frac{\partial}{\partial \phi}(F_r \, \mathbf{e}_r + F_\phi \, \mathbf{e}_\phi) = \frac{\partial F_r}{\partial \phi} \mathbf{e}_r + F_r \frac{\partial \mathbf{e}_r}{\partial \phi} + \frac{\partial F_\phi}{\partial \phi} \mathbf{e}_\phi + F_\phi \frac{\partial \mathbf{e}_\phi}{\partial \phi}$$

$$= \frac{\partial F_r}{\partial \phi} \mathbf{e}_r + F_r \, \mathbf{e}_\phi + \frac{\partial F_\phi}{\partial \phi} \mathbf{e}_\phi - F_\phi \, \mathbf{e}_r. \tag{58}$$

To complete the evaluation of equation (56), we must first take the scalar products of equations (57) and (58) with respect to $\mathbf{e}_r$ and $\mathbf{e}_\phi/r$, and then add the results. Since $\mathbf{e}_r$ and $\mathbf{e}_\phi$ are orthogonal unit vectors, we get

$$\mathbf{e}_r \cdot \frac{\partial}{\partial r}(F_r \, \mathbf{e}_r + F_\phi \, \mathbf{e}_\phi) = \frac{\partial F_r}{\partial r},$$

$$\frac{1}{r} \mathbf{e}_\phi \cdot \frac{\partial}{\partial \phi}(F_r \, \mathbf{e}_r + F_\phi \, \mathbf{e}_\phi) = \frac{1}{r}\left(F_r + \frac{\partial F_\phi}{\partial \phi} \right).$$

Adding these results, and using the product rule of differentiation, we get

$$\nabla \cdot \mathbf{F} = \frac{\partial F_r}{\partial r} + \frac{F_r}{r} + \frac{1}{r}\frac{\partial F_\phi}{\partial \phi} = \frac{1}{r}\frac{\partial(r F_r)}{\partial r} + \frac{1}{r}\frac{\partial F_\phi}{\partial \phi},$$

which confirms equation (44), a special case of equation (43).

A similar argument can be used for curl in polar coordinates. We start from the expression

$$\nabla \times \mathbf{F} = \left(\mathbf{e}_r \frac{\partial}{\partial r} + \frac{1}{r} \mathbf{e}_\phi \frac{\partial}{\partial \phi} \right) \times (F_r \, \mathbf{e}_r + F_\phi \, \mathbf{e}_\phi),$$

which is like equation (56), but with a vector product rather than a scalar product.

Using equations (57) and (58), we get

$$\nabla \times \mathbf{F} = \mathbf{e}_r \times \left(\frac{\partial F_r}{\partial r} \mathbf{e}_r + \frac{\partial F_\phi}{\partial r} \mathbf{e}_\phi \right)$$
$$+ \frac{1}{r} \mathbf{e}_\phi \times \left(\frac{\partial F_r}{\partial \phi} \mathbf{e}_r + F_r \, \mathbf{e}_\phi + \frac{\partial F_\phi}{\partial \phi} \mathbf{e}_\phi - F_\phi \, \mathbf{e}_r \right).$$

We now evaluate the vector products. The vector product of any vector with itself is equal to zero, so $\mathbf{e}_r \times \mathbf{e}_r = \mathbf{0}$ and $\mathbf{e}_\phi \times \mathbf{e}_\phi = \mathbf{0}$. Also, as shown in Figure 36, the unit vectors $\mathbf{e}_r$, $\mathbf{e}_\phi$ and $\mathbf{e}_z$ (in that order) form a right-handed system, so

$$\mathbf{e}_r \times \mathbf{e}_\phi = \mathbf{e}_z \quad \text{and} \quad \mathbf{e}_\phi \times \mathbf{e}_r = -\mathbf{e}_z.$$

Multiplying out the brackets and using these results in our expression for the curl, we conclude that

$$\nabla \times \mathbf{F} = \left(\frac{\partial F_\phi}{\partial r} - \frac{1}{r} \frac{\partial F_r}{\partial \phi} + \frac{F_\phi}{r} \right) \mathbf{e}_z = \frac{1}{r} \left(\frac{\partial (r F_\phi)}{\partial r} - \frac{\partial F_r}{\partial \phi} \right) \mathbf{e}_z,$$

which confirms equation (54), a special case of equation (52).

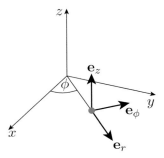

Figure 36 The unit vectors $\mathbf{e}_r$, $\mathbf{e}_\phi$ and $\mathbf{e}_z$ form a right-handed system

General proof of the divergence formula

We now generalise to any orthogonal coordinate system. For this purpose, it is helpful to use a slightly different notation in which we refer to coordinates u_i, with unit vectors $\mathbf{e}_i$ and scale factors h_i, where the index i can be 1, 2 or 3. The unit vectors are mutually orthogonal and right-handed so that, for example, $\mathbf{e}_1 \cdot \mathbf{e}_2 = 0$ and $\mathbf{e}_1 \times \mathbf{e}_2 = \mathbf{e}_3$.

In this notation the del operator and a vector field $\mathbf{F}$ can be written compactly as

$$\nabla = \sum_i \mathbf{e}_i \frac{1}{h_i} \frac{\partial}{\partial u_i} \quad \text{and} \quad \mathbf{F} = \sum_i F_i \, \mathbf{e}_i,$$

where it is understood that the sums range from $i = 1$ to $i = 3$.

The divergence of $\mathbf{F}$ in orthogonal coordinates can then be written as

$$\nabla \cdot \mathbf{F} = \left(\sum_j \mathbf{e}_j \frac{1}{h_j} \frac{\partial}{\partial u_j} \right) \cdot \left(\sum_i F_i \, \mathbf{e}_i \right). \tag{59}$$

Notice that we have used the index j in the first summation, and the index i in the second summation. This is an essential precaution. In any single summation it makes no difference whether we call the index i or j, but when we combine two summations in the same formula, we would run into problems if we used the same index throughout. We would be in danger of leaving out terms such as

$$\mathbf{e}_1 \cdot \frac{1}{h_1} \frac{\partial}{\partial u_1}(F_2 \, \mathbf{e}_2),$$

where the two indices take *different* values.

Multiplying out the brackets in equation (59) gives

$$\boldsymbol{\nabla} \cdot \mathbf{F} = \sum_{i,j} \frac{1}{h_j} \mathbf{e}_j \cdot \frac{\partial (F_i \, \mathbf{e}_i)}{\partial u_j},$$

which is a sum of *nine* terms corresponding to $i = 1, 2, 3$ and $j = 1, 2, 3$.

The crucial step is the evaluation of the derivatives, especially the derivatives of the unit vectors. When we considered the case of polar coordinates, the unit vectors $\mathbf{e}_r$ and $\mathbf{e}_\phi$ were known, so their derivatives could be found explicitly. Now we need a route that works more generally, in any orthogonal coordinate system.

The key is to remember the relationship between unit vectors and tangent vectors given in equations (25) and (26). In our present notation,

$$\mathbf{e}_i = \frac{1}{h_i} \mathbf{T}_i, \quad \text{where } \mathbf{T}_i = \left(\frac{\partial x}{\partial u_i}, \frac{\partial y}{\partial u_i}, \frac{\partial z}{\partial u_i} \right).$$

The mixed partial derivative theorem of Unit 7 tells us that it does not matter which order is used to carry out two partial differentiations in a second-order derivative. Hence

$$\frac{\partial \mathbf{T}_i}{\partial u_j} = \frac{\partial}{\partial u_j} \left(\frac{\partial x}{\partial u_i}, \frac{\partial y}{\partial u_i}, \frac{\partial z}{\partial u_i} \right) = \frac{\partial}{\partial u_i} \left(\frac{\partial x}{\partial u_j}, \frac{\partial y}{\partial u_j}, \frac{\partial z}{\partial u_j} \right) = \frac{\partial \mathbf{T}_j}{\partial u_i}. \tag{60}$$

This equation implicitly contains all the information that we need about the spatial rates of change of the unit vectors. To take advantage of it, we write equation (59) in terms of the tangent vectors, giving

$$\boldsymbol{\nabla} \cdot \mathbf{F} = \sum_{i,j} \frac{1}{h_j^2} \mathbf{T}_j \cdot \frac{\partial}{\partial u_j} \left(\frac{F_i}{h_i} \mathbf{T}_i \right).$$

Using the product rule of differentiation, we then have

$$\boldsymbol{\nabla} \cdot \mathbf{F} = \sum_{i,j} \frac{1}{h_j^2} \left[\frac{\partial}{\partial u_j} \left(\frac{F_i}{h_i} \right) \mathbf{T}_j \cdot \mathbf{T}_i + \frac{F_i}{h_i} \mathbf{T}_j \cdot \frac{\partial \mathbf{T}_i}{\partial u_j} \right],$$

so applying equation (60), we get

$$\boldsymbol{\nabla} \cdot \mathbf{F} = \sum_{i,j} \frac{1}{h_j^2} \left[\frac{\partial}{\partial u_j} \left(\frac{F_i}{h_i} \right) \mathbf{T}_j \cdot \mathbf{T}_i + \frac{F_i}{h_i} \mathbf{T}_j \cdot \frac{\partial \mathbf{T}_j}{\partial u_i} \right]. \tag{61}$$

This equation is ripe for simplification! In an orthogonal coordinate system, the tangent vectors are orthogonal, so the scalar product in the first term is equal to zero unless $j = i$, in which case it is equal to $\mathbf{T}_i \cdot \mathbf{T}_i = |\mathbf{T}_i|^2 = h_i^2$. The scalar product in the last term can be written as

$$\mathbf{T}_j \cdot \frac{\partial \mathbf{T}_j}{\partial u_i} = \frac{1}{2} \frac{\partial (\mathbf{T}_j \cdot \mathbf{T}_j)}{\partial u_i} = \frac{1}{2} \frac{\partial h_j^2}{\partial u_i} = h_j \frac{\partial h_j}{\partial u_i}.$$

Using these results in equation (61), we obtain

$$\boldsymbol{\nabla} \cdot \mathbf{F} = \sum_i \left[\frac{\partial}{\partial u_i} \left(\frac{F_i}{h_i} \right) + \frac{F_i}{h_i} \left(\sum_j \frac{1}{h_j} \frac{\partial h_j}{\partial u_i} \right) \right]. \tag{62}$$

This can be tidied up by noting that

$$\sum_j \frac{1}{h_j} \frac{\partial h_j}{\partial u_i} = \frac{\partial}{\partial u_i} \sum_j \ln h_j = \frac{\partial}{\partial u_i} \ln(h_1 h_2 h_3).$$

Then, introducing the Jacobian factor $J = h_1 h_2 h_3$, we get

$$\sum_j \frac{1}{h_j} \frac{\partial h_j}{\partial u_i} = \frac{\partial}{\partial u_i} \ln J = \frac{1}{J} \frac{\partial J}{\partial u_i}.$$

Returning to equation (62) and using the product rule of differentiation, we conclude that

$$\boldsymbol{\nabla} \cdot \mathbf{F} = \sum_i \frac{\partial}{\partial u_i} \left(\frac{F_i}{h_i} \right) + \left(\frac{F_i}{h_i} \right) \left(\frac{1}{J} \frac{\partial J}{\partial u_i} \right)$$

$$= \sum_i \frac{1}{J} \frac{\partial}{\partial u_i} \left(\frac{F_i}{h_i} J \right),$$

which is the required result (equation (43)).

General proof of the curl formula

We again consider orthogonal coordinates u_i, with unit vectors $\mathbf{e}_i$ and scale factors h_i (for $i = 1, 2, 3$). The coordinate system is assumed to be right-handed, so

$$\mathbf{e}_1 \times \mathbf{e}_2 = \mathbf{e}_3, \quad \mathbf{e}_2 \times \mathbf{e}_3 = \mathbf{e}_1, \quad \mathbf{e}_3 \times \mathbf{e}_1 = \mathbf{e}_2. \tag{63}$$

Note the cyclic pattern based on $1 \to 2 \to 3 \to 1 \to 2 \to \ldots$.

In such a coordinate system, the curl of $\mathbf{F}$ is given by

$$\boldsymbol{\nabla} \times \mathbf{F} = \left(\sum_j \mathbf{e}_j \frac{1}{h_j} \frac{\partial}{\partial u_j} \right) \times \mathbf{F} = \left(\sum_j \frac{1}{h_j} \mathbf{e}_j \times \frac{\partial \mathbf{F}}{\partial u_j} \right). \tag{64}$$

In contrast with the divergence calculation, we do not need to expand $\mathbf{F}$ in terms of its components.

Let us focus on a single component of the curl. We consider $(\boldsymbol{\nabla} \times \mathbf{F})_3$, the component in the local direction of the unit vector $\mathbf{e}_3$. This is found by taking the scalar product of equation (64) with $\mathbf{e}_3$, giving

$$(\boldsymbol{\nabla} \times \mathbf{F})_3 = \frac{1}{h_1} \mathbf{e}_3 \cdot \left(\mathbf{e}_1 \times \frac{\partial \mathbf{F}}{\partial u_1} \right) + \frac{1}{h_2} \mathbf{e}_3 \cdot \left(\mathbf{e}_2 \times \frac{\partial \mathbf{F}}{\partial u_2} \right)$$

$$+ \frac{1}{h_3} \mathbf{e}_3 \cdot \left(\mathbf{e}_3 \times \frac{\partial \mathbf{F}}{\partial u_3} \right).$$

You may remember that equation (37) of Unit 4 gave the identity

$$\mathbf{a} \cdot (\mathbf{b} \times \mathbf{c}) = (\mathbf{a} \times \mathbf{b}) \cdot \mathbf{c},$$

which is valid for any vectors $\mathbf{a}$, $\mathbf{b}$ and $\mathbf{c}$.

Using this identity, we get

$$(\boldsymbol{\nabla} \times \mathbf{F})_3 = \frac{1}{h_1} \left(\mathbf{e}_3 \times \mathbf{e}_1\right) \cdot \frac{\partial \mathbf{F}}{\partial u_1} + \frac{1}{h_2} \left(\mathbf{e}_3 \times \mathbf{e}_2\right) \cdot \frac{\partial \mathbf{F}}{\partial u_2}$$
$$+ \frac{1}{h_3} \left(\mathbf{e}_3 \times \mathbf{e}_3\right) \cdot \frac{\partial \mathbf{F}}{\partial u_3}.$$

The last term is equal to zero because the vector product of any vector with itself is equal to the zero vector. Equations (63) then give

$$(\boldsymbol{\nabla} \times \mathbf{F})_3 = \frac{1}{h_1} \mathbf{e}_2 \cdot \frac{\partial \mathbf{F}}{\partial u_1} - \frac{1}{h_2} \mathbf{e}_1 \cdot \frac{\partial \mathbf{F}}{\partial u_2}.$$

Expressing this in terms of the tangent vectors $\mathbf{T}_i = h_i \, \mathbf{e}_i$, we have

$$(\boldsymbol{\nabla} \times \mathbf{F})_3 = \frac{1}{h_1 h_2} \left(\mathbf{T}_2 \cdot \frac{\partial \mathbf{F}}{\partial u_1} - \mathbf{T}_1 \cdot \frac{\partial \mathbf{F}}{\partial u_2}\right). \tag{65}$$

Using the product rule, the term in brackets can be expressed as

$$\mathbf{T}_2 \cdot \frac{\partial \mathbf{F}}{\partial u_1} - \mathbf{T}_1 \cdot \frac{\partial \mathbf{F}}{\partial u_2}$$
$$= \left(\frac{\partial (\mathbf{T}_2 \cdot \mathbf{F})}{\partial u_1} - \frac{\partial \mathbf{T}_2}{\partial u_1} \cdot \mathbf{F}\right) - \left(\frac{\partial (\mathbf{T}_1 \cdot \mathbf{F})}{\partial u_2} - \frac{\partial \mathbf{T}_1}{\partial u_2} \cdot \mathbf{F}\right).$$

Now, the second terms in each bracket cancel out because equation (60) ensures that $\partial \mathbf{T}_2 / \partial u_1 = \partial \mathbf{T}_1 / \partial u_2$. So returning to equation (65), we have

$$(\boldsymbol{\nabla} \times \mathbf{F})_3 = \frac{1}{h_1 h_2} \left(\frac{\partial (\mathbf{T}_2 \cdot \mathbf{F})}{\partial u_1} - \frac{\partial (\mathbf{T}_1 \cdot \mathbf{F})}{\partial u_2}\right).$$

Finally, noting that

$$\mathbf{T}_i \cdot \mathbf{F} = h_i \, \mathbf{e}_i \cdot \mathbf{F} = h_i F_i,$$

we conclude that

$$(\boldsymbol{\nabla} \times \mathbf{F})_3 = \frac{1}{h_1 h_2} \left(\frac{\partial (h_2 F_2)}{\partial u_1} - \frac{\partial (h_1 F_1)}{\partial u_2}\right).$$

This is equivalent to the third component of equation (52), as required. Corresponding results for the other components can be found by permuting the indices from $(1, 2, 3)$ to $(2, 3, 1)$ and $(3, 1, 2)$.

Solutions to exercises

Solution to Exercise 1

(a) Substituting $x = r \cos \phi$ and $y = r \sin \phi$, we get

$$U(r, \phi) = r^2 \cos^2 \phi - r^2 \sin^2 \phi = r^2 \cos(2\phi),$$

Recall the identity $\cos 2x = \cos^2 x - \sin^2 x$.

(b) We have

$$V(r, \phi) = 2r^2 \cos \phi \sin \phi = r^2 \sin(2\phi).$$

Recall the identity $\sin 2x = 2 \sin x \cos x$.

(c) We have

$$W(r, \phi) = (r^2 \cos^2 \phi + r^2 \sin^2 \phi)^{-1/2} = (r^2)^{-1/2} = \frac{1}{r},$$

where we have taken the positive square root because $r = \sqrt{x^2 + y^2} > 0$.

Solution to Exercise 2

In cylindrical coordinates, $r^2 = x^2 + y^2$, and the field is expressed as

$$T(r, \phi, z) = 100 \, e^{-(r^2 + z^2)} \quad (r^2 + z^2 \leq 1).$$

The point $(r, \phi, z) = (0.5, 0, 0.5)$ gives $r^2 + z^2 = 0.25 + 0.25 = 0.5 < 1$, so it lies within the domain of the function. The value of the temperature at this point is

$$T(0.5, 0, 0.5) = 100 \, e^{-0.5} \simeq 60.7,$$

so the temperature is $60.7°\text{C}$.

Solution to Exercise 3

(a) In cylindrical coordinates, we use the equations $x = r \cos \phi$, $y = r \sin \phi$ and $z = z$ to get

$$U(r, \phi, z) = \frac{z}{(r^2 \cos^2 \phi + r^2 \sin^2 \phi + z^2)^{1/2}} = \frac{z}{(r^2 + z^2)^{1/2}}.$$

Alternatively, equation (6) can be used in the denominator of $U(x, y, z)$.

Here, r is the radial coordinate of cylindrical coordinates, which is the distance from the z-axis (not the distance from the origin).

(b) In spherical coordinates, we use the equations $x = r \sin \theta \cos \phi$, $y = r \sin \theta \sin \phi$ and $z = r \cos \theta$ to get

$$U(r, \theta, \phi) = \frac{r \cos \theta}{(r^2 \sin^2 \theta (\cos^2 \phi + \sin^2 \phi) + r^2 \cos^2 \theta)^{1/2}}$$

$$= \frac{r \cos \theta}{(r^2 \sin^2 \theta + r^2 \cos^2 \theta)^{1/2}}$$

$$= \frac{r \cos \theta}{r}$$

$$= \cos \theta.$$

Alternatively, equation (8) can be used in the denominator of $U(x, y, z)$.

Solution to Exercise 4

The magnitude of the vector $\mathbf{e}_r$ is

$$|\mathbf{e}_r| = \sqrt{(\cos\phi)^2 + (\sin\phi)^2} = \sqrt{\cos^2\phi + \sin^2\phi} = 1,$$

and the magnitude of the vector $\mathbf{e}_\phi$ is

$$|\mathbf{e}_\phi| = \sqrt{(-\sin\phi)^2 + (\cos\phi)^2} = \sqrt{\sin^2\phi + \cos^2\phi} = 1.$$

So $\mathbf{e}_r$ and $\mathbf{e}_\phi$ are unit vectors.

To show that $\mathbf{e}_r$ and $\mathbf{e}_\phi$ are orthogonal, we evaluate their scalar product:

$$\mathbf{e}_r \cdot \mathbf{e}_\phi = (\cos\phi)(-\sin\phi) + (\sin\phi)(\cos\phi) = 0.$$

Because the scalar product is zero, and neither $\mathbf{e}_r$ nor $\mathbf{e}_\phi$ is equal to the zero vector, the two vectors must be orthogonal.

Solution to Exercise 5

In cylindrical coordinates, the vector field takes the form

$$\mathbf{F}(r,\phi,z) = F_r\,\mathbf{e}_r + F_\phi\,\mathbf{e}_\phi + F_z\,\mathbf{e}_z,$$

where

$$\mathbf{e}_r = \cos\phi\,\mathbf{i} + \sin\phi\,\mathbf{j}, \quad \mathbf{e}_\phi = -\sin\phi\,\mathbf{i} + \cos\phi\,\mathbf{j}, \quad \mathbf{e}_z = \mathbf{k}.$$

Using Procedure 1, we get

$$F_r = \mathbf{e}_r \cdot \mathbf{F} = (\cos\phi\,\mathbf{i} + \sin\phi\,\mathbf{j}) \cdot ((x+y)\,\mathbf{i} + (y-x)\,\mathbf{j} + 3z\,\mathbf{k})$$
$$= (x+y)\cos\phi + (y-x)\sin\phi,$$

$$F_\phi = \mathbf{e}_\phi \cdot \mathbf{F} = (-\sin\phi\,\mathbf{i} + \cos\phi\,\mathbf{j}) \cdot ((x+y)\,\mathbf{i} + (y-x)\,\mathbf{j} + 3z\,\mathbf{k})$$
$$= -(x+y)\sin\phi + (y-x)\cos\phi,$$

$$F_z = \mathbf{e}_z \cdot \mathbf{F} = \mathbf{k} \cdot ((x+y)\,\mathbf{i} + (y-x)\,\mathbf{j} + 3z\,\mathbf{k})$$
$$= 3z.$$

The coordinate transformation equations for cylindrical coordinates are

$$x = r\cos\phi, \quad y = r\sin\phi, \quad z = z,$$

so we get

$$F_r = r(\cos\phi + \sin\phi)\cos\phi + r(\sin\phi - \cos\phi)\sin\phi$$
$$= r(\cos^2\phi + \sin^2\phi)$$
$$= r,$$

$$F_\phi = -r(\cos\phi + \sin\phi)\sin\phi + r(\sin\phi - \cos\phi)\cos\phi$$
$$= -r(\sin^2\phi + \cos^2\phi)$$
$$= -r,$$

$$F_z = 3z.$$

Hence in cylindrical coordinates,

$$\mathbf{F}(r,\phi,z) = r\,\mathbf{e}_r - r\,\mathbf{e}_\phi + 3z\,\mathbf{e}_z.$$

Solution to Exercise 6

In spherical coordinates, the vector field takes the form

$$\mathbf{F}(r, \theta, \phi) = F_r\,\mathbf{e}_r + F_\theta\,\mathbf{e}_\theta + F_\phi\,\mathbf{e}_\phi,$$

where

$$\mathbf{e}_r = \sin\theta\cos\phi\,\mathbf{i} + \sin\theta\sin\phi\,\mathbf{j} + \cos\theta\,\mathbf{k},$$
$$\mathbf{e}_\theta = \cos\theta\cos\phi\,\mathbf{i} + \cos\theta\sin\phi\,\mathbf{j} - \sin\theta\,\mathbf{k},$$
$$\mathbf{e}_\phi = -\sin\phi\,\mathbf{i} + \cos\phi\,\mathbf{j}.$$

Using Procedure 1, we get

$$F_r = \mathbf{e}_r \cdot \mathbf{F} = (\sin\theta\cos\phi\,\mathbf{i} + \sin\theta\sin\phi\,\mathbf{j} + \cos\theta\,\mathbf{k}) \cdot z\mathbf{k} = z\cos\theta,$$
$$F_\theta = \mathbf{e}_\theta \cdot \mathbf{F} = (\cos\theta\cos\phi\,\mathbf{i} + \cos\theta\sin\phi\,\mathbf{j} - \sin\theta\,\mathbf{k}) \cdot z\mathbf{k} = -z\sin\theta,$$
$$F_\phi = \mathbf{e}_\phi \cdot \mathbf{F} = (-\sin\phi\,\mathbf{i} + \cos\phi\,\mathbf{j}) \cdot z\mathbf{k} = 0.$$

The coordinate transformation equations for spherical coordinates are

$$x = r\sin\theta\cos\phi, \quad y = r\sin\theta\sin\phi, \quad z = r\cos\theta,$$

so

$$F_r = r\cos^2\theta, \quad F_\theta = -r\sin\theta\cos\theta, \quad F_\phi = 0.$$

Hence in spherical coordinates,

$$\mathbf{F}(r, \theta, \phi) = r\cos^2\theta\,\mathbf{e}_r - r\sin\theta\cos\theta\,\mathbf{e}_\theta.$$

Solution to Exercise 7

Using equations (17), the vector field is

$$\begin{aligned}\mathbf{F} = \ &\cos\theta(\sin\theta\cos\phi\,\mathbf{i} + \sin\theta\sin\phi\,\mathbf{j} + \cos\theta\,\mathbf{k}) \\ &- \sin\theta(\cos\theta\cos\phi\,\mathbf{i} + \cos\theta\sin\phi\,\mathbf{j} - \sin\theta\,\mathbf{k}) \\ = \ &(\cos^2\theta + \sin^2\theta)\,\mathbf{k} = \mathbf{k}.\end{aligned}$$

Solution to Exercise 8

The three tangent vectors are

$$\mathbf{T}_r = \frac{\partial x}{\partial r}\,\mathbf{i} + \frac{\partial y}{\partial r}\,\mathbf{j} + \frac{\partial z}{\partial r}\,\mathbf{k},$$
$$\mathbf{T}_\theta = \frac{\partial x}{\partial\theta}\,\mathbf{i} + \frac{\partial y}{\partial\theta}\,\mathbf{j} + \frac{\partial z}{\partial\theta}\,\mathbf{k},$$
$$\mathbf{T}_\phi = \frac{\partial x}{\partial\phi}\,\mathbf{i} + \frac{\partial y}{\partial\phi}\,\mathbf{j} + \frac{\partial z}{\partial\phi}\,\mathbf{k}.$$

In spherical coordinates we have

$$x = r\sin\theta\cos\phi, \quad y = r\sin\theta\sin\phi, \quad z = r\cos\theta,$$

so

$$\mathbf{T}_r = \sin\theta\cos\phi\,\mathbf{i} + \sin\theta\sin\phi\,\mathbf{j} + \cos\theta\,\mathbf{k},$$
$$\mathbf{T}_\theta = r\cos\theta\cos\phi\,\mathbf{i} + r\cos\theta\sin\phi\,\mathbf{j} - r\sin\theta\,\mathbf{k},$$
$$\mathbf{T}_\phi = -r\sin\theta\sin\phi\,\mathbf{i} + r\sin\theta\cos\phi\,\mathbf{j}.$$

The magnitudes of these vectors are

$$h_r = \sqrt{\sin^2\theta(\cos^2\phi + \sin^2\phi) + \cos^2\theta} = 1,$$

$$h_\theta = \sqrt{r^2\cos^2\theta(\cos^2\phi + \sin^2\phi) + r^2\sin^2\theta} = r,$$

$$h_\phi = \sqrt{r^2\sin^2\theta(\sin^2\phi + \cos^2\phi)} = r\sin\theta,$$

which are the familiar scale factors for spherical coordinates. Hence the required unit vectors are

$$\mathbf{e}_r = \sin\theta\cos\phi\,\mathbf{i} + \sin\theta\sin\phi\,\mathbf{j} + \cos\theta\,\mathbf{k},$$

$$\mathbf{e}_\theta = \cos\theta\cos\phi\,\mathbf{i} + \cos\theta\sin\phi\,\mathbf{j} - \sin\theta\,\mathbf{k},$$

$$\mathbf{e}_\phi = -\sin\phi\,\mathbf{i} + \cos\phi\,\mathbf{j},$$

in agreement with equations (17).

Solution to Exercise 9

(a) With $V(x,y) = e^{x^2+y^2}$, we have

$$\mathbf{grad}\,V = \frac{\partial V}{\partial x}\,\mathbf{i} + \frac{\partial V}{\partial y}\,\mathbf{j}$$

$$= 2x\,e^{x^2+y^2}\,\mathbf{i} + 2y\,e^{x^2+y^2}\,\mathbf{j} = 2e^{x^2+y^2}\,(x\,\mathbf{i} + y\,\mathbf{j}).$$

(b) With $V(x,y,z) = e^{x^2+y^2+z^2}$, we have

$$\mathbf{grad}\,V = \frac{\partial V}{\partial x}\,\mathbf{i} + \frac{\partial V}{\partial y}\,\mathbf{j} + \frac{\partial V}{\partial z}\,\mathbf{k}$$

$$= 2x\,e^{x^2+y^2+z^2}\,\mathbf{i} + 2y\,e^{x^2+y^2+z^2}\,\mathbf{j} + 2z\,e^{x^2+y^2+z^2}\,\mathbf{k}$$

$$= 2e^{x^2+y^2+z^2}\,(x\,\mathbf{i} + y\,\mathbf{j} + z\,\mathbf{k}).$$

Solution to Exercise 10

The required figure is shown in the margin.

Note the following points.

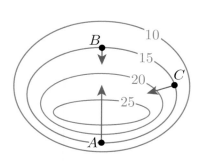

- The arrows representing $\mathbf{grad}\,V$ at A, B and C are perpendicular to the contour lines passing through A, B and C, respectively.

- The arrows all point 'uphill', from lower values to higher values of V.

- The arrows are longer where the contour lines are closer together; this is because the scalar field V varies more rapidly where the contour lines are closer together.

Solution to Exercise 11

To simplify the partial differentiations, we rearrange the expression for $V(x,y)$ to give

$$V(x,y) = \ln((x^2 + y^2)^{1/2}) = \tfrac{1}{2}\ln(x^2 + y^2).$$

Then

$$\frac{\partial V}{\partial x} = \frac{1}{2}\frac{1}{x^2 + y^2} \times 2x = \frac{x}{x^2 + y^2},$$

and similarly,

$$\frac{\partial V}{\partial y} = \frac{y}{x^2 + y^2}.$$

The gradient of the scalar field is therefore given by

$$\nabla V = \frac{x\,\mathbf{i} + y\,\mathbf{j}}{x^2 + y^2}.$$

(This is not defined at the origin – but this is not a problem because the origin is not in the domain of the field.)

$V(x, y)$ remains constant along curves for which $x^2 + y^2$ is constant, so the contour lines are circles centred on the origin. The diagram in the margin shows the contour line through the point $(1, 1)$. At this point, ∇V points in the direction of the radial vector $\mathbf{i} + \mathbf{j}$. An arrow representing ∇V is shown on the diagram. This is perpendicular to the contour line, as expected.

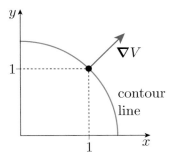

Solution to Exercise 12

Partially differentiating $V(x, y, z)$ with respect to x gives

$$\begin{aligned}
\frac{\partial V}{\partial x} &= \frac{\partial}{\partial x}(x^2 + y^2 + z^2)^{-3/2} \\
&= -\tfrac{3}{2}(x^2 + y^2 + z^2)^{-5/2} \times 2x \\
&= -\frac{3x}{(x^2 + y^2 + z^2)^{5/2}}.
\end{aligned}$$

Similarly,

$$\frac{\partial V}{\partial y} = -\frac{3y}{(x^2 + y^2 + z^2)^{5/2}} \quad \text{and} \quad \frac{\partial V}{\partial z} = -\frac{3z}{(x^2 + y^2 + z^2)^{5/2}}.$$

Hence the gradient is

$$\nabla V = -\frac{3x\,\mathbf{i} + 3y\,\mathbf{j} + 3z\,\mathbf{k}}{(x^2 + y^2 + z^2)^{5/2}} \quad ((x, y, z) \neq (0, 0, 0)).$$

Solution to Exercise 13

(a) The gradient of the scalar field is

$$\begin{aligned}
\nabla T &= -1000 \exp(-(x^2 + 2y^2 + 2z^2)) \times (2x\,\mathbf{i} + 4y\,\mathbf{j} + 4z\,\mathbf{k}) \\
&= -2000 \exp(-(x^2 + 2y^2 + 2z^2))\,(x\,\mathbf{i} + 2y\,\mathbf{j} + 2z\,\mathbf{k}).
\end{aligned}$$

At the point $(1, 1, 1)$, the gradient is

$$\nabla T|_{(1,1,1)} = -2000\,e^{-5}\,(\mathbf{i} + 2\,\mathbf{j} + 2\,\mathbf{k}) \simeq -13.5\,(\mathbf{i} + 2\,\mathbf{j} + 2\,\mathbf{k}),$$

to three significant figures, measured in degrees Celsius per metre.

(b) On moving away from $(1, 1, 1)$, the temperature increases most rapidly in the direction of the gradient at $(1, 1, 1)$. This is the direction of the vector $-(\mathbf{i} + 2\,\mathbf{j} + 2\,\mathbf{k})$, which has magnitude $\sqrt{1^2 + 2^2 + 2^2} = 3$, so the corresponding unit vector is

$$\widehat{\mathbf{n}} = -\tfrac{1}{3}(\mathbf{i} + 2\,\mathbf{j} + 2\,\mathbf{k}).$$

Solution to Exercise 14

(a) The gradient is given by

$$\boldsymbol{\nabla}V = \tfrac{3}{2}(x^2 + y^2 + z^2)^{1/2}\,(2x\,\mathbf{i} + 2y\,\mathbf{j} + 2z\,\mathbf{k})$$
$$= 3(x^2 + y^2 + z^2)^{1/2}\,(x\,\mathbf{i} + y\,\mathbf{j} + z\,\mathbf{k}).$$

So at the point $(1, 2, 2)$, the gradient has the value

$$\boldsymbol{\nabla}V|_{(1,2,2)} = 9(\mathbf{i} + 2\,\mathbf{j} + 2\,\mathbf{k}).$$

The displacement vector from $(1, 2, 2)$ to $(0.98, 1.99, 2.01)$ is

$$\delta\mathbf{s} = -0.02\,\mathbf{i} - 0.01\,\mathbf{j} + 0.01\,\mathbf{k},$$

so the change in V is

$$\delta V \simeq \boldsymbol{\nabla}V \cdot \delta\mathbf{s}$$
$$= 9(\mathbf{i} + 2\,\mathbf{j} + 2\,\mathbf{k}) \cdot (-0.02\,\mathbf{i} - 0.01\,\mathbf{j} + 0.01\,\mathbf{k})$$
$$= 9(-0.02 - 0.02 + 0.02)$$
$$= -0.18.$$

(b) The rate of change of V at the point $(1, 2, 2)$ in the direction of the unit vector $\widehat{\mathbf{n}} = (3\,\mathbf{i} + 4\,\mathbf{k})/5$ is

$$\frac{dV}{ds} = \boldsymbol{\nabla}V \cdot \widehat{\mathbf{n}}$$
$$= 9(\mathbf{i} + 2\,\mathbf{j} + 2\,\mathbf{k}) \cdot \tfrac{1}{5}(3\,\mathbf{i} + 4\,\mathbf{k})$$
$$= \tfrac{99}{5}$$
$$= 19.8.$$

Solution to Exercise 15

In spherical coordinates, the gradient is

$$\boldsymbol{\nabla}V = \frac{\partial V}{\partial r}\,\mathbf{e}_r + \frac{1}{r}\frac{\partial V}{\partial \theta}\,\mathbf{e}_\theta + \frac{1}{r\sin\theta}\frac{\partial V}{\partial \phi}\,\mathbf{e}_\phi.$$

The required partial derivatives are

$$\frac{\partial V}{\partial r} = -\frac{3}{r^4}, \quad \frac{\partial V}{\partial \theta} = 0, \quad \frac{\partial V}{\partial \phi} = 0.$$

So

$$\boldsymbol{\nabla}V = -\frac{3}{r^4}\,\mathbf{e}_r.$$

This gradient field has magnitude $3/r^4$ and points radially inwards, towards the origin.

Solution to Exercise 16

In cylindrical coordinates, the gradient is

$$\boldsymbol{\nabla}f = \frac{\partial f}{\partial r}\,\mathbf{e}_r + \frac{1}{r}\frac{\partial f}{\partial \phi}\,\mathbf{e}_\phi + \frac{\partial f}{\partial z}\,\mathbf{e}_z.$$

The required partial derivatives are

$$\frac{\partial f}{\partial r} = 2r \sin(2\phi), \quad \frac{\partial f}{\partial \phi} = 2r^2 \cos(2\phi), \quad \frac{\partial f}{\partial z} = 2z.$$

So the gradient is

$$\boldsymbol{\nabla} f = 2r \sin(2\phi)\,\mathbf{e}_r + 2r \cos(2\phi)\,\mathbf{e}_\phi + 2z\,\mathbf{e}_z.$$

The unit vectors $\mathbf{e}_r$, $\mathbf{e}_\phi$ and $\mathbf{e}_z$ are mutually orthogonal, so the *square* of the magnitude of the gradient is given by the sum of the squares of its components:

$$|\boldsymbol{\nabla} f|^2 = 4r^2 \sin^2(2\phi) + 4r^2 \cos^2(2\phi) + 4z^2 = 4(r^2 + z^2).$$

Hence the magnitude of the gradient is

$$|\boldsymbol{\nabla} f| = 2\sqrt{r^2 + z^2}.$$

Solution to Exercise 17

(a) In spherical coordinates, the gradient vector field is

$$\boldsymbol{\nabla} T = \frac{\partial T}{\partial r}\,\mathbf{e}_r + \frac{1}{r}\frac{\partial T}{\partial \theta}\,\mathbf{e}_\theta + \frac{1}{r \sin \theta}\frac{\partial T}{\partial \phi}\,\mathbf{e}_\phi.$$

The required partial derivatives are

$$\frac{\partial T}{\partial r} = \sin \theta, \quad \frac{\partial T}{\partial \theta} = r \cos \theta, \quad \frac{\partial T}{\partial \phi} = 0.$$

So

$$\boldsymbol{\nabla} T = \sin \theta\,\mathbf{e}_r + \cos \theta\,\mathbf{e}_\theta.$$

(b) The rate of change of T in the direction of the unit vector $\widehat{\mathbf{n}} = (\mathbf{e}_\theta + \mathbf{e}_\phi)/\sqrt{2}$ is

$$\widehat{\mathbf{n}} \cdot \boldsymbol{\nabla} T = \frac{1}{\sqrt{2}}(\mathbf{e}_\theta + \mathbf{e}_\phi) \cdot (\sin \theta\,\mathbf{e}_r + \cos \theta\,\mathbf{e}_\theta)$$

$$= \frac{1}{\sqrt{2}} \cos \theta.$$

The vectors $\mathbf{e}_r$, $\mathbf{e}_\theta$ and $\mathbf{e}_\phi$ are mutually orthogonal and of unit magnitude.

Note that the required rate of change is the component of the gradient in the direction of the unit vector $\widehat{\mathbf{n}}$, which is most readily evaluated in spherical coordinates in this case.

Solution to Exercise 18

In polar coordinates,

$$\boldsymbol{\nabla} = \mathbf{e}_r \frac{\partial}{\partial r} + \mathbf{e}_\phi \frac{1}{r}\frac{\partial}{\partial \phi}.$$

In cylindrical coordinates,

$$\boldsymbol{\nabla} = \mathbf{e}_r \frac{\partial}{\partial r} + \mathbf{e}_\phi \frac{1}{r}\frac{\partial}{\partial \phi} + \mathbf{e}_z \frac{\partial}{\partial z}.$$

In spherical coordinates,

$$\boldsymbol{\nabla} = \mathbf{e}_r \frac{\partial}{\partial r} + \mathbf{e}_\theta \frac{1}{r}\frac{\partial}{\partial \theta} + \mathbf{e}_\phi \frac{1}{r \sin \theta}\frac{\partial}{\partial \phi}.$$

Solution to Exercise 19

(a) $\quad \nabla \cdot \mathbf{F} = \dfrac{\partial F_x}{\partial x} + \dfrac{\partial F_y}{\partial y} + \dfrac{\partial F_z}{\partial z}$

$\qquad\quad = 2xy + 2yz - 2yz = 2xy.$

(b) $\quad \nabla \cdot \mathbf{G} = \dfrac{\partial G_x}{\partial x} + \dfrac{\partial G_y}{\partial y} + \dfrac{\partial G_z}{\partial z}$

$\qquad\quad = 2(x+y) + 2(y+z) + 2(x+z) = 4(x+y+z).$

Solution to Exercise 20

(a) It makes no sense to take the divergence of a scalar field. The formula for divergence involves the components of a vector field, but a scalar field has no direction so there are no components to use.

(b) Given that $V = x^4 + y^4 + z^4$, the gradient of V is

$$\nabla V = \frac{\partial V}{\partial x}\,\mathbf{i} + \frac{\partial V}{\partial y}\,\mathbf{j} + \frac{\partial V}{\partial z}\,\mathbf{k} = 4x^3\,\mathbf{i} + 4y^3\,\mathbf{j} + 4z^3\,\mathbf{k}.$$

Hence

$$\nabla \cdot (\nabla V) = \frac{\partial}{\partial x}(4x^3) + \frac{\partial}{\partial y}(4y^3) + \frac{\partial}{\partial z}(4z^3)$$

$$= 12(x^2 + y^2 + z^2).$$

Solution to Exercise 21

(a) To partially differentiate $F_x = x/\sqrt{x^2 + y^2}$ with respect to x, we use the quotient rule:

$$\frac{\partial F_x}{\partial x} = \frac{(x^2+y^2)^{1/2} - x\left(\frac{1}{2}(x^2+y^2)^{-1/2} \times 2x\right)}{x^2+y^2}$$

$$= \frac{x^2+y^2-x^2}{(x^2+y^2)^{3/2}} = \frac{y^2}{(x^2+y^2)^{3/2}}.$$

Because of the symmetry between F_x and F_y, a similar result is obtained for $\partial F_y/\partial y$, but with x and y interchanged. There is no z-component in this two-dimensional case, so $\partial F_z/\partial z = 0$. Hence

$$\nabla \cdot \mathbf{F} = \frac{y^2}{(x^2+y^2)^{3/2}} + \frac{x^2}{(x^2+y^2)^{3/2}} + 0$$

$$= \frac{x^2+y^2}{(x^2+y^2)^{3/2}} = \frac{1}{\sqrt{x^2+y^2}} \quad ((x,y) \neq (0,0)).$$

(b) The divergence $\nabla \cdot \mathbf{F}$ calculated in part (a) is positive at all points (except the origin $(0,0)$, where neither $\mathbf{F}$ nor its divergence is defined). We therefore expect $\mathbf{F}$ to diverge away from a typical point, such as that marked by the blue dot in the figure provided with the question.

This interpretation is supported by examining the figure. Let us suppose that $\mathbf{F}$ represents the flow of a fluid. Compare the arrows that enter the square on sides AB and AD with those that leave the square on sides BC and CD. All these arrows have the same length, but those on sides AB and AD are more closely parallel to the sides of the square than those on sides BC and CD. This means that less fluid is carried into the square across sides AB and AD than is carried out across sides BC and CD. So there is a net flow of fluid out of the square, as expected for a field with positive divergence. A more systematic discussion of the flow of fluids across surfaces will be given in the next unit.

Solution to Exercise 22

(a) Using equation (45) for divergence in cylindrical coordinates, and noting that $F_r = 4r^3$, $F_\phi = 0$ and $F_z = 0$, we get

$$\nabla \cdot \mathbf{F} = \frac{1}{r} \frac{\partial (4r^4)}{\partial r} = 16r^2.$$

(b) Similarly, with $G_r = r^2 \sin \phi$, $G_\phi = 0$ and $G_z = z^2$, we get

$$\nabla \cdot \mathbf{G} = \frac{1}{r} \frac{\partial (r^3 \sin \phi)}{\partial r} + \frac{\partial (z^2)}{\partial z} = 3r \sin \phi + 2z.$$

Solution to Exercise 23

(a) Using equation (46) for divergence in spherical coordinates, with $F_r = 4r^3$, $F_\phi = 0$ and $F_z = 0$, we get

$$\nabla \cdot \mathbf{F} = \frac{1}{r^2} \frac{\partial (4r^5)}{\partial r} = 20r^2.$$

Note that the vector field $\mathbf{F}$ is different to that in Exercise 22(a) because the unit vector $\mathbf{e}_r$ in spherical coordinates is not the same as the unit vector $\mathbf{e}_r$ in cylindrical coordinates. It is therefore not surprising that the divergences of these fields are different.

(b) Similarly, with $G_r = 0$, $G_\theta = r \sin^2 \theta$ and $G_\phi = r \cos \theta \cos \phi$, we get

$$\nabla \cdot \mathbf{G} = \frac{1}{r \sin \theta} \frac{\partial (r \sin^3 \theta)}{\partial \theta} + \frac{1}{r \sin \theta} \frac{\partial (r \cos \theta \cos \phi)}{\partial \phi}$$
$$= \frac{3r \sin^2 \theta \cos \theta}{r \sin \theta} - \frac{r \cos \theta \sin \phi}{r \sin \theta}$$
$$= 3 \sin \theta \cos \theta - \cot \theta \sin \phi.$$

Solution to Exercise 24

Using the expression for divergence in spherical coordinates, and the given fact that div $\mathbf{F} = 0$ at all points except the origin, we get

$$\frac{1}{r^2} \frac{\partial (r^2 f(r))}{\partial r} = 0 \quad \text{for } r > 0.$$

So

$$\frac{\partial (r^2 f(r))}{\partial r} = 0.$$

Integrating both sides of this equation, we conclude that $r^2 f(r) = C$, where C is a constant, so $f(r) = C/r^2$, which is proportional to $1/r^2$.

Solution to Exercise 25

We have

$$
\begin{aligned}
\boldsymbol{\nabla} \times \mathbf{V} &= \left(\frac{\partial}{\partial x}\left(\frac{x}{x^2+y^2}\right) - \frac{\partial}{\partial y}\left(\frac{-y}{x^2+y^2}\right) \right) \mathbf{k} \\
&= \left(\frac{(x^2+y^2)\times 1 - x\times 2x}{(x^2+y^2)^2} - \frac{(x^2+y^2)\times(-1)-(-y)\times 2y}{(x^2+y^2)^2}\right)\mathbf{k} \\
&= \left(\frac{(y^2-x^2)-(y^2-x^2)}{(x^2+y^2)^2}\right)\mathbf{k} = \mathbf{0} \quad ((x,y)\neq(0,0)).
\end{aligned}
$$

Solution to Exercise 26

(a)
$$
\boldsymbol{\nabla}\times\mathbf{F} = \begin{vmatrix} \mathbf{i} & \mathbf{j} & \mathbf{k} \\ \dfrac{\partial}{\partial x} & \dfrac{\partial}{\partial y} & \dfrac{\partial}{\partial z} \\ z-y & x-z & y-x \end{vmatrix}.
$$

Expanding the determinant, we obtain

The minus sign in front of $\mathbf{j}$ comes from the rule for expanding a 3×3 determinant.

$$
\begin{aligned}
\boldsymbol{\nabla}\times\mathbf{F} &= \mathbf{i}\left(\frac{\partial(y-x)}{\partial y} - \frac{\partial(x-z)}{\partial z}\right) - \mathbf{j}\left(\frac{\partial(y-x)}{\partial x} - \frac{\partial(z-y)}{\partial z}\right) \\
&\quad + \mathbf{k}\left(\frac{\partial(x-z)}{\partial x} - \frac{\partial(z-y)}{\partial y}\right) \\
&= \mathbf{i}\,(1-(-1)) - \mathbf{j}\,(-1-1) + \mathbf{k}\,(1-(-1)) \\
&= 2\,\mathbf{i} + 2\,\mathbf{j} + 2\,\mathbf{k}.
\end{aligned}
$$

(b)
$$
\begin{aligned}
\boldsymbol{\nabla}\times\mathbf{G} &= \begin{vmatrix} \mathbf{i} & \mathbf{j} & \mathbf{k} \\ \dfrac{\partial}{\partial x} & \dfrac{\partial}{\partial y} & \dfrac{\partial}{\partial z} \\ zy^2 & xz^2 & yx^2 \end{vmatrix} \\
&= \mathbf{i}\left(\frac{\partial(yx^2)}{\partial y} - \frac{\partial(xz^2)}{\partial z}\right) - \mathbf{j}\left(\frac{\partial(yx^2)}{\partial x} - \frac{\partial(zy^2)}{\partial z}\right) \\
&\quad + \mathbf{k}\left(\frac{\partial(xz^2)}{\partial x} - \frac{\partial(zy^2)}{\partial y}\right) \\
&= \mathbf{i}\,(x^2-2xz) - \mathbf{j}\,(2xy-y^2) + \mathbf{k}\,(z^2-2yz).
\end{aligned}
$$

So
$$
\boldsymbol{\nabla}\times\mathbf{G} = x(x-2z)\,\mathbf{i} + y(y-2x)\,\mathbf{j} + z(z-2y)\,\mathbf{k}.
$$

Solution to Exercise 27

The required curl is

$$
\boldsymbol{\nabla}\times\boldsymbol{\nabla}U = \begin{vmatrix} \mathbf{i} & \mathbf{j} & \mathbf{k} \\ \dfrac{\partial}{\partial x} & \dfrac{\partial}{\partial y} & \dfrac{\partial}{\partial z} \\ \dfrac{\partial U}{\partial x} & \dfrac{\partial U}{\partial y} & \dfrac{\partial U}{\partial z} \end{vmatrix}.
$$

This evaluates to

$$\boldsymbol{\nabla} \times \boldsymbol{\nabla}U = \mathbf{i}\left(\frac{\partial^2 U}{\partial y\,\partial z} - \frac{\partial^2 U}{\partial z\,\partial y}\right) - \mathbf{j}\left(\frac{\partial^2 U}{\partial x\,\partial z} - \frac{\partial^2 U}{\partial z\,\partial x}\right)$$
$$+ \mathbf{k}\left(\frac{\partial^2 U}{\partial x\,\partial y} - \frac{\partial^2 U}{\partial y\,\partial x}\right).$$

Within each of the brackets on the right-hand side, the two mixed partial derivatives are equal:

$$\frac{\partial^2 U}{\partial y\,\partial z} = \frac{\partial^2 U}{\partial z\,\partial y}, \quad \frac{\partial^2 U}{\partial x\,\partial z} = \frac{\partial^2 U}{\partial z\,\partial x}, \quad \frac{\partial^2 U}{\partial x\,\partial y} = \frac{\partial^2 U}{\partial y\,\partial x}.$$

We conclude that $\boldsymbol{\nabla} \times \boldsymbol{\nabla}U = \mathbf{0}$ for any scalar field U.

Solution to Exercise 28

(a) The field $\mathbf{F}$ has cylindrical components $F_r = 0$, $F_\phi = 0$, $F_z = r^2$, so

$$\boldsymbol{\nabla} \times \mathbf{F} = \frac{1}{r}\begin{vmatrix} \mathbf{e}_r & r\,\mathbf{e}_\phi & \mathbf{e}_z \\ \dfrac{\partial}{\partial r} & \dfrac{\partial}{\partial \phi} & \dfrac{\partial}{\partial z} \\ 0 & 0 & r^2 \end{vmatrix}$$

$$= \frac{1}{r}\left(\mathbf{e}_r\,(0) - r\,\mathbf{e}_\phi\,(2r) + \mathbf{e}_z\,(0)\right)$$

$$= -2r\,\mathbf{e}_\phi.$$

(b) The field $\mathbf{G}$ has cylindrical components $G_r = 0$, $G_\phi = rz$, $G_z = 0$, so

$$\boldsymbol{\nabla} \times \mathbf{G} = \frac{1}{r}\begin{vmatrix} \mathbf{e}_r & r\,\mathbf{e}_\phi & \mathbf{e}_z \\ \dfrac{\partial}{\partial r} & \dfrac{\partial}{\partial \phi} & \dfrac{\partial}{\partial z} \\ 0 & r^2 z & 0 \end{vmatrix}$$

$$= \frac{1}{r}\left(\mathbf{e}_r\,(-r^2) - r\,\mathbf{e}_\phi\,(0) + \mathbf{e}_z\,(2rz)\right)$$

$$= -r\,\mathbf{e}_r + 2z\,\mathbf{e}_z.$$

(c) The field $\mathbf{H}$ has cylindrical components $H_r = rz\sin\phi$, $H_\phi = 0$, $H_z = 0$, so

$$\boldsymbol{\nabla} \times \mathbf{H} = \frac{1}{r}\begin{vmatrix} \mathbf{e}_r & r\,\mathbf{e}_\phi & \mathbf{e}_z \\ \dfrac{\partial}{\partial r} & \dfrac{\partial}{\partial \phi} & \dfrac{\partial}{\partial z} \\ rz\sin\phi & 0 & 0 \end{vmatrix}$$

$$= \frac{1}{r}\left(\mathbf{e}_r\,(0) - r\,\mathbf{e}_\phi\,(-r\sin\phi) + \mathbf{e}_z\,(-rz\cos\phi)\right)$$

$$= r\sin\phi\,\mathbf{e}_\phi - z\cos\phi\,\mathbf{e}_z.$$

Solution to Exercise 29

The polar components of $\mathbf{F}$ are $F_r = 0$ and $F_\phi = 1/r$, so equation (54) gives

$$\boldsymbol{\nabla} \times \mathbf{F} = \frac{1}{r} \left(\frac{\partial(1)}{\partial r} - \frac{\partial(0)}{\partial \phi} \right) \mathbf{e}_z$$
$$= \mathbf{0} \quad (r \neq 0).$$

Solution to Exercise 30

(a) The field $\mathbf{F}$ has spherical components $F_r = 0$, $F_\theta = r$ and $F_\phi = 0$, so equation (55) gives

$$\boldsymbol{\nabla} \times \mathbf{F} = \frac{1}{r^2 \sin\theta} \begin{vmatrix} \mathbf{e}_r & r\,\mathbf{e}_\theta & r\sin\theta\,\mathbf{e}_\phi \\ \dfrac{\partial}{\partial r} & \dfrac{\partial}{\partial \theta} & \dfrac{\partial}{\partial \phi} \\ 0 & r^2 & 0 \end{vmatrix}$$
$$= \frac{1}{r^2 \sin\theta} \left(\mathbf{e}_r\,(0) - r\,\mathbf{e}_\theta\,(0) + r\sin\theta\,\mathbf{e}_\phi\,(2r) \right)$$
$$= 2\,\mathbf{e}_\phi.$$

(b) $\mathbf{G}$ has spherical components $G_r = 0$, $G_\theta = 0$ and $G_\phi = r\sin\theta$, so

$$\boldsymbol{\nabla} \times \mathbf{G} = \frac{1}{r^2 \sin\theta} \begin{vmatrix} \mathbf{e}_r & r\,\mathbf{e}_\theta & r\sin\theta\,\mathbf{e}_\phi \\ \dfrac{\partial}{\partial r} & \dfrac{\partial}{\partial \theta} & \dfrac{\partial}{\partial \phi} \\ 0 & 0 & r^2\sin^2\theta \end{vmatrix}$$
$$= \frac{1}{r^2 \sin\theta} \left(\mathbf{e}_r\,(2r^2 \sin\theta \cos\theta) - r\,\mathbf{e}_\theta\,(2r\sin^2\theta) + r\sin\theta\,\mathbf{e}_\phi\,(0) \right)$$
$$= 2\cos\theta\,\mathbf{e}_r - 2\sin\theta\,\mathbf{e}_\theta.$$

(c) $\mathbf{H}$ has spherical components $H_r = r^2$, $H_\theta = 0$ and $H_\phi = 0$, so

$$\boldsymbol{\nabla} \times \mathbf{H} = \frac{1}{r^2 \sin\theta} \begin{vmatrix} \mathbf{e}_r & r\,\mathbf{e}_\theta & r\sin\theta\,\mathbf{e}_\phi \\ \dfrac{\partial}{\partial r} & \dfrac{\partial}{\partial \theta} & \dfrac{\partial}{\partial \phi} \\ r^2 & 0 & 0 \end{vmatrix}$$
$$= \mathbf{0}.$$

Acknowledgements

Grateful acknowledgement is made to the following sources:

Figure 2: Hans G / www.flickr.com/photos/48351129@N08/10223373043. This file is licensed under the Creative Commons Attribution-Share Alike Licence http://creativecommons.org/licenses/by-sa/3.0.

Figure 35: NASA.

Every effort has been made to contact copyright holders. If any have been inadvertently overlooked, the publishers will be pleased to make the necessary arrangements at the first opportunity.

Integrating scalar and vector fields

Introduction

Unit 8 explained how to carry out area integrals over flat surfaces, surface integrals over curved surfaces, and volume integrals in three-dimensional space. However, there is another type of integral that is important to us – an integral along a curve, known as a *line integral*.

You are familiar with the idea of integrating along a straight line. Figure 1 shows a straight rod lying along the x-axis with one end at $x = 0$ and the other end at $x = L$. The rod may have an uneven distribution of mass. Its linear density (its mass per unit length) is then a function of position, which we denote by $\lambda(x)$. The mass of a short segment of the rod between x and $x + \delta x$ is given by

$$\delta m \simeq \lambda(x)\,\delta x,$$

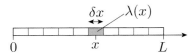

Figure 1 A straight rod

and the mass of the whole rod is found by adding up the masses of all of its segments. In the limit where the rod is divided into an infinite number of infinitesimally short segments, the sum becomes an integral and the total mass of the rod is expressed as

$$M = \int_0^L \lambda(x)\,dx.$$

A new feature introduced in this unit is to allow the rod to be curved (Figure 2). The task of finding the mass of a curved rod can again be approached by dividing the rod into many short segments, finding the mass of each segment, and adding all the contributions together. In the limit where the segments become infinitesimally short, the sum becomes an integral. However, this integral is not along the x-axis, but is along the curved path occupied by the rod. Such an integral is called a *line integral*.

Figure 2 A curved rod

There are a couple of problems that must be solved before we can evaluate a line integral of this sort. When we split the curved rod into segments, we must have a way of labelling the different segments. This is done by choosing a parameter t that increases smoothly from one end of the rod to the other. We can then talk about a segment of the rod for which the parameter has values between t and $t + \delta t$. We also need to find an expression for the length of a segment in terms of t and δt. Once these problems have been solved, the line integral can be expressed as a definite integral over the parameter t. You will see how this works in Section 1.

In Section 2, you will also see how to define and evaluate the line integrals of vector fields. The idea is simple enough: at each point along the path, we take the component of the field that is parallel to the path, and then integrate this component along the path. This turns out to be a very powerful tool in physical applications.

For example, when you lift an object, you expend energy working against gravity (Figure 3) and the lifted object gains energy as a result. The object may be lifted straight upwards, or in a circular arc, or in a spiral – however you like. Whichever path is chosen, the energy transferred to the object by

Figure 3 Lifting weights

the applied force is given by the line integral of the force along the object's path. This is the line integral of a vector field. Such calculations give physicists a precise language for talking about energy transfers.

You might ask whether the energy needed to move an object from one point A to another point B depends on the detailed path taken, or just the points A and B. The answer depends on the forces acting. In mathematical terms, we need to find the conditions under which line integrals depend only on their start and end points. Section 3 will show that some types of vector field have line integrals that are always path-independent. Such fields are said to be *conservative*.

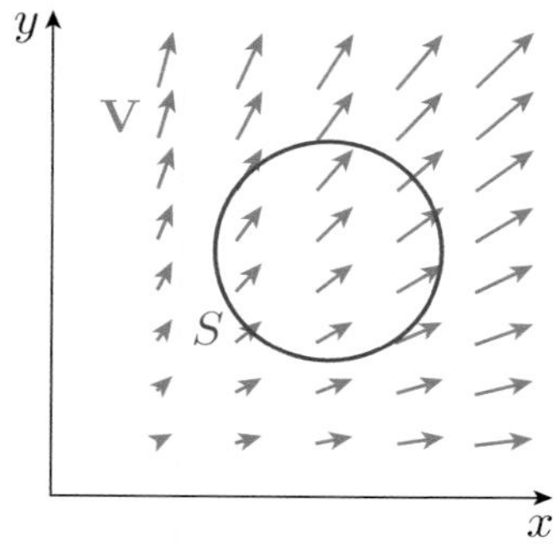

The remainder of the unit uses integrals to get a deeper, and more powerful, understanding of divergence and curl. You will remember that Unit 9 made tentative interpretations of divergence and curl: divergence was associated with the local outflow of a vector field, and curl with a local rotation or swirling. In this unit we will be more precise.

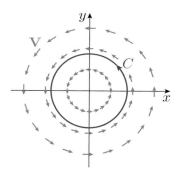

Figure 4 A diverging vector field **V** and a spherical surface S (cross-sectional view)

Figure 4 shows a vector field **V**, together with an imaginary spherical surface S. Let us suppose that the field represents the flow of a fluid. Then it is apparent from the diagram that there is a net flow outwards, from the inside of the sphere into the exterior space. We can quantify this outward flow by integrating the outward normal component of the field over the surface of the sphere. This involves a type of surface integral called the *flux* of the vector field. We will use this idea to establish a precise link between divergence and outflow.

Something similar can be achieved for curl. Figure 5 shows a vector field **V** that represents a different type of fluid flow – one that circulates rather than radiates outwards. The figure also shows an imaginary closed path C, traversed in an anticlockwise sense (as indicated by the blue arrow). Then we can calculate the line integral of the vector field **V** around the path C. This gives a quantity called the *circulation* of the field around C. We will use this idea to establish a precise link between curl and rotation.

The links between flux and divergence, and between circulation and curl, are encapsulated by two important theorems – the *divergence theorem* and the *curl theorem* – which are discussed and used in Sections 4 and 5. These theorems give physicists and engineers powerful tools for exploring real phenomena involving fields, and are essential knowledge for anyone who wants to understand electromagnetic fields or fluid flow.

Figure 5 A circulating vector field **V** and a closed path C

Study guide

This unit builds on all the previous units in this book. You need to be familiar with partial derivatives from Unit 7, surface and volume integrals from Unit 8, and gradients, divergences and curls from Unit 9.

The first half of the unit deals with line integrals of various types. Section 1 covers line integrals of scalar fields, while Section 2 covers line integrals of vector fields. Special vector fields with path-independent line integrals are discussed in Section 3.

The second half of the unit uses integrals to gain more powerful insights into divergence and curl. Section 4 defines the flux of a vector field, and relates it to divergence using the divergence theorem. Section 5 defines the concept of circulation, and relates it to curl using the curl theorem.

1   Line integrals of scalar fields

Imagine a whale taking a meandering journey through the ocean. Within the ocean there are huge numbers of plankton, the whale's staple food supply. The plankton are distributed unevenly, so the number of plankton per unit volume is a function $n(\mathbf{r})$ of position $\mathbf{r}$.

Let us break down the whale's journey into many short steps or segments. The ith step starts at position $\mathbf{r}_i$ and is of length δl_i. The number of plankton encountered by the whale during this step is

$$\delta N_i \simeq n(\mathbf{r}_i)\, A\, \delta l_i,$$

where A is the area of the whale's open mouth (assumed to be permanently open). We can also write this as

$$\delta N_i \simeq \lambda_i\, \delta l_i,$$

where $\lambda_i = n(\mathbf{r}_i)\, A$ is the number of plankton per unit length that are within range of the whale's open mouth in step i.

The total number of plankton N encountered by the whale during its journey is found by adding together contributions from each step, so

$$N \simeq \sum_i \lambda_i\, \delta l_i.$$

This is an approximation because the number of plankton per unit length may vary *within* a step. We really ought to consider the sum in the limit of an infinite number of steps, each of vanishingly small size. In this limit, the sum becomes an integral and the total number of plankton encountered is written as

$$N = \int_C \lambda(\mathbf{r})\, dl.$$

An integral like this is called a **line integral**. Of course, we have not told you how to evaluate such an integral – we will do that shortly; for the moment, we focus on the concept and the notation that expresses it. Notice that the integral sign does not have lower and upper limits. Instead, it carries the symbol C, which labels the whale's path. In general, the detailed path C matters, not just its start and end points. Along some paths between given start and end points, a whale may encounter many plankton; along others, it may find very few.

Another example of a line integral arises when we calculate the length of a path. How far does the whale swim as it travels along a path C? We again divide the path into many segments. The total length of the path is then approximated by

$$L \simeq \sum_i \delta l_i,$$

where δl_i is the length of the ith segment.

Taking the limit of an infinite number of segments, each of vanishingly small length, the total length of the path is given by the line integral

$$L = \int_C 1 \, dl.$$

The notation is deceptively simple. Remember that the integral is along the path C, and of course the length obtained depends on the path. In general, you cannot just do the integral over l and then substitute in limits. There is a special technique for doing line integrals, which we now explain.

1.1   Line integrals in Cartesian coordinates

In this subsection, we discuss line integrals of scalar fields along given *paths*, calculated using Cartesian coordinates (x, y, z).

A path is more than a curve!

> A **path** is a curve with a definite sense of progression from a start point to an end point. In diagrams, the sense of progression may be indicated by an arrow, as in Figure 6.

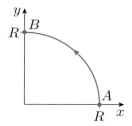

Figure 6   An anticlockwise path around a quarter-circle

Parametric representation of a path

The concept of a line integral along a path is based on the idea of splitting the path into many short segments. In the discussion above we labelled the segments by an index i, but this is not convenient for calculations. Instead, we choose a continuous parameter t that increases smoothly from the beginning of the path to the end. We can then talk about a segment of the path for which the parameter has values between t and $t + \delta t$.

We must specify the shape of the path. This is done by expressing the coordinates of points on the path as functions of the parameter t. For a path in three-dimensional space, we write

$$x = x(t), \quad y = y(t), \quad z = z(t) \quad (t_1 \leq t \leq t_2),$$

The minimum and maximum values of t always correspond to the start and end points of the path, respectively.

where $t = t_1$ at the start point and $t = t_2$ at the end point. Such a set of equations is said to give a **parametric representation**, or a **parametrisation**, of the path. For two-dimensional paths in the xy-plane, $z(t) = 0$, but this is usually left out of the description.

Let us take the path in Figure 6 as an example. This path starts at the point $A = (R, 0)$ on the x-axis, progresses anticlockwise around a circular arc of radius R, and ends at the point $B = (0, R)$ on the y-axis. You can imagine an insect crawling along this path, starting from A at time $t = 0$, and travelling at a steady rate until it reaches B at time $t = \pi/2$. Then at time t, the x- and y-coordinates of the insect are

$$x(t) = R \cos t, \quad y(t) = R \sin t \quad (0 \leq t \leq \pi/2). \tag{1}$$

These equations provide a parametric representation of the path. They can also be written in the vector form

$$\mathbf{r}(t) = R \cos t \, \mathbf{i} + R \sin t \, \mathbf{j},$$

where $\mathbf{r}(t)$ is the position vector of the insect at time t. The relationship between $\mathbf{r}(t)$ and the components in equations (1) is shown in Figure 7.

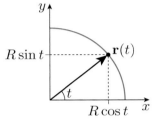

Figure 7   Cartesian components of a point on a path

The parameter t always increases along the path, so in our analogy, the insect always moves forwards. However, the insect could progress in a variety of ways, giving a variety of parametric representations. For example, we could have

$$x(t) = R \cos(t^2), \quad y(t) = R \sin(t^2) \quad (0 \leq t \leq \sqrt{\pi/2}). \tag{2}$$

This is an equally valid parametric representation of the path in Figure 6, but corresponds to a non-uniform rate of progression.

The picture of an insect crawling along a path is just a device to aid understanding. The parameter t need not represent time – it could be any quantity that increases along the path. In particular, if we consider the path traced out by a whale as it swims through the ocean, the parametric representation of this path need not describe the location of the whale as a function of time!

Each parametrisation defines a certain path. The following parametric equations correspond to the path in Figure 8, which is a quarter-circle traversed *clockwise*:

$$x(t) = R \sin t, \quad y(t) = R \cos t \quad (0 \leq t \leq \pi/2).$$

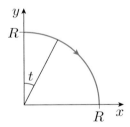

Figure 8   A clockwise path around a quarter-circle

This is not the same as the path in Figure 6 because the sense of progression has been reversed.

In some cases, the start point and end point are identical. For example, the equations

$$x(t) = R \cos t, \quad y(t) = R \sin t \quad (0 \leq t \leq 2\pi)$$

represent the circular path shown in Figure 9, which starts and ends at the point $(R, 0)$ on the x-axis. In general, paths that have distinct start and end points are said to be **open**, while paths with identical start and end points are said to be **closed**. Any journey where you leave your house in the morning and return in the evening is a closed path.

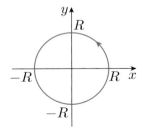

Figure 9   An anticlockwise path around a circle

The length of a short segment of a path

Figure 10 shows a short segment of a path that lies in the xy-plane. This segment begins at point P, with parameter value t and coordinates (x, y), and ends at point Q, with parameter value $t + \delta t$ and coordinates $(x + \delta x, y + \delta y)$.

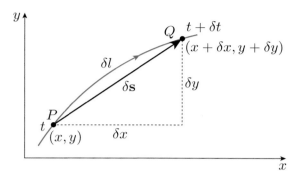

Figure 10   A short segment of a path

The displacement vector from P to Q is given by

$$\delta \mathbf{s} = \delta x \, \mathbf{i} + \delta y \, \mathbf{j}. \tag{3}$$

Dividing and multiplying the right-hand side by δt, we get

$$\delta \mathbf{s} = \left(\frac{\delta x}{\delta t} \, \mathbf{i} + \frac{\delta y}{\delta t} \, \mathbf{j} \right) \delta t \simeq \left(\frac{dx}{dt} \, \mathbf{i} + \frac{dy}{dt} \, \mathbf{j} \right) \delta t, \tag{4}$$

where the last step follows because we are assuming that δt is very small. The magnitude of this displacement is the square root of the sum of the squares of the components. Because $\delta t > 0$, we get

Recall that if $\mathbf{a} = a_x \, \mathbf{i} + a_y \, \mathbf{j}$, then $|\mathbf{a}| = \sqrt{a_x^2 + a_y^2}$.

$$|\delta \mathbf{s}| \simeq \sqrt{\left(\frac{dx}{dt} \right)^2 + \left(\frac{dy}{dt} \right)^2} \, \delta t.$$

This approximates the *distance* between the points P and Q. We are interested in the *curved segment* of path between P and Q, which has length δl. However, if the curve is reasonably smooth, and P and Q are very close together, then δl is well approximated by $|\delta \mathbf{s}|$. In the limit where the points P and Q approach one another, any error introduced by this approximation becomes negligible. We can therefore say that the length of a tiny segment of the path, with parameter values between t and $t + \delta t$, is

$$\delta l \simeq \sqrt{\left(\frac{dx}{dt} \right)^2 + \left(\frac{dy}{dt} \right)^2} \, \delta t. \tag{5}$$

This result applies to any path confined to the xy-plane.

For a path in three-dimensional space, we go through a similar argument but include the z-coordinate. The displacement vector then becomes

$$\delta \mathbf{s} = \delta x \, \mathbf{i} + \delta y \, \mathbf{j} + \delta z \, \mathbf{k},$$

and the expression for the length of a tiny segment of the path is

$$\delta l \simeq \sqrt{\left(\frac{dx}{dt}\right)^2 + \left(\frac{dy}{dt}\right)^2 + \left(\frac{dz}{dt}\right)^2} \, \delta t. \tag{6}$$

The length of a path

The simplest use of line integrals is to find the total length of a path. We begin with the two-dimensional case.

Suppose that we have a path C in the xy-plane, starting at point A and ending at point B. To find the length of this path, we must add up the lengths of all of its segments, taking the limit of an infinite number of segments, each of infinitesimal length. In this limit, the sum becomes an integral, and the total length L of the path is given by the following definite integral, where t_1 and t_2 are the parameter values at the start and end of the path.

Length of a path in the xy-plane

$$L = \int_{t_1}^{t_2} \sqrt{\left(\frac{dx}{dt}\right)^2 + \left(\frac{dy}{dt}\right)^2} \, dt. \tag{7}$$

Example 1

Use the parametrisation of equations (1) to find the length of the quarter-circle path in Figure 6.

Solution

The parametric equations are

$$x(t) = R\cos t, \quad y(t) = R\sin t \quad (0 \le t \le \pi/2),$$

so

$$\frac{dx}{dt} = -R\sin t \quad \text{and} \quad \frac{dy}{dt} = R\cos t.$$

Hence

$$\left(\frac{dx}{dt}\right)^2 + \left(\frac{dy}{dt}\right)^2 = (-R\sin t)^2 + (R\cos t)^2$$
$$= R^2(\sin^2 t + \cos^2 t) = R^2.$$

Using equation (7), the total length of the path is

$$L = \int_0^{\pi/2} \sqrt{R^2} \, dt = \int_0^{\pi/2} R \, dt = \frac{\pi}{2}R,$$

as expected for a quarter of the circumference of a circle of radius R.

We can calculate the length of the same path using the alternative parametrisation of equations (2). In this case, the parametric equations are

$$x(t) = R\cos(t^2), \quad y(t) = R\sin(t^2) \quad (0 \le t \le \sqrt{\pi/2}),$$

and the chain rule of ordinary differentiation gives

$$\frac{dx}{dt} = -R\sin(t^2) \times 2t \quad \text{and} \quad \frac{dy}{dt} = R\cos(t^2) \times 2t.$$

Hence

$$\left(\frac{dx}{dt}\right)^2 + \left(\frac{dy}{dt}\right)^2 = 4R^2t^2\left(\sin^2(t^2) + \cos^2(t^2)\right) = 4R^2t^2,$$

and the total length of the path is

$$L = \int_0^{\sqrt{\pi/2}} 2Rt\,dt = 2R\left[\tfrac{1}{2}t^2\right]_0^{\sqrt{\pi/2}} = \tfrac{1}{2}\pi R,$$

as before.

Any valid parametrisation can be used, and the answer will always be the same, but some choices make life easier than others!

A line integral along a given path does not depend on the choice of parametrisation. You are free to choose any parametrisation you like, provided that it gives a correct representation of the path.

You need not worry about which parametrisation to use; where it is not obvious, we will always suggest an appropriate choice.

We can also consider the reverse path, shown in Figure 8. This occupies the same quarter-circle curve as before, but the start and end points are interchanged, so the path is traversed in the reverse sense. This reverse path is parametrised by the equations

$$x(t) = R\sin t, \quad y(t) = R\cos t \quad (0 \le t \le \pi/2).$$

It is intuitively obvious that this path must have the same length as before, and this can be easily verified. We have

$$\frac{dx}{dt} = R\cos t, \quad \frac{dy}{dt} = -R\sin t,$$

so

$$\left(\frac{dx}{dt}\right)^2 + \left(\frac{dy}{dt}\right)^2 = (R\cos t)^2 + (-R\sin t)^2 = R^2,$$

giving

$$L = \int_0^{\pi/2} R\,dt = \tfrac{1}{2}\pi R,$$

as before.

In general, the lengths of curves, and the line integrals of scalar functions, do not depend on the sense in which a path is traversed.

Why do we bother to distinguish between curves and paths? You will see that this distinction *does* matter for the line integrals of vector fields. Our terminology bears this in mind.

Exercise 1

The parabolic arc shown in the margin has parametric representation

$$x(t) = 2t, \quad y(t) = t^2 \quad (-1 \le t \le 1).$$

What is the length of this arc? You may use the standard integral

$$\int \sqrt{1 + x^2}\, dx = \tfrac{1}{2}\left(x\sqrt{1 + x^2} + \ln(x + \sqrt{1 + x^2})\right) + C.$$

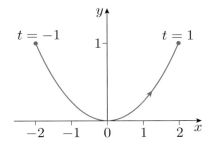

The method is easily extended to paths in three-dimensional space. In this case, the parametric representation gives x, y and z as functions of the parameter t. The formula for the length of a segment is given by equation (6), and the total length of the path is given by the following expression.

Length of a path in three dimensions

$$L = \int_{t_1}^{t_2} \sqrt{\left(\frac{dx}{dt}\right)^2 + \left(\frac{dy}{dt}\right)^2 + \left(\frac{dz}{dt}\right)^2}\, dt, \tag{8}$$

where t_1 and t_2 are the parameter values at the start and end of the path.

Exercise 2

One turn of a helical path has the parabolic representation

$$x = a\cos t, \quad y = a\sin t, \quad z = bt \quad (0 \le t \le 2\pi),$$

where a and b are positive constants. Find the length of this path.

Line integrals of scalar functions

We sometimes need to integrate a scalar function along a given path. For example, we might find the total mass of a curved rod by integrating its linear density (its mass per unit length) along the rod.

Starting at one end of the rod, we follow a path C that tracks along the rod and stops at the other end. Then the total mass of the rod can be expressed as the line integral

$$M = \int_C \lambda\, dl,$$

where λ is the linear density at points along the curved rod.

In two dimensions, the path is described by parametric equations

$$x = x(t), \quad y = y(t) \quad (t_1 \le t \le t_2),$$

and the linear density of the rod is given by a function

$$\lambda = \lambda(x(t), y(t)).$$

We also know that a short segment of the rod has length

$$\delta l \simeq \sqrt{\left(\frac{dx}{dt}\right)^2 + \left(\frac{dy}{dt}\right)^2}\, \delta t.$$

This leads to the following expression for the total mass of the rod.

$$M = \int_{t_1}^{t_2} \lambda(x(t), y(t)) \sqrt{\left(\frac{dx}{dt}\right)^2 + \left(\frac{dy}{dt}\right)^2}\, dt. \tag{9}$$

A similar formula applies in three dimensions, with obvious adjustments to include $z(t)$ and $(dz/dt)^2$. Formulas like this also apply to other quantities that are given per unit length of a path. For example, λ could represent the number of accessible plankton per unit length along a whale's path.

Example 2

A non-uniform curved rod lies in the xy-plane. Its coordinates (in metres) are given by the parametric equations

$$x(t) = 2t, \quad y(t) = 1 - t^2 \quad (-1 \le t \le 1).$$

The linear density of the rod (in kilograms per metre) is

$$\lambda(x, y) = \frac{1}{(x^2 + y^2)^{1/2}}.$$

What is its mass?

Solution

From the given parametric equations, we have

$$x^2(t) + y^2(t) = 4t^2 + (1 - t^2)^2 = t^4 + 2t^2 + 1 = (1 + t^2)^2,$$

so

$$\lambda(x(t), y(t)) = \frac{1}{1 + t^2}.$$

Also,

$$\frac{dx}{dt} = 2 \quad \text{and} \quad \frac{dy}{dt} = -2t,$$

so

$$\sqrt{\left(\frac{dx}{dt}\right)^2 + \left(\frac{dy}{dt}\right)^2} = 2\sqrt{1 + t^2}.$$

The mass of the rod is therefore

$$M = \int_{-1}^{1} \frac{1}{1+t^2} \times 2\sqrt{1+t^2}\, dt = 2 \int_{-1}^{1} \frac{1}{\sqrt{1+t^2}}\, dt.$$

Using a standard integral given in the Handbook, we get

$$M = 2 \left[\ln\left(t + \sqrt{1+t^2}\,\right) \right]_{-1}^{1}$$
$$= 2\ln(\sqrt{2}+1) - 2\ln(\sqrt{2}-1) \simeq 3.53.$$

So the mass of the rod is approximately 3.53 kilograms.

Exercise 3

A semicircular path C has parametric representation

$$x(t) = R\cos t, \quad y(t) = R\sin t \quad (0 \le t \le \pi),$$

where R is a positive constant. On this path, the linear number density of ants (i.e. the number of ants per unit length of path) is given by

$$\lambda(x,y) = \frac{A}{R^4}\, x^2 y,$$

where A is a positive constant. What is the total number of ants on the path?

1.2   Line integrals in orthogonal coordinates

Line integrals can also be evaluated using non-Cartesian coordinates. In this subsection, we describe how this is done. This is optional material, and will not be assessed. However, you should read it if you are interested in physics or astronomy, as there are close links with the mathematics used in Einstein's theory of relativity.

As an example, let us see how the length of a path is calculated in polar coordinates. We consider a path in the xy-plane that is defined using polar coordinates (r, ϕ). This means that its parametric representation is given in the form

$$r = r(t), \quad \phi = \phi(t) \quad (t_1 \le t \le t_2).$$

Figure 11 shows the short segment between points P and Q. The point P has polar coordinates (r, ϕ) and parameter value t, and the point Q has polar coordinates $(r + \delta r, \phi + \delta\phi)$ and parameter value $t + \delta t$.

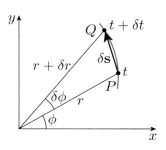

Figure 11   A path segment in polar coordinates (the angle $\delta\phi$ is magnified for clarity)

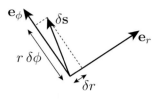

Figure 12 Resolving $\delta\mathbf{s}$ along polar unit vectors

The displacement vector $\delta\mathbf{s}$ from P to Q can be resolved into a radial component δr in the direction of the unit vector $\mathbf{e}_r$, and a transverse component $r\,\delta\phi$ in the direction of the unit vector $\mathbf{e}_\phi$ (see Figure 12). We therefore have

$$\delta\mathbf{s} = \delta r\,\mathbf{e}_r + r\,\delta\phi\,\mathbf{e}_\phi. \tag{10}$$

Note the factor r in the last term on the right-hand side. This is the *scale factor* needed to convert a change in angle, $\delta\phi$, into an appropriate length.

Bearing the scale factor in mind, we can follow the same argument as that given earlier for Cartesian coordinates. In polar coordinates, the expression for the length of a small segment of the path is

$$\delta l \simeq \sqrt{\left(\frac{dr}{dt}\right)^2 + r^2\left(\frac{d\phi}{dt}\right)^2}\,\delta t,$$

and the total length of path between points with parameter values $t = t_1$ and $t = t_2$ is

$$L = \int_{t_1}^{t_2} \sqrt{\left(\frac{dr}{dt}\right)^2 + r^2\left(\frac{d\phi}{dt}\right)^2}\,dt. \tag{11}$$

To illustrate this result, consider an anticlockwise circular path of radius R, centred on the origin. This may be described by the parametric equations

$$r(t) = R, \quad \phi(t) = t \quad (0 \le t \le 2\pi).$$

Since $dr/dt = 0$ and $d\phi/dt = 1$, the total length of the path is

$$L = \int_0^{2\pi} \sqrt{0^2 + R^2 \times 1}\,dt = \int_0^{2\pi} R\,dt = 2\pi R.$$

Exercise 4

In polar coordinates, the spiral path shown in the margin has parametric representation

$$r(t) = 2t, \quad \phi(t) = t \quad (0 \le t \le 5).$$

Find the length of this path.

(*Hint:* You may use the standard integral given in Exercise 1.)

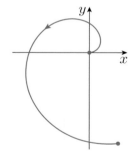

The formula for the length of a path in polar coordinates can be generalised to other orthogonal coordinate systems.

Suppose that a path in three-dimensional space is described in orthogonal coordinates (u, v, w). The corresponding scale factors are denoted by h_u, h_v and h_w, and the unit vectors by $\mathbf{e}_u$, $\mathbf{e}_v$ and $\mathbf{e}_w$.

The path is then specified by parametric equations of the form

$$u = u(t), \quad v = v(t), \quad w = w(t) \quad (t_1 \le t \le t_2).$$

We consider two neighbouring points on the path: P with coordinates (u, v, w) and parameter value t, and Q with coordinates $(u + \delta u, v + \delta v, w + \delta w)$ and parameter value $t + \delta t$ (see Figure 13).

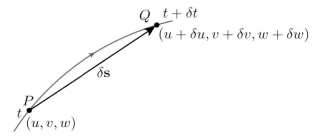

Figure 13   Neighbouring points P and Q on a path in (u, v, w) coordinates. Inevitably, this sketch is two-dimensional, but the path need not be planar.

The displacement vector $\delta \mathbf{s}$ from P to Q can be resolved in the directions of the $\mathbf{e}_u$, $\mathbf{e}_v$ and $\mathbf{e}_w$ unit vectors. For example, the component in the direction of $\mathbf{e}_u$ is $h_u \, \delta u$. This follows directly from the definition of scale factors. There are similar results for the other components, so the displacement vector from P to Q is given by

$$\delta \mathbf{s} = h_u \, \delta u \, \mathbf{e}_u + h_v \, \delta v \, \mathbf{e}_v + h_w \, \delta w \, \mathbf{e}_w. \tag{12}$$

Using the same argument as before, we reach the following conclusion.

Length of a path in an orthogonal coordinate system

In an orthogonal coordinate system (u, v, w), with scale factors h_u, h_v and h_w, the length of a path between points with parameter values $t = t_1$ and $t = t_2$ is

$$L = \int_{t_1}^{t_2} \sqrt{h_u^2 \left(\frac{du}{dt}\right)^2 + h_v^2 \left(\frac{dv}{dt}\right)^2 + h_w^2 \left(\frac{dw}{dt}\right)^2} \, dt. \tag{13}$$

The main point to note about this formula is the presence of the scale factors. These were not apparent in Cartesian coordinates (x, y, z) because all the scale factors are equal to 1 in this case. In polar coordinates (r, ϕ), the scale factors are $h_r = 1$ and $h_\phi = r$, and there is no third coordinate, so in this special case we recover equation (11). For reference, some useful scale factors are listed in Table 1.

Table 1   Some scale factors

Coordinate system		Scale factors
Polar coordinates	(r, ϕ)	$h_r = 1, \, h_\phi = r$
Cylindrical coordinates	(r, ϕ, z)	$h_r = 1, \, h_\phi = r, \, h_z = 1$
Spherical coordinates	(r, θ, ϕ)	$h_r = 1, \, h_\theta = r, \, h_\phi = r \sin \theta$

We can apply equation (13) to paths on the surface of a sphere, such as those that describe journeys on the surface of the Earth. It is natural to use spherical coordinates (r, θ, ϕ) in this case. The advantage of this choice is that the radial coordinate does not vary: it has the constant value R, the radius of the sphere.

The parametric equations of a path on the surface of the sphere then take the form

$$\theta = \theta(t), \quad \phi = \phi(t), \quad r = R \quad (t_1 \leq t \leq t_2).$$

Using equation (13), and taking scale factors from Table 1, the length of a path on the surface of a sphere is given by

$$L = R \int_{t_1}^{t_2} \sqrt{\left(\frac{d\theta}{dt}\right)^2 + \sin^2\theta \left(\frac{d\phi}{dt}\right)^2} \, dt. \tag{14}$$

Numerical methods are often needed to evaluate this integral, but the cases considered in the following exercise can be done by hand.

Exercise 5

Paths A and B lie on the surface of a sphere of radius R, and have the following parametric representations.

Path A: $\theta(t) = t, \quad \phi = \pi/4 \quad (0 \leq t \leq \pi/2).$
Path B: $\theta(t) = \pi/6, \quad \phi = t \quad (0 \leq t \leq \pi/2).$

Use equation (14) to find the lengths of these paths.

Figure 14   A geodesic path from London to Los Angeles

Figure 15   Albert Einstein (1882–1955)

Towards Einstein's theory of general relativity

When considering paths on a curved surface, it is natural to ask: what is the shortest path between two given points? Such paths are called **geodesics**. Long-distance plane routes generally follow geodesics, although slight adjustments may be made for winds and weather (Figure 14). The first step in finding geodesics is to have a formula for the length of a path, and this is provided by equation (13), although more work is needed to identify the geodesics. It turns out that in Exercise 5, path A is a geodesic but path B is not.

In 1916, after years of struggle, Albert Einstein (Figure 15) created his theory of **general relativity**. This is a theory of motion under gravity. Rather than dealing with ordinary space, general relativity deals with **spacetime**, which combines the three dimensions of space with time. Along the track of a particle in spacetime, a quantity called **proper time** increases steadily; this is analogous to the length of a curve in ordinary space.

General relativity is based on two extraordinary ideas. First, it asserts that spacetime is curved by matter. Then it says that when moving under gravity, a body follows the path of maximum proper time. By analogy with ordinary space, such a path is called a *geodesic*. So to predict motion under gravity, we must find the geodesics in spacetime, and this brings line integrals into the heart of general relativity.

2   Line integrals of vector fields

You have seen how to integrate *scalar fields* along given paths. It is also possible to integrate *vector fields* along paths, and this section explains how this is done.

2.1   The basic concept

A simple example will lead us towards the main idea. In a 100 metre race, competitors sprint along a straight track. When analysing the times achieved, officials often record the component of wind velocity in the direction of the race. Fast times are less impressive in a strong following wind, and world records cannot be claimed if such a wind is present.

Longer races generally follow curved paths. For distances above 400 metres, the runners complete one or more laps of the stadium. In these cases, it is not relevant to record the component of the wind velocity in any single direction. Assuming that the wind velocity field remains constant in time, a more suitable measure of wind assistance may be obtained as follows.

- At each point along the path of the race, measure the component of the wind velocity along the direction of the path.

- Integrate this component round the path, from its start point to its end point.

In races round complete laps, we might expect the wind to be in the runners' backs at some points, and in their faces at others. But we can also imagine situations where the wind swirls around the stadium like a gentle eddy, consistently helping the runners on their way. In practice, athletics officials do not concern themselves with such details, but this does not matter. The main point of our example is that it suggests a way of defining the line integral of a vector field.

The concept of the line integral of a vector field

Given a vector field $\mathbf{v}$, and a path C leading from a start point to an end point, the line integral of $\mathbf{v}$ along C is defined as follows.

At each point along the path, we take the component of $\mathbf{v}$ in the direction of the path, and then integrate this along the path.

As a simple example, consider the line integral of the vector field

$$\mathbf{v}(x,y) = x^2(y+1)\,\mathbf{i} + x(y-1)^2\,\mathbf{j}$$

along a path C that travels along the x-axis, starting at $x = 0$ and ending at $x = 3$. Figure 16 is an arrow map of this vector field, with the path C shown in blue.

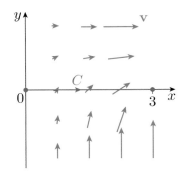

Figure 16   A vector field $\mathbf{v}(x,y)$ and a path C

In this case, the component of $\mathbf{v}$ in the direction of the path is v_x. Along the path C, the component v_x has the value $x^2(0+1) = x^2$. So the line integral of the vector field $\mathbf{v}$ along the path C is

$$\int_{x=0}^{x=3} x^2 \, dx = \left[\tfrac{1}{3}x^3\right]_0^3 = 9.$$

Notice that the answer is a number. A similar result applies to all line integrals of vector fields – their values are scalars (i.e. numbers, or numbers with associated units).

This illustrates the concept of the line integral of a vector field in the special case where the path of integration is along a coordinate axis. But it does not give us a reliable way of calculating line integrals in general. More usually, the path of integration is curved, and the coordinates of points on the path are given by parametric equations. The next subsection will show you how to evaluate line integrals of vector fields in this general case. Once we have a suitable formula, the line integrals of vector fields are just as easy to evaluate as those of scalar fields.

2.2 Line integrals in Cartesian coordinates

Suppose that we are given a two-dimensional vector field $\mathbf{F}(x, y)$, and we want to calculate its line integral along a given path C, with start point A and end point B (Figure 17).

Figure 17 An arrow map of a vector field $\mathbf{F}(x, y)$ (orange) and a path C (blue)

We can imagine approximating the path C by a succession of straight-line steps, as shown in Figure 18. We do this by selecting points along the path, with position vectors $\mathbf{r}_1, \mathbf{r}_2, \ldots, \mathbf{r}_{n+1}$. The sequence starts from A, with position vector $\mathbf{r}_1$, and ends at B, with position vector $\mathbf{r}_{n+1}$. We take a succession of straight-line steps: from $\mathbf{r}_1$ to $\mathbf{r}_2$, from $\mathbf{r}_2$ to $\mathbf{r}_3$, and so on, until we take the last step from $\mathbf{r}_n$ to $\mathbf{r}_{n+1}$. The line integral of $\mathbf{F}$ along the path C is approximated by a sum of contributions from all these steps.

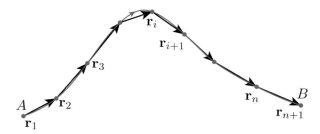

Figure 18 A path approximated by straight-line steps

Figure 19 takes a closer look at the step from $\mathbf{r}_i$ to $\mathbf{r}_{i+1}$, which involves the displacement vector

$$\delta \mathbf{s}_i = \mathbf{r}_{i+1} - \mathbf{r}_i.$$

At the beginning of the step, the vector field has value $\mathbf{F}(\mathbf{r}_i)$. The contribution of this step to the complete line integral is given by multiplying the component of the field in the direction of the step

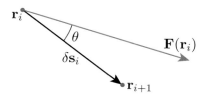

Figure 19 The ith step

(which is $|\mathbf{F}(\mathbf{r}_i)|\cos\theta$) by the length of the step, $|\delta\mathbf{s}_i|$. Using the definition of the scalar product of two vectors, we therefore have

contribution of ith step $= |\mathbf{F}(\mathbf{r}_i)|\cos\theta \times |\delta\mathbf{s}_i| = \mathbf{F}(\mathbf{r}_i)\cdot\delta\mathbf{s}_i$,

Recall that $\mathbf{a}\cdot\mathbf{b} = |\mathbf{a}|\,|\mathbf{b}|\cos\theta$.

where the last equality follows from the definition of the scalar product.

The value of the line integral along C can be closely approximated by adding similar contributions from all the steps:

$$\text{line integral} \simeq \sum_{i=1}^{n} \mathbf{F}(\mathbf{r}_i)\cdot\delta\mathbf{s}_i. \tag{15}$$

We consider this sum in the limit of an infinite number of infinitesimal steps. In this limit, any approximation involved in using a succession of straight-line steps disappears, and the sum gives the exact value of the line integral, which is written as

$$\text{line integral} = \int_C \mathbf{F}\cdot d\mathbf{s}. \tag{16}$$

Note that integral sign carries the label C, which indicates the path followed. It is *not* safe, in general, to write the line integral as

$$\int_{\mathbf{r}_A}^{\mathbf{r}_B} \mathbf{F}\cdot d\mathbf{s},$$

because this indicates only the start and end points, and makes no reference to the path taken between them. In general, we need to specify the *full* path before evaluating the line integral.

Using parametric representations

The concept of a line integral is straightforward, but there remains the task of evaluating equation (16) for a given vector field $\mathbf{F}$ and a given path C. As for the line integrals of scalar functions, the key is to express the path in parametric form.

Let us suppose that the path C lies in the xy-plane, and that points on the path have the parametric representation

$$x = x(t), \quad y = y(t) \quad (t_1 \le t \le t_2),$$

where, as usual, $t = t_1$ refers to the start point of the path and $t = t_2$ refers to the end point. We consider the small displacement $\delta\mathbf{s}$ produced when we move from a point P with parameter value t to a neighbouring point Q with parameter value $t + \delta t$ (see Figure 20).

An expression for this displacement was obtained in equation (3),

$$\delta\mathbf{s} = \delta x\,\mathbf{i} + \delta y\,\mathbf{j},$$

so

$$\begin{aligned}\mathbf{F}\cdot\delta\mathbf{s} &= (F_x\,\mathbf{i} + F_y\,\mathbf{j})\cdot(\delta x\,\mathbf{i} + \delta y\,\mathbf{j}) \\ &= F_x\,\delta x + F_y\,\delta y.\end{aligned}$$

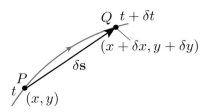

Figure 20   The small displacement from P to Q

Dividing and multiplying by δt then gives

$$\mathbf{F} \cdot \delta \mathbf{s} = \mathbf{F} \cdot \frac{\delta \mathbf{s}}{\delta t} \, \delta t$$

$$\simeq \mathbf{F} \cdot \frac{d\mathbf{s}}{dt} \, \delta t$$

$$= \left(F_x \frac{dx}{dt} + F_y \frac{dy}{dt} \right) \delta t.$$

To obtain the line integral, we take the sum of expressions like this all along the path in the limit of an infinite number of infinitesimal steps. This gives the following result.

$$\int_C \mathbf{F} \cdot d\mathbf{s} = \int_{t_1}^{t_2} \mathbf{F} \cdot \frac{d\mathbf{s}}{dt} \, dt$$

$$= \int_{t_1}^{t_2} \left(F_x \frac{dx}{dt} + F_y \frac{dy}{dt} \right) dt. \tag{17}$$

This formula is very important. It expresses the line integral of a vector field as a definite integral over the parameter t. To evaluate the definite integral, we must express the integrand on the right-hand side as a function of t. The following example shows how this is done.

Example 3

Calculate the line integral of the vector field

$$\mathbf{F} = (x - y)\,\mathbf{i} + (x + y)\,\mathbf{j}$$

along the quarter-circle path C_1 in Figure 21.

This path can be parametrised by the equations

$$x = 2\cos t, \quad y = 2\sin t \quad (0 \le t \le \pi/2).$$

Solution

Differentiating the parametric equations gives

$$\frac{dx}{dt} = -2\sin t, \quad \frac{dy}{dt} = 2\cos t.$$

Expressing the components of $\mathbf{F}$ in terms of t gives

$$F_x = x - y = 2(\cos t - \sin t),$$
$$F_y = x + y = 2(\cos t + \sin t).$$

Hence

$$\mathbf{F} \cdot \frac{d\mathbf{s}}{dt} = F_x \frac{dx}{dt} + F_y \frac{dy}{dt}$$

$$= -4(\cos t - \sin t)\sin t + 4(\cos t + \sin t)\cos t$$

$$= 4(\sin^2 t + \cos^2 t)$$

$$= 4.$$

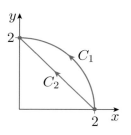

Figure 21   Two paths between the same points

Substituting into equation (17), the required line integral is

$$\int_{C_1} \mathbf{F} \cdot d\mathbf{s} = \int_0^{\pi/2} 4\,dt = \left[4t\right]_0^{\pi/2} = 2\pi.$$

Line integrals generally depend on the path between their start and end points. For example, the line integral of $\mathbf{F}$ over the path C_2 in Figure 21 has a different value to that calculated in Example 3, as you can confirm.

Exercise 6

Calculate the line integral of the vector field

$$\mathbf{F} = (x - y)\,\mathbf{i} + (x + y)\,\mathbf{j}$$

along the straight-line path C_2 shown in Figure 21. This path can be parametrised by the equations

$$x = 2 - t, \quad y = t \quad (0 \le t \le 2).$$

The method used in the above example and exercise applies to all line integrals of vector fields. In three dimensions, the parametric equations also include a function $z(t)$, and the expression for $d\mathbf{s}/dt$ has a component dz/dt. The following procedure refers to this three-dimensional case, but it is readily adapted to curves in the xy-plane by omitting the terms involving z.

Procedure 1   Finding the line integral of a vector field

Given a vector field $\mathbf{F} = F_x\,\mathbf{i} + F_y\,\mathbf{j} + F_z\,\mathbf{k}$, and a path C with the parametric representation

$$x = x(t), \quad y = y(t), \quad z = z(t) \quad (t_1 \le t \le t_2),$$

the line integral of $\mathbf{F}$ along the path C can be found as follows.

1.   Use the parametric representation to find the components of

$$\frac{d\mathbf{s}}{dt} = \frac{dx}{dt}\,\mathbf{i} + \frac{dy}{dt}\,\mathbf{j} + \frac{dz}{dt}\,\mathbf{k}. \tag{18}$$

2.   Express the components of $\mathbf{F}$ as functions of the parameter t.

3.   Find the scalar product

$$\mathbf{F} \cdot \frac{d\mathbf{s}}{dt} = F_x\frac{dx}{dt} + F_y\frac{dy}{dt} + F_z\frac{dz}{dt}$$

as a function of t.

4.   Evaluate the line integral as a definite integral over t:

$$\int_C \mathbf{F} \cdot d\mathbf{s} = \int_{t_1}^{t_2} \mathbf{F} \cdot \frac{d\mathbf{s}}{dt}\,dt. \tag{19}$$

219

Example 4

Evaluate the line integral of the vector field

$$\mathbf{F} = x^2\,\mathbf{i} + y^2\,\mathbf{j} + z^2\,\mathbf{k}$$

along a path C with the parametric equations

$$x = 3t^2, \quad y = 4t^2, \quad z = 5t^2 \quad (0 \le t \le 1).$$

Solution

Differentiating the parametric equations, we get

$$\frac{dx}{dt} = 6t, \quad \frac{dy}{dt} = 8t, \quad \frac{dz}{dt} = 10t.$$

Expressing the components of $\mathbf{F}$ in terms of t gives

$$F_x = x^2 = 9t^4, \quad F_y = y^2 = 16t^4, \quad F_z = z^2 = 25t^4.$$

So

$$\mathbf{F} \cdot \frac{d\mathbf{s}}{dt} = 9t^4 \times 6t + 16t^4 \times 8t + 25t^4 \times 10t$$

$$= 432t^5.$$

Substituting into equation (19), the line integral is

$$\int_C \mathbf{F} \cdot d\mathbf{s} = \int_0^1 432t^5 \, dt$$

$$= 432 \left[\tfrac{1}{6} t^6 \right]_0^1 = 72.$$

Exercise 7

Calculate the line integral of the vector field

$$\mathbf{F} = yz\,\mathbf{i} + xz\,\mathbf{j} + xy\,\mathbf{k}$$

along a path C with parametric equations

$$x = t, \quad y = 1 + 2t, \quad z = 4 \quad (0 \le t \le 1).$$

This is different to the behaviour of the lengths of curves and the line integrals of scalar functions, which are unchanged by a reversal of the path.

If we reverse the direction of the path of a line integral of a vector field, tracing out the same curve but in the opposite sense, the magnitude of the line integral remains unchanged, but its sign is reversed.

This follows directly from equation (15), which expresses the line integral of a vector field $\mathbf{F}$ as a sum of contributions of the form $\mathbf{F}(\mathbf{r}_i) \cdot \delta\mathbf{s}_i$. When we reverse the direction of the path, the sign of each small displacement $\delta\mathbf{s}_i$ changes, so the contribution changes to

$$\mathbf{F}(\mathbf{r}_i) \cdot (-\delta\mathbf{s}_i) = -\mathbf{F}(\mathbf{r}_i) \cdot \delta\mathbf{s}_i.$$

Since this is true for all contributions along the path, the line integral along the reverse path is *minus* the line interval along the original path.

You can check this in the following exercise.

Exercise 8

Calculate the line integral of the vector field

$$\mathbf{F} = yz\,\mathbf{i} + xz\,\mathbf{j} + xy\,\mathbf{k}$$

along the path C_{rev}, with parametric equations

$$x = 1 - t, \quad y = 3 - 2t, \quad z = 4 \quad (0 \le t \le 1).$$

This is the reverse of the path C in Exercise 7, obtained by replacing t with $1 - t$ in the parametric equations.

The following optional box makes a link between line integrals and the concept of energy; this link is of fundamental importance in physics.

Line integrals and energy

Think of a particle of mass m, moving along a path C. For example, it could be a ball that has been thrown in the air, and follows a parabolic arc back to the ground (Figure 22). At each point $\mathbf{r}$, the particle experiences a force $\mathbf{F}(\mathbf{r})$, and we can calculate the line integral of $\mathbf{F}(\mathbf{r})$ along the particle's path:

$$\int_C \mathbf{F} \cdot d\mathbf{s} = \int_{t_1}^{t_2} \mathbf{F} \cdot \frac{d\mathbf{s}}{dt}\, dt, \tag{20}$$

where t is the parameter used to label points along the path, with $t = t_1$ at the start point, and $t = t_2$ at the end point.

The parameter t need not have any physical significance. However, we are free to choose it to be the time elapsed, which increases as the particle traces out its path. This choice does not affect the value of the line integral, but helps us to interpret its meaning.

With t interpreted as time, $d\mathbf{s}/dt$ is the velocity $\mathbf{v}$ of the particle. Also, Newton's second law tells us that 'force is equal to mass times acceleration'. Since acceleration is the rate of change of velocity, we can express this as $\mathbf{F} = m\,d\mathbf{v}/dt$. Putting these results together, the integrand on the right-hand side of equation (20) is

$$
\begin{aligned}
\mathbf{F} \cdot \frac{d\mathbf{s}}{dt} &= m\,\frac{d\mathbf{v}}{dt} \cdot \mathbf{v} \\
&= m\left(\frac{dv_x}{dt}\,v_x + \frac{dv_y}{dt}\,v_y + \frac{dv_z}{dt}\,v_z\right) \\
&= m\,\frac{d}{dt}\left[\tfrac{1}{2}(v_x^2 + v_y^2 + v_z^2)\right] \\
&= \frac{d}{dt}\left(\tfrac{1}{2}mv^2\right),
\end{aligned}
\tag{21}
$$

where $v = |\mathbf{v}|$ is the speed of the particle, which is a function of time as the particle progresses along its path.

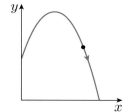

Figure 22 A thrown ball follows a parabolic arc

Combining equations (20) and (21), we conclude that

$$\int_C \mathbf{F} \cdot d\mathbf{s} = \int_{t_1}^{t_2} \frac{d}{dt}\left(\tfrac{1}{2}mv^2\right) dt = \tfrac{1}{2}mv_2^2 - \tfrac{1}{2}mv_1^2, \tag{22}$$

where $v_1 = v(t_1)$ is the particle's initial speed at the beginning of the path, and $v_2 = v(t_2)$ is its final speed at the end.

Scientists place a special interpretation on these results. The quantity $\tfrac{1}{2}mv^2$ is called the **kinetic energy** of the particle, and is interpreted as the energy that the particle has by virtue of being in motion. If $v_2 > v_1$ in equation (22), the particle gains kinetic energy as it moves along the path C.

It is a fundamental principle of science that energy is conserved, so the energy gained by the particle must come from somewhere. If you push the particle in the absence of other forces, it comes from energy stored in your muscles. If the particle falls under gravity, it comes from a type of energy known as **potential energy**, which is stored in the gravitational field. You need not worry about the details – the important point is that the line integral on the left-hand side of equation (22) quantifies the energy transferred to the particle by the force $\mathbf{F}$. This is a major application of line integrals.

The final conclusion does not depend on the use of time as the parameter in the line integral.

We note in passing that it is also possible to evaluate the line integrals of vector fields in non-Cartesian coordinate systems. If (u, v, w) are orthogonal coordinates with unit vectors $\mathbf{e}_u$, $\mathbf{e}_v$ and $\mathbf{e}_w$, then a vector field $\mathbf{F}$ may be expressed as

$$\mathbf{F} = F_u\,\mathbf{e}_u + F_v\,\mathbf{e}_v + F_w\,\mathbf{e}_w.$$

In terms of these coordinates, a path C is represented by parametric equations of the form

$$u = u(t), \quad v = v(t), \quad w = w(t) \quad (t_1 \leq t \leq t_2),$$

and the line integral of $\mathbf{F}$ along C is given by the general formula

$$\int_C \mathbf{F} \cdot d\mathbf{s} = \int_{t_1}^{t_2} \left(F_u h_u \frac{du}{dt} + F_v h_v \frac{dv}{dt} + F_w h_w \frac{dw}{dt} \right) dt, \tag{23}$$

where h_u, h_v and h_w are the appropriate scale factors. In the special case of Cartesian coordinates, all these scale factors are equal to 1, and we recover equation (18). You will not be asked to use equation (23) in this module, but we quote it to give you a more complete picture, and because you may come across it in your future studies.

3 Line integrals of gradient fields

You have seen how to calculate the line integral of any vector field. This section considers a restricted class of vector fields – those that are proportional to the gradients of scalar fields. The line integrals of these fields have a special property: *they are independent of the path taken between their start and end points.* This property is very useful in applications, including many that arise in physics and engineering.

3.1 Gradient fields

We often meet vector fields that are expressed in the form

$$\mathbf{F} = -\boldsymbol{\nabla}U,$$

where U is a scalar field. The minus sign in this equation means that the vector field $\mathbf{F}$ points in the direction in which the scalar field U *decreases* most rapidly. This is usually what is needed. For example, heat flows in the direction in which temperature decreases most rapidly. We retain the minus sign throughout our discussion because this is what you are most likely to meet in real-world applications beyond this module.

> A vector field $\mathbf{F}$ is called a **gradient field** if it can be expressed in the form
>
> $$\mathbf{F} = -\boldsymbol{\nabla}U, \tag{24}$$
>
> where U is a scalar field.
>
> U is called the **scalar potential field** associated with $\mathbf{F}$.

Not all vector fields are gradient fields, and a test for gradient fields will be given later in this section.

Example 5

Show that the vector field $\mathbf{F} = x\,\mathbf{i} - y\,\mathbf{j}$ is a gradient field with an associated scalar potential field $U = \frac{1}{2}(y^2 - x^2)$.

Solution

Taking the partial derivatives of $U = \frac{1}{2}(y^2 - x^2)$, we get

$$\frac{\partial U}{\partial x} = -x \quad \text{and} \quad \frac{\partial U}{\partial y} = y,$$

so

$$\boldsymbol{\nabla}U = \frac{\partial U}{\partial x}\,\mathbf{i} + \frac{\partial U}{\partial y}\,\mathbf{j} = -x\,\mathbf{i} + y\,\mathbf{j} = -\mathbf{F}.$$

Gradient fields have a very important property: their line integrals depend on the start and end points of the path, but are independent of the detailed shape of the path joining these points.

To see why this is so, let us consider a gradient field

$$\mathbf{F} = -\boldsymbol{\nabla} U.$$

We can take the line integral of this vector field along a path C with start point A and end point B. Points on this path are labelled by a parameter t, with $t = t_A$ at the start point, and $t = t_B$ at the end point. The line integral is given by

$$\int_C \mathbf{F} \cdot d\mathbf{s} = \int_{t_A}^{t_B} \mathbf{F} \cdot \frac{d\mathbf{s}}{dt} \, dt = -\int_{t_A}^{t_B} \boldsymbol{\nabla} U \cdot \frac{d\mathbf{s}}{dt} \, dt. \qquad (25)$$

Now, the integrand on the right-hand side can be simplified:

$$\begin{aligned}
\boldsymbol{\nabla} U \cdot \frac{d\mathbf{s}}{dt} &= \left(\frac{\partial U}{\partial x}\mathbf{i} + \frac{\partial U}{\partial y}\mathbf{j} + \frac{\partial U}{\partial z}\mathbf{k} \right) \cdot \left(\frac{dx}{dt}\mathbf{i} + \frac{dy}{dt}\mathbf{j} + \frac{dz}{dt}\mathbf{k} \right) \\
&= \frac{\partial U}{\partial x}\frac{dx}{dt} + \frac{\partial U}{\partial y}\frac{dy}{dt} + \frac{\partial U}{\partial z}\frac{dz}{dt} = \frac{dU}{dt},
\end{aligned}$$

where the last step uses a version of the chain rule (equation (23) of Unit 7). Using this result in the integral on the far right-hand side of equation (25), we get

$$\int_C \mathbf{F} \cdot d\mathbf{s} = -\int_{t_A}^{t_B} \frac{dU}{dt} \, dt = U_A - U_B, \qquad (26)$$

where $U_A = U(t_A)$ is the value of U at the start point of the path, and $U_B = U(t_B)$ is the value of U at the end point.

The same answer $U_A - U_B$ is obtained no matter which route is taken between the given start and end points. For example, Figure 23 shows several paths leading from A to B. The line integral of a gradient field $\mathbf{F} = -\boldsymbol{\nabla} U$ has the same value for all these paths. For a closed loop, the start point A is the same as the end point B, so $U_A = U_B$. Hence the line integral of a gradient field around a closed loop is equal to zero.

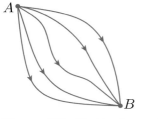

Figure 23 Paths from A to B

A line integral that does not depend on the path between given start and end points is said to be **path-independent**. We can therefore make the following statements.

- Any line integral of a gradient field is *path-independent*.
- Any line integral of a gradient field around a *closed loop* is equal to zero.

It is easy to find the line integral of a gradient field if we know its associated scalar potential field, as the following example shows.

Example 6

The vector field $\mathbf{F} = 3x^2 y\,\mathbf{i} + (x^3 + 4y^3)\,\mathbf{j}$ is a gradient field with associated scalar potential field $U(x,y) = 1 - x^3 y - y^4$. Find the line integral of $\mathbf{F}$ along a path C with parametric equations

$$x = 1 - \cos t, \quad y = 1 + \sin t \quad (0 \le t \le \pi).$$

Solution

Because **F** is a gradient field, its line integrals are path-independent. Although the path is specified in detail, only its start and end points matter. Substituting $t = 0$ and $t = \pi$ in the parametric equations gives start point $(0, 1)$ and end point $(2, 1)$. Using equation (26), we then get

$$\int_C \mathbf{F} \cdot d\mathbf{s} = U(0, 1) - U(2, 1) = 0 - (1 - 8 - 1) = 8.$$

Exercise 9

The vector field $\mathbf{F} = x\,\mathbf{i} - y\,\mathbf{j}$ is a gradient field with an associated scalar potential field $U = \frac{1}{2}(y^2 - x^2)$. Find the line integral of **F** along any path C that starts from $(1, 1)$ and ends at $(7, 3)$.

3.2   Conservative vector fields

You have seen that the line integrals of gradient fields are always *path-independent*, and this simplifies the evaluation of these line integrals. In order to focus on the property of path-independence, we make a definition.

Conservative fields

A vector field **F** is said to be **conservative** if, throughout its domain, all of its line integrals are path-independent.

Using this definition, it is clear that all gradient fields are conservative fields. But can we say that all conservative fields are gradient fields? Our definitions do not exclude the possibility that a field could be conservative, and yet not be expressible in the form $\mathbf{F} = -\boldsymbol{\nabla}U$. You will soon see that all conservative fields *are* gradient fields, but a little more work is needed to establish this fact.

Why conservative?

The word 'conservative' is used for historical reasons. An early application of line integrals was to calculate the energy transferred by a force when a particle moves from one point to another. If these line integrals are path-independent, it turns out that the law of conservation of energy can be expressed by a simple formula involving kinetic and potential energies. The term *conservative field* derives from *conservation of energy*, but is now a far more general concept.

If we are told that a given vector field is conservative, we can often simplify the evaluation of its line integrals, as the following example shows.

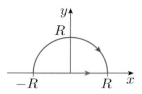

Figure 24   A semicircular path and its straight-line replacement

Example 7

The vector field $\mathbf{F} = (x^2 + y^2)\,\mathbf{i} + 2xy\,\mathbf{j}$ is conservative. Calculate its line integral along the red semicircular path in Figure 24.

Solution

We are told that $\mathbf{F}$ is a conservative field, so we are free to replace the semicircular path by a straight-line path along the x-axis, shown in blue in Figure 24. Along this straight-line path, the component of $\mathbf{F}$ in the direction of the path is $F_x = x^2 + 0 = x^2$, so the line integral is

$$\int_{-R}^{R} F_x \, dx = \int_{-R}^{R} x^2 \, dx = \left[\tfrac{1}{3}x^3\right]_{-R}^{R} = \tfrac{2}{3}R^3.$$

This is equal to the required line integral because the blue and red paths share the same start and end points, and the field is conservative.

Exercise 10

The vector field $\mathbf{F} = 3x^2 y\,\mathbf{i} + (x^3 + y^3)\,\mathbf{j}$ is conservative. Find the line integral of $\mathbf{F}$ along any path that starts at the origin and ends at $(1, 2)$.

But be very careful: you *cannot* adjust the path of a line integral of a vector field *unless* you know that the field is conservative. If the field is not conservative, changing the path will generally give the wrong answer!

We can use an alternative notation for the line integrals of conservative fields, reflecting the fact that they are path-independent. The line integral of the conservative field $\mathbf{F}$ along a path C with start point A and end point B can be written in any of the forms

$$\int_C \mathbf{F} \cdot d\mathbf{s} = \int_{A \to B} \mathbf{F} \cdot d\mathbf{s} = \int_{\mathbf{r}_A \to \mathbf{r}_B} \mathbf{F} \cdot d\mathbf{s},$$

where $\mathbf{r}_A$ and $\mathbf{r}_B$ are the position vectors of A and B. The notations used on the right have the advantage of explicitly indicating the start and end points without giving *irrelevant* information about the precise shape of the path. Using this notation, and referring to Figure 25, it is easy to see that for any *conservative* vector field $\mathbf{F}$,

$$\int_{\mathbf{r}_0 \to \mathbf{r}_B} \mathbf{F} \cdot d\mathbf{s} = \int_{\mathbf{r}_0 \to \mathbf{r}_A} \mathbf{F} \cdot d\mathbf{s} + \int_{\mathbf{r}_A \to \mathbf{r}_B} \mathbf{F} \cdot d\mathbf{s}. \tag{27}$$

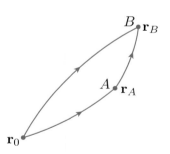

Figure 25   Two routes from $\mathbf{r}_0$ to $\mathbf{r}_B$

This expresses the fact that the line integral from $\mathbf{r}_0$ to $\mathbf{r}_B$ is the same whether the route goes via $\mathbf{r}_A$ or not.

We now show that any conservative field $\mathbf{F}$ must also be a gradient field. We do this by constructing a scalar function $U(\mathbf{r})$ for which $\mathbf{F} = -\boldsymbol{\nabla}U$. This is done by first choosing a fixed reference point $\mathbf{r}_0$ at which $U(\mathbf{r}_0) = 0$, and then defining

The choice of $\mathbf{r}_0$ is arbitrary, but this does not matter – we just make some definite choice.

$$U(\mathbf{r}) = -\int_{\mathbf{r}_0 \to \mathbf{r}} \mathbf{F} \cdot d\mathbf{s}. \tag{28}$$

For a conservative vector field $\mathbf{F}$ and a fixed reference point $\mathbf{r}_0$, the line integral on the right-hand side depends only on the end point $\mathbf{r}$. So $U(\mathbf{r})$ is a well-defined function, which is equal to zero at $\mathbf{r} = \mathbf{r}_0$. Because the line integral involves a scalar product, $U(\mathbf{r})$ is a scalar quantity – in fact, it is the *scalar potential field* associated with $\mathbf{F}$, as we will now show.

When we move from a point $\mathbf{r}_A$ to another point $\mathbf{r}_B$, equation (28) tells us that U changes by

$$U(\mathbf{r}_B) - U(\mathbf{r}_A) = - \int_{\mathbf{r}_0 \to \mathbf{r}_B} \mathbf{F} \cdot d\mathbf{s} + \int_{\mathbf{r}_0 \to \mathbf{r}_A} \mathbf{F} \cdot d\mathbf{s}.$$

Using equation (27), this is equivalent to

$$U(\mathbf{r}_B) - U(\mathbf{r}_A) = - \int_{\mathbf{r}_A \to \mathbf{r}_B} \mathbf{F} \cdot d\mathbf{s}. \tag{29}$$

Now let us take $\mathbf{r}_A = (x, y, z)$ and $\mathbf{r}_B = (x + \delta x, y, z)$, where δx is a tiny increment in x. Then the line integral on the right-hand side of equation (29) can be taken parallel to the x-axis. If δx is very small, we get

$$U(x + \delta x, y, z) - U(x, y, z) \simeq - F_x(x, y, z)\, \delta x.$$

For a point $\mathbf{r} = (x, y, z)$, we use the notations $U(\mathbf{r})$ and $U(x, y, z)$ interchangeably.

Then dividing both sides by δx and taking the limit as δx tends to zero, we get

$$\frac{\partial U}{\partial x} = - F_x.$$

Similar results for $\partial U / \partial y$ and $\partial U / \partial z$ are obtained by making tiny displacements in the y- and z-directions. Collecting these results together, we conclude that

$$F_x = - \frac{\partial U}{\partial x}, \quad F_y = - \frac{\partial U}{\partial y}, \quad F_z = - \frac{\partial U}{\partial z},$$

or in vector form,

$$\mathbf{F} = - \boldsymbol{\nabla} U.$$

This shows that any conservative field is a gradient field. We already know that any gradient field is a conservative field, so we reach the following memorable and important conclusion.

> The terms *conservative field* and *gradient field* are synonymous and can be used interchangeably.

Given a conservative field $\mathbf{F}$, we often want to find the corresponding scalar potential field U. This is useful because once we know U, we can easily evaluate any line integral of $\mathbf{F}$ using equation (29). To obtain a formula for U, we can use equation (28) with any convenient choice of path for the line integral. This technique is illustrated in the following example.

Example 8

A conservative vector field takes the form $\mathbf{F} = xy^2\,\mathbf{i} + x^2y\,\mathbf{j}$. Find the associated scalar potential field $U(x, y)$, taking $U = 0$ at the origin $\mathbf{0}$.

Solution

From equation (28), the scalar potential field is given by

$$U(\mathbf{r}) = -\int_{\mathbf{0}\to\mathbf{r}} \mathbf{F} \cdot d\mathbf{s}.$$

Because the vector field is conservative, we can evaluate this line integral over any convenient path. Let us consider an arbitrary point (a, b). We choose a straight-line path from the origin to this point, as shown in Figure 26.

This path can be described by the parametric equations

$$x = at, \quad y = bt \quad (0 \le t \le 1).$$

The values of a and b are constant along the path, so

$$\frac{dx}{dt} = a \quad \text{and} \quad \frac{dy}{dt} = b.$$

Hence

$$\mathbf{F} \cdot \frac{d\mathbf{s}}{dt} = (at)(bt)^2 a + (at)^2(bt)b = 2a^2b^2t^3$$

and

$$U(a, b) = -\int_{t=0}^{t=1} 2a^2b^2t^3\,dt = -\tfrac{1}{2}a^2b^2.$$

However, the point (a, b) is arbitrary, so for any point (x, y), we conclude that the scalar potential field is

$$U(x, y) = -\tfrac{1}{2}x^2y^2.$$

This answer can (and should) be checked by taking its gradient:

$$\nabla U = -xy^2\,\mathbf{i} - x^2y\,\mathbf{j} = -\mathbf{F},$$

as required.

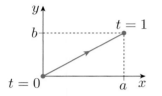

Figure 26 A straight-line path from the origin to (a, b)

Exercise 11

A conservative vector field takes the form $\mathbf{F} = \cos x\,\mathbf{i} + \sin y\,\mathbf{j}$. Find the associated scalar potential field $U(x, y)$, taking $U(0, 0) = 0$.

3.3 The curl test

This subsection gives a test that allows us to decide whether or not a given vector field is conservative. We start by noting that if $\mathbf{F}$ is a conservative vector field, then it is also a gradient field and can be written in the form

$$\mathbf{F} = -\nabla U.$$

Taking the curl of both sides of this equation, we get

$$\nabla \times \mathbf{F} = -\nabla \times (\nabla U) = - \begin{vmatrix} \mathbf{i} & \mathbf{j} & \mathbf{k} \\ \dfrac{\partial}{\partial x} & \dfrac{\partial}{\partial y} & \dfrac{\partial}{\partial z} \\ \dfrac{\partial U}{\partial x} & \dfrac{\partial U}{\partial y} & \dfrac{\partial U}{\partial z} \end{vmatrix}.$$

Expanding the determinant on the right-hand side in the usual way, and using the mixed partial derivative theorem of Unit 7, we get the zero vector $\mathbf{0} = (0,0,0)$. For example, the x-component is

$$-\frac{\partial}{\partial y}\left(\frac{\partial U}{\partial z}\right) + \frac{\partial}{\partial z}\left(\frac{\partial U}{\partial y}\right) = 0.$$

This calculation was done in Exercise 27 of Unit 9.

So any conservative field has zero curl throughout its domain.

In most circumstances, the converse statement is also true; so if a vector field $\mathbf{F}$ has $\nabla \times \mathbf{F} = \mathbf{0}$ throughout its domain, then $\mathbf{F}$ is conservative. We do not have the tools to prove this yet, but a proof is given at the end of the unit. Taking the result on trust, and assuming that all the necessary conditions are met, leads to the following *curl test*. This is the normal way of deciding whether or not a given vector field is conservative.

Curl test for conservative fields

To test whether the vector field $\mathbf{F}$ is conservative, evaluate $\nabla \times \mathbf{F}$.

If $\nabla \times \mathbf{F} = \mathbf{0}$ everywhere in the domain of $\mathbf{F}$, then $\mathbf{F}$ is conservative. Otherwise, it is not conservative.

Strictly speaking, the curl test assumes that the domain of $\mathbf{F}$ is 'simple' in a certain sense (technically, it must be *simply-connected*). We will return to this point in Subsection 5.3.

Example 9

Determine whether or not the following vector fields are conservative.

(a) $\mathbf{F} = yz\,\mathbf{i} + xz\,\mathbf{j} + xy\,\mathbf{k}$ (b) $\mathbf{G} = z^2\,\mathbf{i} + x^2\,\mathbf{j} + y^2\,\mathbf{k}$

Solution

(a) We have

$$\nabla \times \mathbf{F} = \begin{vmatrix} \mathbf{i} & \mathbf{j} & \mathbf{k} \\ \dfrac{\partial}{\partial x} & \dfrac{\partial}{\partial y} & \dfrac{\partial}{\partial z} \\ yz & xz & xy \end{vmatrix} = \mathbf{i}\,(x-x) - \mathbf{j}\,(y-y) + \mathbf{k}\,(z-z) = \mathbf{0}.$$

So the curl test shows that $\mathbf{F}$ is conservative.

(b) We have

$$\nabla \times \mathbf{G} = \begin{vmatrix} \mathbf{i} & \mathbf{j} & \mathbf{k} \\ \dfrac{\partial}{\partial x} & \dfrac{\partial}{\partial y} & \dfrac{\partial}{\partial z} \\ z^2 & x^2 & y^2 \end{vmatrix} = \mathbf{i}\,(2y) - \mathbf{j}\,(-2z) + \mathbf{k}\,(2x).$$

This is not equal to $\mathbf{0}$ everywhere, so $\mathbf{G}$ is *not* conservative.

Exercise 12

Determine whether or not the following vector fields are conservative.

(a) $\mathbf{F} = y\,\mathbf{i} + x\,\mathbf{j} + z\,\mathbf{k}$ (b) $\mathbf{G} = -y\,\mathbf{i} + x\,\mathbf{j} + z\,\mathbf{k}$

4 Flux and the divergence theorem

This section introduces the concept of the *flux of a vector field*, which is a type of surface integral. Unit 8 showed you how to integrate scalar functions over surfaces. Here, we explain how to calculate surface integrals of vector functions. These integrals are found throughout science and engineering. For example, they are used to calculate the amount of air flowing out of a given region or the rate at which heat energy is lost through the walls, roof and ground floor of a house. They are also important in electromagnetism.

The concept of flux allows us to quantify the extent to which a vector field diverges outwards from a given point. Once this has been understood, we can return to a major theme of Unit 9 – *divergence* and its interpretation. An important result called the *divergence theorem* will cast further light on the meaning of divergence.

4.1 Flux over a planar surface element

You probably think of area as a scalar quantity – a certain number of square metres or square inches, say. This is fine for areas drawn on a sheet of paper. More generally, we can consider a planar element that is oriented in three-dimensional space. Such an element is characterised by its area δS *and* its orientation in space.

Figure 27   A planar element and its unit normal $\widehat{\mathbf{n}}$

The simplest way of describing the orientation is to specify a unit vector $\widehat{\mathbf{n}}$ that is perpendicular to the surface of the element (Figure 27). There are actually two vectors that could be used for this purpose, pointing in opposite directions. This is not a problem – we just pick one of these vectors and specify our selection clearly. The chosen unit vector is then called the **unit normal** of the planar element.

Information about the area of the element and its orientation can be combined. We define the **oriented area** of the element to be

$$\delta \mathbf{S} = \delta S\,\widehat{\mathbf{n}}. \tag{30}$$

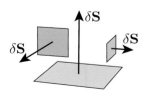

Figure 28   Some oriented areas

This is a vector quantity. Its magnitude is the (scalar) area of the element, δS, and its direction gives the direction of the unit normal to the element. Figure 28 shows the oriented area vectors of some planar elements. The magnitudes of these vectors are larger for elements of larger area, and this is indicated by the relative lengths of the arrows.

Now consider a fluid such as water or air moving in three-dimensional space. We can imagine a tiny planar element inside this fluid. This element is a mathematical construction rather than a tangible object, so it does not interfere with the flow of the fluid. We can then ask: how much fluid passes through the planar element per unit time?

In the simplest case, the planar element is perpendicular to the flow of the fluid, with its unit normal $\widehat{\mathbf{n}}$ in the same direction as the fluid flow, as in Figure 29(a). If the fluid has velocity $\mathbf{v}$ and speed $v = |\mathbf{v}|$, then the volume of fluid passing through the element in a small time δt is equal to the volume of the red box in Figure 29(a). This box has length $v\,\delta t$ and cross-sectional area δS, so the volume of fluid passing through the element in time δt is

$$\delta V = v\,\delta t\,\delta S.$$

Now let us see what happens when the planar element is *not* perpendicular to the flow. Figure 29(b) shows a case where the unit normal $\widehat{\mathbf{n}}$ makes an angle θ with the velocity vector $\mathbf{v}$ of the fluid. In this general case, the volume of fluid passing through the element in time δt is equal to the volume of the red skewed box in Figure 29(b).

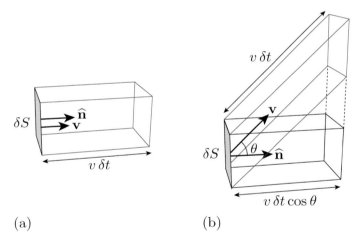

(a)   (b)

Figure 29   Flow through planar elements that are: (a) perpendicular to the flow; (b) not perpendicular to the flow

However, geometry tells us that the red skewed box has the same volume as the black box in Figure 29(b), so its volume is

$$\delta V = (v\,\delta t\cos\theta)\,\delta S = (v\cos\theta)\,\delta t\,\delta S.$$

The quantity $v\cos\theta$ that appears in this equation is the component of the fluid velocity in the direction of the unit normal, since

$$\widehat{\mathbf{n}}\cdot\mathbf{v} = |\widehat{\mathbf{n}}|\,|\mathbf{v}|\cos\theta = v\cos\theta.$$

Hence

$$\delta V = (\widehat{\mathbf{n}}\cdot\mathbf{v})\,\delta t\,\delta S.$$

Using the definition of the oriented area of a planar element in equation (30), this can also be written as

$$\delta V = (\mathbf{v} \cdot \delta \mathbf{S})\,\delta t.$$

Dividing both sides by δt, and taking the limit as δt tends to zero, we see that the rate of flow of fluid volume through the planar element is

$$\frac{dV}{dt} = \mathbf{v} \cdot \delta \mathbf{S}. \tag{31}$$

The right-hand side of equation (31) is what we have been building towards. The quantity $\mathbf{v} \cdot \delta \mathbf{S}$ is called the *flux* of $\mathbf{v}$ over the planar element with oriented area $\delta \mathbf{S}$, and we have shown that this is equal to the rate of flow of fluid through the element.

More generally, we can define the flux of *any* vector field.

Flux of a vector field over a planar element

Given any vector field $\mathbf{F}$ and a planar element with oriented area $\delta \mathbf{S}$, the **flux** of the vector field over the element is defined as

$$\text{flux} = \mathbf{F} \cdot \delta \mathbf{S} = F\,\delta S \cos \theta, \tag{32}$$

where the field $\mathbf{F}$ is evaluated at the position of the element, and θ is the angle between the directions of $\mathbf{F}$ and the unit normal $\widehat{\mathbf{n}}$ to the planar element.

We have

$$\mathbf{F} \cdot \delta \mathbf{S} = (\widehat{\mathbf{n}} \cdot \mathbf{F})\,\delta S.$$

Since $\widehat{\mathbf{n}} \cdot \mathbf{F}$ is the normal component of the field, we can also state the following.

The flux of a vector field over a planar element is the *normal component* of the field multiplied by the area of the element.

Flux is a scalar quantity, which can be positive, negative or zero depending on the relative orientations of $\mathbf{F}$ and the unit normal $\widehat{\mathbf{n}}$.

The word 'flux' derives from a Latin word for flow, and you have seen that it allows us to describe the rate of flow of a fluid through a planar element. However, equation (32) defines flux for *any* vector field. When describing electric and magnetic fields, for example, we may be interested in their fluxes, even though these fields do not actually flow.

Exercise 13

The figure in the margin shows two planar elements A and B, with their unit normals indicated. Find the flux of the vector field $\mathbf{F} = 2\mathbf{i} + 3\mathbf{j} + 5\mathbf{k}$ over both of these elements.

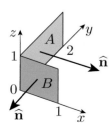

4.2 Flux over an extended surface

In general, we are interested in the flux of a vector field over an *extended surface*, which may be curved. This can be found by integrating over the surface, as we now explain.

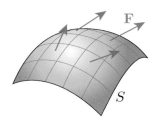

Figure 30 shows a vector field $\mathbf{F}$ and an extended curved surface S. The vector field, and its angle to the normal to the surface, may vary from point to point. However, we can imagine dividing the surface into many tiny elements, each of which can be approximated by a tiny planar area element, with oriented area $\delta\mathbf{S}_i$, at position $\mathbf{r}_i$. For each planar element, we have a choice of two directions for the unit normal. We require these choices to be made consistently so that neighbouring elements have unit normals that are nearly parallel rather than nearly antiparallel.

Figure 30 A vector field $\mathbf{F}$ and an extended surface S

The flux of $\mathbf{F}$ over the extended surface S is then approximated by

$$\text{flux over } S \simeq \sum_i \mathbf{F}(\mathbf{r}_i) \cdot \delta\mathbf{S}_i,$$

where the sum is over all the planar elements approximating the surface. We take the limit where the size of each element tends to zero and the number of elements tends to infinity. In this limit, the sum is written as

$$\text{flux over } S = \int_S \mathbf{F}(\mathbf{r}) \cdot d\mathbf{S}, \tag{33}$$

where the expression on the right-hand side is called the **surface integral** of $\mathbf{F}$ over the surface S. We will explain how to evaluate this surface integral shortly.

Note that the notation $d\mathbf{S}$ is used in surface integrals, while $d\mathbf{s}$ appears in line integrals.

First, it is important to distinguish between two types of surface. An **open surface** has at least one **boundary curve** marking the furthest extent of the surface; an example is shown in Figure 30. A **closed surface** has no boundary curves, and divides three-dimensional space into two parts: the space inside the surface and the space outside the surface. (The shell of an egg forms a closed surface until you break it open.) In the case of an open surface, there are two choices for the set of unit normals, and it is necessary to state which choice has been made by, for example, drawing a diagram showing the unit normals at a few points. For any closed surface, a standard convention is used.

Unit normal convention for closed surfaces

For any closed surface, all the unit normals are chosen to point *outwards* into the exterior space, rather than inwards towards the enclosed volume (see Figure 31).

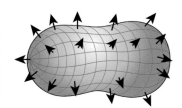

Figure 31 A closed surface and its outward-pointing unit normals

This convention has an important consequence for any vector field that represents a flow. If the flux of the field over a closed surface is positive, the net flow is outwards; if the flux is negative, the net flow is inwards.

We now turn to the calculation of surface integrals of vector fields. Fortunately, the key ideas were introduced in Section 5 of Unit 8 in the context of finding the area of a curved surface.

The first idea is to label points on the surface by a pair of parameters, (u, v). For example, points on the surface of a sphere, centred on the origin, can be labelled by the angular coordinates (θ, ϕ) of a spherical coordinate system. The radial coordinate r takes a constant value R all over the surface of the sphere. Since r does not distinguish different points on the surface, it is not regarded as one of the parameters that label points on the surface.

Points on the surface can also be labelled by their Cartesian coordinates (x, y, z), and there is a set of equations linking (x, y, z) to (u, v) for any point on the surface:

$$x = x(u, v), \quad y = y(u, v), \quad z = z(u, v).$$

On a spherical surface of radius R, for example, the relevant equations are

$$x = R \sin \theta \cos \phi, \quad y = R \sin \theta \sin \phi, \quad z = R \cos \theta.$$

This is reminiscent of the parametric description of a curve, but while each point on a curve is labelled by a single parameter t, each point on a curved surface is labelled by two parameters, (u, v).

When u and v increase by tiny amounts δu and δv, a tiny patch is generated on the surface, as shown in Figure 32. Unit 8 showed that the area of such a patch is

$$\delta S = |\mathbf{J}| \, \delta u \, \delta v, \tag{34}$$

where $\mathbf{J}$ is the *Jacobian vector*, given by

$$\mathbf{J} = \begin{vmatrix} \mathbf{i} & \mathbf{j} & \mathbf{k} \\ \dfrac{\partial x}{\partial u} & \dfrac{\partial y}{\partial u} & \dfrac{\partial z}{\partial u} \\ \dfrac{\partial x}{\partial v} & \dfrac{\partial y}{\partial v} & \dfrac{\partial z}{\partial v} \end{vmatrix}. \tag{35}$$

Unit 8 noted that this vector is perpendicular to the surface. We can always choose the order of the parameters u and v to ensure that $\mathbf{J}$ is *parallel* to the chosen unit normal $\hat{\mathbf{n}}$ of the surface. Assuming that this has been done, the *oriented area* of the tiny surface patch is simply

$$\delta \mathbf{S} = \mathbf{J} \, \delta u \, \delta v,$$

and the flux of a vector field $\mathbf{F}$ over the patch is given by

$$\mathbf{F} \cdot \delta \mathbf{S} = \mathbf{F} \cdot \mathbf{J} \, \delta u \, \delta v.$$

The flux over the entire surface S is found by adding up contributions like this from each of its patches. In the limit where the patches shrink to zero size, the sum becomes an integral over suitable ranges of u and v.

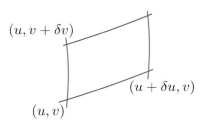

Figure 32   A patch generated by tiny increments in u and v

Evaluating the flux of a vector field over an extended surface

If points on a surface S are parametrised by (u, v), where $u_1 \le u \le u_2$ and $v_1 \le v \le v_2$, then the flux of a vector field $\mathbf{F}$ over the surface is given by the integral

$$\int_S \mathbf{F} \cdot d\mathbf{S} = \int_{v=v_1}^{v=v_2} \left(\int_{u=u_1}^{u=u_2} \mathbf{F} \cdot \mathbf{J} \, du \right) dv. \qquad (36)$$

To evaluate this integral, the integrand $\mathbf{F} \cdot \mathbf{J}$ must be expressed in terms of the parameters u and v.

We assume that the limits of integration, u_1, u_2, v_1 and v_2, are all constants.

To avoid duplicated effort, we skip the step of calculating $\mathbf{J}$ from the determinant in equation (35). You have had practice at doing this in Unit 8, and there is nothing to be gained by going through similar steps again. To understand how equation (36) is used, it is sufficient to look at surfaces that are spheres or portions of spheres. The Jacobian vector $\mathbf{J}$ for a spherical surface was calculated in Unit 8, and we quote that result here for ease of reference.

The calculation of $\mathbf{J}$ for a spherical surface is in Exercise 26 of Unit 8.

The Jacobian vector J on the surface of a sphere

On the surface of a sphere of radius R, centred on the origin and parametrised by (θ, ϕ) of spherical coordinates,

$$\mathbf{J} = R^2 \sin\theta \, \mathbf{e}_r, \qquad (37)$$

where

$$\mathbf{e}_r = \sin\theta \cos\phi \, \mathbf{i} + \sin\theta \sin\phi \, \mathbf{j} + \cos\theta \, \mathbf{k} \qquad (38)$$

is the radial unit vector of spherical coordinates.

This vector points radially outwards away from the centre of the sphere.

A simple but important case arises when a vector field expressed in spherical coordinates takes the form

$$\mathbf{F} = \frac{A}{r^2} \mathbf{e}_r \quad (r \ne 0),$$

where A is a constant. To calculate the flux of this field over a spherical surface of radius R, centred on the origin, we set $r = R$ in the expression for $\mathbf{F}$ and take $\mathbf{J}$ from equation (37). This gives

$$\mathbf{F} \cdot \mathbf{J} = \left(\frac{A}{R^2} \mathbf{e}_r \right) \cdot (R^2 \sin\theta \, \mathbf{e}_r) = A \sin\theta.$$

Since $\mathbf{e}_r$ is a unit vector, $\mathbf{e}_r \cdot \mathbf{e}_r = 1$.

The flux of $\mathbf{F}$ over the surface of the sphere is then given by

$$\int_S \mathbf{F} \cdot d\mathbf{S} = A \int_{\phi=0}^{\phi=2\pi} \left(\int_{\theta=0}^{\theta=\pi} \sin\theta \, d\theta \right) d\phi$$

$$= A \int_{\phi=0}^{\phi=2\pi} \left[-\cos\theta \right]_{\theta=0}^{\theta=\pi} d\phi = 4\pi A.$$

Remarkably enough, this flux does not depend on the radius of the sphere. This can be understood with very little calculation. The outward normal component of the field has the constant value A/R^2 all over the surface of the sphere. Hence all surface elements of the same area make the same contribution to the surface integral. Under these circumstances, the total flux of $\mathbf{F}$ over the spherical surface can be found by multiplying the constant outward radial component of the field by the surface area of the sphere. This gives $A/R^2 \times 4\pi R^2 = 4\pi A$, in agreement with our more explicit calculation. Shortcuts like this are useful when the normal component of the field is constant at all points on the surface.

Example 10

Calculate the flux of the vector field $\mathbf{F} = x\,\mathbf{i} + y\,\mathbf{j}$ over the surface of a sphere of radius R, centred on the origin. You may use the standard integral

$$\int_0^\pi \sin^3\theta\, d\theta = \tfrac{4}{3}.$$

Solution

The coordinate transformation equations for spherical coordinates are

$$x = r\sin\theta\cos\phi, \quad y = r\sin\theta\sin\phi, \quad z = r\cos\theta.$$

On the surface of the sphere we have $r = R$, so on this surface the vector field is

$$\begin{aligned}\mathbf{F} &= R\sin\theta\cos\phi\,\mathbf{i} + R\sin\theta\sin\phi\,\mathbf{j} \\ &= R\sin\theta\,(\cos\phi\,\mathbf{i} + \sin\phi\,\mathbf{j}).\end{aligned}$$

The Jacobian vector on the surface of the sphere is

$$\mathbf{J} = R^2\sin\theta\,\mathbf{e}_r,$$

so

$$\mathbf{F}\cdot\mathbf{J} = R^2\sin^2\theta\,(\cos\phi\,\mathbf{i} + \sin\phi\,\mathbf{j})\cdot\mathbf{e}_r.$$

Using equation (38), we get

$$\mathbf{F}\cdot\mathbf{J} = R^3\sin^3\theta\,(\cos^2\phi + \sin^2\phi) = R^3\sin^3\theta.$$

To find the flux of $\mathbf{F}$ over the surface of the sphere, we integrate $\mathbf{F}\cdot\mathbf{J}$ over the ranges $0 \le \theta \le \pi$ and $0 \le \phi \le 2\pi$ that cover the sphere:

$$\int_S \mathbf{F}\cdot d\mathbf{S} = R^3 \int_{\phi=0}^{\phi=2\pi} \left(\int_{\theta=0}^{\theta=\pi} \sin^3\theta\, d\theta \right) d\phi.$$

Using the standard integral given in the question, we conclude that

$$\int_S \mathbf{F}\cdot d\mathbf{S} = R^3 \int_{\phi=0}^{\phi=2\pi} \tfrac{4}{3}\, d\phi = \tfrac{8}{3}\pi R^3.$$

Exercise 14

Calculate the flux of the vector field $\mathbf{F} = z\,\mathbf{k}$ over the curved surface of a hemisphere of radius R shown in the margin, with its unit normals in the sense marked. (The flat base of the hemisphere is not included.)

Exercise 15

Calculate the flux of the vector field $\mathbf{F} = 3\,\mathbf{k}$ over the same hemispherical surface as in Exercise 14.

4.3 Divergence revisited

Unit 9 introduced the important concept of the divergence of a vector field:

$$\boldsymbol{\nabla} \cdot \mathbf{F} = \frac{\partial F_x}{\partial x} + \frac{\partial F_y}{\partial y} + \frac{\partial F_z}{\partial z}. \tag{39}$$

We claimed that this gives a measure of the extent to which $\mathbf{F}$ diverges or flows away from any point. Various examples were used to illustrate this claim, but no proof was given. The concept of *flux* allows us to quantify this idea. If we surround a given point P by a tiny closed surface, the flux of a vector field $\mathbf{F}$ over that surface gives us a measure of the flow of the field away from P. According to Unit 9, there should be a link between this flux and the divergence of the field at P. We now investigate this link.

Some discussion is needed to reach the main result – the *divergence theorem*. You should follow this discussion in outline to ensure that you understand the main ideas, but you will not be asked to reproduce the steps. The most important point is the divergence theorem itself (equation (43)) and its applications (e.g. Examples 11 and 12).

First, we choose a surface over which to calculate the flux. This choice will not affect our conclusions, but the working is simplified by using the surface of a tiny cube with sides of length δL, whose faces are aligned with the x-, y- and z-axes (see Figure 33). To find the flux over the surface of this cube, we must calculate the fluxes over each of its six faces and add them together. We take the faces in pairs, starting with the two shaded faces in Figure 33, which are perpendicular to the x-axis.

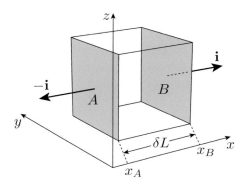

Figure 33   An enlarged view of a tiny cube with sides of length δL aligned with the x-, y- and z-axes

The faces are labelled A and B; the left-hand face is at $x = x_A$, and the right-hand face is at $x = x_B$. It is important to recall that the unit normals of a closed surface always point *outwards* into the exterior space. This means that the unit normal for face A points in the negative x-direction and is equal to $-\mathbf{i}$, while the unit normal for face B is $+\mathbf{i}$. Consequently, the flux of $\mathbf{F}$ over face A is

$$\text{flux over } A = \int_A \mathbf{F} \cdot d\mathbf{S} = \int_A \left(-F_x(x_A, y, z)\right) dy\, dz,$$

and the flux over face B is

$$\text{flux over } B = \int_B \mathbf{F} \cdot d\mathbf{S} = \int_B \left(+F_x(x_B, y, z)\right) dy\, dz.$$

Because the cube is aligned with the coordinate axes, the ranges of integration over y and z are identical in both these integrals. This allows us to express the total flux over both faces as an integral over the x- and y-values associated with face A:

$$\text{flux over } (A + B) = \int_A \left(F_x(x_B, y, z) - F_x(x_A, y, z)\right) dy\, dz.$$

Now, the integrand can be simplified. Dividing and multiplying by $x_B - x_A = \delta L$ and assuming that the cube is very small, we get

$$F_x(x_B, y, z) - F_x(x_A, y, z) = \frac{F_x(x_B, y, z) - F_x(x_A, y, z)}{x_B - x_A} (x_B - x_A)$$

$$\simeq \frac{\partial F_x}{\partial x} \delta L.$$

We therefore obtain

$$\text{flux over } (A + B) \simeq \int_A \left(\frac{\partial F_x}{\partial x} \delta L\right) dy\, dz.$$

Because the cube is assumed to be very small, the integrand can be taken to be constant over face A. The integral is then just the product of the integrand and the area $(\delta L)^2$ of the face. We therefore conclude that

$$\text{flux over } (A + B) \simeq \frac{\partial F_x}{\partial x} (\delta L)^3 = \frac{\partial F_x}{\partial x} \delta V, \tag{40}$$

where δV is the volume of the cube.

There is nothing special about the x-axis. If we consider the pair of faces perpendicular to the y-axis, we get a similar result with x replaced everywhere by y. And if we consider the pair of faces perpendicular to the z-axis, we again get a similar result with x replaced everywhere by z. The total flux of $\mathbf{F}$ over the entire surface of a small cube is found by adding these three contributions together:

$$\text{flux over surface of cube} \simeq \left(\frac{\partial F_x}{\partial x} + \frac{\partial F_y}{\partial y} + \frac{\partial F_z}{\partial z} \right) \delta V.$$

Using the definition of divergence in Cartesian coordinates in equation (39), we see that

$$\text{flux over surface of cube} \simeq \boldsymbol{\nabla} \cdot \mathbf{F}\, \delta V. \tag{41}$$

This is a remarkable result. It establishes the link between divergence and flux. All the approximations made in deriving it become exact in the limit as the volume of the cube shrinks to zero. The result has been derived in a special case, but it is true for all tiny elements of volume no matter what their shape. This allows us to think about divergence in a new way.

Divergence as flux per unit volume

The divergence of a vector field $\mathbf{F}$ at a given point is related to the flux of $\mathbf{F}$ over a tiny surface enclosing the point. In the limit where the surface area and its enclosed volume shrink to zero, we have

$$\boldsymbol{\nabla} \cdot \mathbf{F} = \frac{\text{flux of } \mathbf{F} \text{ over surface}}{\text{volume enclosed by surface}}. \tag{42}$$

So the divergence of a vector field at any point can be interpreted as the *flux per unit volume* at that point.

4.4   Additivity of flux and the divergence theorem

The interpretation of divergence in equation (42) involves the limit of a tiny surface surrounding a point. With a little more effort, we can get a more powerful result – *the divergence theorem* – that applies over extended surfaces and is very useful in applications. To achieve this, we need to establish a rule that allows fluxes to be added together.

The additivity of flux

Suppose that a given volume is subdivided into smaller volume elements. Then the *additivity of flux* relates the flux of a vector field over the surface of the whole volume to its fluxes over the surfaces of the volume elements.

The additivity of flux

If a volume is subdivided into smaller volume elements, the flux of a vector field over the surface of the whole volume is the sum of its fluxes over the surfaces of all the volume elements.

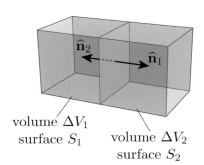

Figure 34   Neighbouring volume elements

To establish this fact, consider two neighbouring volume elements ΔV_1 and ΔV_2 with surfaces S_1 and S_2 (Figure 34). The surfaces S_1 and S_2 share a common boundary wall (shown in green). At any point on this boundary wall, the unit normal of S_1 points in the *opposite* direction to the unit normal of S_2. This is because the unit normals of a closed surface always point outwards, away from the enclosed volume. It follows that the flux of a vector field $\mathbf{F}$ contributed by the boundary wall section of S_1 is equal in magnitude and opposite in sign to the flux contributed by the boundary wall section of S_2. So when we add up the fluxes of $\mathbf{F}$ over the surfaces of all the volume elements, the contributions from the boundary walls all cancel out. The only surviving contributions come from the external surfaces, which form the surface of the whole volume.

The divergence theorem

Finally, we combine the additivity of flux with the interpretation of divergence as flux per unit volume. Suppose that we want to find the flux of a vector field $\mathbf{F}$ over the surface S of a region V (which need not be small). Then we can divide the region into tiny subregions, with surfaces S_i. The additivity of flux tells us that

$$\int_S \mathbf{F} \cdot d\mathbf{S} \simeq \sum_i (\text{flux over } S_i),$$

where the sum is over the surfaces of all the volume elements that make up the region.

The volume elements are assumed to be tiny, so we can use equation (41) to express each flux in terms of divergence. This gives

$$\int_S \mathbf{F} \cdot d\mathbf{S} \simeq \sum_i \boldsymbol{\nabla} \cdot \mathbf{F}(\mathbf{r}_i)\, \delta V_i.$$

Taking the limit of an infinite number of infinitesimal volume elements, the approximations become exact, and we conclude that

$$\int_S \mathbf{F} \cdot d\mathbf{S} = \int_V \boldsymbol{\nabla} \cdot \mathbf{F}\, dV.$$

This is the celebrated *divergence theorem*.

This is the key result of this section. It links surface integrals to related volume integrals.

Divergence theorem

Given a vector field $\mathbf{F}$ and a closed surface S enclosing a volume V, the divergence theorem states that

$$\int_S \mathbf{F} \cdot d\mathbf{S} = \int_V \boldsymbol{\nabla} \cdot \mathbf{F}\, dV. \tag{43}$$

In other words, the surface integral of $\mathbf{F}$ over a closed surface is equal to the volume integral of $\boldsymbol{\nabla} \cdot \mathbf{F}$ over the interior of the surface.

It is easy to remember where the symbol $\boldsymbol{\nabla}$ goes. Divergence involves spatial derivatives, so its units are those of the field divided by length. To get the same units on both sides of equation (43), the divergence must be in the volume integral, rather than in the surface integral.

Origins of the divergence theorem

The divergence theorem is frequently called **Gauss's theorem**. In fact, it was discovered independently by several people: Joseph-Louis Lagrange in 1764, Carl Friedrich Gauss in 1813, George Green in 1828 and Mikhail Ostrogradsky in 1831.

The first two did not publish the theorem, but kept it in their personal papers. Green was an amateur mathematician with no connections to the academic world, and he published his findings in an obscure pamphlet. It was not until the 1830s that the theorem became well known, thanks to its applications in the newly-developing sciences of fluid mechanics and electromagnetism.

The divergence theorem allows us to convert tricky surface integrals into easier volume integrals. The following example illustrates this application.

Example 11

Use the divergence theorem to calculate the surface integral of $\mathbf{F} = 12z\,\mathbf{k}$ over the surface S of the rugby ball in Figure 35. The volume of this rugby ball was found to be $4\pi a^2 b/3$ in Exercise 19 of Unit 8.

Solution

The divergence of $\mathbf{F}$ is

$$\boldsymbol{\nabla} \cdot \mathbf{F} = \frac{\partial(0)}{\partial x} + \frac{\partial(0)}{\partial y} + \frac{\partial(12z)}{\partial z}$$
$$= 12.$$

The divergence theorem allows us to express the required surface integral as a volume integral of $\boldsymbol{\nabla} \cdot \mathbf{F}$ over the volume V of the rugby ball. Using the result given in the question, we get

$$\int_S \mathbf{F} \cdot d\mathbf{S} = \int_V \boldsymbol{\nabla} \cdot \mathbf{F}\, dV$$
$$= \int_V 12\, dV$$
$$= 12 \times \tfrac{4}{3}\pi a^2 b = 16\pi a^2 b.$$

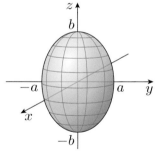

Figure 35   The surface of a rugby ball

With a slight modification of this technique, we can convert difficult surface integrals into easier ones.

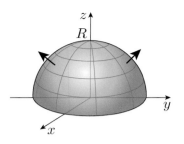

Figure 36   A hemispherical surface with its circular base in the xy-plane, centred on the origin

Example 12

Use the divergence theorem to find the flux of $\mathbf{F} = 3\mathbf{k}$ over the curved dome of the hemisphere in Figure 36, with unit normals as shown.

Solution

In order to apply the divergence theorem, we need a closed surface S. We take this to be the whole surface of the hemisphere, including the curved dome S_1 and the flat base S_2, so

$$\int_S \mathbf{F} \cdot d\mathbf{S} = \int_{S_1} \mathbf{F} \cdot d\mathbf{S} + \int_{S_2} \mathbf{F} \cdot d\mathbf{S},$$

where the normals of S_1 and S_2 both point outwards.

The field $\mathbf{F}$ is constant, so its divergence is equal to zero everywhere. The divergence theorem then tells us that

$$\int_S \mathbf{F} \cdot d\mathbf{S} = 0,$$

so

$$\int_{S_1} \mathbf{F} \cdot d\mathbf{S} + \int_{S_2} \mathbf{F} \cdot d\mathbf{S} = 0.$$

Now, the surface integral over the flat base S_2 is trivial. Because the field $\mathbf{F}$ is constant, and is perpendicular to this surface, we have

$$\int_{S_2} \mathbf{F} \cdot d\mathbf{S} = -3 \times (\pi R^2) = -3\pi R^2.$$

Here, the minus sign arises because the unit normals on the flat base point in the opposite direction to the field. Hence the required surface integral is

$$\int_{S_1} \mathbf{F} \cdot d\mathbf{S} = 3\pi R^2,$$

which agrees with the answer to Exercise 15.

Exercise 16

Use the divergence theorem to calculate the surface integral of the vector field $\mathbf{F} = x\,\mathbf{i} + y\,\mathbf{j} + z\,\mathbf{k}$ over the surface S of a sphere of radius R.

Exercise 17

Use the divergence theorem to calculate the surface integral of the vector field $\mathbf{F} = z\,\mathbf{k}$ over the curved part of the hemispherical surface in Figure 36.

4.5   The equation of continuity

This subsection illustrates an important application of the divergence theorem, but will not be assessed. You can skip it if you are short of time.

Many quantities are neither created nor destroyed, but just move around from place to place. Such quantities are said to be **conserved**. For example, to a good approximation there is a fixed amount of air in the atmosphere. The air can move, and its local density may vary, but the total mass of air remains constant. We say that the mass of air is conserved. Something similar can be said about electric charge and energy. The divergence theorem allows us to express such behaviour in a precise way.

To take a definite case, we consider a fluid of constant total mass. At each point $\mathbf{r}$ and time t, the fluid is described by its velocity $\mathbf{v}(\mathbf{r}, t)$ and its density $\rho(\mathbf{r}, t)$. We consider a fixed surface S enclosing a volume V. The total mass of fluid inside this surface is

$$M = \int_V \rho \, dV.$$

As the fluid moves around, the mass of fluid contained in the region V may change, and the rate of change of the enclosed mass is

$$\frac{dM}{dt} = \frac{d}{dt} \int_V \rho \, dV. \tag{44}$$

Naturally, we assume that there is no spontaneous creation or annihilation of fluid, so any change of fluid mass in the region V must be caused by a flow across the surface S. A net inward flow produces an increase in local mass, while a net outward flow leads to a decrease.

Equation (31) tells us that the rate of flow of fluid volume across a tiny planar element is $\mathbf{v} \cdot \delta\mathbf{S}$, where $\delta\mathbf{S}$ is the oriented area of the element. The corresponding rate of flow of fluid mass is $(\rho\mathbf{v}) \cdot \delta\mathbf{S}$. Hence the rate of flow of fluid mass out of the region V is given by the surface integral

$$\text{rate of outflow} = \int_S (\rho\mathbf{v}) \cdot d\mathbf{S}.$$

Because the unit normals of a closed surface point outwards, this is the rate of flow of fluid mass *out* of the region V, and is equal to $-dM/dt$, the rate of loss of mass from the enclosed region V. We therefore have

$$-\frac{dM}{dt} = \int_S (\rho\mathbf{v}) \cdot d\mathbf{S}. \tag{45}$$

Comparing equations (44) and (45), we conclude that

$$-\frac{d}{dt} \int_V \rho \, dV = \int_S (\rho\mathbf{v}) \cdot d\mathbf{S}. \tag{46}$$

This equation expresses the fact that any change in fluid mass in a region is related to a flow into or out of that region. The focus of interest here is that it can be recast in an alternative form using the divergence theorem.

First, the differentiation on the left-hand side can be brought inside the integral. This is allowed because the region of integration V does not change with time, so any change in the integral must be due to a change in its integrand. For any given region, the integral depends only on t, which is why straight dees have been used in equation (46). However, the density ρ can depend on both t and $\mathbf{r}$, so we must use the curly dees of partial differentiation inside the integral. Thus

$$\frac{d}{dt} \int_V \rho \, dV = \int_V \frac{\partial \rho}{\partial t} \, dV.$$

We can also use the divergence theorem to express the right-hand side of equation (46) as a volume integral:

$$\int_S (\rho \mathbf{v}) \cdot d\mathbf{S} = \int_V \mathbf{\nabla} \cdot (\rho \mathbf{v}) \, dV.$$

Equation (46) can therefore be written as

$$\int_V \left(\frac{\partial \rho}{\partial t} + \mathbf{\nabla} \cdot (\rho \mathbf{v}) \right) dV = 0, \tag{47}$$

where the two volume integrals over V have been combined into a single integral.

When a definite integral is equal to zero, it is normally unsafe to argue that its integrand must be equal to zero – there could, after all, be cancellations of positive and negative contributions. However, we are in a different position. Because equation (47) is valid for *any* region of integration, no matter how small or where it is located, the only possibility is for the integrand to be equal to zero everywhere. This leads to the following conclusion.

> **Equation of continuity**
>
> If the mass of a fluid is conserved, then at each point, its density ρ and velocity $\mathbf{v}$ are related by
>
> $$\frac{\partial \rho}{\partial t} + \mathbf{\nabla} \cdot (\rho \mathbf{v}) = 0. \tag{48}$$
>
> This is known as the **equation of continuity** for fluid mass.

The vector field $\rho \mathbf{v}$ is sometimes called the *mass flux density*, and given the symbol $\mathbf{J}$.

Equations like this appear throughout physics – wherever a quantity that flows like a fluid is conserved. For example, the flow of electric charge and the flow of energy both obey equations of continuity. You will meet this equation again in Unit 12 when we discuss diffusion.

We are sometimes interested in steady-state situations where the density ρ does not change in time at any point in the fluid. In this case, the equation of continuity gives $\mathbf{\nabla} \cdot (\rho \mathbf{v}) = 0$. This restricts the possible flows that can occur in steady-state situations.

Exercise 18

Which of the following vector fields could describe $\rho \mathbf{v}$ in a steady-state flow in a fluid?

(a) $\rho \mathbf{v} = 2y^2 \, \mathbf{i} - 14yz \, \mathbf{j} + 7z^2 \, \mathbf{k}$ (b) $\rho \mathbf{v} = 2x \, \mathbf{i} - 3y \, \mathbf{j} + 4z \, \mathbf{k}$

5   Circulation and the curl theorem

This section brings our discussion of the calculus of fields to a close by investigating the meaning of the curl of a vector field. Its main result is the *curl theorem*, which is the counterpart of the divergence theorem of the previous section.

Recall that Unit 9 introduced the curl of a vector field as

$$\nabla \times \mathbf{F} = \begin{vmatrix} \mathbf{i} & \mathbf{j} & \mathbf{k} \\ \dfrac{\partial}{\partial x} & \dfrac{\partial}{\partial y} & \dfrac{\partial}{\partial z} \\ F_x & F_y & F_z \end{vmatrix}. \tag{49}$$

This is a vector field. We claimed that the curl vector measures the extent to which **F** is associated with rotation or swirling. A few examples supported this claim, but no proof was given. In this section, we use line integrals around closed paths to quantify the concept of curl.

5.1   Circulation of a vector field

We begin by establishing a convention. Figure 37 shows a planar surface element, with unit normal $\hat{\mathbf{n}}$. The perimeter of this element is a closed loop C, which we would like to treat as a path with some sense of positive progression. If the surface element were in the xy-plane, viewed from above, we might talk about progression in a clockwise or anticlockwise sense, but terms like this become ambiguous for planar elements with arbitrary orientations, viewed from arbitrary directions.

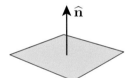

Figure 37   A planar surface element

There are two possible choices for the unit normal of a planar element. A particular choice has been made in Figure 37. Having made this choice, we now fix the sense of positive progression around the perimeter curve C by the following convention.

Right-hand grip rule

See Figure 38: with the thumb of your right hand pointing in the direction of the unit normal of a planar element, the curled fingers of your right hand indicate the sense of positive progression around the perimeter of the element.

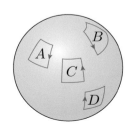

Figure 38   The right-hand grip rule

Exercise 19

The arrows in the figure in the margin show senses of progression around the perimeters of four shaded patches A, B, C and D on the surface of a sphere. For which of these patches do the arrows indicate a sense of positive progression?

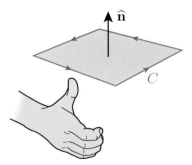

Given a planar element $\delta \mathbf{S}$, we can define a closed path C that goes once round the perimeter of the element in the positive sense defined by the right-hand grip rule. Around this path, we can evaluate the line integral of a vector field $\mathbf{F}$. This line integral is called the *circulation* of the vector field around C. We write

$$\text{circulation} = \int_C \mathbf{F} \cdot d\mathbf{s} = \oint_C \mathbf{F} \cdot d\mathbf{s}.$$

The last expression has a circle in the middle of the integral sign. This symbol is sometimes used as a reminder that the path of integration is closed, but otherwise makes no difference to the meaning.

> **Circulation of a vector field**
>
> Given a vector field $\mathbf{F}$ and a closed path C, the **circulation** of $\mathbf{F}$ around C is given by the line integral
>
> $$\text{circulation} = \oint_C \mathbf{F} \cdot d\mathbf{s}. \tag{50}$$
>
> If C is a path around a planar element with a given unit normal, it is understood that C is traversed in the positive sense determined by the right-hand grip rule.

Section 2 explained how to calculate line integrals of this type. There is nothing new here except that the path is closed, which means that the start and end points of the path are identical. So if the path is described by the parametric equations

$$x = x(t), \quad y = y(t), \quad z = z(t) \quad (t_1 \le t \le t_2),$$

then the extreme parameter values t_1 and t_2 refer to the same point.

Exercise 20

(a) Calculate the circulation of the vector field $\mathbf{F} = x\,\mathbf{j}$ around a closed path C with parametric representation

$$x(t) = \cos t, \quad y(t) = \sin t \quad (0 \le t \le 2\pi).$$

(b) What is the circulation of a conservative vector field $\mathbf{G}$ around the closed path C?

5.2   Curl revisited

Circulation measures the amount of rotation or swirling associated with a vector field. You might therefore expect there to be a link between circulation and curl, similar to the link between flux and divergence. This is indeed the case, and we will now explore the nature of this link.

The following argument justifies the main result – the *curl theorem*. You should follow this discussion in outline to ensure that you understand the main ideas, but you will not be asked to reproduce the steps. The most important point is the curl theorem itself (equation (57)) and its applications (e.g. Examples 14 and 15).

We begin by considering a tiny square surface element with sides of length δL (Figure 39). The element lies in the xy-plane, with its edges aligned with the x- and y-axes, and its unit normal is chosen to be in the positive z-direction (towards you).

We will calculate the circulation of a vector field **F** around the perimeter of this element. To do this, we must first use the right-hand grip rule to determine the positive sense of progression around the perimeter. This is in the order $ABCD$, as indicated by arrows in Figure 39. The path $ABCD$ consists of four straight-line segments, which we consider in pairs, starting with BC and DA, which vary in the y-direction.

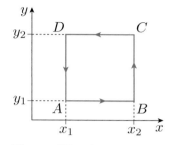

Figure 39 A square surface element in the xy-plane

Line integrals are usually evaluated in parametric form, but these paths are simple enough to make this unnecessary. We can revert to the fundamental concept of a line integral – that of integrating the component of a field in the direction of travel along a path. With the coordinates shown in Figure 39, the line integral contributed by the side BC is

$$I_{BC} = \int_{y_1}^{y_2} F_y(x_2, y, 0)\, dy,$$

and the contribution from the side DA is

$$I_{DA} = -\int_{y_1}^{y_2} F_y(x_1, y, 0)\, dy.$$

The minus sign on the right makes good sense because in the limit where x_1 approaches x_2, the paths BC and DA become the reverse of one another, and must have opposite signs. The combined contribution from sides BC and DA is therefore

$$I_{BC+DA} = \int_{y_1}^{y_2} \big(F_y(x_2, y, 0) - F_y(x_1, y, 0)\big)\, dy.$$

Now, the integrand can be simplified. Dividing and multiplying by $x_2 - x_1 = \delta L$, and assuming that the square is very small, we get

$$F_y(x_2, y, 0) - F_y(x_1, y, 0) = \frac{F_y(x_2, y, 0) - F_y(x_1, y, 0)}{x_2 - x_1}(x_2 - x_1)$$

$$\simeq \frac{\partial F_y}{\partial x}\, \delta L,$$

so

$$I_{BC+DA} \simeq \int_{y_1}^{y_2} \left(\frac{\partial F_y}{\partial x}\, \delta L\right) dy.$$

Because the square is assumed to be very small, the integrand can be taken to be constant over the range of integration. The integral is then approximated by the product of the integrand and the length $y_2 - y_1 = \delta L$.

So we have

$$I_{BC+DA} \simeq \frac{\partial F_y}{\partial x} (\delta L)^2. \tag{51}$$

A similar calculation can be done for the other two sides of the square. Their contribution is

$$I_{AB+CD} = \int_{x_1}^{x_2} \left(F_x(x, y_1, 0) - F_x(x, y_2, 0) \right) dx.$$

In this case, the x-component of the field appears in an integral over x, and the signs are different – the larger value of y (namely y_2) now appears in the term that carries a minus sign. Bearing these changes in mind, and working through the same steps as before, leads to

$$I_{AB+CD} \simeq \int_{x_1}^{x_2} \left(-\frac{\partial F_x}{\partial y} \delta L \right) dx = -\frac{\partial F_x}{\partial y} (\delta L)^2. \tag{52}$$

Finally, combining the contributions from equations (51) and (52), we conclude that the circulation of $\mathbf{F}$ around the square $ABCD$ is

$$\text{circulation} \simeq \left(\frac{\partial F_y}{\partial x} - \frac{\partial F_x}{\partial y} \right) \delta S, \tag{53}$$

where $\delta S = (\delta L)^2$ is the area of the square.

You may recognise the combination of partial derivatives in round brackets. Using the definition of curl in Cartesian coordinates in equation (49), you can see that

$$\frac{\partial F_y}{\partial x} - \frac{\partial F_x}{\partial y} = (\boldsymbol{\nabla} \times \mathbf{F})_z = (\boldsymbol{\nabla} \times \mathbf{F}) \cdot \mathbf{k}. \tag{54}$$

Because the square has its unit normal in the z-direction, its oriented area is $\delta \mathbf{S} = \delta S \, \mathbf{k}$. Combining this with equations (53) and (54), we see that

$$\text{circulation} \simeq (\boldsymbol{\nabla} \times \mathbf{F}) \cdot \delta \mathbf{S}. \tag{55}$$

This is a remarkable result. It establishes the link we have been seeking between curl and circulation. All the approximations made in deriving it become exact in the limit where the area of the square shrinks to zero. The result has been derived in a particular case, but there is nothing special about our choice of axes, or the location of the square. In fact, equation (55) applies to all tiny planar elements of any shape. This enables us to think about curl in a new way.

Curl as circulation per unit area

Given a vector field $\mathbf{F}$ in the vicinity of a given point, the component of $\boldsymbol{\nabla} \times \mathbf{F}$ in the direction of the unit vector $\hat{\mathbf{n}}$ can be found by taking a planar element with unit normal $\hat{\mathbf{n}}$ at the point. The component is given by

$$(\boldsymbol{\nabla} \times \mathbf{F}) \cdot \hat{\mathbf{n}} = \frac{\text{circulation around perimeter of element}}{\text{area of element}}, \tag{56}$$

in the limit where the element becomes very small.

So each component of the curl at a given point can be interpreted as a *circulation per unit area* at that point.

Example 13

Consider the vector field

$$\mathbf{F} = -y\,\mathbf{i} + x\,\mathbf{j}.$$

(a) Calculate the circulation of this vector field around the perimeter C of a tiny circular element of radius R, centred on the origin and lying in the xy-plane. The unit normal of this element is chosen to point in the positive z-direction.

(b) Calculate the z-component of the curl of $\mathbf{F}$ at the origin.

(c) Do your answers to parts (a) and (b) agree with equation (56)?

Solution

(a) Using the given direction of the unit normal, the right-hand grip rule tells us that the path must be traversed anticlockwise (when viewed from the positive z-axis). This path can be represented by parametric equations of the form

$$x = R\cos t, \quad y = R\sin t \quad (0 \le t \le 2\pi).$$

We have

$$\mathbf{F} = -y\,\mathbf{i} + x\,\mathbf{j} = -R\sin t\,\mathbf{i} + R\cos t\,\mathbf{j},$$
$$\frac{d\mathbf{s}}{dt} = \frac{dx}{dt}\,\mathbf{i} + \frac{dy}{dt}\,\mathbf{j} = -R\sin t\,\mathbf{i} + R\cos t\,\mathbf{j},$$

so

$$\begin{aligned}
\mathbf{F} \cdot \frac{d\mathbf{s}}{dt} &= F_x\frac{dx}{dt} + F_y\frac{dy}{dt} \\
&= R^2(\sin^2 t + \cos^2 t) \\
&= R^2.
\end{aligned}$$

The circulation around C is therefore

$$\begin{aligned}
\oint_C \mathbf{F} \cdot d\mathbf{s} &= \int_0^{2\pi} R^2\, dt \\
&= 2\pi R^2.
\end{aligned}$$

(b) At any point, the z-component of the curl of $\mathbf{F}$ is

$$\begin{aligned}
(\boldsymbol{\nabla} \times \mathbf{F}) \cdot \mathbf{k} &= \frac{\partial F_y}{\partial x} - \frac{\partial F_x}{\partial y} \\
&= \frac{\partial(x)}{\partial x} - \frac{\partial(-y)}{\partial y} \\
&= 2.
\end{aligned}$$

In particular, $(\boldsymbol{\nabla} \times \mathbf{F}) \cdot \mathbf{k} = 2$ at the origin.

(c) Because the area of the circular element is πR^2, the right-hand side of equation (56) is equal to $2\pi R^2/\pi R^2 = 2$. This is equal to the left-hand side, calculated at the centre of the element.

Exercise 21

Compare the two sides of equation (56) for a vector field $\mathbf{F} = x^2 \mathbf{j}$ and a square element in the xy-plane with corners A, B, C and D at (x, y), $(x + a, y)$, $(x + a, y + a)$ and $(x, y + a)$, respectively, where a is a small constant length. The unit normal of the element is taken to be in the positive z-direction.

5.3   Additivity of circulation and the curl theorem

You have seen that the divergence of a vector field at a given point can be interpreted as the flux per unit volume in a tiny region around the point. Moreover, the additivity of flux allowed us to derive a more powerful result – the divergence theorem – which applies over *extended* regions. Now we will do something similar for curl.

The additivity of circulation

Consider an open surface in the plane of the page, divided into a number of subregions. As always, the unit normals of the subregions are required to have consistent orientations. To consider a definite case, we take them to point out of the page towards you. Then the right-hand grip rule ensures that the perimeters of the subregions are all traversed in the same sense – in this case, anticlockwise.

The *additivity of circulation* relates the circulation of a vector field around the surface to the sum of its circulations around the subregions.

> **The additivity of circulation**
>
> If an open surface is subdivided into consistently-oriented surface elements, the circulation of a vector field $\mathbf{F}$ around the perimeter of the surface is the sum of the circulations of $\mathbf{F}$ around the perimeters of all the elements.

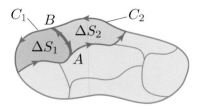

Figure 40   The additivity of circulation

To see why this is true, look at Figure 40; this shows two neighbouring subregions ΔS_1 and ΔS_2, with perimeters C_1 (in red) and C_2 (in blue). These perimeters share a common segment AB, which is traversed in one sense for C_1 and in the *opposite* sense for C_2. So when we add the circulations around C_1 and C_2, the contributions from the common section AB cancel out. More generally, all the contributions from boundaries between subregions cancel out, leaving only contributions from sections that are not shared. But these non-shared sections form the perimeter of the whole surface.

In fact, the surface need not be flat. All we need is an open surface, such as that in Figure 41, divided into surface elements. (Recall that an open surface is one that has a perimeter.) If the surface elements are oriented consistently – with neighbouring elements having similar, rather than opposing, unit normals – the additivity of circulation continues to apply.

The curl theorem

Finally, we can combine the additivity of circulation with the interpretation of curl as circulation per unit area. Suppose that we want to find the circulation of a vector field $\mathbf{F}$ around the perimeter C of an open surface. We can divide the surface into many tiny surface elements S_i with perimeters C_i. The additivity of circulation tells us that

$$\oint_C \mathbf{F} \cdot d\mathbf{s} = \sum_i (\text{circulation around } C_i),$$

where the sum is over the perimeters of all the surface elements that make up the surface.

The surface elements are assumed to be tiny, so we can use equation (55) to express each circulation in terms of curl. This gives

$$\oint_C \mathbf{F} \cdot d\mathbf{s} \simeq \sum_i (\boldsymbol{\nabla} \times \mathbf{F}) \cdot \delta \mathbf{S}_i.$$

In the limit where the surface elements approach zero size, the approximation becomes exact and the right-hand side becomes an integral. We arrive at the following important result.

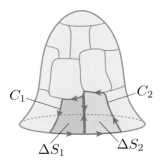

Figure 41   The additivity of circulation on a curved surface

Curl theorem

If $\mathbf{F}$ is a vector field and S is an open surface with perimeter C, then

$$\oint_C \mathbf{F} \cdot d\mathbf{s} = \int_S (\boldsymbol{\nabla} \times \mathbf{F}) \cdot d\mathbf{S}. \tag{57}$$

This is the key result of this section. It links line integrals to related surface integrals.

The curl theorem is just as important as the divergence theorem, and plays a central role in electromagnetism and fluid mechanics.

Origins of the curl theorem

The curl theorem is often called **Stokes's theorem** after the mathematician George Stokes (Figure 42), although the connection with Stokes is rather shaky.

The theorem was actually discovered by Lord Kelvin in 1850. Stokes learned about it in a letter from Kelvin, and set an exam question asking students to prove it. Exams must have been tough in those days! One of the students taking the exam was James Clerk Maxwell, who went on to use the theorem to help to frame the fundamental laws of electromagnetism. Stokes himself is famous for his work on fluid mechanics, wave motion and optics.

Figure 42   George Stokes (1819–1903)

The curl theorem is useful because it can simplify the evaluation of integrals. For example, we can convert a line integral around a closed path into a simpler surface integral, as shown in the following example.

Example 14

Use the curl theorem to find the line integral of $\mathbf{F} = -y\,\mathbf{i} + x\,\mathbf{j}$ around a circular path C in the xy-plane, centred on the origin and of radius R. The path is traversed anticlockwise when seen from the positive z-axis.

Solution

The curl of the two-dimensional vector field $\mathbf{F}$ is

$$\mathbf{\nabla} \times \mathbf{F} = \left(\frac{\partial F_y}{\partial x} - \frac{\partial F_x}{\partial y}\right)\mathbf{k} = \left(\frac{\partial(x)}{\partial x} - \frac{\partial(-y)}{\partial y}\right)\mathbf{k} = 2\mathbf{k}.$$

The path C is the perimeter of a circular disc of radius R, centred on the origin and in the xy-plane. Since C is traversed in an anticlockwise sense, the right-hand grip rule shows that the unit normal of this surface is $\mathbf{k}$ (rather than $-\mathbf{k}$).

Hence, using the curl theorem, the required line integral is

$$\int_C \mathbf{F} \cdot d\mathbf{s} = \int_{\text{disc}} 2\mathbf{k} \cdot \mathbf{k}\, dS = 2\pi R^2,$$

which agrees with the calculation in Example 13(a).

Exercise 22

Use the method of Example 14 to calculate the line integral of the vector field $\mathbf{F} = x^2\,\mathbf{i} + y^2\,\mathbf{j}$ around a rectangular path in the xy-plane with corners at $(0,0)$, $(2,0)$, $(2,1)$, $(1,1)$, traversed in that order, and returning to $(0,0)$.

It is worth noting that the curl theorem applies to all open surfaces, whether flat or not. In Figure 43, the surfaces S_1 and S_2 share the same perimeter path C. In this case, the curl theorem tells us that

$$\int_C \mathbf{F} \cdot d\mathbf{s} = \int_{S_1} (\mathbf{\nabla} \times \mathbf{F}) \cdot d\mathbf{S} = \int_{S_2} (\mathbf{\nabla} \times \mathbf{F}) \cdot d\mathbf{S},$$

for any vector field $\mathbf{F}$.

So if the vector field $\mathbf{G}$ is the curl of $\mathbf{F}$ (so that $\mathbf{G} = \mathbf{\nabla} \times \mathbf{F}$), we have

$$\int_{S_1} \mathbf{G} \cdot d\mathbf{S} = \int_{S_2} \mathbf{G} \cdot d\mathbf{S}, \tag{58}$$

for any open surfaces S_1 and S_2 that share the same perimeter path.

This gives us the freedom to replace the surface integral of a vector field $\mathbf{G}$ over a complicated surface by one over a much nicer surface – *but only if* $\mathbf{G}$ *is a* **curl field** (i.e. a field that is the curl of another vector field). This is reminiscent of the freedom that we have to adjust the paths of *gradient fields* between fixed start and end points.

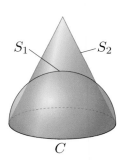

Figure 43   Two surfaces with the same perimeter path

Example 15

The vector field $\mathbf{G} = z^2\,\mathbf{j} + x^2\,\mathbf{k}$ is a curl field. Use this fact to find the surface integral of $\mathbf{G}$ over the curved hemispherical surface S in Figure 44, with its unit normals pointing upwards as shown.

You can check that $\mathbf{G} = \nabla \times \mathbf{F}$, where $\mathbf{F} = \frac{1}{3}(z^3\,\mathbf{i} + x^3\,\mathbf{j})$.

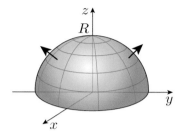

Figure 44 A hemispherical surface

Solution

The perimeter of the hemispherical surface is a circle in the xy-plane, centred on the origin and of radius R. The circular disc at the base of the hemisphere shares this perimeter path. The curl theorem can be applied to both these surfaces, but to ensure that the perimeter path is traversed in the same sense in both cases, the unit normal of the disc must be chosen to be $\mathbf{k}$ (rather than $-\mathbf{k}$). Because $\mathbf{G}$ is a curl field, we can replace the surface integral over the hemisphere by one over the disc.

Hence

$$\int_S \mathbf{G} \cdot d\mathbf{S} = \int_{\text{disc}} \mathbf{G} \cdot d\mathbf{S} = \int_{\text{disc}} \left(z^2\,\mathbf{j} + x^2\,\mathbf{k}\right) \cdot \mathbf{k}\, dS = \int_{\text{disc}} x^2\, dS.$$

So we just need to integrate x^2 over a circular disc. Using polar coordinates, we get

$$\int_S \mathbf{G} \cdot d\mathbf{S} = \int_{\phi=0}^{\phi=2\pi} \left(\int_{r=0}^{r=R} r^2 \cos^2\phi \times r\, dr \right) d\phi$$

$$= \int_0^{2\pi} \cos^2\phi\, d\phi \times \int_0^R r^3\, dr$$

$$= \pi \times \tfrac{1}{4}R^4 = \tfrac{1}{4}\pi R^4.$$

Exercise 23

The vector field $\mathbf{G} = -2xz\,\mathbf{i} + (x^2 + z^2)\,\mathbf{k}$ is a curl field. Use the method of Example 15 to calculate the surface integral of $\mathbf{G}$ over the curved surface of the bell shown in the margin. The open mouth of this bell is a circle in the xy-plane, centred on the origin and of radius R. The body of the bell lies in the region $z > 0$, and its unit normals point in the sense of increasing z.

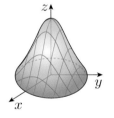

Finally, there is some unfinished technical business. Subsection 3.3 proved that every conservative field has zero curl. The curl test assumes that the converse is true; so if the curl of $\mathbf{F}$ is equal to zero throughout its domain, it assumes that $\mathbf{F}$ is conservative. This is clearly unsafe logic: every owl is a bird, but every bird is not an owl! The curl test is usually reliable, but there is a proviso that can now be explained.

Suppose that $\mathbf{F}$ is defined throughout the *whole of space*, and that $\nabla \times \mathbf{F} = \mathbf{0}$ *everywhere*. Then for any closed path C, the curl theorem tells us that

$$\int_C \mathbf{F} \cdot d\mathbf{s} = \int_S (\nabla \times \mathbf{F}) \cdot d\mathbf{S} = 0,$$

where S is an open surface with C as its perimeter.

Figure 45   Two paths; reversing a path reverses the sign of a line integral

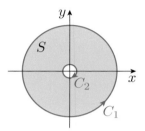

Figure 46   A case in which the domain of a two-dimensional vector field $\mathbf{F}(x, y)$ excludes the origin

Under these circumstances, we can say that $\mathbf{F}$ has zero circulation around any closed loop C. It is easy to see that this implies that all the line integrals of $\mathbf{F}$ are path-independent. For example, Figure 45 shows red and blue paths leading from A to B. The line integral of $\mathbf{F}$ around a closed path C that follows the red path and the *reverse* of the blue path is

$$\int_C \mathbf{F} \cdot d\mathbf{s} = \int_{A \to B \text{ (red)}} \mathbf{F} \cdot d\mathbf{s} - \int_{A \to B \text{ (blue)}} \mathbf{F} \cdot d\mathbf{s}.$$

If this is equal to zero, the line integrals along the red and blue paths must be equal. This independence of path allows us to conclude that $\mathbf{F}$ is conservative, and almost proves the curl test – but there is a loophole.

To see what can go wrong, consider the two-dimensional situation shown in Figure 46, where the vector field $\mathbf{F}$ is not defined at the origin. If we consider a closed loop C_1 that encircles the origin, we can see that this is part of the boundary of an open surface S within the domain of $\mathbf{F}$. But it is not the complete boundary – there is also another portion C_2, closer to the origin. Now the fact that $\nabla \times \mathbf{F} = \mathbf{0}$ tells us that the circulations around C_1 and C_2 cancel one another out – but they might not individually vanish. Under these circumstances, the curl test fails. In technical language, the curl test requires the domain of the field to be *simply-connected*.

A region is **simply-connected** if any closed loop in the region can be continuously shrunk to a point without leaving the region. For example, the whole of space is simply-connected. A typical Swiss cheese (with isolated holes) is also simply-connected. However, a plane with the origin removed, and three-dimensional space with the z-axis removed, are not simply-connected. In such domains, the condition $\nabla \times \mathbf{F} = \mathbf{0}$ does not guarantee the path-independence of all line integrals, so the curl test fails.

Learning outcomes

After studying this unit, you should be able to do the following.

- Calculate the line integral of a scalar field in Cartesian coordinates.
- Calculate the line integral of a vector field in Cartesian coordinates.
- State and apply the properties of conservative fields. Simplify line integrals involving conservative fields by choosing appropriate paths.
- Calculate the conservative vector field corresponding to a given scalar potential field, and find a scalar potential field corresponding to a given conservative vector field.
- Use the curl test to decide whether or not a given vector field is conservative.
- Define the terms closed surface, open surface, flux and oriented area, and understand the convention for the unit normals of a closed surface.

- Calculate the surface integral (or flux) of a vector field over a given surface (in simple cases).

- Interpret divergence as flux per unit volume. State and apply the additivity of flux and the divergence theorem.

- Use the right-hand grip rule to find the positive sense of progression around a given closed loop. Define and calculate circulation of a vector field.

- Interpret curl as flux per unit area. State and apply the additivity of circulation and the curl theorem.

Appendix: two insights

This Appendix is for interest and enjoyment only. It will not help you with calculations, but it contains two interesting insights that unify different topics in this book. You can read it when you have the time (possibly after studying the module).

Unifying various types of integral

In ordinary calculus, we can say that

$$\int_a^b \frac{df}{dx}\, dx = f(b) - f(a), \tag{59}$$

a result known as the **fundamental theorem of calculus** because it brings together derivatives and integrals.

A similar result applies to gradients and line integrals:

$$\int_{A \to B} \boldsymbol{\nabla} U \cdot d\mathbf{s} = U_B - U_A. \tag{60}$$

This is the content of equations (24) and (26), although the sign convention relating $\mathbf{F}$ and U inserted minus signs in those equations. Equation (60) is sometimes called the **gradient theorem**.

Two other important results relating derivatives and integrals were discussed in this unit. The curl theorem can be written as

$$\int_S (\boldsymbol{\nabla} \times \mathbf{F}) \cdot d\mathbf{S} = \oint_C \mathbf{F} \cdot d\mathbf{s}, \tag{61}$$

and the divergence theorem can be written as

$$\int_V \boldsymbol{\nabla} \cdot \mathbf{F}\, dV = \int_S \mathbf{F} \cdot d\mathbf{S}. \tag{62}$$

There is a feature that unifies these four theorems. In each case, the left-hand side involves something that is differentiated and then integrated over a region, while the right-hand side contains no derivative, and is formed from values on the *boundary* of the region.

- In equation (59), the region is an interval along the x-axis, and its boundary is the pair of points $x = a$ and $x = b$ at either end of the interval.

- In equation (60), the region is a curved path, and its boundary consists of the pair of points A and B at either end of the path.

- In equation (61), the region is an open surface S, and its boundary is the closed path C that forms its perimeter.

- In equation (62), the region is a volume V, and its boundary is the surface S of this volume.

From this perspective, all of these theorems belong to the same family.

Expressions for divergence and curl in orthogonal coordinates

Unit 9 gave general formulas for divergence and curl in orthogonal coordinates. The optional Appendix of Unit 9 justified these formulas in a direct way, but it involved lengthy calculations. The divergence and curl theorems allow us to give alternative justifications that are simpler and more attractive.

According to Unit 9, in any orthogonal coordinate system (u, v, w), divergence is given by

$$\boldsymbol{\nabla} \cdot \mathbf{F} = \frac{1}{J} \left[\frac{\partial}{\partial u} \left(\frac{J F_u}{h_u} \right) + \frac{\partial}{\partial v} \left(\frac{J F_v}{h_v} \right) + \frac{\partial}{\partial w} \left(\frac{J F_w}{h_w} \right) \right], \tag{63}$$

where h_u, h_v and h_w are scale factors, and $J = h_u h_v h_w$ is the Jacobian factor.

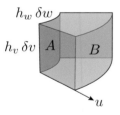

Figure 47   A volume element in (u, v, w) coordinates

The divergence theorem tells us that divergence can be interpreted as flux per unit volume. We can show that equation (63) is a direct expression of this fact. To see why, look at Figure 47, which shows a small volume element for the (u, v, w) orthogonal coordinate system. The volume of this element is

$$\delta V = h_u h_v h_w \, \delta u \, \delta v \, \delta w. \tag{64}$$

We need to calculate the flux of a vector field $\mathbf{F}$ over the surface of the volume element. First, consider the two curved faces A (red) and B (green), which are perpendicular to the u-axis.

The calculation goes along the same lines as that given in Subsection 4.3 for Cartesian coordinates, but there is one significant difference. The faces A and B are generated by the same increments δv and δw, but they may have different areas. We must take account of this when we evaluate the fluxes. The area of each face is

$$\delta A = (h_v \, \delta v) \times (h_w \, \delta w), \tag{65}$$

and the faces have different areas if the scale factors h_u and h_w depend on u. Not surprisingly, equation (40) is replaced by

$$\text{flux over } (A + B) = \frac{\partial (F_u \, \delta A)}{\partial u} \, \delta u,$$

where the area of a face is now *inside* the partial derivative.

Using equation (65) and recalling that δv and δw are the same for both faces, we get

$$\text{flux over } (A+B) = \frac{\partial(F_u h_v h_w)}{\partial u}\,\delta u\,\delta v\,\delta w = \frac{\partial}{\partial u}\left(\frac{JF_u}{h_u}\right)\delta u\,\delta v\,\delta w.$$

Of course, there are similar expressions for the other two pairs of faces, perpendicular to the v- and w-axes. Adding together all these fluxes gives the total flux over the surface of the volume element:

$$\text{total flux} = \left[\frac{\partial}{\partial u}\left(\frac{JF_u}{h_u}\right) + \frac{\partial}{\partial v}\left(\frac{JF_v}{h_v}\right) + \frac{\partial}{\partial w}\left(\frac{JF_w}{h_w}\right)\right]\delta u\,\delta v\,\delta w. \quad (66)$$

Divergence is flux per unit volume. We therefore divide equation (66) by equation (64), and take the limit of a tiny volume element. In this limit, all our approximations become exact, and we recover equation (63).

We can also justify the formula for curl in orthogonal coordinates. In any right-handed orthogonal coordinate system (u, v, w), with scale factors h_u, h_v and h_w, Unit 9 gave the following formula for curl:

$$\boldsymbol{\nabla}\times\mathbf{F} = \frac{1}{h_u h_v h_w}\begin{vmatrix} h_u\,\mathbf{e}_u & h_v\,\mathbf{e}_v & h_w\,\mathbf{e}_w \\ \dfrac{\partial}{\partial u} & \dfrac{\partial}{\partial v} & \dfrac{\partial}{\partial w} \\ h_u F_u & h_v F_v & h_w F_w \end{vmatrix}. \quad (67)$$

Figure 48 shows a tiny area element based on the orthogonal coordinates (u, v, w). This element is perpendicular to the w-axis, and we can obtain an expression for the w-component of $\boldsymbol{\nabla}\times\mathbf{F}$ by finding the circulation per unit area of $\mathbf{F}$ around it.

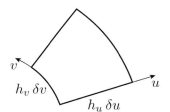

Figure 48 A surface element in the (u, v, w) coordinate system

The calculation goes along similar lines to that given in Subsection 5.2 for Cartesian coordinates. The main new feature is that opposite sides of the element need not be equal in length. Their lengths depend on scale factors, which may vary from point to point. Taking this into account, it is not difficult to show that the circulation around the element in Figure 48 is

$$\text{circulation} = \left(\frac{\partial(h_v F_v)}{\partial u} - \frac{\partial(h_u F_u)}{\partial v}\right)\delta u\,\delta v, \quad (68)$$

while the area of the element is

$$\delta A = h_u h_v\,\delta u\,\delta v.$$

Curl is circulation per unit volume. We therefore divide equation (68) by δA, and take the limit of a tiny area element. In this limit, all our approximations become exact, and we recover the w-component of equation (67). Similar arguments give the other two components of the curl.

Solutions to exercises

Solution to Exercise 1

We have $dx/dt = 2$ and $dy/dt = 2t$, so

$$\left(\frac{dx}{dt}\right)^2 + \left(\frac{dy}{dt}\right)^2 = 2^2 + (2t)^2 = 4(1 + t^2).$$

The length of the parabolic arc is

$$L = \int_{-1}^{1} \sqrt{\left(\frac{dx}{dt}\right)^2 + \left(\frac{dy}{dt}\right)^2}\, dt = 2\int_{-1}^{1} \sqrt{1 + t^2}\, dt.$$

Using the standard integral given in the question, we conclude that

$$L = \left[t\sqrt{1 + t^2} + \ln(t + \sqrt{1 + t^2}) \right]_{t=-1}^{t=1}$$
$$= 2\sqrt{2} + \ln(\sqrt{2} + 1) - \ln(\sqrt{2} - 1) \simeq 4.59.$$

Solution to Exercise 2

We have

$$\frac{dx}{dt} = -a\sin t, \quad \frac{dy}{dt} = a\cos t, \quad \frac{dz}{dt} = b,$$

so

$$\left(\frac{dx}{dt}\right)^2 + \left(\frac{dy}{dt}\right)^2 + \left(\frac{dz}{dt}\right)^2 = (-a\sin t)^2 + (a\cos t)^2 + b^2$$
$$= a^2 + b^2.$$

The length of the helical path is therefore

$$L = \int_0^{2\pi} \sqrt{a^2 + b^2}\, dt = 2\pi\sqrt{a^2 + b^2}.$$

Check: In the limit where $b = 0$, our answer reduces to $2\pi a$, which is the circumference of a circle, as expected.

Solution to Exercise 3

The total number of ants is given by the line integral

$$N = \int_C \lambda\, dl.$$

From the given parametric representation, we have

$$\lambda(x(t), y(t)) = \frac{A}{R^4}(R\cos t)^2 (R\sin t) = \frac{A}{R}\cos^2 t \sin t.$$

Also,

$$\frac{dx}{dt} = -R\sin t, \quad \frac{dy}{dt} = R\cos t,$$

so

$$\delta l \simeq \sqrt{(-R\sin t)^2 + (R\cos t)^2}\,\delta t = R\,\delta t.$$

Hence

$$N = \int_0^\pi \frac{A}{R} \cos^2 t \sin t \times R \, dt = A \int_0^\pi \cos^2 t \sin t \, dt.$$

The integral can be completed by substituting $u = \cos t$. Then $du/dt = -\sin t$. The lower limit $t = 0$ corresponds to $u = \cos 0 = 1$, and the upper limit $t = \pi$ corresponds to $u = \cos \pi = -1$, so

$$N = A \int_{t=0}^{t=\pi} u^2 \left(-\frac{du}{dt} \right) dt$$

$$= -A \int_{u=1}^{u=-1} u^2 \, du = -A \left[\tfrac{1}{3} u^3 \right]_1^{-1} = \tfrac{2}{3} A.$$

Solution to Exercise 4

We have $dr/dt = 2$ and $d\phi/dt = 1$, so

$$L = \int_0^5 \sqrt{4 + 4t^2 \times 1} \, dt = 2 \int_0^5 \sqrt{1 + t^2} \, dt.$$

Using the standard integral given in Exercise 1, we get

$$L = \left[t\sqrt{1 + t^2} + \ln\left(t + \sqrt{1 + t^2} \right) \right]_0^5$$

$$= 5\sqrt{26} + \ln(\sqrt{26} + 5) \simeq 27.8.$$

Solution to Exercise 5

Along path A, $d\theta/dt = 1$ and $d\phi/dt = 0$, so equation (14) gives

$$L = R \int_0^{\pi/2} \sqrt{1} \, dt = \frac{\pi}{2} R.$$

Along path B, $d\theta/dt = 0$, $d\phi/dt = 1$ and $\sin\theta = \sin(\pi/6) = \tfrac{1}{2}$, so

$$L = R \int_0^{\pi/2} \sqrt{\tfrac{1}{4}} \, dt = \frac{\pi}{4} R.$$

Solution to Exercise 6

Differentiating the parametric equations $x = 2 - t$ and $y = t$ gives

$$\frac{dx}{dt} = -1, \quad \frac{dy}{dt} = 1.$$

Expressing the components of $\mathbf{F}$ in terms of t, we get

$$F_x = x - y = (2 - t) - t = 2(1 - t),$$
$$F_y = x + y = (2 - t) + t = 2.$$

So

$$\mathbf{F} \cdot \frac{d\mathbf{s}}{dt} = F_x \frac{dx}{dt} + F_y \frac{dy}{dt} = -2(1 - t) + 2 = 2t.$$

The required line integral is

$$\int_{C_2} \mathbf{F} \cdot d\mathbf{s} = \int_0^2 2t \, dt = \left[t^2 \right]_0^2 = 4.$$

Solution to Exercise 7

Differentiating the parametric equations gives

$$\frac{dx}{dt} = 1, \quad \frac{dy}{dt} = 2, \quad \frac{dz}{dt} = 0.$$

Expressing the components of $\mathbf{F}$ in terms of t, we get

$$F_x = yz = 4(1 + 2t), \quad F_y = xz = 4t, \quad F_z = xy = t(1 + 2t).$$

Hence

$$\mathbf{F} \cdot \frac{d\mathbf{s}}{dt} = 4(1 + 2t) + 8t = 4 + 16t.$$

The required line integral is therefore

$$\int_C \mathbf{F} \cdot d\mathbf{s} = \int_0^1 (4 + 16t)\, dt = \left[4t + 8t^2\right]_0^1 = 12.$$

Solution to Exercise 8

Differentiating the parametric equations gives

$$\frac{dx}{dt} = -1, \quad \frac{dy}{dt} = -2, \quad \frac{dz}{dt} = 0.$$

Expressing the components of $\mathbf{F}$ in terms of t, we get

$$F_x = yz = 4(3 - 2t), \quad F_y = xz = 4(1 - t), \quad F_z = xy = (1 - t)(3 - 2t).$$

Hence

$$\mathbf{F} \cdot \frac{d\mathbf{s}}{dt} = -4(3 - 2t) - 8(1 - t) = -20 + 16t.$$

The required line integral is therefore

$$\int_{C_{\text{rev}}} \mathbf{F} \cdot d\mathbf{s} = \int_0^1 (-20 + 16t)\, dt = \left[-20t + 8t^2\right]_0^1 = -12,$$

which is minus the answer of Exercise 7, as expected.

Solution to Exercise 9

Because $\mathbf{F}$ is a gradient field, any line integral with start point $(1, 1)$ and end point $(7, 3)$ has value

$$\int_C \mathbf{F} \cdot d\mathbf{s} = U(1, 1) - U(7, 3) = 0 - (-20) = 20.$$

Solution to Exercise 10

Because the field is conservative, we can choose any convenient path with the given start and end points. A simple choice is the straight-line path C from the origin $(0, 0)$ to $(1, 2)$. Along this path $y = 2x$, so a suitable parametrisation is

$$x = t, \quad y = 2t \quad (0 \leq t \leq 1).$$

Then we have $dx/dt = 1$ and $dy/dt = 2$, so

$$\mathbf{F} \cdot \frac{d\mathbf{s}}{dt} = F_x \frac{dx}{dt} + F_y \frac{dy}{dt} = (3t^2 \times 2t) \times 1 + (t^3 + 8t^3) \times 2$$
$$= 6t^3 + 18t^3 = 24t^3.$$

So the line integral is

$$\int_C \mathbf{F} \cdot d\mathbf{s} = \int_0^1 24t^3 \, dt = 6.$$

Solution to Exercise 11

The scalar potential field is given by

$$U(\mathbf{r}) = -\int_{0 \to \mathbf{r}} \mathbf{F} \cdot d\mathbf{s}.$$

We consider an arbitrary point $\mathbf{r} = (a, b)$, and choose a straight-line path from the origin to this point. This path can be described by the parametric equations

$$x = at, \quad y = bt \quad (0 \le t \le 1).$$

The values of a and b are constant along the path, so

$$\frac{dx}{dt} = a \quad \text{and} \quad \frac{dy}{dt} = b.$$

Hence

$$\mathbf{F} \cdot \frac{d\mathbf{s}}{dt} = F_x \frac{dx}{dt} + F_y \frac{dy}{dt} = a \cos(at) + b \sin(bt)$$

and

$$U(a, b) = -\int_{t=0}^{t=1} \big(a \cos(at) + b \sin(bt)\big) \, dt$$
$$= -\big[\sin(at) - \cos(bt)\big]_{t=0}^{t=1}$$
$$= \cos b - \sin a - 1.$$

However, the point (a, b) is arbitrary, so for any point (x, y),

$$U(x, y) = \cos y - \sin x - 1.$$

This answer can be checked by taking its gradient:

$$\nabla U = \frac{\partial U}{\partial x} \mathbf{i} + \frac{\partial U}{\partial y} \mathbf{j} = -\cos x \, \mathbf{i} - \sin y \, \mathbf{j} = -\mathbf{F}.$$

Solution to Exercise 12

(a) We have

$$\nabla \times \mathbf{F} = \begin{vmatrix} \mathbf{i} & \mathbf{j} & \mathbf{k} \\ \frac{\partial}{\partial x} & \frac{\partial}{\partial y} & \frac{\partial}{\partial z} \\ y & x & z \end{vmatrix} = \mathbf{i}\,(0) - \mathbf{j}\,(0) + \mathbf{k}\,(1 - 1) = \mathbf{0}.$$

So the curl test shows that $\mathbf{F}$ is conservative.

(b) We have

$$\nabla \times \mathbf{G} = \begin{vmatrix} \mathbf{i} & \mathbf{j} & \mathbf{k} \\ \dfrac{\partial}{\partial x} & \dfrac{\partial}{\partial y} & \dfrac{\partial}{\partial z} \\ -y & x & z \end{vmatrix} = \mathbf{i}\,(0) - \mathbf{j}\,(0) + \mathbf{k}\,(1+1).$$

This is not equal to $\mathbf{0}$ everywhere, so $\mathbf{G}$ is *not* conservative.

Solution to Exercise 13

For element A, the unit normal is $\mathbf{i}$, so the normal component of the field is $\mathbf{i} \cdot \mathbf{F} = 2$. This element has area 2, so the flux over it is equal to 4.

For element B, the unit normal is $-\mathbf{j}$, so the normal component of the field is $-\mathbf{j} \cdot \mathbf{F} = -3$. This element has area 1, so the flux over it is equal to -3.

Solution to Exercise 14

The coordinate transformation equations for spherical coordinates are

$$x = r \sin\theta \cos\phi, \quad y = r \sin\theta \sin\phi, \quad z = r \cos\theta.$$

So on the curved surface of the hemisphere, where $r = R$, the vector field is

$$\mathbf{F} = z\,\mathbf{k} = R\cos\theta\,\mathbf{k}.$$

The unit normals shown in the figure point in the same outward direction as those for a complete sphere, so the formula for $\mathbf{J}$ in equation (37) can be used for the hemisphere. We therefore have

$$\begin{aligned} \mathbf{F} \cdot \mathbf{J} &= (R\cos\theta\,\mathbf{k}) \cdot (R^2 \sin\theta\,\mathbf{e}_r) \\ &= R^3 \cos\theta \sin\theta\,\mathbf{k} \cdot \mathbf{e}_r \\ &= R^3 \cos^2\theta \sin\theta. \end{aligned}$$

From equation (38),
$\mathbf{k} \cdot \mathbf{e}_r = \cos\theta$.

The surface of the hemisphere is defined by $0 \le \theta \le \pi/2$ and $0 \le \phi \le 2\pi$, so the required flux is

$$\int_S \mathbf{F} \cdot d\mathbf{S} = R^3 \int_{\phi=0}^{\phi=2\pi} \left(\int_{\theta=0}^{\theta=\pi/2} \cos^2\theta \sin\theta\, d\theta \right) d\phi.$$

To carry out the integral over θ, we make the substitution $u = \cos\theta$. Then $du/d\theta = -\sin\theta$. The limit $\theta = 0$ corresponds to $u = 1$, and the limit $\theta = \pi/2$ corresponds to $u = 0$, so

$$\int_{\theta=0}^{\theta=\pi/2} \cos^2\theta \sin\theta\, d\theta = \int_{\theta=0}^{\theta=\pi/2} u^2 \left(-\frac{du}{d\theta} \right) d\theta$$

$$= -\int_1^0 u^2\, du = \tfrac{1}{3}.$$

Hence

$$\int_S \mathbf{F} \cdot d\mathbf{S} = R^3 \int_0^{2\pi} \tfrac{1}{3}\, d\phi = \tfrac{2}{3}\pi R^3.$$

Solution to Exercise 15

Following the same method as in Exercise 14, we have

$$\mathbf{F} = 3\mathbf{k} \quad \text{and} \quad \mathbf{J} = R^2 \sin\theta\, \mathbf{e}_r,$$

so

$$\mathbf{F} \cdot \mathbf{J} = 3R^2 \sin\theta\, \mathbf{k} \cdot \mathbf{e}_r = 3R^2 \sin\theta \cos\theta = \tfrac{3}{2} R^2 \sin(2\theta).$$

The flux over the hemispherical surface is

$$\int_S \mathbf{F} \cdot d\mathbf{S} = \tfrac{3}{2} R^2 \int_{\phi=0}^{\phi=2\pi} \left(\int_{\theta=0}^{\theta=\pi/2} \sin(2\theta)\, d\theta \right) d\phi$$

$$= \tfrac{3}{2} R^2 \int_{\phi=0}^{\phi=2\pi} \left[-\tfrac{1}{2} \cos(2\theta) \right]_0^{\pi/2} d\phi$$

$$= \tfrac{3}{2} R^2 \int_0^{2\pi} 1\, d\phi = 3\pi R^2.$$

Solution to Exercise 16

The divergence of $\mathbf{F}$ is

$$\mathbf{\nabla} \cdot \mathbf{F} = \frac{\partial(x)}{\partial x} + \frac{\partial(y)}{\partial y} + \frac{\partial(z)}{\partial z} = 3.$$

Using the divergence theorem, the required surface integral is

$$\int_S \mathbf{F} \cdot d\mathbf{S} = \int_V \mathbf{\nabla} \cdot \mathbf{F}\, dV = \int_V 3\, dV,$$

where the volume integral is over the volume of a sphere of radius R.
Hence

$$\int_S \mathbf{F} \cdot d\mathbf{S} = 3 \times \tfrac{4}{3} \pi R^3 = 4\pi R^3.$$

Solution to Exercise 17

As in Example 12, we consider the whole surface of the hemisphere, S, which includes the curved dome S_1 and the flat base S_2. Then

$$\int_S \mathbf{F} \cdot d\mathbf{S} = \int_{S_1} \mathbf{F} \cdot d\mathbf{S} + \int_{S_2} \mathbf{F} \cdot d\mathbf{S}.$$

On the flat base of the hemisphere, $z = 0$, so in this case

$$\int_{S_2} \mathbf{F} \cdot d\mathbf{S} = 0$$

and

$$\int_{S_1} \mathbf{F} \cdot d\mathbf{S} = \int_S \mathbf{F} \cdot d\mathbf{S} = \int_V \mathbf{\nabla} \cdot \mathbf{F}\, dV,$$

where V is the region bounded by the hemispherical surface and its base.

The divergence of $\mathbf{F} = z\,\mathbf{k}$ is

$$\boldsymbol{\nabla}\cdot\mathbf{F} = \frac{\partial(0)}{\partial x} + \frac{\partial(0)}{\partial y} + \frac{\partial(z)}{\partial z} = 1,$$

so

$$\int_{S_1} \mathbf{F}\cdot d\mathbf{S} = \int_V 1\, dV = \tfrac{2}{3}\pi R^3,$$

where we have used the fact that a hemisphere of radius R has half the volume of a complete sphere (i.e. $\tfrac{1}{2} \times \tfrac{4}{3}\pi R^3$). The answer agrees with that of Exercise 14.

Solution to Exercise 18

(a) In order for the flow to be steady-state, we must have $\boldsymbol{\nabla}\cdot(\rho\mathbf{v}) = 0$. In this case,

$$\boldsymbol{\nabla}\cdot(\rho\mathbf{v}) = \frac{\partial(2y^2)}{\partial x} + \frac{\partial(-14yz)}{\partial y} + \frac{\partial(7z^2)}{\partial z} = 0 - 14z + 14z = 0,$$

so this can be a steady-state flow.

(b) In this case,

$$\boldsymbol{\nabla}\cdot(\rho\mathbf{v}) = \frac{\partial(2x)}{\partial x} + \frac{\partial(-3y)}{\partial y} + \frac{\partial(4z)}{\partial z} = 2 - 3 + 4 = 3 \neq 0,$$

so this cannot be a steady-state flow.

Solution to Exercise 19

The unit normals of a closed surface all point outwards into the exterior space. Using the right-hand grip rule, we see that the perimeters of B and C are traversed in a positive sense, and the perimeters of A and D are traversed in a negative sense.

Solution to Exercise 20

(a) We have

$$\frac{d\mathbf{s}}{dt} = \frac{dx}{dt}\,\mathbf{i} + \frac{dy}{dt}\,\mathbf{j} = -\sin t\,\mathbf{i} + \cos t\,\mathbf{j}$$

and

$$\mathbf{F} = \cos t\,\mathbf{j}.$$

Hence

$$\mathbf{F}\cdot\frac{d\mathbf{s}}{dt} = \cos^2 t,$$

and the circulation of $\mathbf{F}$ around C is

$$\oint_C \mathbf{F}\cdot d\mathbf{s} = \int_0^{2\pi} \cos^2 t\, dt = \int_0^{2\pi} \tfrac{1}{2}\big(1 + \cos(2t)\big)\, dt = \pi.$$

(b) The line integral of a conservative field around a closed path is equal to zero, so the circulation of $\mathbf{G}$ around C is equal to zero.

Solution to Exercise 21

The left-hand side of equation (56) is $(\nabla \times \mathbf{F}) \cdot \mathbf{k}$, which is equal to

$$\frac{\partial F_y}{\partial x} - \frac{\partial F_x}{\partial y} = \frac{\partial(x^2)}{\partial x} - \frac{\partial(0)}{\partial y} = 2x.$$

With the unit normal in the positive z-direction, the perimeter of $ABCD$ must be traversed in an anticlockwise sense, as shown in the diagram. The field acts in the y-direction, so only sides BC and DA contribute to the circulation. Along side BC, the component of the field in the direction of the path has the constant value $(x + a)^2$. When this is integrated along the length of BC, it makes a contribution $(x + a)^2 a$ to the circulation. Along side DA, the component of the field in the direction of the path has the constant value $-x^2$. When this is integrated along the length of DA, it makes a contribution $-x^2 a$ to the circulation. So the total circulation of $\mathbf{F}$ around $ABCD$ is

$$\text{circulation} = (x + a)^2 a - x^2 a = (x^2 + 2ax + a^2)a - x^2 a = 2a^2 x + a^3.$$

The area of the square is a^2, so

$$\text{circulation per unit area} = \frac{2a^2 x + a^3}{a^2} = 2x + a.$$

In the limit where a tends to zero, the left- and right-hand sides of equation (56) become equal, as required. (Note that in general, equation (56) applies only in the limit of a vanishingly small element.)

Solution to Exercise 22

Using the curl theorem, the required line integral can be calculated from the surface integral of $\nabla \times \mathbf{F}$ over a rectangular area. However, we have

$$\nabla \times \mathbf{F} = \begin{vmatrix} \mathbf{i} & \mathbf{j} & \mathbf{k} \\ \dfrac{\partial}{\partial x} & \dfrac{\partial}{\partial y} & \dfrac{\partial}{\partial z} \\ x^2 & y^2 & 0 \end{vmatrix} = \mathbf{0},$$

so the surface integral, and hence the required line integral, is equal to zero.

Solution to Exercise 23

Because $\mathbf{F}$ is a curl field, we can replace the curved surface of the bell by the flat circular disc at its mouth. To ensure that both surfaces have the same perimeter path, traversed in the same sense, the unit normal of the disc must be taken to be $\mathbf{k}$ (rather than $-\mathbf{k}$). We therefore get

Although it is not part of the question, you could check that $\mathbf{G} = \nabla \times \mathbf{F}$, where $\mathbf{F} = -x^2 y \mathbf{i} + xz^2 \mathbf{j}$.

$$\int_{\text{bell}} \mathbf{G} \cdot d\mathbf{S} = \int_{\text{disc}} \mathbf{G} \cdot d\mathbf{S} = \int_{\text{disc}} \left(-2xz\,\mathbf{i} + (x^2 + z^2)\,\mathbf{k} \right) \cdot \mathbf{k}\,dS.$$

The disc lies in the xy-plane, so $z = 0$. Hence the integral reduces to

$$\int_{\text{bell}} \mathbf{G} \cdot d\mathbf{S} = \int_{\text{disc}} x^2\,dS.$$

This integral was evaluated in Example 15, so the answer is $\pi R^4 / 4$.

Acknowledgements

Grateful acknowledgement is made to the following source:

Figure 3: Russian International News Agency / http://commons.wikimedia.org/wiki/File:RIAN_archive_497570_ Weight_lifter_Sultan_Rakhmanov.jpg. This file is licensed under the Creative Commons Attribution-Share Alike Licence http://creativecommons.org/licenses/by-sa/3.0.

Every effort has been made to contact copyright holders. If any have been inadvertently overlooked, the publishers will be pleased to make the necessary arrangements at the first opportunity.

Index

Index